SAY IT IN SPANISH

A Guide for Health Care Professionals

SAY IT IN SPANISH

A Guide for Health Care Professionals

Esperanza Villanueva Joyce,
Ed.D., CNS, RN

Assistant Professor
University of Texas Health Science Center
San Antonio, Texas

Maria Elena Villanueva, M.D.
Mexico, D.F.

W. B. SAUNDERS COMPANY
A Division of Harcourt Brace & Company

PHILADELPHIA   LONDON   TORONTO

MONTREAL   SYDNEY   TOKYO

W.B. SAUNDERS COMPANY

A Division of Harcourt Brace & Company

The Curtis Center
Independence Square West
Philadelphia, PA 19106

Library of Congress Cataloging-in-Publication Data

Joyce, Esperanza Villanueva.
　　Say it in Spanish : a guide for health care
professionals / Esperanza Villanueva Joyce,
Maria Elena Villanueva. — 1st ed.
　　　p.　cm.
　　ISBN 0-7216-4955-6
　　1. Spanish language—Conversation and
phrase books (for medical personnel)
I. Villanueva, Maria Elena. II. Title.
PC4120.M3J68　1996
468.3'421'02461—dc20　　　　　　　95-9345

SAY IT IN SPANISH　　　　ISBN 0-7216-4955-6

Printed in the United States of America

Last digit is the print number:　9　8　7　6　5　4

With gratitude to my husband Raymond, who diligently typed much of the manuscript. He also carefully edited each unit and provided feedback that was not only useful but very practical. My thanks to my daughter Leslie Ann, who was very patient when told many times, "You have to wait."

E. V. Joyce

For Jose, Claudia, Jose Luis, and Roberto, who contributed their support. Special thanks to Jose Luis, who photographed many of the figures used in this book.

M. E. Villanueva

Contents

CONTENTS

UNIT V

UNIDAD V

UNIT VI

UNIDAD VI

Preface

THE IDEA for this text grew from multiple observations in clinical settings where the frustrations of non–Spanish-speaking providers are evident. These frustrations stem from the lack of control providers feel when they are not in command of the language of their patients and must depend on translators for the collection of data. My bicultural background and my bilingual abilities (I was born in Mexico and have spent over 20 years in the United States) have afforded me the opportunity to translate for many Spanish-speaking patients. This has allowed me to understand the predicament that Spanish-speaking patients find themselves in when they require medical care. The communication of simple facts can be difficult, and miscommunication can have lethal consequences.

As a faculty member in schools of nursing I was often amused by my students' comments: "Don't assign me a Spanish-speaking patient," or "I don't know how to speak Spanish." I had little choice, since 46 percent of our large medical center patient population was Hispanic. From 1982 through 1991 I taught a course entitled "Communicating with the Spanish-Speaking Patient." This was the only such course being taught in a nursing school in the state of Texas. Evaluations confirmed that the course helped students provide better care to their Spanish-speaking patients. Students were able to interact with families, collect data, and make meaningful contributions to their patients' care. In this setting, as in others, it was clear that the opportunities gained by knowledge of a second language were innumerable!

APPROACH

Say It in Spanish is designed primarily to meet the needs of health care professionals and students who anticipate contact with Spanish-speaking patients. Health providers in hospitals, clinics, physician's offices, outpatient and community centers, as well as students in nursing schools and allied health schools, can benefit from the use of this textbook. This text can also be used as a self-instructional program for those whose occupations bring them into daily contact with patients whose native language is Spanish. To facilitate the self-instructional approach, all translations are accompanied by their pronunciation.

Over the past decade there has been a growing recognition in health care settings of the importance of communicating with Spanish-speaking patients. Clinicians who can communicate with their patients will be able to assess more effectively the success of the treatment they are providing. The Spanish expressions used in this book are primarily those used in Spanish-speaking countries close to the United States and Spanish communities within the United States.

This text provides an introduction to the Spanish language, but it is not a comprehensive grammar textbook. Our intent is to present practical language that can be used in clinical settings in which intervention with a Spanish-speaking patient may be short term or long term. Those who use this text will be able to express in simple Spanish what they need to say. Special emphasis is placed on the use of meaningful medical vocabulary. Medical situations mentioned in the text are those experienced in everyday life.

FEATURES OF THE TEXT

For the convenience of the health provider, Units I through IV include English-Spanish usage. This bilingual text eliminates the time-consuming process of looking up words in the dictionary.

The questioning techniques presented have been selected to elicit "yes" or "no" answers. These will assist those providers who have a limited knowledge of Spanish.

Dialogues are presented as situations with corresponding appropriate basic vocabulary. The dialogues deal with familiar situations in the medical setting. And they are simple and interesting, so the provider has the opportunity to use repetition that will enhance his or her retention.

An overview of physical assessment, with the use of commands specific to the body part being examined, is included.

Scenes are illustrated using basic vocabulary. This will help health providers to link the object with its Spanish equivalent without reference to English.

English phrases are not always translated literally. Instead, the most common Spanish words have been selected and presented.

Tables in each unit help the provider review key words, ideas, and concepts.

A cultural perspective that increases the awareness of the health care provider for the needs of the Spanish-speaking population is included.

ORGANIZATION

The text is comprised of six units organized to present a patient's usual movement from the community to the hospital setting. The first unit focuses on practical language skills that are used in first aid and emergency situations as well as in routine home visits. The use of short dialogues that will elicit "yes" and "no" answers will facilitate data collection essential for immediate care. Unit I also includes a section on a visit to the home. Home health care workers will be able to ask pertinent questions related to the health status of family members.

Unit II concentrates on approaches used in the hospital. It includes a description of the admission of the patient, the patient's room, and hospital meals. This unit also presents the most common vocabulary that a patient will encounter in specific departments such as pharmacy, laboratory, and x-ray. The health provider can refer quickly to the appropriate chapter, thus increasing his or her communication skills and not delaying treatment while waiting for a translator.

Unit III provides specific content related to greetings and common expressions that will assist in creating a welcoming environment for the patient. The sections on phrases and commands will facilitate the completion of a physical assessment. The discussion of physical assessment specifically relates to internal and external parts of the body.

Unit IV presents the terminology of numbers, time, colors, and members of the family. These sections have been selected to enhance the health provider's knowledge of everyday terms that will be useful in the clinical setting.

Unit V presents an overview of the most essential grammatical concepts. The pronunciation and spelling of Spanish sounds are explained in detail. Most of the Spanish sounds are similar to sounds in English and therefore are easy to learn. These sections provide the basis for appropriate use of the language and also serve as a quick reference.

Unit VI describes cultural variations among Spanish-speaking groups as well as the common health beliefs and popular health cures practiced by each group. The intent in this unit is to increase the health provider's awareness of cultural differences in the health perceptions of Spanish-speaking patients.

The English-Spanish index is divided into two sections: a sentence index and a word index. The unique sentence index is a useful tool that will save the health care worker time when determining which question to ask.

Difficult terms, important terms, and useful vocabulary are highlighted in tables that appear throughout the book.

Esperanza Villanueva Joyce

UNIT I

—
—
—
—
—
—
—
—
—
—
—
—
—
—
—
—
—
—
—
—
—
—
—
—
—
—
—

UNIDAD 1

—
—
—
—
—
—
—
—
—
—
—
—
—
—
—
—
—
—
—
—
—
—
—
—
—
—
—
—
—
—

First Aid

Primeros Auxilios

Injury or sudden illness becomes an emergency when a life is threatened. Injured persons depend on others for their well-being. Health providers must communicate accurately and in language a person can understand. In an emergency, there is no time for lengthy conversation. Use short phrases that elicit either a "yes" or "no" response. Use your hands when talking, pantomime, point, use facial expressions! There are several expressions you can use to get someone's attention. Table 1-1 lists some commonly used phrases.

Una herida o enfermedad repentina se convierte en una emergencia cuando la vida corre peligro. Las personas que han sufrido daños dependen de otros para sobrevivir. Los proveedores de salud deben comunicarse con exactitud para hacerse entender. En un caso de emergencia no hay tiempo para conversar. Use frases cortas para que las respuestas sean "sí" o "no." ¡Use las manos al hablar, haga pantomimas, apunte, use expresiones faciales! Hay varias expresiones que puede usar para atraer la atención. La tabla 1-1 muestra algunas expresiones comunes.

Miss	**señorita**
	(seh-nyoh-ree-tah)
Mrs.	**señora**
	(seh-nyoh-rah)
Mr.	**señor**
	(seh-nyohr)
hello!	**¡hola!**
	(oh-lah)
Can you hear me?	**¿Puede oírme?**
	(Poo-eh-deh oh-eer-meh)
Can you talk?	**¿Puede hablar?**
	(Poo-eh-deh ah-blahr)

FIGURE 1-1 *Injury or sudden illness becomes an emergency when life is threatened. Health providers must communicate accurately and in language a person can understand.*

TABLE 1-1 ATTENTION GETTING PHRASES	TABLA 1-1 FRASES PARA ATRAER ATENCION	
ENGLISH	SPANISH	PRONUNCIATION
Mr.	señor	*seh-nyohr*
Mrs.	señora	*seh-nyoh-rah*
Miss	señorita	*seh-nyoh-ree-tah*
Listen!	¡Oiga!	*¡Oh-ee-gah!*
Excuse me!	¡Perdón!	*¡Pehr-dohn!*
young man/woman	joven	*hoh-behn*
boy/girl	muchacho(a)	*moo-chah-choh (chah)*
boy/girl	niño(a)	*nee-nyoh (nyah)*

Can you breathe?	**¿Puede respirar?** *(Poo-eh-deh rehs-pee-rahr)*
What is your name?	**¿Cómo se llama?** *(Koh-moh seh yah-mah)*
Do you know where you are?	**¿Sabe dónde está?** *(Sah-beh dohn-deh ehs-tah)*
Do you know what day today is?	**¿Que día es hoy?** *(Keh dee-ah ehs oh-ee)*
Please don't move.	**Por favor, no se mueva.** *(Pohr fah-bohr noh seh moo-eh-bah)*
I need to see if you are hurt.	**Necesito ver si está lastimado.** *(Neh-seh-see-toh behr see ehs-tah lahs-tee-mah-doh)*

Unless an emergency is life threatening, a person needs to participate in his own care to maintain a sense of control. Tell the patient to speak slowly when speaking Spanish and remind him to respond with

FIGURE 1-2 *In an emergency, tell the patient to speak slowly and to respond with "yes" or "no" as much as possible.*

"yes" or "no" as much as possible. Table 1-2 shows a list of common commands you can use.

A menos que su vida esté en peligro, una persona necesita participar en su propio cuidado para mantener el sentido de control. Dígale al paciente que hable despacio cuando hable en español y recuérdele que responda "sí" o "no" lo máximo posible. La tabla 1-2 muestra una lista de mandatos comunes que puede usar.

English	Spanish
Open your eyes.	Abra los ojos.
	(Ah-brah lohs oh-hos)
Don't turn.	No voltee.
	(Noh bohl-teh-eh)
Where does it hurt?	¿Dónde le duele?
	(Dohn-deh leh doo-eh-leh)
Point.	Apunte/señale.
	(Ah-poon-teh/seh-nyah-leh)
Did you fall?	¿Se cayó?
	(Seh kah-yoh)
Were you hit by a car?	¿Lo atropelló un carro?
	(Loh ah-troh-peh-yoh oon kah-rroh)
Did you lose consciousness?	¿Perdió el conocimiento?
	(Pehr-dee-oh ehl koh-noh-see-mee-ehn-toh)
Where do you live?	¿Dónde vive?
	(Dohn-deh bee-beh)

TABLE 1-2 PRONUNCIATION OF COMMANDS		TABLA 1-2 PRONUNCIACION DE MANDATOS
ENGLISH	*SPANISH*	*PRONUNCIATION*
Sit down!	¡Siéntese!	*¡See-ehn-teh-seh!*
Move!	¡Muévase!	*¡Moo-eh-bah-seh!*
Don't move!	¡No se mueva!	*¡Noh seh moo-eh-bah!*
Breathe!	¡Respire!	*¡Rehs-pee-reh!*
Speak!	¡Hable!	*¡Ah-bleh!*
Open!	¡Abra!	*¡Ah-brah!*
Turn!	¡Voltee!	*¡Bohl-teh-eh!*
Be still!	¡Quieto!	*¡Kee-eh-toh!*
Point!	¡Apunte!/¡Señale!	*¡Ah-poon-teh!/¡Seh-nyah-leh!*
Bend!	¡Doble!	*¡Doh-bleh!*

Do you remember the street?	**¿Recuerda la calle?** *(Reh-koo-ehr-dah lah kah-yeh)*
Where were you going?	**¿A dónde iba?** *(Ah dohn-deh ee-bah)*
Your leg is broken.	**Tiene la pierna quebrada/fracturada.** *(Tee-eh-neh lah pee-ehr-nah keh-brah-dah/frahk-too-rah-dah)*
I need to cut your pants.	**Necesito cortar el pantalón.** *(Neh-seh-see-toh kohr-tahr ehl pahn-tah-lohn)*
I am going to put a splint on your leg.	**Voy a ponerle una tablilla en la pierna.** *(Boy ah poh-nehr-leh oo-nah tah-blee-yah ehn lah pee-ehr-nah)*
Do not bend your leg!	**¡No doble la pierna!** *(Noh doh-bleh lah pee-ehr-nah)*
Keep your leg straight.	**Mantenga la pierna derecha.** *(Mahn-tehn-gah lah pee-ehr-nah deh-reh-chah)*
I am going to cover you.	**Lo voy a cubrir.** *(Loh boy ah koo-breer)*
I am going to put you on a stretcher.	**Voy a ponerlo en la camilla.** *(Boy ah poh-nehr-loh ehn lah kah-mee-yah)*
We are going to the hospital.	**Vamos al hospital.** *(Bah-mohs ahl ohs-pee-tahl)*
We are going in an ambulance.	**Vamos en la ambulancia.** *(Bah-mohs ehn lah ahm-boo-lahn-see-ah)*
It will take 10 minutes.	**Tomará diez minutos.** *(Toh-mah-rah dee-ehs mee-noo-tohs)*
Have you been hospitalized before?	**¿Ha estado hospitalizado alguna vez?** *(Ah ehs-tah-doh ohs-pee-tah-lee-sah-doh ahl-goo-nah behs)*
Have you had any accidents?	**¿Ha tenido algún accidente?** *(Ah teh-nee-doh ahl-goon ahk-see-dehn-teh)*

While traveling to the emergency room, and if the patient's condition is stable, ask him or her for information. This will help the staff complete forms and will decrease delays in calling family or friends. Some important questions to ask are listed in table 1-3.

Mientras viaja al cuarto de emergencias y si la condición del paciente es estable, hágale más preguntas. Esto ayudará a los empleados a com-

FIGURE 1-3 *When an accident occurs, the health provider must gather as much information as possible and must give instructions to relatives.*

pletar los formularios y disminuirá la demora en llamar a la familia o a los amigos del paciente. La tabla 1-3 muestra algunas preguntas importantes.

What kind of . . . ?	¿Qué clase de . . . ? *(Keh klah-seh deh)*
Have you ever broken any bones?	¿Se ha quebrado alguna vez? *(Seh ah keh-brah-doh ahl-goo-nah behs)*
How long ago?	¿Hace cuanto tiempo? *(Ah-seh koo-ahn-toh tee-ehm-poh)*
Were you hospitalized?	¿Lo hospitalizaron? *(Loh ohs-pee-tah-lee-sah-rohn)*
Do you know the name of the hospital?	¿Sabe el nombre del hospital? *(Sah-beh ehl nohm-breh dehl ohs-pee-tahl)*
The doctor will see you in the emergency room.	El doctor lo verá en el cuarto de emergencias. *(Ehl dohk-tohr loh beh-rah ehn ehl koo-ahr-toh deh eh-mehr-hehn-see-ahs)*

TABLE 1-3   TABLA 1-3
IMPORTANT QUESTIONS TO   PREGUNTAS IMPORTANTES QUE HACER
ASK IF AN ACCIDENT   SI OCURRIO UN ACCIDENTE
OCCURRED

ENGLISH	SPANISH	PRONUNCIATION
Did you faint?	¿Se desmayó?	¿Seh dehs-mah-yoh?
Do you feel nauseated?	¿Siente náusea?	¿See-ehn-teh nah-oo-seh-ah?
Do you feel weak?	¿Se siente débil?	¿Seh see-ehn-teh deh-beel?
Do you feel dizzy?	¿Se siente mareado?	¿Seh see-ehn-teh mah-reh-ah-doh?
Are you cold?	¿Tiene frío?	¿Tee-eh-neh free-oh?
Are you hot?	¿Tiene calor?	¿Tee-eh-neh kah-lohr?

The doctor will give you something for pain.
El doctor le dará algo para el dolor.
(Ehl dohk-tohr leh dah-rah ahl-goh pah-rah ehl doh-lohr)

The nurse will ask how you feel.
La enfermera le preguntará cómo se siente.
(Lah ehn-fehr-meh-rah leh preh-goon-tah-rah koh-moh seh see-ehn-teh)

They will let you talk to your family.
Le permitirán hablar con su familia.
(Leh pehr-mee-tee-rahn ah-blahr kohn soo fah-mee-lee-ah)

Do you have a phone?
¿Tiene teléfono?
(Tee-eh-neh teh-leh-foh-noh)

Give it to the clerk.
Déselo a la secretaria.
(Deh-seh-loh ah lah seh-kreh-tah-ree-ah)

Is your family in town?
¿Está su familia en la ciudad?
(Ehs-tah soo fah-mee-lee-ah ehn lah see-oo-dahd)

Add *es* to a singular noun that ends in a consonant or in *z* to make it plural. Add *s* to a singular noun that ends in a vowel to make it plural. Table 1-4 lists examples of singular and plural nouns and articles.

Añada *es* a la palabra singular que termina en una consonante o en *z* para hacerla plural. Añada *s* a la palabra singular que termina en una

vocal para hacerla plural. La tabla 1-4 muestra una lista de ejemplos
de sustantivos y artículos singulares y plurales.

Do you have any children?	¿Tiene niños? *(Tee-eh-neh nee-nyohs)*
How many?	¿Cuántos? *(koo-ahn-tohs)*
How many boys/girls?	¿Cuántos niños/niñas? *(koo-ahn-tohs nee-nyohs/nee-nyahs)*
How old are they?	¿Cuántos años tienen? *(koo-ahn-tohs ah-nyohs tee-eh-nehn)*
Do they all go to school?	¿Todos van a la escuela? *(Toh-dohs bahn ah lah ehs-koo-eh-lah)*
What is the name of the school?	¿Cómo se llama la escuela? *(koh-moh seh yah-mah lah ehs-koo-eh-lah)*
Do you have a husband?	¿Tiene esposo? *(Tee-eh-neh ehs-poh-soh)*
Is he at work?	¿Está trabajando? *(Ehs-tah trah-bah-hahn-doh)*
Do you know his work phone number?	¿Sabe el teléfono de su trabajo? *(Sah-beh ehl teh-leh-foh-noh deh soo trah-bah-ho)*

TABLE 1-4
SINGULAR AND PLURAL

TABLA 1-4
SINGULAR Y PLURAL

SINGULAR		PLURAL	
the girl	la niña *(lah nee-nyah)*	the girls	las niñas *(lahs nee-nyahs)*
the boy	el niño *(ehl nee-nyoh)*	the boys	los niños *(lohs nee-nyohs)*
the doctor	el doctor *(ehl dohk-tohr)*	the doctors	los doctores *(lohs dohk-toh-rehs)*
the hospital	el hospital *(ehl ohs-pee-tahl)*	the hospitals	los hospitales *(lohs ohs-pee-tah-lehs)*
a heart	un corazón *(oon koh-rah-sohn)*	some hearts	unos corazones *(oo-nohs koh-rah-sohn-ehs)*
a table	una mesa *(oo-nah meh-sah)*	some tables	unas mesas *(oo-nahs meh-sahs)*

Do you have any brothers/ sisters?	**¿Tiene hermanos/hermanas?** *(Tee-eh-neh ehr-mah-nohs/ehr-mah-nahs)*
Do they live close to you?	**¿Viven cerca de usted?** *(Bee-behn sehr-kah deh oos-tehd)*
What do you do?	**¿Qué hace usted?** *(Keh ah-seh oos-tehd)*
Are you employed?	**¿Trabaja?** *(Trah-bah-hah)*
Where do you work?	**¿Dónde trabaja?** *(Dohn-deh trah-bah-hah)*
Do you know the name of the street?	**¿Sabe el nombre de la calle?** *(Sah-beh ehl nohm-breh deh lah kah-yeh)*
Do you work every day?	**¿Trabaja todos los días?** *(Trah-bah-hah toh-dohs lohs dee-ahs)*
How many hours a day do you work?	**¿Cuántas horas por día trabaja?** *(Koo-ahn-tahs oh-rahs pohr dee-ah trah-bah-hah)*
Who can take care of the children?	**¿Quién puede cuidar a los niños?** *(Kee-ehn poo-eh-deh koo-ee-dahr ah lohs nee-nyohs)*
You will need a cast.	**Necesitará un yeso.** *(Neh-seh-see-tah-rah oon yeh-soh)*
You can walk with crutches.	**Puede caminar con muletas.** *(Poo-eh-deh kah-mee-nahr kohn moo-leh-tahs)*
Keep your leg elevated.	**Mantenga la pierna elevada.** *(Mahn-tehn-gah lah pee-ehr-nah eh-leh-bah-dah)*
Can you take time off from work?	**¿Puede faltar al trabajo?** *(Poo-eh-deh fahl-tahr ahl trah-bah-hoh)*
Are you on vacation?	**¿Está de vacaciones?** *(Ehs-tah deh bah-kah-see-ohn-ehs)*
Can you take a vacation?	**¿Puede tomar vacaciones?** *(Poo-eh-deh toh-mahr bah-kah-see-ohn-ehs)*
Do you have another car?	**¿Tiene otro carro?** *(Tee-eh-neh oh-troh kah-rroh)*
Do you have car insurance?	**¿Tiene seguro de carro?** *(Tee-eh-neh seh-goo-roh deh kah-rroh)*
Do you have hospital insurance?	**¿Tiene seguro de hospital?** *(Tee-eh-neh seh-goo-roh deh ohs-pee-tahl)*

Do you have help at home?	**¿Tiene ayuda en casa?** *(Tee-eh-neh ah-yoo-dah ehn kah-sah)*
Will you need help?	**¿Va a necesitar ayuda?** *(Bah ah neh-seh-see-tahr ah-yoo-dah)*
Call your friends.	**Llame a sus amigos.** *(Yah-meh ah soos ah-mee-gohs)*
They can help clean.	**Ellos pueden ayudar a limpiar.** *(Eh-yohs poo-eh-dehn ah-yoo-dahr ah leem-pee-ahr)*
Try to calm down.	**Trate de calmarse.** *(Trah-teh deh kahl-mahr-seh)*
You will get help.	**Se le ayudará.** *(Seh leh ah-yoo-dah-rah)*

TABLE 1-5
NOUNS AND ARTICLES

TABLA 1-5
SUSTANTIVOS Y ARTICULOS

		NOUNS ENDING IN o, or, al, ador ARE *MASCULINE. MALE NOUNS ARE*	
NOUNS ENDING IN a, d, ion, OR z ARE *FEMININE. FEMALE NOUNS ARE FEMININE.*		*MASCULINE EVEN THOUGH THE NOUN* *MAY END IN a.*	

the	**la (feminine)** *(lah)*	the	**el (masculine)** *(ehl)*
a or an	**una (feminine)** *(oo-nah)*	a or an	**un (masculine)** *(oon)*
the house	**la casa** *(lah kah-sah)*	the man	**el hombre** *(ehl ohm-breh)*
a door	**una puerta** *(oo-nah poo-ehr-tah)*	an author	**un autor** *(oon ah-oo-tohr)*
the daughter	**la hija** *(lah ee-hah)*	the son	**el hijo** *(ehl ee-hoh)*
the friend	**la amiga (feminine)** *(lah ah-mee-gah)*	the friend	**el amigo (masculine)** *(ehl ah-mee-goh)*
the woman	**la mujer** *(lah moo-hehr)*	the hospital	**el hospital** *(ehl ohs-pee-tahl)*
the health	**la salud** *(lah sah-lood)*	the month	**el mes** *(ehl mehs)*

Important exception: *the hand, la mano.* Note the ending *o; la mano* is feminine.

The days of the week, months of the year, and names of a language are all masculine.

We know the gender of a Spanish word by its ending. If the word ends in *a*, it is usually feminine. If the word ends in *o*, it is usually masculine. Table 1-5 lists some nouns and articles.

Se determina el género de la palabra en español al ver su terminación. Si la palabra termina en *a* generalmente es femenina. Si la palabra termina en *o* generalmente es masculina. La tabla 1-5 muestra algunos sustantivos y artículos.

Emergency Care

Cuidado de Urgencia (Emergencia)

Emergency rooms are frequently very busy. There is a tendency to rush through procedures. When possible, take a few extra minutes to attempt to communicate so your diagnosis is accurate. This saves time in the long run.

Los cuartos (salas) de urgencia (emergencia) frecuentemente están ocupados. Hay una tendencia a apurarse en los procedimientos. Cuando le sea posible tome unos minutos adicionales para intentar la comuni-

FIGURE 2-1   *Emergency rooms are often busy places.*

cación, para que su diagnóstico sea exacto. Esto ahorra tiempo a largo plazo.

Mrs. García, a pregnant 32-year-old woman was involved in a car accident. She just arrived at the emergency room.

La señora García, tiene 32 años de edad, está embarazada, y tuvo un accidente automovilístico. Acaba de llegar al cuarto de urgencias (emergencias).

Hello, Mrs. García.	**Hola, señora García.** *(Oh-lah seh-nyoh-rah Gahr-see-ah)*
I am going to ask you some questions.	**Voy a hacerle algunas preguntas.** *(Boy ah ah-sehr-leh ahl-goo-nahs preh-goon-tahs.)*
What is your name?	**¿Cómo se llama?** *(Koh-moh seh yah-mah)*
What is your last name?	**¿Cuál es su apellido?** *(Koo-ahl ehs soo ah-peh-yee-doh)*

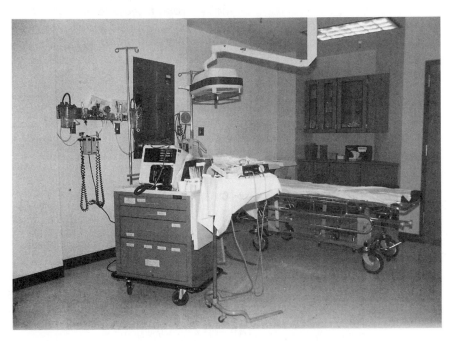

FIGURE 2-2 *Emergency rooms are often impersonal and may frighten the patient. Ensure privacy and accept reactions to fear and pain.*

Answer "yes" or "no."	**Conteste "sí" o "no."**
	(Kohn-tehs-teh "see" oh "noh")
Did you lose consciousness?	**¿Perdió el conocimiento/se desmayó?**
	(Pehr-dee-oh ehl koh-noh-see-mee-ehn-toh/seh dehs-mah-yoh)
Do you know where you are?	**¿Sabe dónde está?**
	(Sah-beh dohn-deh ehs-tah)
Do you know what day of the week today is?	**¿Sabe qué día de la semana es hoy?**
	(Sah-beh keh dee-ah deh lah seh-mah-nah ehs ohy)
Are you nauseated?	**¿Tiene náuseas?**
	(Tee-eh-neh nah-oo-seh-ahs)
Are you bleeding?	**¿Está sangrando?**
	(Ehs-tah sahn-grahn-doh)
How many months pregnant are you?	**¿Cuántos meses tiene de embarazo?**
	(Koo-ahn-tohs meh-sehs tee-eh-neh deh ehm-bah-rah-soh)
When was your last normal period?	**¿Cuándo tuvo su última menstruación normal?**
	(Koo-ahn-doh too-boh soo ool-tee-mah mehns-troo-ah-see-ohn nohr-mahl)
Did your water break?	**¿Se reventó su bolsa de agua?**
	(Seh rreh-behn-toh soo bohl-sah deh ah-goo-ah)
When?	**¿Cuándo?**
	(Koo-ahn-doh)
Did you feel warm water run out of your vagina?	**¿Sintió que salió agua tibia de su vagina?**
	(Seen-tee-oh keh sah-lee-oh ah-goo-ah tee-bee-ah deh soo bah-hee-nah)

In an emergency situation, the objective is to obtain as much information as correctly as possible. Get to the point!

En una situación urgente el objetivo es obtener información lo más correcta posible. ¡Sea breve!

Have you eaten?	**¿Ha comido?**
	(Ah koh-mee-doh)
At what time?	**¿A que hora?**
	(Ah keh oh-rah)
What did you eat?	**¿Que comió?**
	(Keh koh-mee-oh)

Mrs. García, I need to help you change your clothes.	**Señora García, necesito ayudarle a cambiar su ropa.** *(Seh-nyoh-rah Gahr-see-ah neh-seh-see-toh ah-yoo-dahr-leh ah kahm-bee-ahr soo roh-pah)*
I have a gown.	**Tengo una bata.** *(Tehn-goh oo-nah bah-tah)*
I am going to examine you.	**Voy a examinarla.** *(Boy ah ehx-ah-mee-nahr-lah)*

Some words are difficult to pronounce because they are too long. Don't hurry; take your time. Table 2-1 gives the pronunciation of some difficult words.

Algunas palabras son difíciles de pronunciar porque son muy largas. No se apure, haga una pausa. La tabla 2-1 muestra la pronunciación de algunas palabras difíciles.

How close are your contractions?	**¿Cada cuánto tiempo le vienen las contracciones?** *(Kah-dah koo-ahn-toh tee-ehm-poh leh bee-eh-nehn lahs kohn-trahk-see-ohn-ehs)*
Tell me when you feel a contraction!	**¡Diga cuando sienta una contracción!** *(Dee-gah koo-ahn-doh see-ehn-tah oo-nah kohn-trahk-see-ohn)*
We need to count.	**Tenemos que contar.** *(Teh-neh-mohs keh kohn-tahr)*

TABLE 2-1 *PRONUNCIATION OF* *SELECTED WORDS*	*TABLA 2-1* ***PRONUNCIACION DE*** ***PALABRAS SELECTAS***	

ENGLISH	*SPANISH*	*PRONUNCIATION*
ambulance	**ambulancia**	*ahm-boo-lahn-see-ah*
consciousness	**conocimiento**	*koh-noh-see-mee-ehn-toh*
contraction	**contracciones**	*kohn-trahk-see-ohn-ehs*
pregnant	**embarazada**	*ehm-bah-rah-sah-dah*
to examine	**examinar**	*ehx-ah-mee-nahr*
receptionist	**recepcionista**	*reh-sehp-see-ohn-ees-tah*
bleeding	**sangrando**	*sahn-grahn-doh*
temperature	**temperatura**	*tehm-peh-rah-too-rah*

Are you cold?

¿Tiene frío?
(Tee-eh-neh free-oh)

Are you hot?

¿Tiene calor?
(Tee-eh-neh kah-lohr)

Where were you hit?

¿Dónde se golpeó?
(Dohn-deh seh gohl-peh-oh)

Point!

¡Apunte! / ¡Señale!
(Ah-poon-teh/seh-nyah-leh)

Do you feel any pain?

¿Tiene dolor?
(Tee-eh-neh doh-lohr)

Where?

¿Dónde?
(Dohn-deh)

Pain at the waist?

¿Dolor en la cintura?
(Doh-lohr ehn lah seen-too-rah)

Back pain?

¿Dolor de espalda?
(Doh-lohr deh ehs-pahl-dah)

Is the pain sharp?

¿El dolor es agudo?
(Ehl doh-lohr ehs ah-goo-doh)

Is the pain in one place?

¿El dolor es en un solo lugar?
(Ehl doh-lohr ehs ehn oon soh-loh loo-gahr)

Does it come and go?

¿Es momentáneo?
(Ehs moh-mehn-tah-neh-oh)

Are you feeling a contraction?

¿Está sintiendo una contracción?
(Ehs-tah seen-tee-ehn-doh oo-nah kohn-trahk-see-ohn)

Tell me when!

¡Dígame cuándo!
(Dee-gah-meh koo-ahn-doh)

I am going to listen to the baby's heart beat.

Voy a escuchar el latido del corazón del bebé.
(Boy ah ehs-koo-chahr ehl lah-tee-doh dehl koh-rah-sohn dehl beh-beh)

Please breathe normally.

Por favor, respire normalmente.
(Pohr fah-bohr, rehs-pee-reh nohr-mahl-mehn-teh)

It sounds good.

Se oye bien.
(Seh oh-yeh bee-ehn)

Do you have any allergies?

¿Tiene alergias?
(Tee-eh-neh ah-lehr-hee-ahs)

Are you allergic to foods/dust/medicines?

¿Tiene alergia a comidas/polvo/medicinas?
(Tee-eh-neh ah-lehr-hee-ah ah koh-mee-dahs/pohl-boh/meh-dee-see-nahs)

How old are you?	**¿Cuántos años tiene?** *(Koo-ahn-tohs ah-nyohs tee-eh-neh)*
How many pregnancies have you had?	**¿Cuántos embarazos ha tenido?** *(Koo-ahn-tohs ehm-bah-rah-sohs ah teh-nee-doh)*
How many children do you have?	**¿Cuántos niños tiene?** *(Koo-ahn-tohs nee-nyohs tee-eh-neh)*
Have you had an abortion?	**¿Ha tenido abortos?** *(Ah teh-nee-doh ah-bohr-tohs)*
How many?	**¿Cuántos?** *(Koo-ahn-tohs)*
When was the last one?	**¿Cuándo fue el último?** *(Koo-ahn-doh foo-eh ehl ool-tee-moh)*
Did you ever have a miscarriage?	**¿Tuvo un aborto natural?** *(Too-boh oon ah-bohr-toh nah-too-rahl)*
Did you ever have an ectopic (tubal) pregnancy?	**¿Tuvo un embarazo fuera de la matriz o en las trompas?** *(Too-boh oon ehm-bah-rah-soh foo-eh-rah deh lah mah-trees oh ehn lahs trohm-pahs)*
Do you work, also?	**¿Trabaja también?** *(Trah-bah-hah tahm-bee-ehn)*
Are you a housewife?	**¿Es ama de casa?** *(Ehs ah-mah deh kah-sah)*
What kind of work do you do?	**¿Qué clase de trabajo hace?** *(Keh klah-seh deh trah-bah-hoh ah-seh)*
How many pounds have you gained?	**¿Cuántas libras ha aumentado?** *(Koo-ahn-tahs lee-brahs ah ah-oo-mehn-tah-doh)*
Do you smoke?	**¿Fuma?** *(Foo-mah)*
Do you drink alcohol?	**¿Toma bebidas alcohólicas?** *(Toh-mah beh-bee-dahs ahl-koh-lee-kahs)*
Do you drink coffee?	**¿Toma café?** *(Toh-mah kah-feh)*
Do you take any medicines?	**¿Toma algunas medicinas?** *(Toh-mah ahl-goo-nahs meh-dee-see-nahs)*
What medicines do you take?	**¿Qué medicinas toma?** *(Keh meh-dee-see-nahs toh-mah)*
For what reason?	**¿Cuál es la razón?** *(Koo-ahl ehs lah rah-sohn)*

Do you take any narcotics?	**¿Toma narcóticos?**
	(Toh-mah nahr-koh-tee-kohs)
Do you habitually take drugs?	**¿Tiene el vicio de tomar drogas?**
	(Tee-eh-neh ehl bee-see-oh deh toh-mahr droh-gahs)
Are you married/single?	**¿Está casada/es soltera?**
	(Ehs-tah kah-sah-dah/ehs sohl-teh-rah)
Do you live with your husband?	**¿Vive con su esposo?**
	(Bee-beh kohn soo ehs-poh-soh)
Where is your husband?	**¿Dónde está su esposo?**
	(Dohn-deh ehs-tah soo ehs-poh-soh)
Do you have relatives/friends?	**¿Tiene parientes/amigos?**
	(Tee-eh-neh pah-ree-ehn-tehs/ah-mee-gohs)
That's all for now—I will see you later.	**Es todo por ahora—la veré luego.**
	(Ehs toh-doh pohr ah-oh-rah—lah beh-reh loo-eh-goh)
Thank you!	**¡Gracias!**
	(Grah-see-ahs)

Table 2-2 will help you with the pronunciation of selected words.
La tabla 2-2 le ayudará con la pronunciación de palabras selectas.

TABLE 2-2 PRONUNCIATION OF SELECTED WORDS	TABLA 2-2 PRONUNCIACION DE PALABRAS SELECTAS	
ENGLISH	*SPANISH*	*PRONUNCIATION*
last name	**apellido**	*ah-peh-yee-doh*
know/knows	**sabe**	*sah-beh*
week	**semana**	*seh-mah-nah*
nausea	**náusea**	*nah-oo-seh-ah*
where	**donde**	*dohn-deh*
how many	**cuántos**	*koo-ahn-tohs*
thank you	**gracias**	*grah-see-ahs*
blood	**sangre**	*sahn-greh*
need	**necesita**	*neh-seh-see-tah*
question	**pregunta**	*preh-goon-tah*

The nurse approaches Mrs. García.
La enfermera se acerca a la señora García.

Hello Mrs. García, I need to take your temperature and blood pressure.	**Hola, señora García, necesito tomarle la temperatura y presión de la sangre.** *(Oh-lah seh-nyoh-rah Gahr-see-ah neh-seh-see-toh toh-mahr-leh lah tehm-peh-rah-too-rah ee lah preh-see-ohn deh lah sahn-greh)*
I also need a urine sample.	**También necesito una muestra de orina.** *(Tahm-bee-ehn neh-seh-see-toh oo-nah moo-ehs-trah deh oh-ree-nah)*
Don't get up!	**¡No se levante!** *(Noh se leh-bahn-teh)*

Supportive measures include ensuring privacy and accepting various reactions to fear and pain. Explain all procedures, even when you think the patient does not understand the language. Try to demonstrate the

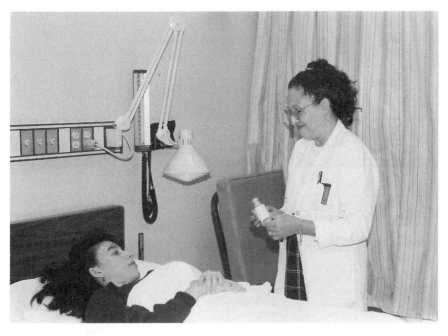

FIGURE 2-3   *The nurse explains the directions on the bottle to the patient and asks a variety of questions.*

procedure you are about to perform and what you expect. Commonly used commands are listed in Table 2-3.

Las medidas que dan apoyo incluyen el asegurar privacidad y aceptar reacciones al miedo y al dolor. Explique todos los procedimientos, aun cuando usted piense que el paciente no entiende la lengua. Trate de demostrar el procedimiento que va a hacer y lo que se espera del paciente. Los mandatos que se usan comúnmente figuran en la tabla 2-3.

I have the bedpan.	**Tengo el bacín/pato.** *(Tehn-goh ehl bah-seen/pah-toh)*
Bend your knees!	**¡Doble las piernas!** *(Doh-bleh lahs pee-ehr-nahs)*
Pull up your hips!	**¡Levante la cadera!** *(Leh-bahn-teh lah kah-deh-rah)*
Are you in pain?	**¿Tiene dolor?** *(Tee-eh-neh doh-lohr)*
Where?	**¿Dónde?** *(Dohn-deh)*
Here is the toilet paper.	**Aquí está el papel del baño/higiénico.** *(Ah-kee ehs-tah ehl pah-pehl dehl bah-nyoh/ee-hee-eh-nee-koh)*
Lower your legs.	**Baje sus piernas.** *(Bah-heh soos pee-ehr-nahs)*
Rest.	**Descanse** *(Des-kahn-seh)*

TABLE 2-3
COMMON COMMANDS

TABLA 2-3
MANDATOS COMUNES

ENGLISH	SPANISH	PRONUNCIATION
Bend!	**¡Doble!**	**¡Doh-bleh!**
Call!	**¡Llame!**	**¡Yah-meh!**
Choose!	**¡Escoja!**	**¡Ehs-koh-hah!**
Get!	**¡Consiga!**	**¡Kohn-see-gah!**
Get out!	**¡Fuera!**	**¡Foo-eh-rah!**
Get up!	**¡Levántese!**	**¡Leh-bahn-teh-seh!**
Lower!	**¡Baje!**	**¡Bah-heh!**
Pull!	**¡Jale!**	**¡Hah-leh!**
Tell me!	**¡Dígame!**	**¡Dee-gah-meh!**
Wake up!	**¡Despierte!**	**¡Dehs-pee-ehr-teh!**

Later on they will take X-rays.	**Más tarde le van a tomar rayos X.** *(Mahs tahr-deh leh bahn ah toh-mahr rah-yohs eh-kiss)*
Then they will take blood samples.	**Luego le van a tomar muestras de sangre.** *(Loo-eh-goh leh bahn ah toh-mahr moo-ehs-trahs deh sahn-greh)*
Here is the bell.	**Aquí está la campana.** *(Ah-kee ehs-tah lah kahm-pah-nah)*
Call if you need help.	**Llame si necesita ayuda.** *(Yah-meh see neh-seh-see-tah ah-yoo-dah)*

In the lobby, Mr. García speaks to the receptionist. See Table 2-4 for pronunciation of selected words.

En la sala de espera, el señor García habla con la recepcionista. Vea la tabla 2-4 para la pronunciación de palabras selectas.

I am going to ask some questions.	**Voy a hacerle unas preguntas.** *(Boy ah ah-sehr-leh oo-nahs preh-goon-tahs)*
What is your address?	**¿Cuál es su dirección?** *(Koo-ahl ehs soo dee-rehk-see-ohn)*
The name of the street . . .	**El nombre de la calle . . .** *(Ehl nohm-breh deh lah kah-yeh)*

TABLE 2-4
PRONUNCIATION OF
SELECTED WORDS

TABLA 2-4
PRONUNCIACION DE
PALABRAS SELECTAS

ENGLISH	*SPANISH*	*PRONUNCIATION*
address	**dirección**	*dee-rehk-see-ohn*
number	**número**	*noo-meh-roh*
health	**salud**	*sah-lood*
work	**trabajo**	*trah-bah-hoh*
insurance	**seguro**	*seh-goo-roh*
sign	**firme**	*feer-meh*
here	**aquí**	*ah-kee*

FIGURE 2-4   *Patient information is carefully documented.*

Telephone number?	**¿Número de teléfono?**
	(Noo-meh-roh deh teh-leh-foh-noh)
Number of your . . .	**Número de su . . .**
	(Noo-meh-roh deh soo)
health insurance?	**seguro de salud?**
	(seh-goo-roh deh sah-lood)
medicaid?	**medicaid?**
	(meh-dee-kah-eed)
social security?	**seguro social?**
	(seh-goo-roh soh-see-ahl)
Where do you work?	**¿Dónde trabaja?**
	(Dohn-deh trah-bah-hah)
What is your work phone number?	**¿Cuál es el teléfono de su trabajo?**
	(Koo-ahl ehs ehl teh-leh-foh-noh deh soo trah-bah-hoh)
Sign here, please.	**Firme aquí, por favor.**
	(Feer-meh ah-kee, pohr fah-bohr)
Thank you!	**¡Gracias!**
	(Grah-see-ahs)

TABLE 2-5 HELPFUL NUMBERS		TABLA 2-5 NUMEROS UTILES	
NUMBER	ENGLISH	SPANISH	PRONUNCIATION
1	one	uno	oo-noh
2	two	dos	dohs
3	three	tres	trehs
4	four	cuatro	koo-ah-troh
5	five	cinco	seen-koh
6	six	seis	seh-ees
7	seven	siete	see-eh-teh
8	eight	ocho	oh-choh
9	nine	nueve	noo-eh-beh
10	ten	diez	dee-ehs
15	fifteen	quince	keen-seh
20	twenty	veinte	beh-een-teh
30	thirty	treinta	treh-een-tah
50	fifty	cincuenta	seen-koo-ehn-tah
100	one hundred	cien	see-ehn

Memorization of numbers is helpful when you are asking for addresses or phone numbers. Table 2-5 lists some helpful numbers.

Memorizar los números es útil al pedir direcciones o números de teléfono. La tabla 2-5 muestra algunos números útiles.

Chapter Three

A Home Visit

Una Visita al Hogar

During a home visit, it is customary to greet each member of the family. Greet adults with a handshake (also with a smile). For younger children, a pat on the head or a light touch on the cheek is acceptable. People are more likely to pay attention to what you do, rather than how you pronounce the language, so don't worry about your accent. During this visit, the health worker will talk to the mother about her baby, to a six-year old, and to the grandfather.

FIGURE 3-1 *All family members must be assessed during a family visit.*

Durante una visita al hogar se acostumbra saludar a cada miembro de la familia. Salude a los adultos con un apretón de manos (también con una sonrisa). A los niños, una palmadita en la cabeza o una caricia en la mejilla es aceptable. La gente le pone más atención a lo que hace que a cómo pronuncia el lenguaje, así que no se preocupe mucho por su acento. En esta visita, el trabajador de la salud hablará con la madre acerca del bebé, con el niño de seis años, y con el abuelo.

Hello, Mrs. Mora.	**Hola, señora Mora.** *(Oh-lah, seh-nyoh-rah Moh-rah)*
How are you?	**¿Cómo está?** *(Koh-moh ehs-tah)*

A variety of greetings and common expressions will help you to get acquainted with the patients. Some common greetings and expressions are listed in Table 3-1.

Una variedad de saludos y expresiones comunes le ayudarán a darse a conocer con los pacientes. La tabla 3-1 muestra algunos saludos y expresiones comúnes.

I am a nurse.	**Yo soy la enfermera.** *(Yoh soh-eeh lah ehn-fehr-meh-rah)*
I am a doctor.	**Yo soy la doctora.** *(Yoh soh-eeh lah dohk-toh-rah)*

TABLE 3-1 *GREETINGS AND COMMON* *EXPRESSIONS*	TABLA 3-1 ***SALUDOS Y EXPRESIONES*** ***COMUNES***

ENGLISH	SPANISH	PRONUNCIATION
Good morning!	**¡Buenos días!**	*¡Boo-eh-nohs dee-ahs!*
Good evening!	**¡Buenas noches!**	*¡Boo-eh-nahs noh-chehs!*
Pardon me!	**¡Perdóneme!**	*¡Pehr-doh-neh-meh!*
Excuse me!	**¡Excúseme!**	*¡Ehx-koo-seh-meh!*
Good afternoon!	**¡Buenas tardes!**	*¡Boo-eh-nahs tahr-dehs!*
Good night!	**¡Buenas noches!**	*¡Boo-eh-nahs noh-chehs!*
Thank you!	**¡Gracias!**	*¡Grah-see-ahs!*
Please!	**¡Por favor!**	*¡Pohr fah-bohr!*
Good!	**¡Bueno!**	*¡Boo-eh-noh!*
Go on!	**¡Siga!**	*¡See-gah!*

I am a social worker.

Yo soy la trabajadora social.
*(Yoh soh-ee lah trah-bah-hah-doh-rah
soh-see-ahl)*

I am a dentist.

Yo soy el dentista.
(Yoh soh-ee ehl dehn-tees-tah)

Today I am here to examine your baby.

Hoy estoy aquí para examinar a su bebé.
*(Oh-ee ehs-tohy ah-kee pah-rah ehx-ah-
mee-nahr ah soo beh-beh)*

I will start by taking his vital signs.

Voy a empezar por tomarle los signos vitales.
*(Boy ah ehm-peh-sahr pohr toh-mahr-leh
lohs seeg-nohs bee-tah-lehs)*

When was he born?

¿Cuándo nació?
(Koo-ahn-doh nah-see-oh)

Where?

¿Dónde?
(Dohn-deh)

Was the delivery normal?

¿Fue normal el parto?
(Foo-eh nohr-mahl ehl pahr-toh)

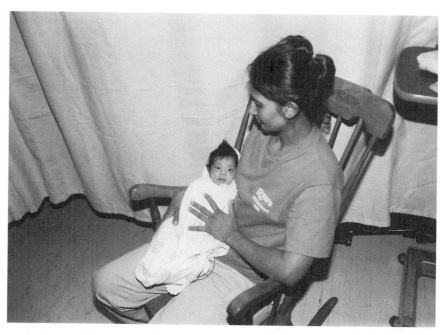

FIGURE 3-2 *During a home visit the health-care worker has an opportunity to talk to the mother about her baby.*

Note that questions in Spanish use the interrogation symbol at the beginning and at the end of the question. It is helpful to memorize some common pronouns used in questions. Table 3-2 lists some commonly used interrogative expressions.

Note que las preguntas en español usan el símbolo interrogativo al principio y al final de las mismas. Es conveniente memorizar algunos pronombres comunes que se usan en las preguntas. La tabla 3-2 muestra algunas expresiones interrogativas comunes.

English	Spanish
Was he premature?	**¿Fue prematuro?** *(Foo-eh preh-mah-too-roh)*
Has he been ill?	**¿Ha estado enfermo?** *(Ah ehs-tah-doh ehn-fehr-moh)*
Is he . . .	**¿Está . . .** *(Ehs-tah)*
eating well?	**comiendo bien?** *(koh-mee-ehn-doh bee-ehn)*
sleeping well?	**durmiendo bien?** *(door-mee-ehn-doh bee-ehn)*
breast-feeding?	**tomando el pecho?** *(toh-mahn-doh ehl peh-choh)*

TABLE 3-2
COMMON INTERROGATIVE
EXPRESSIONS

TABLA 3-2
EXPRESIONES INTERROGATIVAS
COMUNES

ENGLISH	SPANISH	PRONUNCIATION
Who?	**¿Quién?**	*Kee-ehn?*
Who? (all)	**¿Quiénes?**	*Kee-ehn-ehs?*
What?	**¿Qué?**	*Keh?*
Which?	**¿Cuál?**	*Koo-ahl?*
Which? (ones)	**¿Cuáles?**	*Koo-ah-lehs?*
How many?	**¿Cuántos? (m)**	*Koo-ahn-tohs? (m)*
	¿Cuántas? (f)	*Koo-ahn-tahs? (f)*
How much?	**¿Cuánto?**	*Koo-ahn-toh?*
How?	**¿Cómo?**	*Koh-moh?*
When?	**¿Cuándo?**	*Koo-ahn-doh?*
Where?	**¿Dónde?**	*Dohn-deh?*
Why?	**¿Por qué?**	*Pohr keh?*
For what?	**¿Para qué?**	*Pah-rah keh?*

taking formula?	tomando fórmula?
	(toh-mahn-doh fohr-moo-lah)
What formula does he take?	¿Qué fórmula toma?
	(Keh fohr-moo-lah toh-mah)
How many ounces does he take?	¿Cuántas onzas toma?
	(Koo-ahn-tahs ohn-sahs toh-mah)
How often do you feed him?	¿Qué tan a menudo lo alimenta?
	(Keh tahn ah meh-noo-doh loh ah-lee-mehn-tah)
Do you feed him every three hours?	¿Le da de comer cada tres horas?
	(Leh dah deh koh-mehr kah-dah trehs oh-rahs)
This is a new formula.	Esta es una fórmula nueva.
	(Ehs-tah ehs oo-nah fohr-moo-lah noo-eh-bah)

Table 3-3 helps you with the pronunciation of selected words.
La table 3-3 le ayuda con la pronunciación de palabras selectas.

| Does he have a fever/diarrhea/colic? | ¿Tiene fiebre/diarrea/cólico? |
| | *(Tee-eh-neh fee-eh-breh/dee-ah-re-ah/koh-lee-koh)* |

TABLE 3-3 PRONUNCIATION OF SELECTED WORDS	TABLA 3-3 PRONUNCIACION DE PALABRAS SELECTAS	
ENGLISH	SPANISH	PRONUNCIATION
family	familia	fah-mee-lee-ah
nurse	enfermera	ehn-fehr-meh-rah
I am	yo soy	yoh soh-ee
diaper	pañal	pah-nyahl
formula	fórmula	fohr-moo-lah
fever	fiebre	fee-eh-breh
diarrhea	diarrea	dee-ah-re-ah
sleep	sueño	soo-eh-nyoh
colic	cólico	koh-lee-koh
cough	tos	tohs
medicine	medicina	meh-dee-see-nah

Does he sleep all night?

¿Duerme toda la noche?
(Doo-ehr-meh toh-dah lah noh-cheh)

How many times a night does he wake up?

¿Cuántas veces se despierta durante la noche?
(Koo-ahn-tahs beh-sehs seh dehs-pee-ehr-tah doo-rahn-teh lah noh-cheh)

Does he cry often?

¿Llora mucho?
(Yoh-rah moo-choh)

When was the last time he had a bowel movement?

¿Cuándo fue la última vez que evacuó/movió el intestino?
(Koo-ahn-doh foo-eh lah ool-tee-mah behs keh eh-bah-koo-oh/moh-bee-oh ehl een-tehs-tee-noh)

Is he urinating well?

¿Orina bien?
(Oh-ree-nah bee-ehn)

Have you seen blood in his urine?

¿Ha visto sangre en su orina?
(Ah bees-toh sahn-greh ehn soo oh-ree-nah)

How many diapers have you changed since yesterday?

¿Cuántos pañales he cambiado desde ayer?
(Koo-ahn-tohs pah-nyah-lehs ah kahm-bee-ah-doh dehs-deh ah-yehr)

When did you notice the skin rash?

¿Cuándo se dió cuenta de la piel rosada?
(Koo-ahn-doh seh dee-oh koo-ehn-tah deh lah pee-ehl roh-sah-dah)

How many times has he vomited?

¿Cuántas veces ha vomitado?
(Koo-ahn-tahs beh-sehs ah boh-mee-tah-doh)

Is it a lot?

¿Es mucho?
(Ehs moo-choh)

Does the vomit have blood in it?

¿Tiene sangre el vómito?
(Tee-eh-neh sahn-greh ehl boh-mee-toh)

What color is the vomit?

¿De qué color es el vómito?
(Deh keh ko-lohr ehs ehl boh-mee-toh)

Does the vomit have any undigested food in it?

¿Tiene restos de comida?
(Tee-eh-neh rehs-tohs deh koh-mee-dah)

Does the vomit smell bad?

¿El vómito huele mal?
(Ehl boo-mee-toh oo-eh-leh mahl)

Is he coughing?

¿Está tosiendo?
(Ehs-tah toh-see-ehn-doh)

Write some of the common verbs from Table 3-4 on an index card. They will come in handy in the clinical setting.

Escriba en una tarjeta algunos verbos útiles de la tabla 3-4. Serán convenientes en el área clínica.

Does he cough only at night?	**¿Tose sólo de noche?**
	(Toh-seh soh-loh deh noh-cheh)
Is it a dry cough?	**¿Es tos seca?**
	(Ehs tohs seh-kah)
Is it a moist cough?	**¿Es tos húmeda?**
	(Ehs tohs oo-meh-dah)
Does the cough produce vomit?	**¿La tos le produce vómito?**
	(Lah tohs leh proh-doo-seh boh-mee-toh)
Dress him with few clothes.	**Vístalo con poca ropa.**
	(Bees-tah-loh kohn poh-kah roh-pah)
Leave the area uncovered.	**Deje el área descubierta.**
	(Deh-heh ehl ah-reh-ah dehs-koo-bee-ehr-tah)
Do not put plastic panties on him.	**No le ponga calzón de plástico.**
	(Noh leh pohn-gah cahl-sohn deh plahs-tee-koh)

TABLE 3-4
USEFUL VERBS

TABLA 3-4
VERBOS UTILES

ENGLISH	SPANISH	PRONUNCIATION
boil	**hervir**	*ehr-beer*
change	**cambiar**	*kahn-bee-ahr*
cough	**toser**	*tohs-ehr*
cry	**llorar**	*yoh-rahr*
dress	**vestir**	*behs-teer*
drink	**beber/tomar**	*beh-behr/toh-mahr*
eat	**comer**	*koh-mehr*
feel	**sentir**	*sehn-teer*
give	**dar**	*dahr*
leave	**dejar**	*deh-hahr*
make	**hacer**	*ah-sehr*
play	**jugar**	*joo-gahr*
see	**ver**	*behr*
take	**tomar/llevar**	*toh-mahr/yeh-bahr*

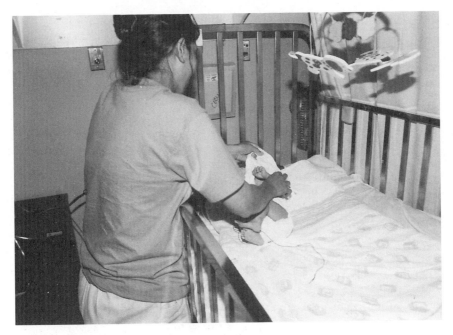

FIGURE 3-3 A home visit provides you an opportunity to assess the environment and see if there are other needs that you need to address.

Take his temperature rectally.	**Tómele la temperatura por el recto.** *(Toh-meh-leh lah tehm-peh-rah-too-rah pohr ehl rehk-toh)*
Normal rectal temperature is 100.4 degrees Fahrenheit.	**La temperatura normal en el recto es de 100.4 grados Fahrenheit.** *(Lah tehm-peh-rah-too-rah nohr-mahl ehn ehl rehk-toh ehs deh see-ehn poon-toh koo-ah-troh grah-dohs fah-rehn-heh-eet)*
Give him this medicine every four hours.	**Déle esta medicina cada cuatro horas.** *(Deh-leh ehs-tah meh-dee-see-nah kah-dah koo-ah-troh oh-rahs)*
Boil any water that he drinks.	**Hierva el agua que él toma.** *(Ee-ehr-bah ehl ah-goo-ah keh ehl toh-mah)*
Sterilize his bottles.	**Esterilice las botellas/biberones** *(Ehs-teh-ree-lee-seh lahs boh-teh-yahs/ bee-beh-roh-nehs)*

You can feed him solid foods.

Puede darle alimentos sólidos.
(Poo-eh-deh dahr-leh ah-lee-mehn-tohs soh-lee-dohs)

Wash well any fruits and vegetables that you give him.

Lave bien las frutas y verduras que le dé.
(Lah-beh bee-ehn lahs froo-tahs ee behr-doo-rahs keh leh deh)

Wash his hands before feeding him.

Lávele las manos antes de darle de comer.
(Lah-beh-leh lahs mah-nohs ahn-tehs deh dahr-leh deh koh-mehr)

Don't let him put dirt in his mouth.

No deje que se meta tierra en la boca.
(Noh deh-heh keh seh meh-tah tee-eh-rrah ehn lah boh-kah)

Burp him.

Haga que eructe/repita.
(Ah-gah keh eh-rook-teh/reh-pee-tah)

Keep him awake.

Manténgalo despierto.
(Mahn-tehn-gah-loh dehs-pee-ehr-toh)

Don't let him sleep more than three hours during the day.

No lo deje dormir más de tres horas durante el día.
(Noh loh deh-heh dohr-meehr mahs deh trehs oh-rahs doo-rahn-teh ehl dee-ah)

Watch to see if he sleeps quietly.

Vigile si su sueño es tranquilo.
(Bee-hee-leh see soo soo-eh-nyoh ehs trahn-kee-loh)

Watch to see if he moves abnormally.

Vigile si presenta movimientos anormales.
(Bee-hee-leh see preh-sehn-tah moh-bee-mee-ehn-tohs ah-nohr-mah-lehs)

Give him the medicine with a dropper.

Déle la medicina con gotero.
(Deh-leh lah meh-dee-see-nah kohn goh-teh-roh)

When you are examining a baby or older children, it is also a good idea to talk to their parents. Be sure to ask direct questions to older children and call them by their first names. Also, observe to see if the parents and the child get along. Table 3-5 lists common questions.

Es una buena idea hablar con los padres cuando esté examinando al bebé o a niños mayores. A los niños mayores hágales preguntas directas y llámelos por su nombre. También observe si los padres y el niño se llevan bien. La tabla 3-5 muestra preguntas comúnes.

TABLE 3-5 SIMPLE QUESTIONS	TABLA 3-5 PREGUNTAS SENCILLAS	
ENGLISH	SPANISH	PRONUNCIATION
Do you understand?	¿Entiende?	¿Ehn-tee-ehn-deh?
What is this?	¿Qué es esto?	¿Keh ehs ehs-toh?
Why not?	¿Por qué no?	¿Pohr keh noh?
What's going on?	¿Qué pasa?	¿Keh pah-sah?
Since when?	¿Desde cuándo?	¿Dehs-deh koo-ahn-doh?
For what?	¿Para qué?	¿Pah-rah keh?
Never?	¿Nunca?	¿Noon-kah?
Are you hungry?	¿Tiene hambre?	¿Tee-eh-neh ahm-breh?
Are you thirsty?	¿Tiene sed?	¿Tee-eh-neh sehd?
Is that enough?	¿Es suficiente?	¿Ehs soo-fee-see-ehn-teh?
Is that too much?	¿Es mucho?	¿Ehs moo-choh?
Can you feel this?	¿Siente esto?	¿See-ehn-teh ehs-toh?

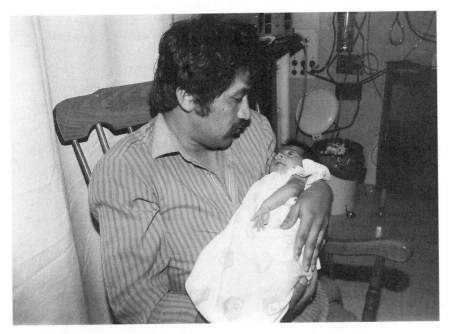

FIGURE 3-4 Observe the father's interaction with his child. Note how they get along.

I want to examine the older child.	**Quiero examinar al niño mayor.** *(Kee-eh-roh ehx-ah-mee-nahr ahl nee-nyoh mah-yohr)*
The one who is six years old.	**El que tiene seis años.** *(Ehl keh tee-eh-neh seh-ees ah-nyohs)*
Does he go to school?	**¿Va a la escuela?** *(Bah ah lah ehs-koo-eh-lah)*
Does he sleep well?	**¿Duerme bien?** *(Doo-ehr-meh bee-ehn)*
Does he wet the bed?	**¿Moja la cama?** *(Moh-hah lah kah-mah)*
Does he play outdoors?	**¿Juega afuera de la casa?** *(Joo-eh-gah ah-foo-eh-rah deh lah kah-sah)*
Does he have any friends?	**¿Tiene amigos?** *(Tee-eh-neh ah-mee-gohs)*
Do any of your children have . . .	**¿Algunos de sus niños tienen . . .** *(Ahl-goo-nohs deh soos nee-nyohs tee-eh-nehn)*
asthma?	**asma?** *(ahs-mah)*
cold/flu?	**resfriado/gripa?** *(rehs-free-ah-doh/gree-pah)*
chickenpox?	**varicela?** *(bah-ree-seh-lah)*
diphtheria?	**difteria?** *(deef-teh-ree-ah)*
measles?	**sarampión?** *(sah-rahm-pee-ohn)*
mumps?	**paperas?** *(pah-peh-rahs)*
pneumonia?	**pulmonía?** *(pool-moh-nee-ah)*
convulsions?	**convulsiones?** *(kohn-bool-see-ohn-ehs)*
nausea and vomiting?	**náusea y vómitos?** *(nah-oo-seh-ah ee boh-mee-tohs)*
hearing defects?	**defectos del oído?** *(deh-fehk-tohs dehl oh-ee-doh)*
delayed speech?	**retraso del habla?** *(reh-trah-soh dehl ah-blah)*
visual defects?	**defectos de la vista?** *(deh-fehk-tohs deh lah bees-tah)*

bad coordination?	**mala coordinación?**
	(mah-lah kohr-dee-nah-see-ohn)
Is he hyperactive?	**Es inquieto/latoso?**
	(Ehs een-kee-eh-toh/lah-toh-soh)
Does his school complain about him?	**¿Tiene quejas de la escuela?**
	(Tee-eh-neh keh-hahs deh lah ehs-koo-eh-lah)

It is all right to use the familiar voice *tú* with adolescents and young children. With adults, however, especially if you do not know them, it is better to use the more formal term *usted*. Address older persons as Mr. or Mrs. and their last name. Table 3-6 contains a list of personal pronouns.

Está bien usar la forma familiar *tú* con personas jovenes o niños. Con los adultos, especialmente si no los conoce, es mejor usar *usted*. Diríjase a las personas mayores por "señor," "señora" y su apellido. La tabla 3-6 muestra una lista de pronombres personales.

FIGURE 3-5 *The nurse must ask questions about the growth and development of each child.*

TABLE 3-6 PERSONAL PRONOUNS	TABLA 3-6 PRONOMBRES PERSONALES	
ENGLISH	SPANISH	PRONUNCIATION
I	Yo	Yoh
You (familiar)	Tú (familiar)	Too
You (formal)	Usted (formal)	Oos-tehd
He	El	Ehl
She	Ella	Eh-yah
We (masculine)	Nosotros (masculino)	Noh-soh-trohs
We (feminine)	Nosotras (femenino)	Noh-soh-trahs
They (masculine)	Ellos (masculino)	Eh-yohs
They (feminine)	Ellas (femenino)	Eh-yahs

What is your name?	¿Cómo se/te llama(s)? *(Koh-moh seh/teh yah-mah[s])*
My name is . . .	Mi nombre es . . . *(Mee nohm-breh ehs)*
I would like to talk to you!	¡Me gustaría hablar con usted/contigo! *(Meh goos-tah-ree-ah ah-blahr kohn oos-tehd/kohn-tee-goh)*
Do you have time?	¿Tiene(s) tiempo? *(Tee-eh-neh[s] tee-ehm-poh)*
Are you in a hurry?	¿Está(s) de prisa? *(Ehs-tah[s] deh pree-sah)*
Do you like going to school?	¿Le/Te gusta ir a la escuela? *(Leh/Teh goos-tah eer ah lah ehs-koo-eh-lah)*
What grade are you in?	¿En qué año está(s)? *(Ehn keh ah-nyoh ehs-tah[s])*
What subject do you like best?	¿Qué materia le/te gusta más? *(Keh mah-teh-ree-ah leh/teh goos-tah mahs)*
What kind of grades do you make?	¿Qué calificaciones saca(s)? *(Keh kah-lee-fee-kah-see-ohn-ehs sah-kah[s])*
Do you play sports?	¿Practica(s) deportes? *(Prahk-tee-kah[s] deh-pohr-tehs)*
Which ones?	¿Cuáles? *(Koo-ah-lehs)*

How many friends do you have?	¿Cuántos amigos tiene(s)?
	(Koo-ahn-tohs ah-mee-gohs tee-eh-neh[s])
Do you need help with your school work?	¿Necesita(s) ayuda con la tarea?
	(Neh-seh-see-tah[s] ah-yoo-dah kohn lah tah-reh-ah)
Who helps you?	¿Quién le/te ayuda?
	(Kee-ehn leh/teh ah-yoo-dah)
Do you have problems seeing?	¿Tiene(s) problemas con la visión?
	(Tee-eh-neh[s] proh-bleh-mahs kohn lah bee-see-ohn)
Do you wear glasses?	¿Usa(s) anteojos/lentes?
	(Oo-sah[s] ahn-teh-oh-hohs/lehn-tehs)
Can you see the blackboard well?	¿Puede(s) ver bien la pizarra/el pizarrón?
	(Poo-eh-deh[s] behr bee-ehn lah pee-sah-rrah/ehl pee-sah-rrohn)
Do you miss school often?	¿Falta(s) mucho a la escuela?
	(Fahl-tah[s] moo-choh ah lah ehs-koo-eh-lah)
Do you get distracted easily?	¿Se/Te distrae(s) fácilmente?
	(Seh/teh dees-trah-eh[s] fah-seel-mehn-teh)
Who takes you to school?	¿Quién lo/te lleva a la escuela?
	(Kee-ehn loh/teh yeh-bah ah lah ehs-koo-eh-lah)
Do you walk to school?	¿Camina(s) a la escuela?
	(Kah-mee-nah[s] ah lah ehs-koo-eh-lah)
Do you eat breakfast?	¿Toma(s) desayuno/almuerzo?
	(Toh-mah[s] deh-sah-yoo-noh/ahl-moo-ehr-soh)
Do you have problems with your teeth?	¿Tiene(s) problemas en los dientes?
	(Tee-eh-neh[s] proh-bleh-mahs ehn lohs dee-ehn-tehs)
At what time do you go to sleep?	¿A qué hora se/te acuesta(s) a dormir?
	(Ah keh oh-rah seh/teh ah-koo-ehs-tah[s] ah dohr-meer)
How many hours do you sleep?	¿Cuántas horas duerme(s)?
	(Koo-ahn-tahs oh-rahs doo-ehr-meh[s])
Do you wake up at night?	¿Se/Te despierta(s) en la noche?
	(Seh/Teh dehs-pee-ehr-tah[s] ehn lah noh-che)

What house chores do you do?	¿Qué quehaceres hace(s)? *(Keh keh-ah-seh-rehs ah-seh[s])*
How do you feel?	¿Cómo se/te siente(s)? *(Koh-moh seh/teh see-ehn-teh[s])*
Have you been sick?	¿Ha(s) estado enfermo? *(Ah[s] ehs-tah-doh ehn-fehr-moh)*
Is there anything that worries you?	¿Hay algo que le/te preocupa(s)? *(Ah-ee ahl-goh keh leh/teh preh-oh-koo-pah[s])*
Who do you talk to?	¿Con quién habla(s)? *(Kohn kee-ehn ah-blah[s])*
Do you have any questions?	¿Tiene(s) preguntas? *(Tee-eh-neh[s] preh-goon-tahs)*
Thank you for talking to me!	¡Gracias por hablar conmigo! *(Grah-see-ahs pohr ah-blahr kohn-mee-goh)*
I will talk to your mother again.	Hablaré con su/tu mamá otra vez. *(Ah-blah-reh kohn soo/too mah-mah oh-trah behs)*
Good-bye!	¡Hasta luego! *(Ahs-tah loo-eh-goh)*

A home visit gives you the opportunity to assess several members of the family. It is also a convenient time to assess the home environment and to determine how family members are coping with their needs. The health worker approaches Mr. Rios, the grandfather. Mr. Rios suffered a stroke five months ago and is recuperating.

Una visita al hogar proporciona la oportunidad de asesorar a varios miembros de la familia. También es una ocasión conveniente para evaluar el ambiente familiar y determinar cómo se están dando abasto con sus necesidades. El trabajador de la salud se dirige al señor Ríos, el abuelo. El señor Ríos sufrió un ataque de apoplejía hace cinco meses y se está recuperando.

Mr. Ríos, how are you?	Señor Ríos, ¿cómo está? *(Seh-nyohr Ree-ohs, koh-moh ehs-tah)*
Good afternoon!	¡Buenas tardes! *(Boo-eh-nahs tahr-dehs)*
Do you remember me?	¿Se acuerda de mí? *(Seh ah-koo-ehr-dah deh mee)*
I am a . . .	Yo soy . . . *(Yo soh-ee)*

medical student.	**el estudiante de medicina.** *(ehl ehs-too-dee-ahn-teh* *deh meh-dee-see-nah)*
nurse.	**el/la enfermero(a).** *(ehl/lah ehn-fehr-meh-roh[ah])*
therapist.	**el/la terapista.** *(ehl/lah teh-rah-pees-tah)*
I want to talk to you.	**Quiero hablar con usted.** *(Kee-eh-roh ah-blahr kohn oos-tehd)*
Can you get out of bed?	**¿Puede salir de la cama?** *(Poo-eh-deh sah-leer deh lah kah-mah)*
Please raise this arm.	**Por favor, levante este brazo.** *(Pohr fah-bohr leh-bahn-teh ehs-teh* *brah-soh)*
Now, raise the left arm.	**Ahora levante el brazo izquierdo.** *(Ah-oh-rah leh-bahn-teh ehl brah-soh* *ees-kee-ehr-doh)*
I will help you to sit down.	**Le ayudaré a sentarse.** *(Leh ah-yoo-dah-reh ah sehn-tahr-seh)*

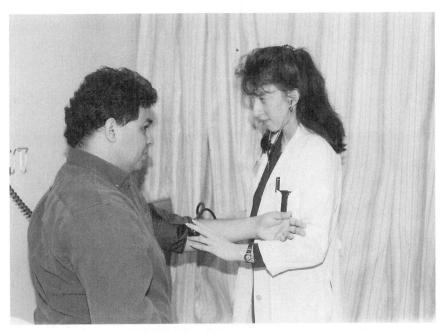

FIGURE 3-6 Vital signs are taken routinely during a home visit.

Remain seated.

Quédese sentado.
(Keh-deh-seh sehn-tah-doh)

I have some paper.

Tengo papel.
(Tehn-goh pah-pehl)

I want you to write your
  name and today's date.

**Quiero que escriba su nombre y la
  fecha de hoy.**
*(Kee-eh-roh keh ehs-kree-bah soo nohm-
  breh ee lah feh-chah deh oh-ee)*

Now, stand up and walk.

Ahora, levántese y camine.
*(Ah-oh-rah, leh-bahn-teh-seh ee kah-
  mee-neh)*

Walk six paces.

Camine seis pasos.
(Kah-mee-neh seh-ees pah-sohs)

Do not hold onto the wall.

No se agarre de la pared.
*(Noh seh ah-gah-rreh deh lah pah-
  rehd)*

Sit in the chair.

Siéntese en la silla.
(See-ehn-teh-seh ehn lah see-yah)

Please cross your legs.

Por favor, cruce la pierna.
*(Pohr fah-bohr, kroo-seh lah pee-ehr-
  nah)*

Lift up your right foot.

Levante el pie derecho.
(Leh-bahn-teh ehl pee-eh deh-reh-choh)

Have you had swelling . . .

Ha tenido hinchazón . . .
(Ah teh-nee-doh een-chah-sohn)

on your feet?

en los pies?
(ehn lohs pee-ehs)

on your ankles?

en los tobillos?
(ehn lohs toh-bee-yohs)

on your eyelids?

en los párpados?
(ehn lohs pahr-pah-dohs)

Are you taking your
  medicine?

¿Está tomando sus medicinas?
*(Ehs-tah toh-mahn-doh soos meh-dee-
  see-nahs)*

How many times a day?

¿Cuántas veces al día?
(Koo-ahn-tahs beh-sehs ahl dee-ah)

Do you sleep during the day?

¿Duerme durante el día?
(Doo-ehr-meh doo-rahn-teh ehl dee-ah)

At what time do you go to
  sleep?

¿A qué hora se acuesta a dormir?
*(Ah keh oh-rah seh ah-koo-ehs-tah ah
  dohr-meer)*

At what time do you get up?

¿A qué hora se levanta?
(Ah keh oh-rah seh leh-bahn-tah)

Do you wake up at night?

¿Se despierta en la noche?
(Seh dehs-pee-ehr-tah ehn lah noh-cheh)

Is your appetite good?

¿Tiene buen apetito?
(Tee-eh-neh boo-ehn ah-peh-tee-toh)

Is your appetite bad?

¿Tiene mal apetito?
(Tee-eh-neh mahl ah-peh-tee-toh)

How many times do you eat per day?

¿Cuántas veces come por día?
(Koo-ahn-tahs beh-sehs koh-meh pohr dee-ah)

What did you eat for breakfast?

¿Qué comió en el desayuno?
(Keh koh-mee-oh ehn ehl deh-sah-yoo-noh)

Tell me what foods.

Dígame qué alimentos.
(Dee-gah-meh keh ah-lee-mehn-tohs)

Do you drink coffee?

¿Toma café?
(Toh-mah kah-feh)

How many cups per day?

¿Cuántas tazas diarias?
(Koo-ahn-tahs tah-sahs dee-ah-ree-ahs)

How many glasses of water do you drink?

¿Cuántos vasos de agua toma?
((Koo-ahn-tohs bah-sohs deh ah-goo-ah toh-mah)

When was the last time you went to the bathroom?

¿Cuándo fue la última vez que movió el intestino?
(Koo-ahn-doh foo-eh lah ool-tee-mah behs keh moh-bee-oh ehl een-tehs-tee-noh)

Are you constipated?

¿Está estreñido?
(Ehs-tah ehs-treh-nyee-doh)

Do you have diarrhea?

¿Tiene diarrea?
(Tee-eh-neh dee-ah-reh-ah)

How often do you urinate?

¿Cuántas veces orina?
(Koo-ahn-tahs beh-sehs oh-ree-nah)

What color is your urine?

¿Cuál es el color de la orina?
(Koo-ahl ehs ehl koh-lohr deh lah oh-ree-nah)

Have you seen blood in your urine?

¿Ha visto sangre en la orina?
(Ah beehs-toh sahn-greh ehn lah oh-ree-nah)

Do you dribble?

¿Se gotea desqués de orinar?
(Seh goh-teh-ah dehs-poo-ehs deh oh-ree-nahr?)

Do you have problems beginning to urinate?

¿Tiene dificultad para empezar a orinar?
*(Tee-eh-neh dee-fee-kool-tahd pah-rah
ehm-peh-sahr ah oh-ree-nahr)*

Do you have any hesitancy
during urination?

¿Se corta el chorro de la orina?
*(Seh kohr-tah ehl choh-roh deh lah oh-
ree-nah)*

Do you have any questions?

¿Tiene preguntas que hacerme?
*(Tee-eh-neh preh-goon-tahs keh ah-sehr-
meh)*

Thank you for the
information.

Gracias por la información.
*(Grah-see-ahs pohr lah een-fohr-mah-
see-ohn)*

Visit to the Dentist

Visita al Dentista

Proper dental hygine requires frequent visits to the dentist. The condition of the teeth allows for proper chewing and thus assists with the digestion of foods. A healthy mouth will always be considered a sign of good health.

Una apropiada higiene dental requiere visitas frecuentes al dentista. El buen estado de los dientes permite una buena masticación y por lo tanto la buena digestión de los alimentos. Una boca sana será siempre un signo del buen cuidado personal.

Good afternoon Miss Gonzalez.	**Buenas tardes, señorita González.** *(Boo-eh-nahs tahr-dehs seh-nyoh-ree-tah Gohn-sah-lehs)*
Come in.	**Pase/entre usted.** *(Pah-seh/ehn-treh oos-tehd)*
Please sit down.	**Siéntese, por favor.** *(See-ehn-teh-seh pohr fah-bohr)*
What is the matter?	**¿Qué le pasa/sucede?** *(Keh leh pah-sah/soo-seh-deh)*
When was the last time you went to the dentist?	**¿Cuándo fue al dentista por última vez?** *(koo-ahn-doh foo-eh ahl dehn-tees-tah pohr ool-tee-mah behs)*
Please open your mouth.	**Abra la boca, por favor.** *(Ah-brah lah boh-kah pohr fah-bohr)*
I am going to check your teeth.	**Voy a revisar sus dientes.** *(Boy ah reh-bee-sahr soos dee-ehn-tehs)*
I am going to hit them gently.	**Voy a darles golpecitos.** *(Boy ah dahr-lehs gohl-peh-see-tohs)*
Point when it hurts.	**Señale cuando duela.** *(Seh-nyah-leh koo-ahn-doh doo-eh-lah)*

Bite!	**¡Muerda!**
	(Moo-ehr-dah)
Please open your mouth wider.	**Por favor, abra más la boca.**
	(Pohr fah-bohr, ah-brah mahs lah boh-kah)
I am going to clean your teeth.	**Voy a limpiarle los dientes.**
	(Boy ah leem-pee-ahr-leh lohs dee-ehn-tehs)
Do your gums bleed?	**¿Le sangran las encías?**
	(Leh sahn-grahn lahs ehn-see-ahs)
Are your teeth sensitive . . .	**¿Tiene sensibilidad . . .**
	(Tee-eh-neh sehn-see-bee-lee-dahd)
to cold?	**al frío?**
	(ahl free-oh)
to shock?	**¿a los toques?**
	(ah lohs toh-kehs)
to pain?	**¿al dolor?**
	(ahl doh-lohr)
Do you have bad breath?	**¿Tiene mal aliento?**
	(Tee-eh-neh mahl ah-lee-ehn-toh)
Do you have frequent blisters/ulcerations?	**¿Tiene ulceraciones frecuentes?**
	(Tee-eh-neh ool-seh-rah-see-oh-nehs freh-koo-ehn-tehs)
Does the air hurt your teeth?	**¿Le molesta el aire?**
	(Leh moh-lehs-tah ehl ah-ee-reh)

TABLE 4-1 *COMMON WORDS*		*TABLA 4-1* *PALABRAS COMUNES*
ENGLISH	*SPANISH*	*PRONUNCIATION*
air	**aire**	*ah-ee-reh*
anesthesia	**anestesia**	*ah-nehs-teh-see-ah*
anticoagulant	**anticoagulante**	*ahn-tee-koh-ah-gool-ahn-teh*
antibiotic	**antibiótico**	*ahn-tee-bee-oh-tee-koh*
baby tooth	**diente de leche**	*dee-ehn-teh deh leh-cheh*
Bite!	**¡Muerda!**	*¡Moo-ehr-dah!*
chemotherapy	**quimioterapia**	*kee-mee-oh-teh-rah-pee-ah*
caries	**caries**	*kah-ree-ehs*
cavity	**cavidad**	*kah-bee-dahd*
cement	**cemento**	*seh-mehn-toh*

Does it hurt when you chew very hard?	**¿Le duele al masticar con fuerza?** *(Leh doo-eh-leh ahl mahs-tee-kahr kohn foo-ehr-sah)*
Rinse your mouth.	**Enjuague su boca.** *(Ehn-hoo-ah-geh soo boh-kah)*
I am going to take X-rays.	**Voy a tomarle radiografías.** *(Boy ah toh-mahr-leh rah-dee-oh-grah-fee-ahs)*
I will return shortly.	**Regreso en seguida.** *(Reh-greh-soh ehn seh-ggee-dah)*
I checked your X-rays.	**Revisé sus radiografías.** *(Reh-bee-seh soos rah-dee-oh-grah-fee-ahs)*
I have to pull your tooth.	**Tengo que extraer/sacar la muela.** *(Tehn-goh keh ehx-trah-ehr/sah-kahr lah moo-eh-lah)*
I am going to use a local anesthetic.	**Voy a ponerle/aplicarle anestesia local.** *(Boy ah poh-nehr-leh/ah-plee-kahr-leh ah-nehs-teh-see-ah loh-kahl)*
Tell me when it feels numb.	**Avíseme cuando sienta dormido.** *(Ah-bee-seh-meh koo-ahn-doh see-ehn-tah dohr-mee-doh)*
Do you feel O.K.?	**¿Se siente bien?** *(Seh see-ehn-teh bee-ehn)*
Does it still hurt?	**¿Todavía le duele?** *(Toh-dah-bee-ah leh doo-eh-leh)*
I pulled your tooth.	**Le saqué la muela.** *(Leh sah-keh lah moo-eh-lah)*
I am putting in a temporary filling.	**Le aplicaré empaste temporal.** *(Leh ah-plee-kah-reh ehm-pahs-teh tehm-poh-rahl)*
I will use resins.	**Usaré resinas.** *(Oo-sah-reh reh-see-nahs)*
I am going to polish your teeth.	**Ahora voy a pulir sus dientes.** *(Ah-oh-rah boy a poo-leer soos dee-ehn-tehs)*
You need to brush your teeth better.	**Necesita cepillar mejor sus dientes.** *(Neh-seh-see-tah seh-pee-yahr meh-hohr soos dee-ehn-tehs)*
Use dental floss.	**Use hilo dental.** *(Oo-seh ee-loh dehn-tahl)*
Come back in ten days.	**Regrese en diez días.** *(Reh-greh-seh ehn dee-ehs dee-ahs)*

TABLE 4-2 *PROPER VOCABULARY*		TABLA 4-2 *VOCABULARIO APROPIADO*
ENGLISH	*SPANISH*	*PRONUNCIATION*
oral floss	hilo dental	*ee-loh dehn-tahl*
oral surgeon	cirujano dentista	*see-roo-hah-noh dehn-tees-tah*
dentist	dentista	*dehn-tees-tah*
dentifrice	dentífrico	*dehn-tee-free-koh*
disclosing solution	solución reveladora	*soh-loo-see-ohn reh-beh-lah-doh-rah*
enamel	esmalte	*ehs-mahl-teh*
extract	extraer/sacar	*ehx-trah-ehr/sah-kahr*
eyetooth	diente canino/ colmillo	*dee-ehn-teh kah-nee-noh/kohl-mee- yoh*
to fill	empastar/rellenar	*ehm-pahs-tahr/reh-yeh-nahr*
fluoride	fluoruro	*floo-oh-roo-roh*

If it is necessary, come back.　　**En caso necesario, puede regresar.**
　　　　　　　　　　　　　　　　(Ehn kah-soh neh-seh-sah-ree-oh, poo-
　　　　　　　　　　　　　　　　eh-deh reh-greh-sahr)
I hope you do well.　　　　　　**Que siga bien.**
　　　　　　　　　　　　　　　　(Keh see-gah bee-ehn)

It is very important to give oral-hygiene instructions to all patients receiving dental care. This will help them prevent long term damage to their teeth and gums.

Es de suma importancia el dar instrucciones de higiene a todos los pacientes que reciben tratamiento dental. Esto evitará daños futuros a sus dientes y encías.

I want to talk to you about plaque.

Quiero platicarle acerca de la placa bacteriana.
(Kee-eh-roh plah-tee-kahr-leh ah-sehr- kah deh lah plah-kah bahk-teh-ree- ah-nah)

Plaque is a sticky, colorless layer of bacteria.

La placa es una capa pegajosa, sin color, y con bacterias.
(Lah plah-kah ehs oo-nah kah-pah peh- gah-hoh-sah seen koh-lohr ee kohn bahk-teh-ree-ahs)

FIGURE 4-1   *When a patient is discharged from the hospital, it is important to give him written instructions for care at home.*

TABLE 4-3 COMMON DISEASES	TABLA 4-3 *ENFERMEDADES COMUNES*	
ENGLISH	*SPANISH*	*PRONUNCIATION*
gumboil	flemón/absceso	*fleh-mohn/ahb-seh-soh*
gingivitis	gingivitis	*heen-hee-bee-tees*
dental plaque	sarro	*sah-roh*
pyorrhea	piorrea	*pee-oh-reh-ah*
tumor	tumor	*too-mohr*
lesions	lesiones	*leh-see-ohn-ehs*
odontalgia/toothache	odontalgia/dolor de muela	*oh-dohn-tahl-hee-ah/doh-lohr deh moo-eh-lah*

TABLE 4-4 DENTAL APPLIANCES	TABLA 4-4 ADITAMENTOS DENTALES	
ENGLISH	SPANISH	PRONUNCIATION
complete dentures	dentadura completa	dehn-tah-doo-rah kohm-pleh-tah
fixed bridge	puente fijo	poo-ehn-teh fee-hoh
movable bridge	puente móvil	poo-ehn-teh moh-beel
partial denture	dentadura parcial	dehn-tah-doo-rah pahr-see-ahl
gold tooth	diente de oro	dee-ehn-teh deh oh-roh
crowns	coronas	koh-roh-nahs
braces	abrazaderas	ah-brah-sah-deh-rahs
implant	implante	eem-plahn-teh
sealant	placa protectora	plah-kah proh-tehk-toh-rah

Plaque causes dental caries.

La placa causa caries dental.
(Lah plah-kah kah-oo-sah kah-ree-ehs dehn-tahl)

Plaque also causes pyorrhea and tooth loss.

La placa causa pérdida de dientes y piorrea.
(Lah plah-kah kah-oo-sah pehr-dee-dah deh dee-ehn-tehs ee pee-oh-reh-ah)

Plaque can be prevented by brushing and flossing.

La placa se evita usando hilo dental y cepillo.
(Lah plah-kah seh eh-bee-tah oo-sahn-doh ee-loh dehn-tahl ee seh-pee-yoh)

Fluoride makes teeth stronger and healthier. It also helps make teeth less sensitive.

El fluoruro ayuda a que los dientes sean fuertes y sanos. También ayuda a que los dientes sean menos sensibles.

Do not eat or drink anything for thirty minutes.

No coma ni beba nada por treinta minutos.
(Noh koh-mah nee beh-bah nah-dah pohr treh-een-tah mee-noo-tohs)

Come back in six months.

Por favor, regrese en seis meses.
(Pohr fah-bohr reh-greh-seh ehn seh-ees meh-sehs)

UNIT II

UNIDAD II

Chapter Five

In the Hospital   **En el Hospital**

When someone asks you for directions in Spanish, knowing key words is essential. Do not hesitate to use your hands or draw a map that the patient can use as a guide; the patient will appreciate it. Table 5-1 will help you with pronunciation of selected words.

Cuando alguien le pregunta por direcciones en español, es esencial conocer palabras claves. No vacile en usar sus manos o dibujar un mapa

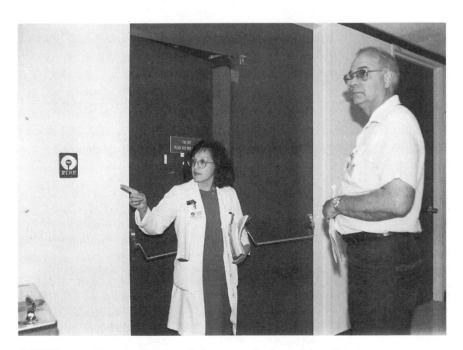

FIGURE 5-1   *Knowing key words is essential when giving directions.*

que el paciente pueda usar como guía. El paciente lo agradecerá. La
tabla 5-1 le ayudará con la pronunciación de palabras selectas.

English	Spanish
Good morning!	**¡Buenos días!** *(Boo-eh-nohs dee-ahs)*
Is this _____ Hospital?	**¿Es éste el Hospital _____?** *(Ehs ehs-teh ehl ohs-pee-tahl _____)*
I need to go to the surgery clinic.	**Necesito ir a la clínica de cirugía.** *(Neh-seh-see-toh eer ah lah klee-nee-kah deh see-roo-hee-ah)*
Can you give me directions?	**¿Me puede dar direcciones?** *(Meh poo-eh-deh dahr dee-rek-see-ohn-ehs)*
Yes, go to the end of the hall.	**Sí, vaya al final del pasillo.** *(See, bah-yah ahl feen-ahl dehl pah-see-yoh)*
Do you see the fire extinguisher?	**¿Ve el extintor de fuego?** *(Beh ehl ehx-teen-tohr deh foo-eh-goh)*
It's in the middle of the wall.	**Está en la mitad de la pared.** *(Ehs-tah ehn lah mee-tahd deh lah pah-rehd)*

TABLE 5-1
PRONUNCIATION OF
SELECTED WORDS

TABLA 5-1
PRONUNCIACIÓN DE
PALABRAS SELECTAS

ENGLISH	SPANISH	PRONUNCIATION
directions	**direcciones**	*dee-rehk-see-ohn-ehs*
hesitate	**vacilar**	*bah-see-lahr*
the tower	**la torre**	*lah toh-reh*
building	**edificio**	*eh-dee-fee-see-oh*
fire escape	**escape de fuego**	*ehs-kah-peh deh foo-eh-goh*
surgery	**cirugía**	*see-roo-hee-ah*
administration	**administración**	*ahd-mee-nees-trah-see-ohn*
arrow	**flecha**	*fleh-chah*
laboratory	**laboratorio**	*lah-boh-rah-toh-ree-oh*
lobby	**vestíbulo**	*behs-tee-boo-loh*
clinic	**clínica**	*klee-nee-kah*
cafeteria	**cafetería**	*kah-feh-teh-ree-ah*
stairs	**escalera**	*ehs-kah-leh-rah*
elevator	**elevador**	*eh-leh-bah-dohr*

When you get there, turn right.	**Cuando llegue ahí, dé vuelta a la derecha.** *(Koo-ahn-doh yeh-geh ah-ee, deh boo-ehl-tah ah lah deh-reh-chah)*
You will pass the cafeteria.	**Va a pasar la cafetería.** *(Bah ah pah-sahr lah kah-feh-teh-ree-ah)*
Go to the glass doors.	**Vaya a las puertas de vidrio.** *(Bah-yah ah lahs poo-ehr-tahs deh bee-dree-oh)*
The clinic is in another building.	**La clínica está en otro edificio.** *(Lah klee-nee-kah ehs-tah ehn oh-troh eh-dee-fee-see-oh)*

You may wish to memorize single words that will help you with directions. Table 5-2 lists some key words.

Puede memorizar palabras que le ayudarán con las direcciones. La tabla 5-2 muestra algunas palabras claves.

You have to cross the street.	**Tiene que cruzar la calle.** *(Tee-eh-neh keh kroo-sahr lah kah-yeh)*
Walk two blocks.	**Camine dos cuadras.** *(Kah-mee-neh dohs koo-ah-drahs)*

TABLE 5-2 *KEY WORDS*		*TABLA 5-2* *PALABRAS CLAVES*
ENGLISH	*SPANISH*	*PRONUNCIATION*
below	**abajo**	*ah-bah-hoh*
above	**arriba**	*ah-ree-bah*
blocks	**cuadras**	*koo-ah-drahs*
right	**derecha**	*deh-reh-chah*
straight	**derecho**	*deh-reh-choh*
corner	**esquina**	*ehs-kee-nah*
left	**izquierda (f)**	*ees-kee-ehr-dah*
	izquierdo (m)	*ees-kee-ehr-doh*
sign	**letrero**	*leh-treh-roh*
wall	**pared**	*pah-rehd*
hallway	**pasillo**	*pah-see-yoh*

Then, turn to the left.

Luego dé vuelta a la izquierda.
(Loo-eh-goh deh boo-ehl-tah ah lah ees-kee-ehr-dah)

It is a beige brick building.

Es un edificio de ladrillo color crema.
(Ehs oon eh-dee-fee-see-oh deh lah-dree-yoh koh-lohr kreh-mah)

It is a six-story building.

Es un edificio de seis pisos.
(Ehs oon eh-dee-fee-see-oh deh seh-ees pee-sohs)

Take the elevator to the sixth floor.

Tome el elevador al sexto piso.
(Toh-meh ehl eh-leh-bah-dohr ahl sehx-toh pee-soh)

The elevators are slow.

Los elevadores son lentos.
(Lohs eh-leh-bah-doh-rehs sohn lehn-tohs)

Exit to the right.

Salga a la derecha.
(Sahl-gah ah lah deh-reh-chah)

FIGURE 5-2 Use your hands or draw a map when giving directions to a non-English-speaking patient.

You will see the sign on the wall.	**Verá el letrero en la pared.** *(Beh-rah ehl leh-treh-roh ehn lah pah-rehd)*
Follow the red arrows.	**Siga las flechas rojas.** *(See-gah lahs fleh-chahs roh-hahs)*
There is a front desk.	**Hay un escritorio al frente.** *(Ah-ee oon ehs-kree-toh-ree-oh ahl frehn-teh)*
Ask the receptionist for a number.	**Pídale un número a la recepcionista.** *(Pee-dah-leh oon noo-meh-roh ah lah reh-sehp-see-ohn-ees-tah)*
Wait in the lobby.	**Espere en el vestíbulo.** *(Ehs-peh-reh ehn ehl behs-tee-boo-loh)*
You have to wait your turn.	**Tendrá que esperar su turno.** *(Tehn-drah keh ehs-peh-rahr soo toor-noh)*
Do you want to take the stairs?	**¿Quiere ir por las escaleras?** *(Kee-eh-reh eer pohr lahs ehs-kah-leh-rahs)*
They are around the corner.	**Están doblando la esquina.** *(Ehs-tahn doh-blahn-doh lah ehs-kee-nah)*
Follow the stairs.	**Siga por las escaleras.** *(See-gah pohr lahs ehs-kah-leh-rahs)*
You can't get lost!	**¡No se puede perder!** *(Noh seh poo-eh-deh pehr-dehr)*

Sometimes, you will remember only a few words. Don't worry! Remembering useful verbs comes in handy because the verb is the essential part of a sentence. You can help patients by recognizing some useful verbs. Table 5-3 lists some useful verbs that you should memorize.

Algunas veces sólo recordará pocas palabras. ¡No se preocupe! Recordar los verbos es importante porque son lo esencial de una oración. Puede ayudar a los pacientes si reconoce algunos verbos útiles. La tabla 5-3 muestra algunos verbos útiles que deberá memorizar.

You can cross at the walkway.	**Puede cruzar por el pasillo.** *(Poo-eh-deh kroo-sahr pohr ehl pah-see-yoh)*
I don't think so.	**No lo creo.** *(Noh loh kreh-oh)*

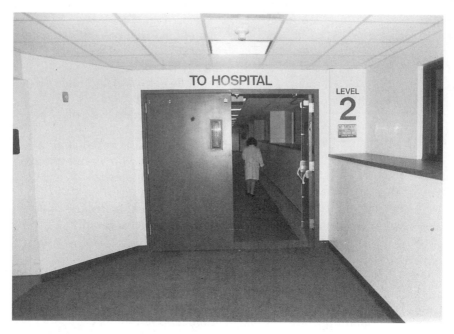

FIGURE 5-3   *Memorizing a few verbs in Spanish will help you give the right directions even when you are unable to carry on a conversation.*

TABLE 5-3 USEFUL VERBS		TABLA 5-3 **VERBOS UTILES**
ENGLISH	*SPANISH*	*PRONUNCIATION*
to see	**ver**	*behr*
to give	**dar**	*dahr*
to take	**tomar**	*toh-mahr*
to ask	**preguntar**	*preh-goon-tahr*
to tell	**decir**	*deh-seer*
to wait	**esperar**	*ehs-peh-rahr*
to hurt	**doler**	*doh-lehr*
to turn	**voltear/dar vuelta**	*bohl-teh-ahr/dahr boo-ehl-tah*
to follow	**seguir**	*seh-geer*
to cross	**cruzar**	*kroo-sahr*

I am in a lot of pain.	**Tengo mucho dolor.** *(Tehn-goh moo-choh doh-lohr)*
If it is far, could I drive?	**Si está lejos, ¿podría manejar?** *(See ehs-tah leh-hohs, poh-dree-ah mah-neh-hahr)*
Is there a policeman there?	**¿Hay algún policía?** *(Ah-ee ahl-goon poh-lee-see-ah)*
I need better directions.	**Necesito mejores direcciones.** *(Neh-seh-see-toh meh-hoh-rehs dee-rehk-see-ohn-ehs)*
I am afraid of getting lost.	**Tengo miedo de perderme.** *(Tehn-goh mee-eh-doh deh pehr-dehr-meh)*
This is a very large place.	**Este es un lugar muy grande.** *(Ehs-teh ehs oon loo-gahr mooy grahn-deh)*
I will not find the street.	**No encontraré la calle.** *(Noh ehn-kohn-trah-reh lah kah-yeh)*
What is the name of the street?	**¿Cuál es el nombre de la calle?** *(Koo-ahl ehs ehl nohm-breh deh lah kah-yeh)*
Can you write down the name?	**¿Puede escribir el nombre?** *(Poo-eh-deh ehs-kree-beer ehl nohm-breh)*
I have a piece of paper.	**Tengo un pedazo de papel.** *(Tehn-goh oon peh-dah-soh deh pah-pehl)*
But, I don't have a pencil.	**Pero no tengo un lápiz.** *(Peh-roh noh tehn-goh oon lah-pees)*
I don't have a pen, either.	**Tampoco tengo una pluma.** *(Tahm-poh-koh tehn-goh oo-nah ploo-mah)*

Because you are sensitive to the patient's needs, you decide that he is going to need more help than written directions to the clinic. Reassurance sometimes does not help.

Como usted es sensitivo a las necesidades del paciente, decide que él necesita más ayuda que sólo escribir las direcciones a la clínica. El volver a indicarlas a veces no ayuda.

Sit down here and wait.	**Siéntese aquí y espere.** *(See-ehn-teh-seh ah-kee ee ehs-peh-reh)*

I'll call for a wheelchair.	**Pediré una silla de ruedas.**
	(Peh-dee-reh oo-nah see-yah deh roo-eh-dahs)
This is an employee from transportation.	**Este es un empleado del departamento de transporte.**
	(Ehs-teh ehs oon ehm-pleh-ah-doh dehl deh-pahr-tah-mehn-toh deh trahns-pohr-teh)
He will take you.	**El lo llevará.**
	(Ehl loh yeh-bah-rah)
Please sit down.	**Siéntese, por favor.**
	(See-ehn-teh-seh pohr fah-bohr)
Place your feet here.	**Ponga sus pies aquí.**
	(Pohn-gah soos pee-ehs ah-kee)
Over the stool.	**Sobre el taburete.**
	(Soh-breh ehl tah-boo-reh-teh)
We have to go far.	**Tenemos que ir lejos.**
	(Teh-neh-mohs keh eer leh-hohs)
Are you o.k.?	**¿Está bien?**
	(Ehs-tah bee-ehn)

FIGURE 5-4   *The secretary helps the patient by verifying his or her appointment.*

Let me know how you feel.	**Dígame cómo se siente.** *(Dee-gah-meh koh-moh seh see-ehn-teh)*
I can stop the wheelchair.	**Puedo parar la silla de ruedas.** *(Poo-eh-doh pah-rahr lah see-yah deh* *roo-eh-dahs)*
Where are you from?	**¿De dónde es usted?** *(Deh dohn-deh ehs oos-tehd)*
How did you get here?	**¿Cómo llegó aquí?** *(Koh-moh yeh-goh ah-kee)*
Is someone here with you?	**¿Hay alguien con usted?** *(Ah-ee ahl-gee-ehn kohn oos-tehd)*
Do you know how to get back?	**¿Sabe cómo regresar?** *(Sah-beh koh-moh reh-greh-sahr)*

The patient has arrived at an unfamiliar place. There are many questions that he could ask. Table 5-4 lists some questions that he might ask.

El paciente llegó a un lugar diferente. El no está familiarizado con su alrededor. Hay muchas preguntas que puede hacer. La tabla 5-4 muestra otras preguntas que él puede hacer.

This is the clinic.	**Esta es la clínica.** *(Ehs-tah ehs lah klee-nee-kah)*
Good morning miss.	**Buenos días señorita.** *(Boo-eh-nohs dee-ahs seh-nyoh-ree-tah)*
I was told to come here.	**Me dijeron que viniera aquí.** *(Meh dee-heh-rohn keh bee-nee-eh-rah* *ah-kee)*
I need to see Doctor White.	**Necesito ver al doctor White.** *(Neh-seh-see-toh behr ahl dohk-tohr* *Joo-ah-eeth)*
Have you been here before?	**¿Ha estado aquí antes?** *(Ah ehs-tah-doh ah-kee ahn-tehs)*
If you have been here before, I will need your card.	**Si ha estado aquí antes, necesitaré su** **tarjeta.** *(See ah ehs-tah-doh ah-kee ahn-tehs,* *neh-seh-see-tah-reh soo tahr-heh-* *tah)*
If you haven't, please fill out these papers.	**Si no, por favor llene estos papeles.** *(See noh, pohr fah-bohr yeh-neh ehs-* *tohs pah-peh-lehs)*

TABLE 5-4   TABLA 5-4
OTHER QUESTIONS   OTRAS PREGUNTAS

ENGLISH	SPANISH	PRONUNCIATION
Is it far?	¿Está lejos?	¿Ehs-tah leh-hohs?
How far?	¿Qué tan lejos?	¿Keh tahn leh-hohs?
Do I have time?	¿Tengo tiempo?	¿Tehn-goh tee-ehm-poh?
At what time do they close?	¿A qué hora cierran?	¿Ah keh oh-rah see-eh-rahn?
What time is it?	¿Qué hora es?	¿Keh oh-rah ehs?
Are there elevators?	¿Hay elevadores?	¿Ah-ee eh-leh-bah-doh-rehs?
Are there ramps?	¿Hay rampas?	¿Ah-ee ram-pahs?
Where is it?	¿Dónde está?	¿Dohn-deh ehs-tah?
Is it the same color?	¿Es del mismo color?	¿Ehs dehl mees-moh koh-lohr?
Should I drive?	¿Debo manejar?	¿Deh-boh mah-neh-hahr?
Is parking available?	¿Hay estacionamiento?	¿Ah-ee ehs-tah-see-ohn-ah-mee-ehn-toh?
What is the name of the street?	¿Cuál es el nombre de la calle?	¿Koo-ahl ehs ehl nohm-breh deh lah kah-yeh?
Can you go with me?	¿Puede ir conmigo?	¿Poo-eh-deh eer kohn-mee-goh?

I cannot read English, can you help me?	No puedo leer inglés, ¿puede ayudarme?
	(Noh poo-eh-doh leh-ehr een-glehs, poo-eh-deh ah-yoo-dahr-meh)
Yes, please wait.	Sí, espere, por favor.
	(See, ehs-peh-reh pohr fah-bohr)
This is my first time here.	Esta es mi primera vez aquí.
	(Ehs-tah ehs mee pree-meh-rah behs ah-kee)
In that case, tell me your full name.	En ese caso, dígame su nombre completo.
	(Ehn eh-seh kah-soh, dee-gah-meh soo nohm-breh kohm-pleh-toh)

What is your date of birth? year? month? day?	**¿Cuál es su fecha de nacimiento? año/ mes/día?** *(Koo-ahl ehs soo feh-chah deh nah-see-mee-ehn-toh ah-nyoh/mehs/dee-ah)*
Your appointment is listed here on the computer.	**Su cita está registrada en la computadora.** *(Soo see-tah ehs-tah reh-hees-trah-dah ehn lah kohm-poo-tah-doh-rah)*
You have to go directly to the floor.	**Debe ir al piso directamente.** *(Deh-beh eer ahl pee-soh dee-rehk-tah-mehn-teh)*
The doctor will see you there.	**El doctor lo verá ahí.** *(Ehl dohk-tohr loh beh-rah ah-ee)*
The surgery floor is in the hospital towers.	**El piso de cirugía está en las torres del hospital.** *(Ehl pee-soh deh see-roo-hee-ah ehs-tah ehn lahs toh-rehs dehl ohs-pee-tahl)*

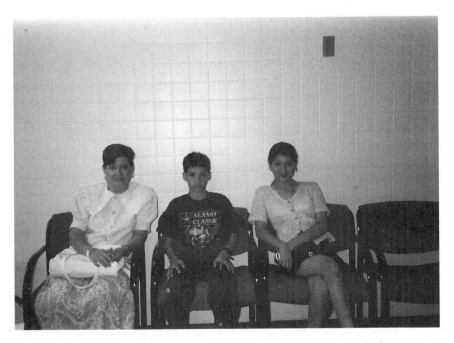

FIGURE 5-5 *It is helpful to verify if the patient has an appointment before you give him or her further directions.*

Ask for unit 6A.

Pregunte por la unidad Seis A.
(Preh-goon-teh pohr lah oo-nee-dahd seh-ees Ah)

From here, turn to the left, then turn to the right.

De aquí, dé vuelta a la izquierda, luego voltée a la derecha.
(Deh ah-kee, deh boo-ehl-tah ah lah ees-kee-ehr-dah, loo-eh-goh bohl-teh-eh ah lah deh-reh-chah)

Follow the green line.

Siga la línea verde.
(See-gah lah lee-neh-ah behr-deh)

The line is on the wall.

La línea está en la pared.
(Lah lee-neh-ah ehs-tah ehn lah pah-rehd)

Watch for the arrow.

Fíjese en la flecha.
(Fee-heh-seh ehn lah fleh-chah)

This will take you to the end of the hall.

Esta la llevará al fin del pasillo.
(Ehs-tah lah yeh-bah-rah ahl feen dehl pah-see-yoh)

There, turn to the left.

Ahí, voltee a la izquierda.
(Ah-ee bohl-teh-eh ah lah ees-kee-ehr-dah)

The secretary will help you.

La secretaria lo ayudará.
(Lah seh-kreh-tah-ree-ah loh ah-yoo-dah-rah)

Good luck!

¡Buena suerte!
(Boo-eh-nah soo-ehr-teh)

The Clerical Staff

Las Secretarias

The clerical staff is very important. They are usually the first to greet the patient as he/she enters the hospital. Their ability to be pleasant, to be courteous, and to give the appropriate information speeds up the process of admitting the patient or referring him/her to another department.

Las secretarias son muy importantes. Ellas generalmente son las

FIGURE 6-1 *Gathering appropriate information helps the patient.*

primeras personas que saludan al paciente cuando ingresa al hospital.
La habilidad de ser amables, atentas y de dar información apropiada,
asegura que el proceso de admitir a el/la paciente en el hospital o de
mandarlo(a) a otro departamento sea más rápido.

Good afternoon!	**¡Buenas tardes!** *(Boo-eh-nahs tahr-dehs)*
Are you the patient?	**¿Es usted el/la paciente?** *(Ehs oos-tehd ehl/lah pah-see-ehn-teh)*
Do you speak English?	**¿Habla usted inglés?** *(Ah-blah oos-tehd een-glehs)*
Is he/she with you?	**¿El/ella viene con usted?** *(Ehl/eh-yah bee-eh-neh kohn oos-tehd)*
Does he/she speak English?	**¿El/ella habla inglés?** *(Ehl/eh-yah ah-blah een-glehs)*
May I help you?	**¿En qué puedo servirle?** *(Ehn keh poo-eh-doh sehr-beer-leh)*
What happened to you?	**¿Qué le pasó?** *(Keh leh pah-soh)*
Please sit down.	**Por favor, siéntese.** *(Pohr fah-bohr, see-ehn-teh-seh)*
I need to ask you some questions.	**Necesito hacerle unas preguntas.** *(Neh-seh-see-toh ah-sehr-leh oo-nahs preh-goon-tahs)*
I have to enter the information into the computer.	**Tengo que poner la información en la computadora.** *(Tehn-goh keh poh-nehr lah een-fohr-mah-see-ohn ehn lah kohm-poo-tah-doh-rah)*
What is your name?	**¿Cómo se llama?** *(Koh-moh seh yah-mah)*
What is your last name?	**¿Cual es su apellido?** *(Koo-ahl ehs soo ah-peh-yee-doh)*
Have you ever been to this hospital before?	**¿Ha estado antes en este hospital?** *(Ah ehs-tah-doh ahn-tehs ehn ehs-teh ohs-pee-tahl)*
Have you ever been to the emergency room?	**¿Ha estado en el cuarto de emergencias/urgencias?** *(Ah ehs-tah-doh ehn ehl koo-ahr-toh deh eh-mehr-hehn-see-ahs/oor-hehn-see-ahs)*

When was the last time you were here?	**¿Cuándo fué la última vez que estuvo aquí?** *(Koo-ahn-doh foo-eh lah ool-tee-mah behs keh ehs-too-boh ah-kee)*
Is this your first time in the hospital?	**¿Es su primera vez en el hospital?** *(Ehs soo pree-meh-rah behs ehn ehl ohs-pee-tahl)*
Do you have a hospital card?	**¿Tiene usted tarjeta de hospital?** *(Tee-eh-neh oos-tehd tahr-heh-tah deh ohs-pee-tahl)*
What is your Social Security number?	**¿Cuál es su número de Seguro Social?** *(Koo-ahl ehs soo noo-meh-roh deh seh-goo-roh soh-see-ahl)*
Please repeat it slowly.	**Por favor, repita despacio.** *(Pohr fah-bohr reh-pee-tah dehs-pah-see-oh)*
What is your date of birth?	**¿Fecha de nacimiento?** *(Feh-chah deh nah-see-mee-ehn-toh)*

FIGURE 6-2 *Most information is entered into the computer.*

When were you born?	**¿En qué año nació?**
	(Ehn keh ah-nyoh nah-see-oh)
How old are you?	**¿Cuántos años tiene?**
	(Koo-ahn-tohs ah-nyohs tee-eh-neh)
Do you have health insurance?	**¿Tiene seguro de salud?**
	(Tee-eh-neh seh-goo-roh deh sah-lood)
What is the name of your insurance?	**¿Cuál es el nombre de su seguro?**
	(Koo-ahl ehs ehl nohm-breh deh soo seh-goo-roh)
Will it pay for your hospitalization?	**¿Paga por su hospitalización?**
	(Pah-gah pohr soo ohs-pee-tah-lee-sah-see-ohn)
Who is going to pay the hospital?	**¿Quién va a pagar el hospital?**
	(Kee-ehn bah ah pah-gahr ehl ohs-pee-tahl)
Do you have Medicare?	**¿Tiene Medicare?**
	(Tee-eh-neh meh-dee-kehr)

FIGURE 6-3 *All the patients' information must be filed.*

Do you have your Medicare card?	**¿Tiene usted su tarjeta de Medicare?** *(Tee-eh-neh oos-tehd soo tahr-heh-tah deh meh-dee-kehr)*
Do you have a driver's license?	**¿Tiene licencia para manejar?** *(Tee-eh-neh lee-sehn-see-ah pah-rah mah-neh-hahr)*
What is your address?	**¿Cuál es su dirección?** *(Koo-ahl ehs soo dee-rehk-see-ohn)*
Where do you live?	**¿Dónde vive?** *(Dohn-deh bee-beh)*
What is the name of the street?	**¿Cuál es el nombre de la calle?** *(Koo-ahl ehs ehl nohm-breh deh lah kah-yeh)*
Is that an apartment?	**¿Es apartamento?** *(Ehs ah-pahr-tah-mehn-toh)*
Is it a house?	**¿Es una casa?** *(Ehs oo-nah kah-sah)*
What is the zip code?	**¿Cuál es el código postal?** *(Koo-ahl ehs ehl koh-dee-goh pohs-tahl)*
What is your phone number?	**¿Cuál es su número de teléfono?** *(Koo-ahl ehs soo noo-meh-roh deh teh-leh-foh-noh)*
Do you work?	**¿Trabaja?** *(Trah-bah-hah)*
Where do you work?	**¿Dónde trabaja?** *(Dohn-deh trah-bah-hah)*
What is the address?	**¿Cuál es la dirección?** *(Koo-ahl ehs lah dee-rehk-see-ohn)*
Is it here in town?	**¿Está en esta ciudad?** *(Ehs-tah ehn ehs-tah see-oo-dahd)*
What work do you do?	**¿Qué trabajo hace?** *(Keh trah-bah-hoh ah-seh)*
Where were you born?	**¿Dónde nació?** *(Dohn-deh nah-see-oh)*
Are you single?	**¿Es usted soltero(a)?** *(Ehs oos-tehd sohl-teh-roh[rah])*
Are you married?	**¿Es usted casado(a)?** *(Ehs oos-tehd kah-sah-doh[dah])*
Are you divorced?	**¿Es usted divorciado(a)?** *(Ehs oos-tehd dee-bohr-see-ah-doh[dah])*
Are you a widow/widower?	**¿Es usted viudo(a)?** *(Ehs oos-tehd bee-oo-doh[dah])*

Are you a common-law wife/ husband?	**¿Es usted concubino(a)?** *(Ehs oos-tehd kohn-koo-bee-noh[nah])*
What is your religion?	**¿Cuál es su religión?** *(Koo-ahl ehs soo reh-lee-hee-ohn)*
Who can we call in case of an emergency?	**¿A quién llamamos en caso de emergencia?** *(Ah kee-ehn yah-mah-mohs ehn kah-soh deh eh-mehr-hehn-see-ah)*
Do you have a family doctor?	**¿Tiene usted doctor familiar?** *(Tee-eh-neh oos-tehd dohk-tohr fah-mee-lee-ahr)*
Do you want to see our doctor?	**¿Quiere ver a nuestro doctor?** *(Kee-eh-reh behr ah noo-ehs-troh dohk-tohr)*
Do you prefer to call your doctor?	**¿Prefiere llamar a su doctor?** *(Preh-fee-eh-reh yah-mahr ah soo dohk-tohr)*
You must pay a deposit.	**Debe pagar un depósito.** *(Deh-beh pah-gahr oon deh-poh-see-toh)*
You don't have to pay cash.	**No tiene que pagar al contado.** *(Noh tee-eh-neh keh pah-gahr ahl kohn-tah-doh)*
You can pay on terms.	**Puede pagar a plazos.** *(Poo-eh-deh pah-gahr ah plah-sohs)*
You need to sign this form.	**Debe firmar esta forma.** *(Deh-beh feer-mahr ehs-tah fohr-mah)*
You are giving us permission to treat you here.	**Usted nos dá permiso de tratarlo(a) aquí.** *(Oos-tehd nohs dah pehr-mee-soh deh trah-tahr-loh[lah] ah-kee)*
Please sign here.	**Por favor, firme aquí.** *(Pohr fah-bohr feer-meh ah-kee)*
Can you write?	**¿Puede escribir?** *(Poo-eh-deh ehs-kree-beer)*
You can write an X.	**Puede escribir una X.** *(Poo-eh-deh ehs-kree-beer oo-nah eh-kiss)*
How long have you been sick?	**¿Desde cuándo está usted enfermo(a)?** *(Dehs-deh koo-ahn-doh ehs-tah oos-tehd ehn-fer-moh[mah])*
Days?/Months?	**¿Días?/¿Meses?** *(Dee-ahs/Meh-sehs)*

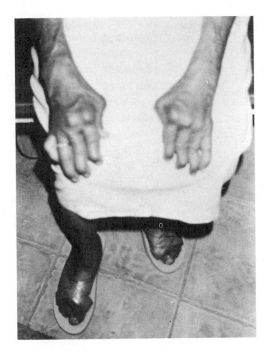

FIGURE 6-4 *Sometimes a person cannot sign his or her name because of a debilitating illness but is able to place a mark on the line.*

Why are you here today?	**¿Cuál es la razón por la que esta aquí?** *(Koo-ahl ehs lah rah-sohn pohr lah keh ehs-tah ah-kee)*
What is the problem?	**¿Cuál es el problema?** *(Koo-ahl ehs ehl proh-bleh-mah)*
What is hurting you?	**¿Qué le duele?** *(Keh leh doo-eh-leh)*
Start at the beginning.	**Comience desde el principio.** *(Koh-mee-ehn-seh dehs-deh ehl preen-see-pee-oh)*
When did this happen?	**¿Cuándo le pasó esto?** *(Koo-ahn-doh leh pah-soh ehs-toh)*
Do you have relatives/ friends?	**¿Tiene parientes/amigos?** *(Tee-eh-neh pah-ree-ehn-tehs/ah-mee-gohs)*
Where are they?	**¿Dónde están?** *(Dohn-deh ehs-tahn)*

What is your brother's name?	**¿Cómo se llama su hermano(a)?** *(Koh-moh seh yah-mah soo ehr-mah-noh[nah])*
What is your husand's/wife's name?	**¿Cómo se llama su esposo(a)?** *(Koh-moh seh yah-mah soo ehs-poh-soh[sah])*
Thank you for the information.	**Gracias por la información.** *(Grah-see-ahs pohr lah een-fohr-mah-see-ohn)*
Please have a seat in the waiting room.	**Por favor, siéntese en la sala de espera.** *(Pohr fah-bohr see-ehn-teh-seh ehn lah sah-lah deh ehs-peh-rah)*
There are many patients waiting.	**Hay muchos pacientes esperando.** *(Ah-ee moo-chohs pah-see-ehn-tehs ehs-peh-rahn-doh)*
You will have to wait.	**Tendrá que esperar.** *(Tehn-drah keh ehs-peh-rahr)*
You will have to wait about 30 minutes.	**Tendrá que esperar treinta minutos.** *(Tehn-drah keh ehs-peh-rahr treh-een-tah mee-noo-tohs)*

FIGURE 6-5 *Many patients have to be hospitalized.*

You may be here for four hours.	**Estará aquí durante cuatro horas.** *(Ehs-tah-rah ah-kee doo-rahn-teh koo-ah-troh oh-rahs)*
A nurse will see you.	**Una/Un enfermera(o) lo/la atenderá.** *(Ooh-nah/Oon ehn-fehr-meh-rah[roh] loh[lah] ah-tehn-deh-rah)*
Do you need to call a taxi?	**¿Necesita llamar un taxi?** *(Neh-seh-see-tah yah-mahr oon tahx-ee)*
Do you want to go home?	**¿Quiere ir a su casa?** *(Kee-eh-reh eer ah soo kah-sah)*
You need to be admitted.	**Necesita internarse.** *(Neh-seh-see-tah een-tehr-nahr-seh)*
Please wait a few minutes.	**Por favor, espere unos minutos.** *(Poh fah-bohr ehs-peh-reh oo-nohs mee-noo-tohs)*
I will call transportation.	**Llamaré al transporte.** *(Yah-mah-reh ahl trahns-pohr-teh)*
Someone will take you to your room.	**Alguien lo llevará a su cuarto.** *(Ahl-gee-ehn loh yeh-bah-rah ah soo koo-ahr-toh)*
You will be all right!	**¡Va a estar bien!** *(Bah ah ehs-tahr bee-ehn)*
Don't worry!	**¡No se preocupe!** *(Noh seh preh-oh-koo-peh)*

Chapter Seven

Admitting a Patient

Admitiendo al Paciente

Often Hispanic patients take someone with them to the hospital to translate for them. However, this does not compare to being able to greet the patient in his/her native language or being able to elicit first-hand information from the patient. Do not become annoyed if the patient brings several members of his family with him. Hispanics tend to be supportive of one another and feel better when family is around. Be patient. Tell the patient that you will be asking many questions.

Frecuentemente los pacientes hispanos llevan a una persona con ellos al hospital. Esta persona sirve de intérprete; pero no hay comparación como el poder saludar al paciente en su lengua nativa y tomar información directa. No se moleste si el paciente va acompañado por varios miembros de su familia. Los Hispanos tienden a apoyarse uno al otro y se sienten mejor cuando hay familiares alrededor. Tenga paciencia. Avísele al paciente que va a hacerle muchas preguntas.

What can I help you with?	**¿En qué puedo ayudarlo?** *(Ehn keh poo-eh-doh ah-yoo-dahr-loh)*
Tell me why you are here?	**¿Dígame por qué está aquí?** *(Dee-gah-meh pohr keh ehs-tah ah-kee)*
What has happened to you?	**¿Qué le ha pasado?** *(Keh leh ah pah-sah-doh)*
How did you get here?	**¿Cómo llegó aquí?** *(koh-moh yeh-goh ah-kee)*
Did you come by car?	**¿Vino en carro?** *(Bee-noh ehn kah-rroh)*
Did you arrive in a wheelchair?	**¿Llegó en silla de ruedas?** *(Yeh-goh ehn see-yah deh roo-eh-dahs)*
Did you walk?	**¿Caminó?** *(Kah-mee-noh)*

You have to give us permission for treatment.

Tiene que darnos su permiso para que le demos tratamiento.
(Tee-eh-neh keh dahr-nohs soo per-mee-soh pah-rah keh leh deh-mohs trah-tah-mee-ehn-toh)

Can you write?

¿Puede escribir?
(Poo-eh-deh ehs-kree-beer)

Please sign here.

Por favor, firme aquí.
(Pohr fah-bohr, feer-meh ah-kee)

Why have you come to the hospital?

¿Por qué ha venido al hospital?
(Pohr keh ah beh-nee-doh ahl ohs-pee-tahl)

What problem do you have?

¿Qué problema tiene?
(Keh proh-bleh-mah tee-eh-neh)

Do you have high blood pressure?

¿Tiene presión alta?
(Tee-eh-neh preh-see-ohn ahl-tah)

Are you dizzy?

¿Tiene mareos?
(Tee-eh-neh mah-reh-ohs)

Do you get headaches?

¿Tiene dolor de cabeza?
(Tee-eh-neh doh-lohr deh kah-beh-sah)

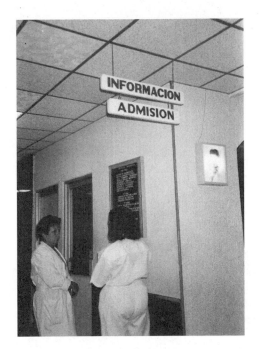

FIGURE 7-1 The admission's office staff will ask you for necessary information.

See table 7-1 for similar medical terms.
Vea la tabla 7-1 con términos médicos similares.

I am going to ask you several questions!	**¡Voy a hacerle muchas preguntas!** *(Boy ah ah-sehr-leh moo-chahs preh-goon-tahs)*
Do you speak English?	**¿Habla inglés?** *(Ah-blah een-glehs)*
Can you read?	**¿Puede leer?** *(Poo-eh-deh leh-ehr)*
Where do you work?	**¿Dónde trabaja?** *(Dohn-deh trah-bah-hah)*
What is your occupation?	**¿Qué clase de trabajo tiene?** *(Keh klah-seh deh trah-bah-hoh tee-eh-neh)*
For how many years did you go to school?	**¿Cuántos años fue a la escuela?** *(Koo-ahn-tohs ah-nyohs foo-eh ah lah ehs-koo-eh-lah)*

FIGURE 7-2   *The patient is asked to sign permission forms for treatment.*

TABLE 7-1
SIMILAR MEDICAL TERMS

TABLA 7-1
TERMINOS MEDICOS SIMILARES

ENGLISH	SPANISH	PRONUNCIATION
anemia	anemia	ah-neh-mee-ah
cardiac	cardíaco	kahr-dee-ah-koh
dehydrated	deshidratado	deh-see-drah-tah-doh
epilepsy	epilepsia	eh-pee-lehp-see-ah
inflammation	inflamación	een-flah-mah-see-ohn
neurotic	neurótico	neh-oo-roh-tee-koh
organ	órgano	ohr-gah-noh
pancreas	páncreas	pahn-kreh-ahs
rheumatic	reumático	reh-oo-mah-tee-koh
valve	válvula	bahl-boo-lah
vision	visión	bee-see-ohn
vomit	vómito	boh-mee-toh

FIGURE 7-3   The floor/unit secretary may need to ask additional questions.

What is your religion?   **¿Cuál es su religión?**
                                    (Koo-ahl ehs soo reh-lee-hee-ohn)
Who takes care of you at   **¿Quién lo cuida en casa?**
    home?   *(Kee-ehn loh koo-ee-dah ehn kah-sah)*

Table 7-2 will help you with the pronunciation of some commonly used words.
La tabla 7-2 le ayudará con la pronunciación de algunas palabras comunes.

Do you have a husband? a   **¿Tiene esposo? ¿esposa? ¿hijos?**
    wife? children?   *(Tee-eh-neh ehs-poh-soh ehs-poh-*
                                    *   sah   ee-hohs)*
Do you have a family doctor?   **¿Tiene un doctor familiar?**
                                    (Tee-eh-neh oon dohk-tohr fah-mee-lee-
                                    *   ahr)*
Do you have any allergies?   **¿Tiene alergias?**
                                    (Tee-eh-neh ah-lehr-hee-ahs)

TABLE 7-2 PRONUNCIATION OF SELECTED WORDS	TABLA 7-2 PRONUNCIACION DE PALABRAS SELECTAS	
ENGLISH	*SPANISH*	*PRONUNCIATION*
help	ayuda	*ah-yoo-dah*
work	trabajo	*trah-bah-hoh*
hospital	hospital	*ohs-pee-tahl*
chest	pecho	*peh-choh*
reason	razón	*rah-sohn*
ask	preguntar	*preh-goon-tahr*
speak	hablar	*ah-blahr*
read	leer	*leh-ehr*
allergies	alergias	*ah-lehr-hee-ahs*
smoke	fumar	*fooh-mahr*
alcohol	alcohol	*ahl-kohl*
visit	visita	*bee-see-tah*
permission	permiso	*pehr-mee-soh*
last	última	*ool-tee-mah*

Are you allergic to any foods?	**¿Es alérgico a ciertas comidas?** *(Ehs ah-lehr-hee-koh ah see-ehr-tahs koh-mee-dahs)*
any drugs? any plants?	**¿a ciertos medicamentos? ¿a ciertas plantas?** *(ah see-ehr-tohs meh-dee-kah-mehn-tohs ah see-ehr-tahs plahn-tahs)*
Do you smoke?	**¿Fuma?** *(Foo-mah)*
How many cigarettes per day?	**¿Cuántos cigarrillos por día?** *(Koo-ahn-tohs see-gah-rree-yohs pohr dee-ah)*
Do you drink alcohol?	**¿Toma bebidas alcohólicas?** *(Toh-mah beh-bee-dahs ahl-koh-lee-kahs)*
What kind of drinks?	**¿Qué clase de bebidas?** *(Keh klah-seh deh beh-bee-dahs)*
How much do you drink per day?	**¿Cuánto alcohol toma por día?** *(Koo-ahn-toh ahl-kohl toh-mah pohr dee-ah)*
Do you take drugs/medicine?	**¿Usa drogas/medicamentos?** *(Oo-sah droh-gahs/meh-dee-kah-mehn-tohs)*
What drugs/medicine do you take?	**¿Qué drogas/medicamentos usa?** *(Keh droh-gahs/meh-dee-kah-mehn-tohs oo-sah)*
Have you ever had a blood transfusion?	**¿Ha tenido transfusiones de sangre?** *(Ah teh-nee-doh trahns-foo-see-ohn-ehs deh sahn-greh)*
Have you ever had a reaction to a blood transfusion?	**¿Alguna vez ha tenido reacción a transfusiones de sangre?** *(Ahl-goo-nah behs ah teh-nee-doh reh-ahk-see-ohn ah trahns-foo-see-ohn-ehs deh sahn-greh)*
When was the last time that you took that medicine?	**¿Cuándo fue la última vez que tomó esa medicina?** *(Koo-ahn-doh foo-eh lah ool-tee-mah behs keh toh-moh eh-sah meh-dee-see-nah)*
Have you ever had surgery?	**¿Ha tenido operaciones?** *(Ah teh-nee-doh oh-peh-rah-see-ohn-ehs)*

What kind of surgery?	¿Qué clase de operaciones? *(Keh klah-seh deh oh-peh-rah-see-ohn-ehs)*
Have you ever broken any bones?	¿Ha tenido huesos rotos/fracturados? *(Ah teh-nee-doh oo-eh-sohs roh-tohs/frahk-too-rah-dohs)*
Have you ever been in a car accident?	¿Ha tenido accidentes de carro? *(Ah teh-nee-doh ahk-see-dehn-tehs deh kah-roh)*
Did you bring . . .	¿Trajo algo . . . *(Trah-hoh ahl-goh)*
valuables?	¿de valor? *(deh bah-lohr)*
glasses?	¿anteojos/lentes? *(ahn-teh-oh-hohs/lehn-tehs)*
jewelry?	¿joyas? *(hoh-yahs)*
cash?	¿dinero? *(dee-neh-roh)*

FIGURE 7-4 *It is important to get correct information. Ask again if you are not sure that the patient understood what you were asking.*

artificial eye?	**¿ojo artificial?**
	(oh-hoh ahr-tee-fee-see-ahl)
hearing aid?	**¿aparato para oír?**
	(ah-pah-rah-toh pah-rah oh-eer)
dentures?	**¿dentadura postiza?**
	(dehn-tah-doo-rah pohs-tee-sah)
The hospital is not responsible for those items.	**El hospital no se hace responsable por esos objetos.**
	(Ehl ohs-pee-tahl noh seh ah-seh rehs-pohn-sah-bleh por eh-sohs ohb-heh-tohs)
Do you have any special problems?	**¿Tiene problemas especiales?**
	(Tee-eh-neh proh-bleh-mahs ehs-peh-see-ah-lehs)
Are you on a special diet?	**¿Hace dieta especial?**
	(Ah-seh dee-eh-tah ehs-peh-see-ahl)
What foods do you like?	**¿Qué alimentos le gustan?**
	(Keh ah-lee-mehn-tohs leh goos-tahn)
What foods do you dislike?	**¿Qué alimentos le disgustan?**
	(Keh ah-lee-mehn-tohs leh dees-goos-tahn)
Do you need to see a dietitian?	**¿Necesita ver a la dietista?**
	(Neh-seh-see-tah behr ah lah dee-eh-tees-tah)

Table 7-3 lists some special diets.
La tabla 7-3 muestra una lista de dietas especiales.

TABLE 7-3 *TYPES OF DIETS*		*TABLA 7-3* *TIPOS DE DIETAS*
ENGLISH	*SPANISH*	*PRONUNCIATION*
regular	**regular**	*reh-goo-lahr*
liquid	**líquida**	*lee-kee-dah*
low-sodium	**baja en sal/poca sal**	*bah-hah ehn sahl/poh-kah sahl*
diabetic	**diabética**	*dee-ah-beh-tee-kah*
low-cholesterol	**poco colesterol**	*poh-koh koh-lehs-teh-rohl*
low-fat	**poca grasa**	*poh-kah grah-sah*
pureed	**puré**	*poo-reh*

Do you have . . .

    tuberculosis?

    chest pain?

    diabetes?

    cancer?

How many people are there in your family?

Do you live by yourself?

How do you spend your day?

At what time do you get up?

At what time do you go to bed?

How many hours a night do you sleep?

Do you sleep during the day?

How long?

Who helps you at home?

Can you do house chores?

Do you get tired easily?

Do you want to see a social worker?

Do you want to see a priest?

¿Tiene . . .
(Tee-eh-neh)

    ¿tuberculosis?
    (too-behr-koo-loh-sees)

    ¿dolor en el pecho?
    (doh-lohr ehn ehl peh-choh)

    ¿diabetes?
    (dee-ah-beh-tehs)

    ¿cáncer?
    (kahn-sehr)

¿Cuántas personas forman su familia?
(koo-ahn-tahs pehr-soh-nahs fohr-mahn soo fah-mee-lee-ah)

¿Vive solo?
(Bee-beh soh-loh)

¿Cómo pasa el día?
(Koh-moh pah-sah ehl dee-ah)

¿A qué hora se levanta?
(Ah keh oh-rah seh leh-bahn-tah)

¿A qué hora se acuesta?
(Ah keh oh-rah seh ah-koo-ehs-tah)

¿Cuántas horas duerme por la noche?
(Koo-ahn-tahs oh-rahs doo-ehr-meh pohr lah noh-cheh)

¿Duerme durante el día?
(Doo-ehr-meh doo-rahn-teh ehl dee-ah)

¿Cuánto tiempo?
(Koo-ahn-toh tee-ehm-poh)

¿Quién le ayuda en casa?
(Kee-ehn leh ah-yoo-dah ehn kah-sah)

¿Puede hacer quehaceres domésticos?
(Poo-eh-deh ah-sehr keh-ah-seh-rehs doh-mehs-tee-kohs)

¿Se cansa con facilidad?
(Seh kahn-sah kohn fah-see-lee-dahd)

¿Necesita ver a la trabajadora social?
(Neh-seh-see-tah behr ah lah trah-bah-hah-doh-rah soh-see-ahl)

¿Necesita ver al sacerdote?
(Neh-seh-see-tah behr ahl sah-sehr-doh-teh)

See Table 7-4 for more helpful words and phrases.
Vea la tabla 7-4 con más palabras y frases útiles.

TABLE 7-4 HELPFUL WORDS AND PHRASES		TABLA 7-4 PALABRAS Y FRASES UTILES
ENGLISH	SPANISH	PRONUNCIATION
hospital policy	reglas del hospital	reh-glahs dehl ohs-pee-tahl
routine	rutina	roo-tee-nah
no smoking	no se permite fumar	noh seh pehr-mee-teh foo-mahr
instructions	instrucciones	eens-trook-see-ohn-ehs
chaplain/priest	capellán/sacerdote/cura	kah-peh-yahn/sah-sehr-doh-teh/ koo-rah
visiting hours	horas de visita	oh-rahs deh bee-see-tah

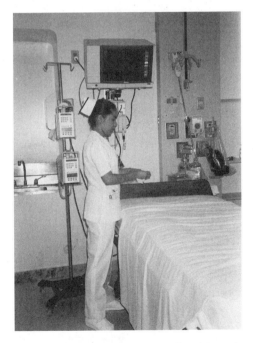

FIGURE 7-5 Hospital rooms are not always comfortable and can be frightening.

I will show you your room.	**Le mostraré su cuarto.** *(Leh mohs-trah-reh soo koo-ahr-toh)*
You cannot smoke in here.	**No puede fumar aquí.** *(Noh poo-eh-deh foo-mahr ah-kee)*
This is the call bell.	**Este es el timbre.** *(Ehs-teh ehs ehl teem-breh)*
The meals are served	**Los alimentos se sirven** *(Lohs ah-lee-mehn-tohs seh seer-behn)*
at 7 A.M.	**a las siete de la mañana.** *(ah lahs see-eh-teh deh lah mah- nyah-nah)*
at 11:30 A.M.	**a las once y media de la mañana** *(ah lahs ohn-seh ee meh-dee-ah deh lah mah-nyah-nah)*
at 5 P.M.	**a las cinco de la tarde.** *(ah lahs seen-koh deh lah tahr-deh)*
You may use the phone to make local calls.	**Puede usar el teléfono para hacer llama- das locales.** *(Poo-eh-deh ooh-sahr ehl teh-leh-foh- noh pah-rah ah-sehr yah-mah-dahs loh-kah-lehs)*
Here is a radio.	**Aquí está el radio.** *(Ah-kee ehs-tah ehl rah-dee-oh)*
The television has four channels.	**El televisor tiene cuatro canales.** *(Ehl teh-leh-bee-sohr tee-eh-neh koo-ah- troh kah-nah-lehs)*
There is an educational channel.	**Hay un canal educativo.** *(Ah-ee oon kah-nahl eh-doo-kah-tee- boh)*
These buttons move the bed up/down.	**Estos botones mueven la cama hacia arriba/abajo.** *(Ehs-tohs boh-toh-nehs moo-eh-behn lah kah-mah ah-see-ah ah-rree-bah/ah- bah-hoh)*
You can raise your head.	**Puede levantar la cabeza.** *(Poo-eh-deh leh-bahn-tahr lah kah-beh- sah)*
You can raise your feet.	**Puede levantar los pies.** *(Poo-eh-deh leh-bahn-tahr lohs pee-ehs)*
The rails lower down.	**El barandal se baja.** *(Ehl bah-rahn-dahl seh bah-hah)*

Visiting hours are from 2 P.M. to 8 P.M.	**Las horas de visita son de las dos a las ocho de la noche.** *(Lahs oh-rahs deh bee-see-tah sohn deh lahs dohs ah lahs oh-choh deh lah noh-cheh)*
While in the hospital, wear this bracelet at all times.	**Use esta pulsera mientras esté en el hospital.** *(Oo-seh ehs-tah pool-seh-rah mee-ehn-trahs ehs-teh chn ehl ohs-pee-tahl)*
Your towels are in the bathroom.	**Sus toallas están en el baño.** *(Soos too-ah-yahs ehs-tahn ehn ehl bah-nyoh)*
There is an emergency light.	**Hay una luz para emergencias.** *(Ah-ee oo-nah loos pah-rah eh-mehr-hehn-see-ahs)*
If you have an emergency, pull the cord in the bathroom.	**Si tiene una emergencia, jale el cordón en el baño.** *(See tee-eh-neh oon-ah eh-mehr-hehn-see-ah, hah-leh ehl kohr-dohn ehn ehl bah-nyoh)*
The bell will sound.	**La campana sonará.** *(Lah kahm-pah-nah soh-nah-rah)*
Your family will bring your clothes to you.	**Su familia le traerá ropa.** *(Soo fah-mee-lee-ah leh trah-eh-rah roh-pah)*
Change into this gown.	**Póngase esta bata.** *(Pohn-gah-seh ehs-tah bah-tah)*
Now, get some rest.	**Ahora descanse.** *(Ah-oh-rah dehs-kahn-seh)*
Do you have any questions?	**¿Tiene dudas?** *(Tee-eh-neh doo-dahs)*
I will be back to ask you some more questions.	**Regresaré para hacerle más preguntas.** *(Reh-greh-sah-reh pah-rah ah-sehr-leh mahs preh-goon-tahs)*

Table 7-5 will help you review some commonly asked questions.
La tabla 7-5 ayudará a repasar algunas preguntas comunes.

TABLE 7-5   *TABLA 7-5*
COMMON QUESTIONS   *PREGUNTAS COMUNES*

ENGLISH	SPANISH	PRONUNCIATION
Do you have . . . ?	¿Tiene . . . ?	¿Tee-eh-neh . . . ?
How did you . . . ?	¿Cómo hizo . . . ?	¿Koh-moh ee-soh . . . ?
What kind . . . ?	¿Qué clase . . . ?	¿Keh klah-seh . . . ?
What's the matter?	¿Qué pasa?	¿Keh pah-sah?
How many . . . ?	¿Cuántos . . . ?	¿Koo-ahn-tohs . . . ?
Have you had . . . ?	¿Ha tenido . . . ?	¿Ah teh-nee-doh . . . ?
What is . . . ?	¿Qué es . . . ?	¿Keh ehs . . . ?
Can you . . . ?	¿Puede usted . . . ?	¿Poo-eh-deh oos-tehd . . . ?

The Patient's Room

El Cuarto del Paciente

Mr. Gonzalez has been admitted to room 569 of the surgery floor.
Al señor González lo admitieron en el cuarto quinientos sesenta y nueve (cinco, seis, nueve) del piso de cirugía.

Hello Mr. Gonzalez, I am the head nurse.	**Hola, señor González, yo soy la/el enfermera(o) encargada(o).** *(Oh-lah seh-nyohr Gohn-sah-lehs, yoh soh-ee lah/ehl ehn-fehr-meh-rah[roh] ehn-kahr-gah-dah[doh])*
This brochure explains the hospital's guidelines.	**Este folleto explica las reglas del hospital.** *(Ehs-teh foh-yeh-toh ex-plee-kah lahs reh-glahs dehl ohs-pee-tahl)*
I am going to give you a tour of the floor.	**Voy a darle un recorrido por el piso.** *(Boy ah dahr-leh oon reh-koh-rree-doh pohr ehl pee-soh)*
This is the lobby.	**Esta es la sala de espera.** *(Ehs-tah es lah sah-lah deh ehs-peh-rah)*
You can bring your family here.	**Puede traer a su familia aquí.** *(Poo-eh-deh trah-ehr ah soo fah-mee-lee-ah ah-kee)*
This is the service area.	**Esta es el área de servicio.** *(Ehs-tah ehs ehl ah-reh-ah deh sehr-bee-see-oh)*
You can order coffee here.	**Puede ordenar café aquí.** *(Poo-eh-deh ohr-deh-nahr kah-feh ah-kee)*
The stairs are at the end of the hallway.	**Las escaleras están al final del pasillo.** *(Lahs ehs-kah-leh-rahs ehs-tahn ahl fee-nahl dehl pah-see-yoh)*

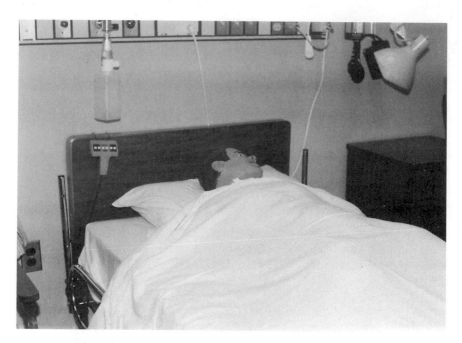

FIGURE 8-1   When a patient is hospitalized he is informed about his room environment and is given general hospital guidelines.

TABLE 8-1 PRONUNCIATION OF SELECTED WORDS	TABLA 8-1 PRONUNCIACION DE PALABRAS SELECTAS	
ENGLISH	SPANISH	PRONUNCIATION
bathroom	baño	bah-nyoh
corner	esquina	ehs-kee-nah
stairs	escaleras	ehs-kah-leh-rahs
room	cuarto	koo-ahr-toh
wall	pared	pah-rehd
patient	paciente	pah-see-ehn-teh
table	mesa	meh-sah
bell	campana	kahm-pah-nah
button	botón	boh-tohn
window	ventana	behn-tah-nah

The elevators work twenty-four hours a day.	**Los elevadores trabajan las veinticuatro horas.** *(Lohs eh-leh-bah-doh-rehs trah-bah-hahn lahs beh-een-tee-koo-ah-troh oh-rahs)*
There are guest bathrooms in the corner.	**Hay baños para las visitas en la esquina.** *(Hay bah-nyohs pah-rah lahs bee-see-tahs ehn lah ehs-kee-nah)*
In case of fire, use the stairs.	**En caso de incendio, use las escaleras.** *(Ehn kah-soh deh eehn-sehn-dee-oh, oo-seh lahs ehs-kah-leh-rahs)*
This is your room.	**Este es el cuarto.** *(Ehs-teh ehs ehl koo-ahr-toh)*
You cannot hang anything from the ceiling.	**No puede colgar nada del techo.** *(Noh poo-eh-deh kohl-gahr nah-dah dehl teh-choh)*
You cannot hang anything from the door.	**No puede colgar nada en la puerta.** *(Noh poo-eh-deh kohl-gahr nah-dah ehn lah poo-ehr-tah)*

FIGURE 8-2   *The visitor's restroom is across the lobby, next to the elevators.*

You can tape pictures to the wall.

Puede pegar retratos en la pared.
(Poo-eh-deh peh-gahr reh-trah-tohs ehn lah pah-rehd)

You can put cards on the shelf.

Puede poner tarjetas en el estante.
(Poo-eh-deh poh-nehr tahr-heh-tahs ehn ehl ehs-tahn-teh)

You can have flowers.

Puede tener flores.
(Poo-eh-deh teh-nehr floh-rehs)

This chair pulls out into a bed.

Esta silla se hace cama.
(Ehs-tah see-yah seh ah-seh kah-mah)

This is the call bell/buzzer.

Esta es la campana/el timbre.
(Ehs-tah ehs lah kahm-pah-nah/ehl teem-breh)

This button lowers (raises) the headboard.

Este botón baja (sube) la cabecera de la cama.
(Ehs-teh boh-tohn bah-hah (soo-beh) lah kah-beh-seh-rah deh lah kah-mah)

Do you need the headboard up?

¿Necesita levantar la cabecera más?
(Neh-seh-see-tah leh-bahn-tahr lah kah-beh-seh-rah mahs)

FIGURE 8-3 It is important to know where emergency equipment is located.

FIGURE 8-4   *In case of fire, use the emergency exits.*

TABLE 8-2 USEFUL VERBS	TABLA 8-2 *VERBOS UTILES*	
ENGLISH	*SPANISH*	*PRONUNCIATION*
can	poder	*poh-dehr*
is	es, está	*ehs, ehs-tah*
there are	hay	*ah-ee*
to bathe	bañar	*bah-nyahr*
to close	cerrar	*seh-rahr*
to cry	llorar	*yoh-rahr*
to go	ir	*eer*
to hang	colgar	*kohl-gahr*
to have	tener	*teh-nehr*
to speak	hablar	*ah-blahr*

TABLE 8-3 USEFUL ITEMS		TABLA 8-3 ARTICULOS UTILES
ENGLISH	SPANISH	PRONUNCIATION
cosmetics	cosméticos	kohs-meh-tee-kohs
perfume	perfume	pehr-foo-meh
toothpaste	pasta de dientes	pahs-tah deh dee-ehn-tehs
toothbrush	cepillo de dientes	seh-pee-yoh deh dee-ehn-tehs
comb	peine	peh-ee-neh
razor	navaja/máquina de afeitar	nah-bah-hah/mah-kee-nah deh ah-feh-ee-tahr
glass	vidrio/vaso/cristal	bee-dree-oh/bah-soh/crees-tahl
nightgown	camisa de dormir/bata	kah-mee-sah deh dohr-meer/bah-tah
lipstick	lápiz de labios	lah-pees deh lah-bee-ohs

The bed has one blanket.

La cama tiene una frazada/colcha.
(Lah kah-mah tee-eh-neh oo-nah frah-sah-dah/kohl-chah)

If you need more sheets, call the assistant.

Si necesita más sábanas, llame a la/el asistente.
(See neh-seh-see-tah mahs sah-bah-nahs, yah-meh ah lah/ehl ah-sees-tehn-teh)

Do you need more pillows?

¿Necesita más almohadas?
(Neh-seh-see-tah mahs ahl-moh-ah-dahs)

Keep the siderails up at night.

Mantenga los barandales levantados durante la noche.
(Mahn-tehn-gah lohs bah-rahn-dah-lehs leh-bahn-tah-dohs doo-rahn-teh lah noh-cheh)

You have a private bathroom.

Tiene un baño privado.
(Tee-eh-neh oon bah-nyoh pree-bah-doh)

There is a shower.

Hay una ducha.
(Ah-ee oo-nah doo-chah)

There is also a bathtub/tub.

También hay una bañera/tina.
(Tahm-bee-ehn ah-ee oo-nah bah-nyeh-rah/tee-nah)

Put your clothes in the closet.

Ponga su ropa en el closet/ropero.
(Pohn-gah soo roh-pah ehn ehl kloh-seht/roh-peh-roh)

Don't walk around barefoot.	**No camine descalzo.** *(No kah-mee-neh dehs-kahl-soh)*
Wear slippers, the floor is cold.	**Use las pantuflas/chanclas, el piso está frío.** *(Oo-seh lahs pahn-too-flahs/chahn-klahs, ehl pee-soh ehs-tah free-oh)*
You can make local phone calls.	**Puede hacer llamadas locales.** *(Poo-eh-deh ah-sehr yah-mah-dahs loh-kah-lehs)*
Dial 9, wait for the tone, and then dial the number you wish to call.	**Marque el nueve, espere el tono, luego marque el número que quiera llamar.** *(Mahr-keh ehl noo-eh-beh, ehs-peh-reh ehl toh-noh, loo-eh-goh mahr-keh ehl noo-meh-roh keh kee-eh-rah yah-mahr)*
You can call collect.	**Puede llamar por cobrar.** *(Poo-eh-deh yah-mahr pohr koh-brahr)*
If you want to watch T.V., you have to pay a fee.	**Si quiere ver el televisor, tiene que pagar una cuota.** *(See kee-eh-reh behr ehl teh-leh-bee-sohr, tee-eh-neh keh pah-gahr oo-nah koo-oh-tah)*

TABLE 8-4   **TABLA 8-4**
ITEMS OF CLOTHING   **ARTICULOS DE VESTIR**

ENGLISH	SPANISH	PRONUNCIATION
skirt	**falda**	*fahl-dah*
blouse	**blusa**	*bloo-sah*
gown	**bata/vestido**	*bah-tah/behs-tee-doh*
suit	**traje**	*trah-heh*
pants/slacks	**pantalones**	*pahn-tah-loh-nehs*
dress	**vestido**	*behs-tee-doh*
coat	**abrigo**	*ah-bree-goh*
shoes	**zapatos**	*sah-pah-tohs*
jacket	**chaqueta**	*chah-keh-tah*
sweater	**chamarra/suéter**	*chah-mah-rrah/soo-eh-tehr*
tie	**corbata**	*kohr-bah-tah*
underwear	**ropa interior**	*roh-pah een-teh-ree-ohr*
socks	**calcetines/calcetas**	*kahl-seh-tee-nehs/kahl-seh-tahs*
hose/stockings	**medias**	*meh-dee-ahs*

You cannot smoke in your room.

No puede fumar en el cuarto.
(Noh poo-eh-deh foo-mahr ehn ehl koo-ahr-toh)

You can smoke on the patio.

Puede fumar en el patio.
(Poo-eh-deh foo-mahr ehn ehl pah-tee-oh)

You cannot open the windows.

No puede abrir las ventanas.
(Noh poo-eh-deh ah-breer lahs behn-tah-nahs)

Visiting hours are from 9 A.M. to 9 P.M.

Las horas de visita son de las nueve de la mañana a las nueve de la noche.
(Lahs oh-rahs deh bee-see-tah sohn deh lahs noo-eh-beh deh lah mah-nyah-nah ah lahs noo-eh-beh deh lah noh-cheh)

Chapter Nine

The X-Ray Department

El Departamento de Rayos X

Mr. Martínez, a sixty-year-old patient, is going to have X-rays taken. He is scheduled for abdomen and chest X-rays.

Al Señor Martínez, un paciente de sesenta años, le van a tomar rayos X. Está en el horario para tomarle rayos X del abdomen y del pecho.

Good morning, Mr. Martinez.	**Buenos días, señor Martínez.** *(Boo-eh-nohs dee-ahs seh-nyohr Mahr-tee-nehs)*
Transportation is here.	**El transporte está aquí.** *(Ehl trahns-pohr-teh ehs-tah ah-kee)*
Good morning!	**¡Buenos días!** *(Boo-eh-nohs dee-ahs)*
Where do I need to go?	**¿A dónde tengo que ir?** *(Ah dohn-deh tehn-goh keh eer)*
We are going to take X-rays.	**Vamos a tomar rayos X.** *(Bah-mohs ah toh-mahr rah-yohs eh-kiss)*
I am going to help you lie on the stretcher.	**Voy a ayudarlo a acostarse en la camilla.** *(Boy ah ah-yoo-dahr-loh ah ah-kohs-tahr-seh ehn lah kah-mee-yah)*
Don't move!	**¡No se mueva!** *(Noh seh moo-eh-bah)*
We are going to pull the sheet at the count of three.	**Vamos a jalar la sábana al contar tres.** *(Bah-mohs ah hah-lahr lah sah-bah-nah ahl kohn-tahr trehs)*
One, two, three . . .	**Uno, dos, tres . . .** *(Oo-noh, dohs, trehs)*

95

Very good!	¡Muy bien!
	(Moo-ee bee-ehn)
Don't hold on to the rail.	No agarre el barandal.
	(Noh ah-gah-rreh ehl bah-rahn-dahl)
I am going to cover you with a sheet.	Voy a cubrirlo con una sábana.
	(Boy ah koo-breer-loh kohn oo-nah sah-bah-nah)
Take your medical file.	Lleve su expediente.
	(Yeh-beh soo ehx-peh-dee-ehn-teh)
Take your hospital card.	Lleve su tarjeta del hospital.
	(Yeh-beh soo tahr-heh-tah dehl ohs-pee-tahl)
Remember to bring them back.	Acuérdese de regresarlos.
	(Ah-koo-ehr-deh-seh deh reh-greh-sahr-lohs)
It's not very far.	No está muy lejos.
	(Noh ehs-tah moo-ee leh-hohs)

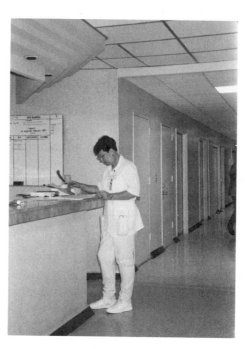

FIGURE 9-1 Transportation will take the patient's chart and card.

We are here!	**¡Ya llegamos/Aquí estamos!** *(Yah yeh-gah-mohs/Ah-kee ehs-tah-mohs)*
Stay/remain as you are.	**Quédese como está.** *(Keh-deh-seh koh-moh ehs-tah)*

Mr. Martínez arrives at the department.
El señor Martínez llega al departamento.

Hello, Mr. Martínez.	**Hola, señor Martínez.** *(Oh-lah seh-nyohr Mahr-tee-nehs)*
I am the technician.	**Yo soy el/la técnico(a).** *(Yoh soh-ee ehl/lah tehk-nee-koh[kah])*
Please change your clothes.	**Por favor, cámbiese de ropa.** *(Por fah-bohr kahm-bee-eh-seh deh roh-pah)*
I am going to take X-rays of your abdomen first.	**Voy a tomarle rayos X del abdomen primero.** *(Boy ah toh-mahr-leh rah-yohs eh-kiss dehl ahb-doh-mehn pree-meh-roh)*

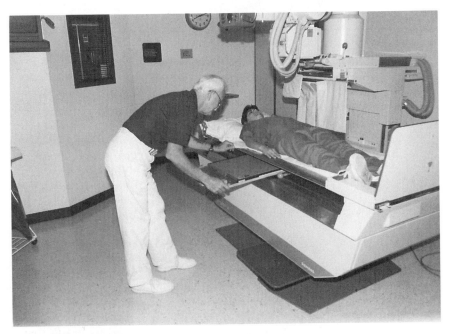

FIGURE 9-2 Lying supine and keeping quiet helps while taking X-rays.

Lie down!

¡Acuéstese!
(Ah-koo-ehs-teh-seh)

I am putting a cassette under your waist.

Estoy poniendo un caset debajo de la cintura.
(Ehs-tohy poh-nee-ehn-doh oon kah-seht deh-bah-hoh deh lah seen-too-rah)

It will feel like a board.

Lo sentirá como una tabla.
(Loh sehn-tee-rah koh-moh oo-nah tah-blah)

It has film inside.

Tiene la película adentro.
(Tee-eh-neh lah peh-lee-koo-lah ah-dehn-troh)

Don't move!

¡No se mueva!
(Noh seh moo-eh-bah)

When I tell you, hold your breath.

Cuando le avise, no respire.
(Koo-ahn-doh leh ah-bee-seh, noh rehs-pee-reh)

Don't breathe!

¡No respire!
(Noh rehs-pee-reh)

You can breathe now.

Ya puede respirar.
(Yah poo-eh-deh rehs-pee-rahr)

TABLE 9-1 *COMMON COMMANDS*	*TABLA 9-1* *ORDENES/MANDATOS COMUNES*	
ENGLISH	*SPANISH*	*PRONUNCIATION*
Tighten your muscle!	**¡Apriete el músculo!**	*¡Ah-pree-eh-teh ehl moos-koo-loh!*
Turn on your side!	**¡Voltéese de lado!**	*¡Bohl-teh-eh-seh deh lah-doh!*
Stand up straight!	**¡Párese derecho!**	*¡Pah-reh-seh deh-reh-choh!*
Keep your feet together!	**¡Mantenga los pies juntos!**	*¡Mahn-tehn-gah lohs pee-ehs hoon-tohs!*
Turn to the right!	**¡Voltée a la derecha!**	*¡Bohl-teh-eh ah lah deh-reh-chah!*
Walk straight ahead!	**¡Camine derecho!**	*¡Kah-mee-neh deh-reh-choh!*
Lift your arms!	**¡Levante los brazos!**	*¡Leh-bahn-teh lohs brah-sohs!*
Stay/remain as you are!	**¡Quédese como está!**	*¡Keh-deh-seh koh-moh ehs-tah!*

Breathe out!	¡Exhale/respire! *(Ehx-ah-leh/rehs-pee-reh)*
Turn onto your side.	Voltéese de lado. *(Bohl-teh-eh-seh deh lah-doh)*
Turn to the right.	Voltee a la derecha. *(Bohl-teh-eh ah lah deh-reh-chah)*
Once more.	Una vez más. *(Oo-nah behs mahs)*
Hold your breath.	No respire. *(Noh rehs-pee-reh)*
Breathe!	¡Respire! *(Rehs-pee-reh)*
Now I need to take an X-ray of your chest.	Ahora necesito tomarle una radiografía del pecho. *(Ah-oh-rah neh-seh-see-toh toh-mahr-leh oo-nah rah-dee-oh-grah-fee-ah dehl peh-choh)*
Stand up straight.	Párese derecho(a). *(Pah-reh-seh deh-reh-choh[chah])*
Keep your feet together.	Ponga los pies juntos. *(Pohn-gah lohs pee-ehs hoon-tohs)*

FIGURE 9-3 Raise your arms and don't breathe!

TABLE 9-2 COMMANDS	TABLA 9-2 ORDENES/MANDATOS	
ENGLISH	SPANISH	PRONUNCIATION
Don't hold on!	¡No se agarre!	¡Noh seh ah-gah-rreh!
Breathe!	¡Respire!	¡Rehs-pee-reh!
Don't breathe!	¡No respire!	¡Noh rehs-pee-reh!
Don't move!	¡No se mueva!	¡Noh seh moo-eh-bah!
Don't laugh!	¡No se ría!	¡Noh seh ree-ah!
Talk!	¡Hable!	¡Ah-bleh!
Lie down!	¡Acuéstese!	¡Ah-koo-ehs-teh-seh!
Don't lie down!	¡No se acueste!	¡Noh seh ah-koo-ehs-teh!
Hold your breath!	¡No respire!	¡Noh rehs-pee-reh!
Keep quiet!	¡Quédese quieto!	¡Keh-deh-seh kee-eh-toh!
	¡No se mueva!	¡Noh seh moo-eh-bah!
Press hard!	¡Presione fuerte!	¡Preh-see-oh-neh foo-ehr-teh!
Sit down!	¡Siéntese!	¡See-ehn-teh-seh!
Stay still!	¡Quédese quieto!	¡Keh-deh-seh kee-eh-toh!

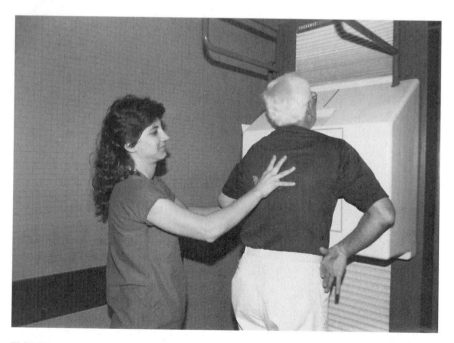

FIGURE 9-4   Give clear directions to your patient.

Lift your arms.

Levante los brazos.
(Leh-bahn-teh lohs brah-sohs)

Stay/remain like this for a moment.

Quédese así por un rato.
(Keh-deh-seh ah-see pohr oon rah-toh)

Now turn toward the screen.

Ahora, voltee hacia la placa.
(Ah-oh-rah bohl-teh-eh ah-see-ah lah plah-kah)

This will feel cold.

Esto se sentirá frío.
(Ehs-toh seh sehn-tee-rah free-oh)

It will take a minute.

Va a tomar un minuto.
(Bah ah toh-mahr oon mee-noo-toh)

Are you in pain?

¿Tiene dolor?
(Tee-eh-neh doh-lohr)

You can breathe.

Puede respirar.
(Poo-eh-deh rehs-pee-rahr)

Stop breathing.

No respire.
(Noh rehs-pee-reh)

I finished.

Ya terminé.
(Yah tehr-mee-neh)

You can breathe now!

¡Puede respirar!
(Poo-eh-deh rehs-pee-rahr)

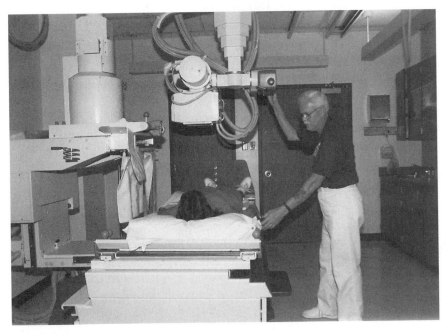

FIGURE 9-5 *You must be perfectly still!*

TABLE 9-3   TABLA 9-3
COMMON QUESTIONS   PREGUNTAS COMUNES

ENGLISH	SPANISH	PRONUNCIATION
Where do I need to go?	¿A dónde necesito ir?	¿Ah dohn-deh neh-seh-see-toh eer?
Do you need help?	¿Necesita ayuda?	¿Neh-seh-see-tah ah-yoo-dah?
Have you had X-rays taken?	¿Le han tomado rayos X?	¿Leh ahn toh-mah-doh rah-yohs eh-kiss?
When was the last time?	¿Cuándo fue la última vez?	¿Koo-ahn-doh foo-eh lah ool-tee-mah behs?
Do you know why?	¿Sabe por qué?	¿Sah-beh pohr keh?
How old are you?	¿Cuántos años tiene?	¿Koo-ahn-tohs ah-nyohs tee-eh-neh?
Are you pregnant?	¿Está embarazada?	¿Ehs-tah ehm-bah-rah-sah-dah?
Have you had cancer?	¿Ha tenido cáncer?	¿Ah teh-nee-doh kahn-sehr?
Do you have a history of cancer in your family?	¿Tiene antecedentes de cáncer en su familia?	¿Tee-eh-neh ahn-teh-seh-dehn-tehs deh kahn-sehr ehn soo fah-mee-lee-ah?

I will return shortly.

Regresaré enseguida.
(Reh-greh-sah-reh ehn-seh-gee-dah)

Please sit down.

Siéntese, por favor.
(See-ehn-teh-seh pohr fah-bohr)

Don't change your clothes.

No se cambie de ropa.
(Noh seh kahm-bee-eh deh roh-pah)

I want to see if the X-rays came out all right.

Quiero ver si los rayos X salieron bien.
(Kee-eh-roh behr see lohs rah-yohs eh-kiss sah-lee-eh-rohn bee-ehn)

I am back.

Ya regresé.
(Yah reh-greh-seh)

Now you can change your clothes.

Ahora se puede cambiar de ropa.
(Ah-oh-rah seh poo-eh-deh kahm-bee-ahr deh roh-pah)

Do you need help?

¿Necesita ayuda?
(Neh-seh-see-tah ah-yoo-dah)

I am going to call the radiologist.

Voy a llamar al radiólogo.
(Boy ah yah-mahr ahl rah-dee-oh-loh-goh)

He will talk to you.

El hablará con usted.
(Ehl ah-blah-rah kohn oos-tehd)

Dr. Blanco, the radiologist, stands by the door and greets the patient.
El doctor Blanco, radiólogo, se para en la puerta y saluda al paciente.

Good morning!

¡Buenos días!
(Boo-eh-nohs dee-ahs)

I am Dr. Blanco.

Yo soy el doctor Blanco.
(Yoh soh-ee ehl dohk-tohr Blahn-koh)

We need to bring you back.

Necesitamos que regrese.
(Neh-seh-see-tah-mohs keh reh-greh-seh)

We need to take another X-ray of your abdomen.

Necesitamos tomarle otras radiografías del abdomen.
(Neh-seh-see-tah-mohs toh-mahr-leh oh-trahs rah-dee-oh-grah-fee-ahs dehl ahb-doh-mehn)

But we have to give you something to drink first.

Pero primero le daremos algo para tomar.
(Peh-roh pree-meh-roh leh dah-reh-mohs ahl-goh pah-rah toh-mahr)

At the same time that we take the X-rays.

Al mismo tiempo que tomamos los rayos X.
(Ahl mees-moh tee-ehm-poh keh toh-mah-mohs lohs rah-yohs eh-kiss)

TABLE 9-4 HELPFUL PHRASES	TABLA 9-4 FRASES UTILES	
ENGLISH	SPANISH	PRONUNCIATION
I am going to help you.	Voy a ayudarlo(a).	Boy ah ah-yoo-dahr-loh(lah)
We are going to pull.	Vamos a jalar.	Bah-mohs ah hah-lahr
Very good!	¡Muy bien!	¡Moo-ee bee-ehn!
Take your medical file.	Lleve su expediente.	Yeh-beh soo ehx-peh-dee-ehn-teh
Take your hospital card.	Lleve su tarjeta.	Yeh-beh soo tahr-heh-tah
It's not very far.	No está muy lejos.	Noh ehs-tah moo-ee leh-hohs
We are here.	Estamos aquí.	Ehs-tah-mohs ah-kee
Please put on this gown.	Por favor, póngase esta bata.	Pohr fah-bohr pohn-gah-seh ehs-tah bah-tah

Tonight, eat lightly.	Esta noche coma poco. *(Ehs-tah noh-cheh koh-mah poh-koh)*
Take these pills after your meal.	Tómese estas pastillas después de la cena. *(Toh-meh-seh ehs-tahs pahs-tee-yahs dehs-poo-ehs deh lah seh-nah)*
You can drink water.	Puede tomar agua. *(Poo-eh-deh toh-mahr ah-goo-ah)*
Please tell the nurse to call me.	Por favor, dígale a la enfermera que me llame. *(Por fah-bohr dee-gah-leh ah lah ehn-fehr-meh-rah keh meh yah-meh)*
Do you have any questions?	¿Tiene preguntas? *(Tee-eh-neh preh-goon-tahs)*
I will see you tomorrow at 9 o'clock.	Lo veré mañana a las nueve. *(Loh beh-reh mah-nyah-nah ah lahs noo-eh-beh)*
Have a nice day!	¡Que pase un buen día! *(Keh pah-seh oon boo-ehn dee-ah)*
Transportation will take you back to your room.	Transportación lo regresará a su cuarto. *(Trahns-pohr-tah-see-ohn loh reh-greh-sah-rah ah soo koo-ahr-toh)*

TABLE 9-5 HELPFUL PHRASES	TABLA 9-5 FRASES UTILES	
ENGLISH	SPANISH	PRONUNCIATION
It will feel like a board.	Se siente como una tabla.	Seh see-ehn-teh koh-moh oo-nah tah-blah
One more time.	Una vez más.	Oo-nah behs mahs
It will take a minute.	Va a tomar un minuto.	Bah ah toh-mahr oon mee-noo-toh
I am through.	Ya terminé.	Yah tehr-mee-neh
I will return!	¡Regresaré!	¡Reh-greh-sah-reh!
You need to return.	Necesita regresar.	Neh-seh-see-tah reh-greh-sahr
You can drink water.	Necesita tomar agua.	Neh-seh-see-tah toh-mahr ah-goo-ah
When I tell you.	Cuando le diga.	Koo-ahn-doh leh dee-gah

TABLE 9-6 COMMON WORDS	TABLA 9-6 PALABRAS COMUNES	
ENGLISH	SPANISH	PRONUNCIATION
division	división	*dee-bee-see-ohn*
nuclear medicine	medicina nuclear	*meh-dee-see-nah noo-kleh-ahr*
ventilation	ventilación	*behn-tee-lah-see-ohn*
thyroid	tiroides/tiroidea	*tee-roh-ee-dehs/tee-roh-ee-deh-ah*
irradiate	irradiar	*ee-rrah-dee-ahr*
gallbladder	vesícula biliar	*beh-see-koo-lah bee-lee-ahr*
liver	hígado	*ee-gah-doh*
contrast	contraste	*kohn-trahs-teh*
laxative	laxante/purgante	*lahx-ahn-teh/poor-gahn-teh*
enema	enema/sonda	*eh-neh-mah/sohn-dah*
ultrasound	ultrasonido	*ool-trah-soh-nee-doh*
bowel	intestino	*een-tehs-tee-noh*
arteriogram	arteriograma	*ahr-teh-ree-oh-grah-mah*

The Laboratory

El Laboratorio

Mrs. Garza is going to have blood drawn in preparation for a 24-hour urine collection. The nurse explains the laboratory procedure and the hospital routine to her.

A la señora Garza le van a tomar muestras de sangre y se prepara para colectar/juntar su orina por veinticuatro horas. La enfermera le explica el procedimiento del laboratorio y la rutina del hospital.

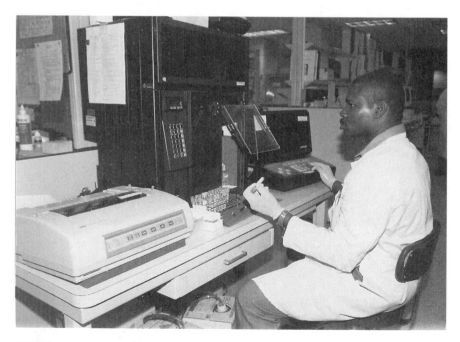

FIGURE 10-1 *Many blood tests are run in the laboratory.*

Mrs. Garza, the doctor has ordered blood samples.	Señora Garza, el doctor ordenó muestras de sangre. *(Seh-nyoh-rah Gahr-sah, ehl dohk-tohr ohr-deh-noh moo-ehs-trahs deh sahn-greh)*
The technician almost always comes at six A.M.	Casi siempre el laboratorista viene a las seis de la mañana. *(Kah-see see-ehm-preh ehl lah-boh-rah-toh-rees-tah bee-eh-neh ah lahs seh-ees deh lah mah-nyah-nah)*
Please do not eat after midnight.	Por favor, no coma después de medianoche. *(Pohr fah-bohr noh koh-mah dehs-poo-ehs deh meh-dee-ah-noh-cheh)*
In your case, do not eat anything after 8 P.M..	En su caso, no coma nada después de las ocho de la noche. *(Ehn soo kah-soh, noh koh-mah nah-dah dehs-poo-ehs deh lahs oh-choh deh lah noh-cheh)*

TABLE 10-1 *PRONUNCIATION OF* *SELECTED WORDS*	*TABLA 10-1* *PRONUNCIACION DE* *PALABRAS SELECTAS*	
ENGLISH	*SPANISH*	*PRONUNCIATION*
laboratory	**laboratorio**	*lah-boh-rah-toh-ree-oh*
technician	**técnico**	*tehk-nee-koh*
sample	**muestra**	*moo-ehs-trah*
in the morning	**en la mañana**	*ehn lah mah-nyah-nah*
tomorrow	**mañana**	*mah-nyah-nah*
after	**después**	*dehs-poo-ehs*
explain	**explique**	*ehx-plee-keh*
every time	**cada vez**	*kah-dah behs*
bottle	**botella**	*boh-teh-yah*
remain	**quédese**	*keh-deh-seh*
next	**siguiente**	*see-gee-ehn-teh*
pinprick	**picadura**	*pee-kah-doo-rah*
tubes	**tubos**	*too-bohs*
blood	**sangre**	*sahn-greh*

Tomorrow they will give you a special test.

Mañana le harán un examen especial.
(Mah-nyah-nah leh ah-rahn oon ehx-ah-mehn ehs-peh-see-ahl)

I am going to explain to you how to collect a urine sample.

Le voy a explicar cómo juntar una muestra de orina.
(Leh boy ah ehx-plee-kahr koh-moh hoon-tahr oo-nah moo-ehs-trah deh oh-ree-nah)

I will wake you up in the morning.

La voy a despertar en la mañana.
(Lah boy ah dehs-pehr-tahr ehn lah mah-nyah-nah)

I will ask you to urinate.

Le diré que orine.
(Leh dee-reh keh oh-ree-neh)

Every time you urinate, put it in this container.

Cada vez que orine, póngala en este frasco.
(Kah-dah behs keh oh-ree-neh, pohn-gah-lah ehn ehs-teh frahs-koh.

The container should be kept in a bucket with ice.

El frasco se mantendrá en un balde con hielo.
(Ehl frahs-koh seh mahn-tehn-drah ehn oon bahl-deh kohn ee-eh-loh)

The following day, the sample will be sent to the laboratory.

Al día siguiente, se mandará al laboratorio.
(Ahl dee-ah see-gee-ehn-teh, seh mahn-dah-rah ahl lah-boh-rah-toh-ree-oh)

Hello Mrs. Garza.

Hola, señora Garza.
(Oh-la seh-nyoh-rah Gahr-sah)

I am here to draw your blood.

Estoy aquí para tomarle una muestra de sangre.
(Ehs-tohy ah-kee pah-rah toh-mahr-leh oo-nah moo-ehs-trah deh sahn-greh)

Please stay/remain in bed.

Por favor, quédese en la cama.
(Pohr fah-bohr keh-deh-seh ehn lah kah-mah)

I am going to lift your sleeve.

Voy a levantar la manga.
(Boy ah leh-bahn-tahr lah mahn-gah)

Make a fist!

¡Cierre la mano/Haga un puño!
(See-eh-reh lah mah-noh/Ah-gah oon poo-nyoh)

Relax, it will not hurt!

¡Relájese, no le va a doler!
(Reh-lah-heh-seh, no leh bah ah doh-lehr)

Open your hand!	**¡Abra la mano!** *(Ah-brah lah mah-noh)*
I want to take a sample from your finger.	**Quiero tomar una muestra del dedo.** *(Kee-eh-roh toh-mahr oo-nah moo-ehs-trah dehl deh-doh)*
I want to check your sugar level.	**Quiero ver el nivel de azúcar.** *(Kee-eh-roh behr ehl nee-behl deh ah-soo-kahr)*
Do not move.	**No se mueva.** *(Noh seh moo-eh-bah)*
This won't take long.	**Esto se hace rápido.** *(Ehs-toh seh ah-seh rah-pee-doh)*
Have you had blood drawn before?	**Le han tomado muestras antes?** *(Leh ahn toh-mah-doh moo-ehs-trahs ahn-tehs)*
You will feel pain, like a pinprick.	**Sentirá dolor como una picadura.** *(Sehn-tee-rah doh-lohr koh-moh oo-nah pee-kah-doo-rah)*

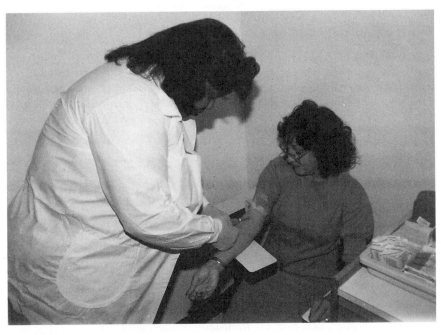

FIGURE 10-2 *Having blood drawn can be a frightening experience.*

TABLE 10-2 COMMON LAB WORDS	TABLA 10-2 PALABRAS COMUNES EN EL LABORATORIO	

ENGLISH	SPANISH	PRONUNCIATION
complete blood count	biometría *hemática completa	bee-oh-meh-tree-ah eh-mah-tee-kah kohm-pleh-tah
needle	aguja	ah-goo-hah
alcohol	*alcohol	ahl-kohl
syringe	jeringa	heh-reen-gah
gloves	guantes	goo-ahn-tehs
pathology	patología	pah-toh-loh-hee-ah
procedure	procedimiento	proh-seh-dee-mee-ehn-toh
STAT/emergency	STAT/emergencia	ehs-taht/eh-mehr-hehn-see-ah
reports	reportes	reh-pohr-tehs
specimen	muestra	moo-ehs-trah
fasting	en ayunas	ehn ah-yoo-nahs

*In Spanish the letter "h" is always silent; therefore, it is never pronounced.

I need two tubes of blood.	**Necesito dos tubos de sangre.** *(Neh-seh-see-toh dohs too-bohs deh sahn-greh)*
One tube for a blood count, another for a serology test.	**Un tubo para una biometría hemática, otro para una prueba serológica.** *(Oon too-boh pah-rah oo-nah bee-oh-meh-tree-ah eh-mah-tee-kah, oh-troh pah-rah oo-nah proo-eh-bah seh-roh-loh-hee-kah)*
Take a deep breath.	**Respire hondo.** *(Rehs-pee-reh ohn-doh)*
Relax, calm down.	**Relájese, cálmese.** *(Reh-lah-heh-seh, kahl-meh-seh)*
I need to use a tourniquet.	**Necesito usar un torniquete.** *(Neh-seh-see-toh oo-sahr oon tohr-nee-keh-teh)*
That is all!	**¡Es todo!** *(Ehs toh-doh)*

Note that the names of many brand-name products are not translated. Their pronunciation does, however, change a bit.

TABLE 10-3 *HELPFUL VERBS*		TABLA 10-3 *VERBOS UTILES*
ENGLISH	*SPANISH*	*PRONUNCIATION*
to ask	**preguntar**	*preh-goon-tahr*
to bend	**doblar**	*doh-blahr*
to come	**venir**	*beh-neer*
to go	**ir**	*eer*
to keep	**guardar/mantener**	*goo-ahr-dahr/mahn-teh-nehr*
to lift	**levantar/elevar**	*leh-bahn-tahr/eh-leh-bahr*
to place	**poner/colocar**	*poh-nehr/koh-loh-kahr*
to wake	**despertar**	*dehs-pehr-tahr*
to draw	**sacar/tirar/dibujar**	*sah-kahr/tee-rahr/dee-boo-hahr*
to eat	**comer**	*koh-mehr*
to drink	**beber/tomar**	*beh-behr/toh-mahr*

Note que hay muchas marcas de productos que no se traducen. La pronunciación cambia un poco.

I am going to put a Band-Aid on your arm.	**Voy a ponerle una cinta adhesiva/una curita/Band-Aid.** *(Boy ah poh-nehr-leh oo-nah seen-tah ah-deh-see-bah/oo-nah koo-ree-tah/ bahn-dah-eed)*
Please apply pressure for about five minutes.	**Por favor, ponga presión por cinco minutos.** *(Pohr fah-bohr pohn-gah preh-see-ohn pohr seen-koh mee-noo-tohs)*
I am through!	**¡Ya terminé!** *(Yah tehr-mee-neh)*
The nurse wants to talk to you.	**La enfermera quiere hablarle.** *(Lah ehn-fehr-meh-rah kee-eh-reh ah-blahr-leh)*
Mrs. Garza, I want you to get up and go urinate.	**Señora Garza, quiero que se levante y vaya a orinar.** *(Seh-nyoh-rah Gahr-sah kee-eh-roh keh seh leh-bahn-teh ee bah-yah ah oh-ree-nahr)*

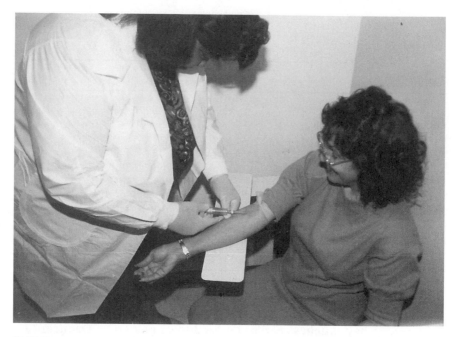

FIGURE 10-3   *Precautions must be observed when drawing blood.*

TABLE 10-4 PRONUNCIATION OF SELECTED WORDS	*TABLA 10-4 PRONUNCIACION DE PALABRAS SELECTAS*	
ENGLISH	*SPANISH*	*PRONUNCIATION*
additive	**aditivo**	*ah-dee-tee-boh*
package	**paquete**	*pah-keh-teh*
limitations	**limitaciones**	*lee-mee-tah-see-ohn-ehs*
spread	**untar/extender**	*oon-tahr/ehx-tehn-dehr*
adhesive	**adhesivo**	*ah-deh-see-boh*
sterile	**estéril**	*ehs-teh-reel*
rub	**frotar/restregar**	*froh-tahr/rehs-treh-gahr*
hematology	**hematología**	*eh-mah-toh-loh-hee-ah*
puncture	**pinchazo/picadura**	*peen-chah-soh/pee-kah-doo-rah*
blood bank	**banco de sangre**	*bahn-koh deh sahn-greh*
coagulated	**coagulado(a)**	*koh-ah-goo-lah-doh(dah)*

Urinate a little, then put it into this cup.

Orine un poco, luego póngala en esta taza.
(Oh-ree-neh oon poh-koh, loo-eh-goh pohn-gah-lah ehn ehs-tah tah-sah)

Remember that you have to put the urine into a container.

Recuerde que debe orinar y poner la orina en el frasco.
(Reh-koo-ehr-deh keh deh-beh oh-ree-nahr ee poh-nehr lah oh-ree-nah ehn ehl frahs-koh)

Remember that you will have to do this for 24 hours.

Recuerde que hará esto por veinticuatro horas.
(Reh-koo-ehr-deh keh ah-rah ehs-toh pohr beh-een-tee-koo-ah-troh oh-rahs)

If there is no ice in the bucket, call me.

Si no hay hielo en el balde, llámeme.
(See noh ahee ee-eh-loh ehn ehl bahl-deh yah-meh-meh)

I will remind you during the day.

Le recordaré durante el día.
(Leh reh-kohr-dah-reh doo-rahn-teh ehl dee-ah)

Do you feel all right?

¿Se siente bien?
(Seh see-ehn-teh bee-ehn)

Are you hungry?

¿Tiene hambre?
(Tee-eh-neh ahm-breh)

Do you want a cup of coffee?

¿Quiere una taza de café?
(Kee-eh-reh oo-nah tah-sah deh kah-feh)

Did you understand?

¿Entendió?
(Ehn-tehn-dee-oh)

Tomorrow, bring a stool sample in this container.

Mañana traiga una muestra de su excremento en este frasco.
(Mah-nyah-nah trah-ee-gah oo-nah moo-ehs-trah deh soo ehx-kreh-mehn-toh ehn ehs-teh frahs-koh)

Chapter Eleven

The Pharmacy

La Farmacia

The pharmacy provides services which are an integral part of total patient care. Drugs are dispensed only upon the order of a physician. The nurse orders the medication from the pharmacy after the doctor has prescribed the treatment for the patient.

La farmacia provee servicios como parte integral del cuidado total del paciente. Los medicamentos son distribuidos solamente por

FIGURE 11-1   *The pharmacy provides services for patients.*

orden del doctor. La/el enfermera(o) ordena la medicina a la farmacia después de que el doctor dejó la receta con el tratamiento para el paciente.

The inpatient pharmacy is open from 7 A.M. to 1 A.M.

La farmacia para pacientes que están internados está abierta de las siete de la mañana a la una de la mañana.
(Lah fahr-mah-see-ah pah-rah pah-see-ehn-tehs keh ehs-tahn een-tehr-nah-dohs ehs-tah ah-bee-ehr-tah deh lahs see-eh-teh deh lah mah-nyah-nah ah lah oo-nah deh lah mah-nyah-nah)

The pharmacy is open Monday through Friday.

La farmacia está abierta de lunes a viernes.
(Lah fahr-mah-see-ah ehs-tah ah-bee-ehr-tah deh loo-nehs ah bee-ehr-nehs)

FIGURE 11-2   The inpatient pharmacy is staffed around the clock.

| TABLE 11-1 | TABLA 11-1 |
| DRUG CATEGORIES | CATEGORIAS DE LOS MEDICAMENTOS |

ENGLISH	SPANISH	PRONUNCIATION
analgesic	analgésicos	ah-nahl-heh-see-kohs
antacid	antiácidos	ahn-tee-ah-see-dohs
antiarrhythmic	antiarritmias	ahn-tee-ah-reet-mee-ahs
antianxiety	contra la ansiedad/	kohn-trah lah ahn-see-eh-dahd/
	ansiolíticos	ahn-see-oh-lee-tee-kohs
antibiotics	antibióticos	ahn-tee-bee-oh-tee-kohs
anticonvulsant	anticonvulsivo	ahn-tee-kohn-bool-see-boh
	antiepiléptico	ahn-tee-eh-pee-lehp-tee-koh
antiemetic	antiemético	ahn-tee-eh-meh-tee-koh
antiviral	antivirales	ahn-tee-bee-rah-lehs
contraceptives	contraceptivos	kohn-trah-sehp-tee-bohs
decongestants	descongestionantes	dehs-kohn-hehs-tee-oh-nahn-tehs
laxatives	laxantes/purgantes	lahx-ahn-tehs/poor-gahn-tehs
narcotics	narcóticos	nahr-koh-tee-kohs
sedatives	sedativo/sedantes	seh-dah-tee-boh/seh-dahn-tehs

It is open on Saturday, Sunday, and holidays.

Esta abierta los sábados, domingos y días festivos.
(Ehs-tah ah-bee-ehr-tah lohs sah-bah-dohs, doh-meen-gohs ee dee-ahs fehs-tee-bohs)

The staff delivers and picks up orders every hour from each floor.

Los empleados recogen y surten órdenes en los pisos cada hora.
(Los ehm-pleh-ah-dohs reh-koh-hehn ee soor-tehn ohr-deh-nehs ehn lohs pee-sohs kah-dah oh-rah)

The nursing staff takes STAT orders to the pharmacy.

Las enfermeras llevan órdenes urgentes a la farmacia.
(Lahs ehn-fehr-meh-rahs yeh-bahn ohr-deh-nehs oor-hehn-tehs ah lah fahr-mah-see-ah)

Nurses control narcotic records on the unit.

Las enfermeras controlan archivos de narcóticos en el piso.
(Lahs ehn-fehr-meh-rahs kohn-troh-lahn ahr-chee-bohs deh nahr-koh-tee-kohs ehn ehl pee-soh)

If they find expired items on the unit, they return them to the pharmacy for replacement.

Si encuentran artículos con fecha vencida, los regresan a la farmacia, donde son reemplazados.
(See ehn-koo-ehn-trahn ahr-tee-koo-lohs kohn feh-chah behn-see-dah lohs reh-greh-sahn ah lah fahr-mah-see-ah dohn-deh sohn rehm-plah-sah-dohs)

The medication area is inspected every month.

Cada mes se inspecciona el área de medicamentos.
(Kah-dah mehs seh eens-pehk-see-ohn-ah ehl ah-reh-ah deh meh-dee-kah-mehn-tohs)

Medication carts are checked for quantity, number, and expiration date of each item.

Los carros con medicamentos se revisan para anotar la cantidad, número y fecha de caducidad de cada artículo.

FIGURE 11-3 Nurses maintain medication records.

TABLE 11-2 POTENTIAL POISONS		TABLA 11-2 POSIBILIDAD DE ENVENENAMIENTO
ENGLISH	SPANISH	PRONUNCIATION
alcohol	alcohol	*ahl-kohl*
antihistamine	antihistamínico	*ahn-tee-ees-tah-mee-nee-koh*
ammonia	amonia/amoníaco	*ah-moh-nee-ah/ah-moh-nee-ah-koh*
barbiturates	barbitúricos	*bahr-bee-too-ree-kohs*
boric acid	ácido bórico	*ah-see-doh boh-ree-koh*
cocaine	cocaína	*koh-kah-ee-nah*
digitalis	digitálicos	*dee-hee-tah-lee-kohs*
lead	plomo	*ploh-moh*
morphine	morfina	*mohr-fee-nah*
nicotine	nicotina	*nee-koh-tee-nah*
nitroglycerin	nitroglicerina	*nee-troh-glee-seh-ree-nah*
aspirin	aspirina	*ahs-pee-ree-nah*

FIGURE 11-4   *Pharmacists interpret doctors' orders and are available to the nursing staff for consultation.*

TABLE 11-3 APOTHECARY MEASURES	TABLA 11-3 MEDIDAS FARMACEUTICAS	
ENGLISH	SPANISH	PRONUNCIATION
ounces	onzas	ohn-sahs
grains	granos	grah-nohs
pound	libra	lee-brah
quart	cuarto	koo-ahr-toh
gallon	galón	gah-lohn

A standard schedule is used.

Se usa un horario estándar.
(Seh oo-sah oon oh-rah-ree-oh ehs-tahn-dahr)

The pharmacist interprets the physician's order.

El farmacéutico interpreta la orden del doctor.
(Ehl fahr-mah-seh-oo-tee-koh een-tehr-preh-tah lah ohr-dehn dehl dohk-tohr)

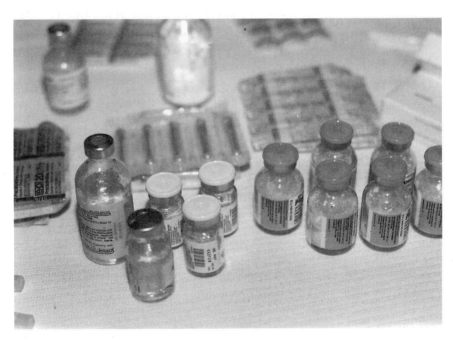

FIGURE 11-5 *Each medication (vial, suppository) must be labeled.*

TABLE 11-4   **TABLA 11-4**
METRIC MEASURES   **MEDIDAS METRICAS**

ENGLISH	SPANISH	PRONUNCIATION
milligram	**miligramo**	*mee-lee-grah-moh*
grams	**gramos**	*grah-mohs*
kilogram	**kilogramos/kilo**	*kee-loh-grah-mohs/kee-loh*
milliliter	**mililitro**	*mee-lee-lee-troh*
liter	**litro**	*lee-troh*
centimeter	**centímetro**	*sehn-tee-meh-troh*
cubic centimeter	**centímetro cúbico**	*sehn-tee-meh-troh koo-bee-koh*
meter	**metro**	*meh-troh*

Vials, pills, capsules, liquids, and IV fluids are dispensed.

Se surten frascos, pastillas, cápsulas, líquidos y sueros.
(Seh soor-tehn frahs-kohs, pahs-tee-yahs, kahp-soo-lahs, lee-kee-dohs ee soo-eh-rohs)

The nurse enters a dosage schedule into the computer.

La enfermera ingresa el horario de dosis en la computadora.
(Lah ehn-fehr-meh-rah een-greh-sah ehl oh-rah-ree-oh deh doh-sees ehn lah kohm-poo-tah-doh-rah)

Four times a day.

Cuatro veces al día.
(Koo-ah-troh beh-sehs ahl dee-ah)

TABLE 11-5   **TABLA 11-5**
HOUSEHOLD MEASURES   **MEDIDAS CASERAS**

ENGLISH	SPANISH	PRONUNCIATION
drop	**gota**	*goh-tah*
teaspoon	**cucharadita**	*koo-chah-rah-dee-tah*
tablespoon	**cucharada**	*koo-chah-rah-dah*
cup	**taza**	*tah-sah*
glass	**vaso**	*bah-soh*

TABLE 11-6 MEDICATION FORMS	TABLA 11-6 FORMAS DE LOS MEDICAMENTOS	

ENGLISH	SPANISH	PRONUNCIATION
fluid	fluido	floo-ee-doh
liquid	líquido	lee-kee-doh
gel	gelatina	heh-lah-tee-nah
capsule	cápsula	kahp-soo-lah
pill	píldora	peel-doh-rah
tablet	tableta	tah-bleh-tah
solid	sólido	soh-lee-doh
inhalant	inhalante	een-ah-lahn-teh
solution	solución	soh-loo-see-ohn
syrup	jarabe/zumo	hah-rah-beh/soo-moh
lotion	loción	loh-see-ohn
ointment	*ungüento	oon-goo-ehn-toh
topical	tópico	toh-pee-koh
rectal suppository	supositorio rectal	soo-poh-see-toh-ree-oh rehk-tahl
vaginal suppository	supositorio vaginal	soo-poh-see-toh-ree-oh bah-he-nahl
semi-solid	semisólido(a)	seh-mee-soh-lee-doh(dah)
diluent	diluente	dee-loo-ehn-teh

*The (¨) sign above the u in ungüento is used for emphasis.

Three times a day.	**Tres veces al día.** *(Trehs beh-sehs ahl dee-ah)*
Twice a day.	**Dos veces al día.** *(Dohs beh-sehs ahl dee-ah)*
Daily.	**Diariamente/Una por día/Cada día.** *(Dee-ah-ree-ah-mehn-teh/Oo-nah pohr dee-ah/Kah-dah dee-ah)*
Before/after meals.	**Antes/después de las comidas.** *(Ahn-tehs/dehs-poo-ehs deh lahs koh-mee-dahs)*
At bedtime.	**Al acostarse.** *(Ahl ah-kohs-tahr-seh)*
The pharmacist assists with patient education.	**El/La farmacéutico(a) asiste con la educación del paciente.** *(Ehl/Lah fahr-mah-seh-oo-tee-koh(kah) ah-sees-teh kohn lah eh-doo-kah-see-ohn dehl pah-see-ehn-teh)*

FIGURE 11-6   *The pharmacist logs the schedules of each medication into the computer.*

TABLE 11-7 ADMINISTRATION ROUTES	TABLA 11-7 VIAS DE ADMINISTRACION	
ENGLISH	SPANISH	PRONUNCIATION
by mouth	**por la boca**	*pohr lah boh-kah*
per rectum	**por el recto/rectal**	*pohr ehl rehk-toh/rehk-tahl*
vaginal	**vaginal**	*bah-hee-nahl*
intravenous	**intravenoso**	*een-trah-beh-noh-soh*
intramuscular	**intramuscular**	*een-trah-moos-koo-lahr*
sublingual	**sublingual**	*soob-leen-goo-ahl*
patch	**parche**	*pahr-cheh*
subcutaneous	**subcutáneo**	*soob-koo-tah-neh-oh*
oral	**oral**	*oh-rahl*
nasal	**nasal**	*nah-sahl*
otic	**ótico**	*oh-tee-koh*
ophthalmic	**oftálmico**	*ohf-tahl-mee-koh*

In case of a medication error, the doctor is notified.

En caso de error en el medicamento, se notifica al doctor.
(Ehn kah-soh deh eh-rohr ehn ehl meh-dee-kah-mehn-toh, seh noh-tee-fee-kah ahl dohk-tohr)

Outpatient prescriptions are also dispensed.

También se surten las recetas para pacientes de consulta externa.
(Tahm-bee-ehn seh soor-tehn lahs reh-seh-tahs pah-rah pah-see-ehn-tehs deh kohn-sool-tah ehx-tehr-nah)

Include in the label:

Incluya en la etiqueta:
(Een-kloo-yah ehn lah eh-tee-keh-tah)

the name of the patient.

el nombre del paciente.
(ehl nohm-breh dehl pah-see-ehn-teh)

the date.

la fecha.
(lah feh-chah)

the doctor's name.

el nombre del doctor.
(ehl nohm-breh dehl dohk-tohr)

the name of the drug.

el nombre de la droga/del medicamento.
(ehl nohm-breh deh lah droh-gah/ dehl meh-dee-kah-mehn-toh)

the dosage.

la dosis.
(lah doh-sees)

the route.

la vía.
(lah bee-ah)

| TABLE 11-8 | TABLA 11-8 | |
| USEFUL WORDS | PALABRAS UTILES | |
ENGLISH	SPANISH	PRONUNCIATION
systemic	sistemático	*sees-teh-mah-tee-koh*
nausea	náusea	*nah-oo-seh-ah*
vomiting	vomitando	*boh-mee-tahn-doh*
lavage	lavado	*lah-bah-doh*
induce	inducir	*een-doo-seer*
lubricant	lubricante	*loo-bree-kahn-teh*
sterile	estéril	*ehs-teh-reel*

the volume.

el volumen.
(ehl boh-loo-mehn)

the total number of pills.

el número total de pastillas.
(ehl noo-meh-roh toh-tahl de pahs-tee-yahs)

the lot number.

el número de lote.
(ehl noo-meh-roh deh loh-teh)

the expiration date.

la caducidad.
(lah kah-doo-see-dahd)

The outpatient pharmacy is open daily from 9:00 A.M. to 6:00 P.M.

La farmacia de consulta externa abre de nueve de la mañana a seis de la tarde todos los días.
(Lah fahr-mah-see-ah deh kohn-sool-tah ehx-tehr-nah ah-breh deh noo-eh-beh deh lah mah-nyah-nah ah seh-ees deh lah tahr-deh toh-dohs lohs dee-ahs)

Please come back in a few minutes.

Por favor, regrese en unos minutos.
(Pohr fah-bohr reh-greh-seh ehn oon-ohs mee-noo-tohs)

Wait your turn.

Espere su turno.
(Ehs-peh-reh soo toor-noh)

You will have to wait.

Tendrá que esperar.
(Tehn-drah keh ehs-peh-rahr)

You will have to wait several minutes!

¡Tendrá que esperar varios minutos!
(Tehn-drah keh ehs-peh-rahr bah-ree-ohs mee-noo-tohs)

You will have to wait at least 30 minutes!

Tendrá que esperar por lo menos treinta minutos!
(Tehn-drah keh ehs-peh-rahr pohr loh meh-nohs treh-een-tah mee-noo-tohs)

The prescription will be ready at _____.

La receta estará lista a las _____.
(Lah reh-seh-tah ehs-tah-rah lees-tah ah lahs _____)

Take this medicine with juice.

Tome la medicina con jugo.
(Toh-meh lah meh-dee-see-nah kohn joo-goh)

Take this medicine with a full glass of water.

Tómela con un vaso lleno de agua.
(Toh-meh-lah kohn oon bah-soh yeh-noh deh ah-goo-ah)

Do not drink alcohol with this medicine.

No tome alcohol con esta medicina.
(No toh-meh ahl-kohl kohn ehs-tah meh-dee-see-nah)

This medicine can cause drowsiness.	**Le puede causar sueño.** *(Leh poo-eh-deh kah-oo-sahr soo-eh-nyoh)*
Do not drive while taking this medicine!	**¡No maneje/conduzca mientras esté tomando esta medicina!** *(Noh mah-neh-heh/kohn-doos-kah mee-ehn-trahs ehs-teh toh-mahn-doh ehs-tah meh-dee-see-nah)*
Do not operate machinery while taking this medicine!	**¡No maneje/opere una máquina/maquinaria mientras esté tomando esta medicina!** *(Noh mah-neh-heh/oh-peh-reh oo-nah mah-kee-nah/mah-kee-nah-ree-ah mee-ehn-trahs ehs-teh toh-mahn-doh ehs-tah meh-dee-see-nah)*
This is an antacid.	**Este es un antiácido.** *(Ehs-teh ehs oon ahn-tee-ah-see-doh)*
This is a sedative.	**Este es un sedante.** *(Ehs-teh ehs oon seh-dahn-teh)*

TABLE 11-9   *TABLA 11-9*
COGNATES   *COGNADOS*

ENGLISH	SPANISH	PRONUNCIATION
anemia	**anemia**	*ah-neh-mee-ah*
angina	**angina**	*ahn-hee-nah*
cataract	**catarata**	*kah-tah-rah-tah*
bronchitis	**bronquitis**	*brohn-kee-tees*
enteritis	**enteritis**	*ehn-teh-ree-tees*
gangrene	**gangrena**	*gahn-greh-nah*
hypertension	**hipertensión**	*ee-pehr-tehn-see-ohn*
laryngitis	**laringitis**	*lah-reen-hee-tees*
pancreatitis	**pancreatitis**	*pahn-kreh-ah-tee-tees*
pneumonia	**pulmonía/neumonía**	*pool-moh-nee-ah/neh-oo-moh-nee-ah*
rubella	**rubéola**	*roo-beh-oh-lah*
tonsillitis	**tonsilitis/amigdalitis**	*tohn-see-lee-tees/ah-meeg-dah-lee-tees*
vaginitis	**vaginitis**	*bah-hee-nee-tees*
constipation	**constipación/ estreñimiento**	*kohns-tee-pah-see-ohn/ehs-treh-nyee- mee-ehn-toh*
cirrhosis	**cirrosis**	*see-roh-sees*

This is a pain killer.

Esta medicina quita/alivia el dolor.
(Ehs-tah meh-dee-see-nah kee-tah/ah-lee-bee-ah ehl doh-lohr)

Take this on an empty stomach.

Tómela con el estómago vacío.
(Toh-meh-lah kohn ehl ehs-toh-mah-goh bah-see-oh)

Take this one hour before eating.

Tómela una hora antes de comer.
(Toh-meh-lah oo-nah oh-rah ahn-tehs deh koh-mehr)

Take this with food.

Tómela con la comida.
(Toh-meh-lah kohn lah koh-mee-dah)

Avoid sunlight.

Evite asolearse/los rayos del sol.
(Eh-bee-teh ah-soh-leh-ahr-seh/lohs rah-yohs dehl sohl)

Follow the instructions carefully.

Siga las instrucciones con cuidado.
(See-gah lahs eens-trook-see-ohn-ehs kohn koo-ee-dah-doh)

Take two aspirins.

Tome dos aspirinas.
(Toh-meh dohs ahs-pee-ree-nahs)

Sleep at least eight hours.

Duerma al menos ocho horas.
(Doo-ehr-mah ahl meh-nohs oh-choh oh-rahs)

You can refill this prescription _____ times.

Puede surtir _____ veces.
(Poo-eh-deh soor-teer _____ beh-sehs)

Take all the medicine indicated in this prescription.

Tome toda la medicina indicada en la receta.
(Toh-meh toh-dah lah meh-dee-see-nah een-dee-kah-dah ehn lah reh-seh-tah)

This prescription may not be refilled.

Esta receta no se puede surtir de nuevo.
(Ehs-tah reh-seh-tah noh seh poo-eh-deh soor-teer deh noo-eh-boh)

If you react to the medicine . . .

Si reacciona mal al medicamento . . .
(See reh-ahk-see-ohn-ah mahl ahl meh-dee-kah-mehn-toh)

Call your physician.

Llame a su médico.
(Yah-meh ah soo meh-dee-koh)

Go to the hospital immediately!

¡Vaya inmediatamente/en seguida al hospital!
(Bah-yah een-meh-dee-ah-tah-mehn-teh/ehn seh-gee-dah ahl ohs-pee-tahl)

Chapter Twelve

The Meals

Las Comidas

For many patients, hospital meals are not very appetizing. Hispanic patients, in general, prefer foods that are spicy and juicy. They are quite attached to special *bocadillos* (appetizers) which may not be available in the hospital. Please explain to patients what foods they are able to bring from home and assist them with the selections that they make from their menus. Table 12-1 lists some diets available at the hospital.

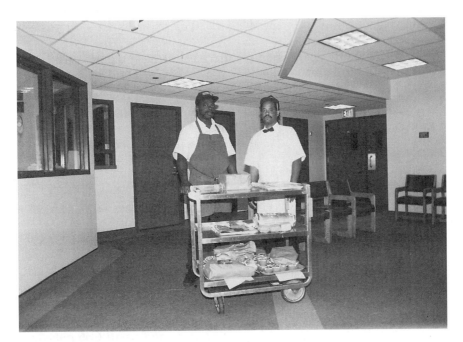

FIGURE 12-1 *Serving foods in the hospital is a complex activity.*

Para muchos pacientes las comidas que se sirven en el hospital no son apetitosas. Los hispanos, en general, prefieren comidas bien condimentadas y jugosas. Están acostumbrados a comer platos especiales que a veces no se pueden encontrar en los hospitales. Por favor, explíqueles a los pacientes que sí pueden traer comida de su casa y ayúdeles con las selecciones que pueden hacer en sus menús. La tabla 12-1 tiene una lista de algunas de las dietas que se ofrecen en el hospital.

There are many diets available to patients.

Hay muchas dietas para los pacientes.
(Ah-ee moo-chahs dee-eh-tahs pah-rah lohs pah-see-ehn-tehs)

The doctor has to prescribe the diet.

El/la doctor(a) debe recetar la dieta.
(Ehl/lah dohk-tohr(ah) deh-beh reh-seh-tahr lah dee-eh-tah)

Can you tell me what kind of diet you have?

¿Puede decirme qué tipo de dieta tiene?
(Poo-eh-deh deh-seer-meh keh tee-poh deh dee-eh-tah tee-eh-neh)

What foods do you like?

¿Qué comidas le gustan?
(Keh koh-mee-dahs leh goos-tahn)

Many patients do not follow a balanced diet and do not eat a variety of needed foods.

Muchos pacientes no llevan una dieta balanceada y no comen la variedad de alimentos necesarios.

The following should be included in your daily diet:

Lo siguiente se debe incluir en la dieta diaria:
(Loh see-gee-ehn-teh seh deh-beh een-kloo-eer ehn lah dee-eh-tah dee-ah-ree-ah)

2 to 4 servings of milk.

de dos a cuatro vasos de leche.
(deh dohs ah koo-ah-troh bah-sohs deh leh-cheh)

2 to 3 servings of meat, fish, or poultry.

de dos a tres porciones de carne, pescado o aves de corral.
(deh dohs ah trehs pohr-see-ohn-ehs deh kahr-neh, pehs-kah-doh oh ah-behs deh ko-rahl)

2 to 4 servings of fruit.

de dos a cuatro porciones de fruta.
(deh dohs ah koo-ah-troh pohr-see-ohn-ehs deh froo-tah)

TABLE 12-1 TYPES OF DIETS		TABLA 12-1 TIPOS DE DIETAS
ENGLISH	*SPANISH*	*PRONUNCIATION*
regular	**regular**	*reh-goo-lahr*
diabetic	**para diabético/a**	*pah-rah dee-ah-beh-tee-koh(kah)*
no-salt	**sin sal**	*seen sahl*
low-cholesterol	**colesterol bajo**	*koh-lehs-teh-rohl bah-hoh*
low-fat	**poca grasa**	*poh-kah grah-sah*
soft	**suave**	*soo-ah-beh*
liquid	**líquida**	*lee-kee-dah*

6 to 11 servings of starches.

de seis a once porciones de almidón/féculas.
(deh seh-ees ah ohn-seh pohr-see-ohn-ehs deh ahl-mee-dohn/feh-koo-lahs)

wheat bread and cereals.

pan de trigo y cereales.
(pahn deh tree-goh ee seh-reh-ah-lehs)

3 to 5 servings of vegetables.

de tres a cinco porciones de vegetales.
(deh trehs ah seen-koh pohr-see-ohn-ehs deh beh-heh-tah-lehs)

I am going to give you a list.

Voy a darle una lista.
(Boy ah dahr-leh oo-nah lees-tah)

For breakfast:

Para el desayuno:
(Pah-rah ehl deh-sah-yoo-noh)

eggs

huevos
(oo-eh-bohs)

toast

pan tostado
(pahn tohs-tah-doh)

coffee

café
(kah-feh)

milk

leche
(leh-cheh)

juice

jugo
(joo-goh)

fruit

fruta
(froo-tah)

What kind of coffee?	**¿Qué clase de café?** *(Keh klah-seh deh kah-feh)*
regular	**regular** *(reh-goo-lahr)*
decaffeinated	**descafeinado** *(dehs-kah-feh-ee-nah-doh)*
instant	**instantáneo** *(eens-tahn-tah-neh-oh)*
How do you like your coffee?	**¿Cómo le gusta el café?** *(Koh-moh leh goos-tah ehl kah-feh)*
black	**negro** *(neh-groh)*
with cream	**con crema** *(kohn kreh-mah)*
with sugar	**con azúcar** *(kohn ah-soo-kahr)*
What kind of juices?	**¿Qué clase de jugos?** *(Keh klah-seh deh joo-gohs)*
orange	**de naranja** *(deh nah-rahn-hah)*
grape	**de uva** *(deh oo-bah)*
apple	**de manzana** *(deh mahn-sah-nah)*
grapefruit	**de toronja** *(deh toh-rohn-hah)*
prune	**de ciruela** *(deh see-roo-eh-lah)*
tomato	**de tomate** *(deh toh-mah-teh)*
How do you like your eggs cooked?	**¿Cómo le gustan los huevos?** *(Koh-moh leh goos-tahn lohs oo-eh-bohs)*
scrambled	**revueltos** *(reh-boo-ehl-tohs)*
over-easy	**volteados** *(bohl-teh-ah-dohs)*
fried	**fritos** *(free-tohs)*
hard-boiled	**duros** *(doo-rohs)*
with ham	**con jamón** *(kohn hah-mohn)*

We have cereals.	**Tenemos cereales.**
	(Teh-neh-mohs seh-reh-ah-lehs)
Do you like them hot/cold?	**¿Le gustan calientes/fríos?**
	(Leh goos-tahn kah-lee-ehn-tehs/free-ohs)
oatmeal	**avena**
	(ah-beh-nah)
Cream of Wheat	**crema de trigo**
	(kreh-mah deh tree-goh)
Corn Flakes	**hojitas de maíz**
	(oh-hee-tahs deh mah-ees)
Kitchen personnel bring the food trays.	**Los empleados de la cocina traen las bandejas con comida.**
	(Lohs ehm-pleh-ah-dohs deh lah koh-see-nah trah-ehn lahs bahn-deh-hahs kohn koh-mee-dah)
We serve lunch at twelve noon.	**Servimos la comida al mediodía.**
	(Sehr-bee-mohs lah koh-mee-dah ahl meh-dee-oh-dee-ah)

TABLE 12-2 COMMON FOODS	TABLA 12-2 COMIDAS COMUNES	
ENGLISH	*SPANISH*	*PRONUNCIATION*
desserts	**postres**	*pohs-trehs*
gelatin	**gelatina**	*geh-lah-tee-nah*
vinegar	**vinagre**	*bee-nah-greh*
custard	**flan**	*flahn*
shrimp	**camarones**	*kah-mah-rohn-ehs*
tuna	**atún**	*ah-toon*
turkey	**pavo/guajolote**	*pah-boh/goo-ah-hoh-loh-teh*
lamb	**cordero**	*kohr-deh-roh*
crab	**cangrejos**	*kahn-greh-hohs*
tamales	**tamales**	*tah-mah-lehs*
crackers	**galletas saladas**	*gah-yeh-tahs sah-lah-dahs*
enchiladas	**enchiladas**	*ehn-chee-lah-dahs*
cereals	**cereales**	*seh-reh-ah-lehs*
vegetables	**vegetales**	*beh-heh-tah-lehs*
coffee	**café**	*kah-feh*
eggs	**huevos**	*oo-eh-bohs*

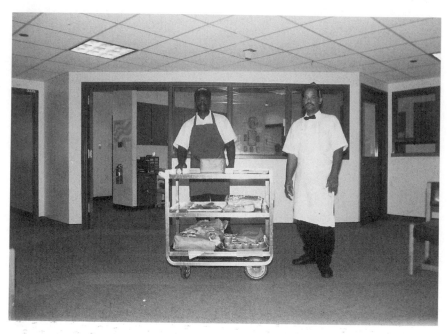

FIGURE 12-2 *Kitchen staff delivers food several times a day.*

We have meats:	Tenemos carnes:
	(Teh-neh-mohs kahr-nehs)
beef	**res**
	(rehs)
hamburger	**hamburğuesa**
	(ahm-boor-geh-sah)
steak	**bistec**
	(bees-tehk)
roast	**rostizado**
	(rohs-tee-sah-doh)
pork	**puerco**
	(poo-ehr-koh)
chops	**chuletas**
	(choo-leh-tahs)
ribs	**costillas**
	(kohs-tee-yahs)
chicken	**pollo**
	(poh-yoh)

fried chicken	**pollo frito**
	(poh-yoh free-toh)
baked chicken	**pollo asado**
	(poh-yoh ah-sah-doh)
breast	**pechuga**
	(peh-choo-gah)
leg	**pierna**
	(pee-ehr-nah)
wings	**alas**
	(ah-lahs)
fish	**pescado**
	(pehs-kah-doh)
breaded	**empanizado**
	(ehm-pah-nee-sah-doh)
broiled fish	**pescado al horno**
	(pehs-kah-doh ahl ohr-noh)
These meats can be substituted.	**Estas carnes se pueden sustituir.**
	(Ehs-tahs kahr-nehs seh poo-eh-dehn soos-tee-too-eer)
Among the vegetables that we serve are:	**Entre los vegetales que servimos hay:**
	(Ehn-treh lohs beh-heh-tah-lehs keh sehr-bee-mohs ah-ee)
potatoes	**papas**
	(pah-pahs)
baked potatoes	**papas asadas**
	(pah-pahs ah-sah-dahs)
french fries	**papas fritas**
	(pah-pahs free-tahs)
mashed potatoes	**puré de papas**
	(poo-reh deh pah-pahs)
green beans	**ejotes/habichuelas**
	(eh-hoh-tehs/ah-bee-choo-eh-lahs)
peas	**chicharos**
	(chee-chah-rohs)
corn	**maíz/elote**
	(mah-ees/eh-loh-teh)
beans	**frijoles/habas**
	(free-hoh-lehs/ah-bahs)
pinto beans	**frijol pinto**
	(free-hol peen-toh)
refried	**refritos**
	(reh-free-tohs)

rice	**arroz**
	(ah-rrohs)
salad	**ensalada**
	(ehn-sah-lah-dah)
lettuce	**lechuga**
	(leh-choo-gah)
We also have desserts.	**También tenemos postres.**
	(Tahm-bee-ehn teh-neh-mohs pohs- *trehs)*
ice cream	**nieve/helado**
	(nee-eh-beh/eh-lah-doh)
vanilla	**vainilla**
	(bah-ee-nee-yah)
chocolate	**chocolate**
	(choh-koh-lah-teh)
strawberry	**fresa**
	(freh-sah)
pies	**pasteles**
	(pahs-teh-lehs)

TABLE 12-3
PRONUNCIATION OF
SELECTED WORDS

TABLA 12-3
PRONUNCIACION DE
PALABRAS SELECTAS

ENGLISH	SPANISH	PRONUNCIATION
alcoholic beverages	**bebidas alcohólicas**	*beh-bee-dahs al-koh-lee-kahs*
minerals	**minerales**	*mee-neh-rah-lehs*
vitamins	**vitaminas**	*bee-tah-mee-nahs*
raw	**crudos**	*kroo-dohs*
frozen	**helado/congelado**	*eh-lah-doh/kohn-heh-lah-doh*
substitutes	**sustitutos**	*soos-tee-too-tohs*
miscellaneous	**miscelánea**	*mee-seh-lah-neh-ah*
soups	**sopas**	*soh-pahs*
cottage cheese	**requesón**	*reh-keh-sohn*
carbonated drinks	**bebidas gaseosas**	*beh-bee-dahs gah-seh-oh-sahs*
toothpick	**palillo**	*pah-lee-yoh*
saccharin	**sacarina**	*sah-kah-ree-nah*
roast beef	**rosbif**	*rohs-beef*

pecan	**nuez** *(noo-ehs)*
apple	**manzana** *(mahn-sah-nah)*
cookies	**galletas** *(gah-yeh-tahs)*
candy	**dulces** *(dool-sehs)*
We don't serve carbonated soda or any other canned drinks.	**No servimos gaseosas u otras bebidas envasadas.** *(Noh sehr-bee-mohs gah-seh-oh-sahs oo oh-trahs beh-bee-dahs ehn-bah-sah-dahs)*
You can buy canned drinks in the cafeteria.	**Puede comprar bebidas envasadas en la cafetería.** *(Poo-eh-deh kohm-prahr beh-bee-dahs ehn-bah-sah-dahs ehn lah kah-feh-teh-ree-ah)*

FIGURE 12-3 Carbonated drinks are sold in the hospital cafeteria.

You can also buy snacks:	También puede comprar aperitivos: *(Tahm-bee-ehn poo-eh-deh kohm-prahr* *ah-peh-ree-tee-bohs)*
juices	jugos *(joo-gohs)*
fruit	fruta *(froo-tah)*
yogurt	yogur *(yoh-goor)*

peanut-butter sandwich	emparedado de crema de
	   cacahuate
	(ehm-pah-reh-dah-doh deh kreh-
	   mah deh kah-kah-oo-ah-teh)

milk	leche *(leh-cheh)*
breads	panes *(pah-nehs)*
corn bread	maíz *(mah-ees)*

FIGURE 12-4   *Prices are usually posted on the wall in the cafeterias.*

wheat	**trigo** *(tree-goh)*
condiments	**condimentos** *(kohn-dee-mehn-tohs)*
spices	**especias** *(ehs-peh-see-ahs)*
butter	**mantequilla** *(mahn-teh-kee-yah)*
mustard	**mostaza** *(mohs-tah-sah)*
hot sauce	**salsa picante** *(sahl-sah pee-kahn-teh)*
mayonnaise	**mayonesa** *(mah-yoh-neh-sah)*
There is water in the glass/ pitcher.	**Hay agua en el vaso/la jarra.** *(Ah-ee ah-goo-ah ehn ehl bah-soh/lah hah-rrah)*
Do you want water?	**¿Quiere agua?** *(Kee-eh-reh ah-goo-ah)*
Do you want ice?	**¿Quiere hielo?** *(Kee-eh-reh ee-eh-loh)*
This is the tray.	**Esta es la bandeja.** *(Ehs-tah ehs lah bahn-deh-hah)*
The fork, spoon, and knife are wrapped in the napkin.	**El tenedor, la cuchara y el cuchillo están envueltos en la servilleta.** *(Ehl teh-neh-dohr lah koo-chah-rah ee ehl koo-chee-yoh ehs-tahn ehn- boo-ehl-tohs ehn lah sehr-bee-yeh- tah)*
There is a straw.	**Hay un popote.** *(Ah-ee oon poh-poh-teh)*
The salt and pepper are in these packets.	**La sal y la pimienta están en estos paquetes.** *(Lah sahl ee lah pee-mee-ehn-tah ehs- tahn ehn ehs-tohs pah-keh-tehs)*
Sorry, we have no toothpicks.	**Lo siento, no hay palillos.** *(Loh see-ehn-toh noh ah-ee pah-lee- yohs)*
The plates are made of plastic.	**Los platos son de plástico.** *(Lohs plah-tohs sohn deh plahs-tee- koh)*
They can't break.	**No se pueden romper.** *(Noh seh poo-eh-dehn rohm-pehr)*

The cover is hot.	**La cubierta está caliente.** *(Lah koo-bee-ehr-tah ehs-tah kah-lee-ehn-teh)*
It keeps the food warm.	**Mantiene la comida tibia.** *(Mahn-tee-eh-neh lah koh-mee-dah tee-bee-ah)*
You can eat in your room or in the visitors' room.	**Puede comer en su cuarto o en el cuarto para visitas.** *(Poo-eh-deh koh-mehr ehn soo koo-ahr-toh oh ehn ehl koo-ahr-toh pah-rah bee-see-tahs)*
Select your foods from the menu after breakfast.	**Seleccione las comidas del menú después del desayuno.** *(Seh-lehk-see-ohn-eh lahs koh-mee-dahs dehl meh-noo dehs-poo-ehs dehl deh-sah-yoo-noh)*
You have to choose three meals a day.	**Tiene que escoger tres comidas diarias.** *(Tee-eh-neh keh ehs-koh-hehr trehs koh-mee-dahs dee-ah-ree-ahs)*

FIGURE 12-5 *Visitors may eat in the lounge.*

TABLE 12-4 LIST OF FRUITS	TABLA 12-4 LISTA DE FRUTAS	
ENGLISH	SPANISH	PRONUNCIATION
strawberry	fresa	freh-sah
lime	lima	lee-mah
cantaloupe/melon	melón	meh-lohn
pineapple	piña	pee-nyah
cherry	cereza	seh-reh-sah
watermelon	sandía	sahn-dee-ah
plum	ciruelo	see-roo-eh-loh
grapefruit	toronja	toh-rohn-hah
banana	plátano	plah-tah-noh
orange	naranja	nah-rahn-hah
pear	pera	peh-rah

You can order one or two portions.	**Puede ordenar una o dos porciones.** *(Poo-eh-deh ohr-deh-nahr oo-nah oh dohs pohr-see-ohn-ehs)*
We send the menu to the kitchen.	**Mandamos el menú a la cocina.** *(Mahn-dah-mohs ehl meh-noo ah lah koh-see-nah)*

Some people cannot tolerate gas-producing foods and should avoid eating them.

Algunas personas no toleran las comidas que producen gases y deberían evitar comerlas.

Gas-producing foods:	**Comidas que producen gases:** *(Koh-mee-dahs keh proh-doo-sehn gah-sehs)*
onions	**cebolla** *(seh-boh-yah)*
beans	**frijoles** *(free-hoh-lehs)*
celery	**apio** *(ah-pee-oh)*
carrots	**zanahoria** *(sah-nah-oh-ree-ah)*

cabbage	col/repollo
	(kohl/reh-poh-yoh)
raisins	pasas
	(pah-sahs)
bananas	plátanos
	(plah-tah-nohs)
prunes	ciruelas
	(see-roo-eh-lahs)

Cholesterol is a type of fat found in the blood. A low-cholesterol diet may help you to lower your blood-cholesterol level if it is too high. Cut down on foods that have high-cholesterol content. The following list gives you a general idea of foods you should avoid.

El colesterol es un tipo de grasa en la sangre. Una dieta baja en colesterol le puede ayudar a rebajar el nivel del mismo si está muy alto. Reduzca las comidas que tienen contenido muy alto de colesterol. La siguiente lista le dá una idea en general de las comidas que debe evitar.

Foods you should not eat:	**Comidas que no debe comer:**
	(Koh-mee-dahs keh noh deh-beh koh-mehr)
butter	mantequilla
	(mahn-teh-kee-yah)
shortening	manteca
	(mahn-teh-kah)
egg yolks	yema de huevos
	(yeh-mah deh oo-eh-bohs)
biscuits	bisquetes/bizcocho
	(bees-keh-tehs/bees-koh-choh)
pancakes	panqueque/hojuela
	(pahn-keh-keh/oh-hoo-eh-lah)
avocados	aguacates
	(ah-goo-ah-kah-tehs)
bacon	tocino
	(toh-see-noh)
sausage	salchicha/chorizo
	(sahl-chee-chah/choh-ree-soh)
hot dog	perro caliente
	(peh-rroh kah-lee-ehn-teh)
whole milk	leche entera
	(leh-cheh ehn-teh-rah)

ice cream	**nieve/helado** *(nee-eh-beh/eh-lah-doh)*
chocolate	**chocolate** *(choh-koh-lah-teh)*
liver	**hígado** *(ee-gah-doh)*
most red meat	**la mayoría de las carnes rojas** *(lah mah-yoh-ree-ah deh lahs kahr-nes roh-hahs)*
most cookies	**la mayoría de las galletas** *(lah mah-yoh-ree-ah deh lahs gah-yeh-tahs)*

Chapter Thirteen

Discharge Planning

Dando de Alta al Paciente

RECOMMENDATIONS FOR A PATIENT BEING DISCHARGED FROM THE HOSPITAL

RECOMENDACIONES PARA UN PACIENTE QUE ES DADO DE ALTA DEL HOSPITAL

Mrs. Garcia is a 32-year-old woman who has just delivered a baby. The doctor is visiting her in her room. He tells her that she will be discharged tomorrow. He also tells her that she must follow directions carefully so that everything turns out all right.

La señora García, de 32 años de edad, tuvo un bebé. El médico la visita en su cuarto. Le comunica que mañana será dada de alta. También le dice que debe seguir cuidadosamente las recomendaciones que se le den para que todo salga bien.

Mrs. Garcia, tomorrow you will be discharged from the hospital.	**Señora García, mañana sale usted del hospital.** *(Seh-nyoh-rah Gahr-see-ah, may-nyah-nah sah-leh oos-tehd dehl ohs-pee-tahl)*
I will give you recommendations for both you and the baby.	**Le daré recomendaciones para usted y para su bebé.** *(Leh dah-reh reh-koh-mehn-dah-see-ohn-ehs pah-rah oos-tehd ee pah-rah soo beh-beh)*
You will have to rest at least seven days.	**Tendrá que guardar reposo al menos siete días.** *(Tehn-drah keh goo-ahr-dahr reh-poh-soh ahl meh-nohs see-eh-teh dee-ahs)*
Your diet should be low in fats and spicy foods.	**Su dieta debe ser baja en grasas y en comidas picantes.**

FIGURE 13-1 *Discharge planning should start upon admission. Once the baby is born, there are too many issues to deal with.*

	(Soo dee-eh-tah deh-beh sehr bah-hah ehn grah-sahs ee ehn koh-mee-dahs pee-kahn-tehs)
Try to have a bowel movement every day.	**Procure mover el intestino diariamente.** *(Proh-koo-reh moh-behr ehl een-tehs-tee-noh dee-ah-ree-ah-mehn-teh)*
Avoid foods which may cause constipation.	**Evite comidas que provoquen estreñimiento.** *(Eh-bee-teh koh-mee-dahs keh proh-boh-kehn ehs-treh-nyeh-mee-en-toh)*
Drink a lot of water and juices.	**Tome mucha agua y jugos.** *(Toh-meh moo-chah ah-goo-ah ee joo-gohs)*
Check your wound to make sure that it doesn't get infected.	**Vigile su herida para asegurarse de que no se infecte.** *(Bee-hee-leh soo eh-ree-dah pah-rah ah-seh-goo-rahr-seh deh keh noh seh een-fehk-teh)*

Watch your bleeding.	**Vigile su sangrado.** *(Bee-hee-leh soo sahn-grah-doh)*
If you bleed a lot, or if you develop a fever, go to the hospital immediately.	**Si es abundante, o si aparece fiebre acuda inmediatamente al hospital.** *(See ehs ah-boon-dahn-teh, oh see ah-pah-reh-seh fee-eh-breh ah-koo-dah een-meh-dee-ah-tah-mehn-teh ahl ohs-pee-tahl)*
Take a bath every day.	**Báñese todos los días.** *(Bah-nyeh-seh toh-dohs lohs dee-ahs)*
Clean your breast thoroughly.	**Lave muy bien sus senos/pechos.** *(Lah-beh moo-eeh bee-ehn soohs seh-nohs/peh-chohs)*
Sleep at least six hours daily.	**Duerma por lo menos seis horas diarias.** *(Doo-ehr-mah pohr loh meh-nohs seh-ees oh-rahs dee-ah-ree-ahs)*
As soon as you can, go see your doctor.	**En cuanto pueda acuda a su médico.** *(Ehn koo-ahn-toh poo-eh-dah ah-koo-dah ah soo meh-dee-koh)*
For the birth control plan that you wish to have.	**Para el control de fertilidad que desee.** *(Pah-rah ehl kohn-trohl deh fehr-tee-lee-dahd keh deh-seh-eh)*

TABLE 13-1 *DISCHARGE* *RECOMMENDATIONS*	*TABLA 13-1* ***RECOMENDACIONES AL DAR DE ALTA***

ENGLISH	SPANISH	PRONUNCIATION
recommendations	**recomendaciones**	*reh-koh-mehn-dah-see-ohn-ehs*
will have	**tendrá**	*tehn-drah*
keep	**guardar**	*goo-ahr-dahr*
rest	**reposo**	*reh-poh-soh*
fats	**grasas**	*grah-sahs*
spicy foods	**comidas picantes**	*koh-mee-dahs pee-kahn-tehs*
wound	**herida**	*eh-ree-dah*
bleeding	**sangrado**	*sahn-grah-doh*
go	**acuda**	*ah-koo-dah*
birth control	**control de fertilidad**	*kohn-trohl deh fehr-tee-lee-dahd*

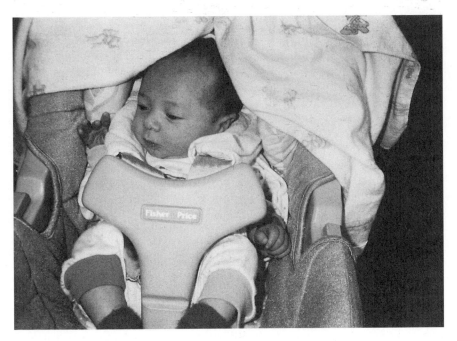

FIGURE 13-2 *It is important to give the mother written recommendations for her baby when she leaves the hospital.*

About your baby.	**En cuanto a su bebé.** *(Ehn koo-ahn-toh ah soo beh-beh)*
Bathe him every day.	**Báñelo diariamente.** *(Bah-nyeh-loh dee-ah-ree-ah-mehn-teh)*
Watch his navel.	**Vigile su ombligo.** *(Bee-hee-leh soo ohm-blee-goh)*
Clean your nipples before you breast-feed.	**Lave sus pezones antes de darle el pecho.** *(Lah-beh soos peh-soh-nehs ahn-tehs deh dahr-leh ehl peh-choh)*
Breast-feed or give him a bottle every three hours.	**Déle el pecho o el biberón cada tres horas.** *(Deh-leh ehl peh-choh oh ehl bee-beh-rohn kah-dah trehs oh-rahs)*
Burp him.	**Hágalo eructar/repetir.** *(Ah-gah-loh eh-rook-tahr/reh-peh-teer)*

Pat his back gently.	**Déle palmaditas en la espalda.** *(Deh-leh pahl-mah-dee-tahs ehn lah ehs-pahl-dah)*
Watch his urine and his bowel movements.	**Vigile su orina y sus evacuaciones.** *(Bee-hee-leh sooh oh-ree-nah ee soos eh-bah-koo-ah-see-oh-nehs)*
Be sure that his nose is clear.	**Vigile que su nariz esté libre.** *(Bee-hee-leh keh soo nah-rees ehs-teh lee-breh)*
Dress him in loose clothes.	**Póngale ropa cómoda.** *(Pohn-gah-leh roh-pah koh-moh-dah)*
Take him for vaccinations at the age of two months.	**Llévelo a vacunar cuando cumpla dos meses.** *(Yeh-beh-loh ah bah-koo-nahr koo-ahn-doh koom-plah dohs meh-sehs)*
Watch his growth and development.	**Vigile su crecimiento y desarrollo.** *(Bee-hee-leh soo kreh-see-mee-ehn-toh ee deh-sah-roh-yoh)*
If you see anything wrong, take him to the doctor.	**Si nota algo malo, llévelo a su médico.** *(See noh-tah ahl-goh mah-loh, yeh-beh-loh ah soo meh-dee-koh)*
If you follow these recommendations everything will be fine.	**Si usted sigue estos consejos todo saldrá con éxito.** *(See oos-tehd see-geh ehs-tohs kohn-seh-hohs toh-doh sahl-drah kohn ehx-ee-toh)*

TABLE 13-2
USEFUL WORDS

TABLA 13-2
PALABRAS UTILES

ENGLISH	*SPANISH*	*PRONUNCIATION*
navel	**ombligo**	*ohm-blee-goh*
burp	**eructar/repetir**	*eh-rook-tahr/reh-peh-teer*
placing it	**colocándolo**	*koh-loh-kahn-doh-loh*
loose clothes	**ropa cómoda**	*roh-pah koh-moh-dah*
vaccinations	**vacunas**	*bah-koo-nahs*
growth	**crecimiento**	*kreh-see-mee-ehn-toh*
development	**desarrollo**	*deh-sah-rroh-yoh*
successful	**con éxito**	*kohn ehx-ee-toh*
I will see you	**la veré**	*lah beh-reh*

I will see you later, Mrs. García.	**Hasta luego, señora García.** *(Ahs-tah loo-eh-goh, seh-nyoh-rah Gahr-see-ah)*
I will see you tomorrow.	**La veré mañana.** *(Lah beh-reh mah-nyah-nah)*

UNIT III

UNIDAD III

Chapter Fourteen

Physical Exam

Examen Físico

The physical exam is very important. Thanks to the physical exam, from the moment that we see a person, we can start to assess and to note the patient's general well-being (pain, mental health, dehydration, etc.). A good review of the body allows us to make a primary diagnosis. With assistance from the laboratory and the X rays, we are able to make a final diagnosis. The physical exam must be done carefully, since it provides a fundamental base for further decision making. The mental exam is part of the physical exam. It gives us the opportunity to see if the patient is nervous, tense, aggressive, vulnerable, restless, or depressed. We are able to assess whether the patient is oriented to time, person, or place.

El examen físico es muy importante. Gracias a éste, desde el momento en que vemos a la persona, podemos darnos cuenta de su estado general (dolor, conciencia, deshidratación, etc.). Una buena revisión del cuerpo nos permitirá hacer un primer diagnóstico. Ayudados por el laboratorio y los rayos X podremos hacer un diagnóstico final. El examen físico debe hacerse con el mayor cuidado posible ya que es una base fundamental para tomar decisiones posteriores. El examen mental es parte del examen físico. Nos permite saber si el paciente está nervioso, tenso, agresivo, vulnerable, inquieto o deprimido. Podremos ver si está orientado en persona, tiempo, lugar y espacio.

Useful commands and phrases that facilitate the physical exam.

Comandos y frases útiles que facilitan el examen físico.
(Koh-mahn-dohs ee frah-sehs oo-tee-lehs keh fah-see-lee-tahn ehl ehx-ah-mehn fee-see-koh)

Note that the familiar *tu* is being used.
Note que se está usando la forma familiar *tu*.

TABLE 14-1 THE PATIENT'S MOODS	TABLA 14-1 ACTITUD DEL PACIENTE	
ENGLISH	SPANISH	PRONUNCIATION
nervous	nervioso	nehr-bee-oh-soh
tense	tenso	tehn-soh
aggressive	agresivo	ah-greh-see-boh
irritable	irritable	ee-ree-tah-bleh
restless	inquieto	een-kee-eh-toh
depressed	deprimido	deh-pree-mee-doh
flat	indiferente	een-dee-feh-rehn-teh
anxious	ansioso	ahn-see-oh-soh
euphoric	eufórico	eh-ooh-foh-ree-koh

I am going to examine you.

Voy a examinarte.
(Boy ah ehx-ah-mee-nahr-teh)

Please sit up on the bed.

Por favor, siéntate en la cama.
(Pohr fah-bohr see-ehn-tah-teh ehn lah kah-mah)

I am going to check your head.

Voy a revisar tu cabeza.
(Boy ah reh-bee-sahr too kah-beh-sah)

Lift your head.

Levanta la cabeza.
(Leh-bahn-tah lah kah-beh-sah)

Lower your head.

Baja la cabeza.
(Bah-hah lah kah-beh-sah)

Move it from side to side.

Muévela de lado a lado.
(Moo-eh-beh-lah deh lah-doh ah lah-doh)

I am going to check your eyes.

Voy a revisar tus ojos.
(Boy ah reh-bee-sahr toos oh-hohs)

Look straight ahead.

Mira hacia adelante.
(Mee-rah ah-see-ah ah-deh-lahn-teh)

Look up.

Mira hacia arriba.
(Mee-rah ah-see-ah ah-rree-bah)

Look down.

Mira hacia abajo.
(Mee-rah ah-see-ah ah-bah-hoh)

Follow my finger.

Sigue mi dedo.
(See-geh mee deh-doh)

Look straight at the light.

Mira directo a la luz.
(Mee-rah dee-rehk-toh ah lah loos)

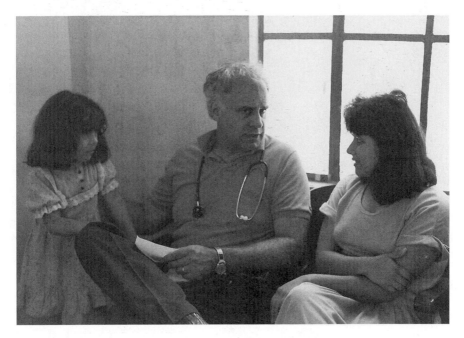

FIGURE 14-1   *The doctor talks to a female patient and her child.*

I am going to check your ears.	**Voy a revisar tus orejas.** *(Boy ah reh-bee-sahr toos oh-reh-hahs)*
Turn your head to the left.	**Voltea la cabeza hacia la izquierda.** *(Bohl-teh-ah lah kah-beh-sah ah-see-ah lah ees-kee-ehr-dah)*
Turn your head to the right.	**Voltea la cabeza hacia la derecha.** *(Bohl-teh-ah lah kah-beh-sah ah-see-ah lah deh-reh-chah)*
I am going to check your nose.	**Voy a revisar tu nariz.** *(Boy ah reh-bee-sar too nah-rees)*
Wrinkle your nose.	**Arruga la nariz.** *(Ah-rooh-gah lah nah-rees)*
I am going to check your throat.	**Voy a revisar tu garganta.** *(Boy ah reh-bee-sahr too gahr-gahn-tah)*
Open your mouth.	**Abre la boca.** *(Ah-breh lah boh-kah)*
Close your mouth.	**Cierra la boca.** *(See-eh-rrah lah boh-kah)*

Open again.

Say "aah".

Please swallow.

Abre otra vez.
(Ah-breh oh-trah behs)
Di "aaa".
(Dee aaah)
Traga, por favor.
(Trah-gah pohr fah-bohr)

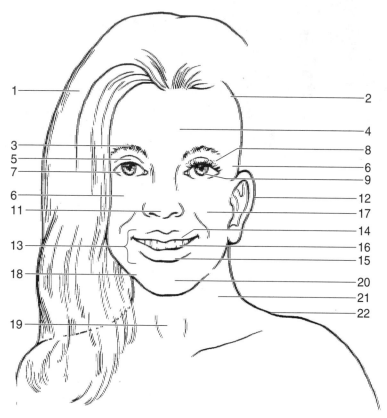

FIGURE 14-2 *The head and neck. (1) El cabello/el pelo (hair), (2) el cráneo (skull),
(3) la ceja (eyebrow), (4) la frente (forehead), (5) el párpado (eyelid), (6) la sien (tem-
ple), (7) la esclerótica (sclera), (8) la pestaña (eyelash), (9) el ojo (eye), (10) el pómulo
(cheekbone), (11) la nariz (nose), (12) la oreja/el oído (ear), (13) la boca (mouth),
(14) el labio superior (upper lip), (15) el labio inferior (lower lip), (16) los dientes
(teeth), (17) la mejilla (cheek), (18) la mandíbula (mandible), (19) la manzanilla/la
nuez de Adán (Adam's apple), (20) la barbilla (chin), (21) el cuello (neck), (22) la
piel (skin).*

Smile.	**Sonríe.** *(Sohn-ree-eh)*
I am going to check your mouth.	**Voy a revisar tu boca.** *(Boy ah reh-bee-sahr too boh-kah)*
Your lips should not be dry.	**Tus labios no deben estar secos.** *(Toos lah-bee-ohs noh deh-behn ehs-tahr seh-kohs)*
Stick out your tongue.	**Saca la lengua.** *(Sah-kah lah lehn-goo-ah)*
I am going to check your gums.	**Voy a revisar tus encías.** *(Boy ah reh-bee-sahr toos ehn-see-ahs)*
I am going to check your teeth.	**Voy a revisar tus dientes.** *(Boy ah reh-bee-sahr toos dee-ehn-tehs)*

UPPER EXTREMITIES	*EXTREMIDADES SUPERIORES*
I am going to check your arm.	**Voy a revisar tu brazo.** *(Boy ah reh-bee-sahr too brah-soh)*
Lift your arm.	**Levanta tu brazo.** *(Leh-bahn-tah too brah-soh)*
Extend it.	**Extiéndelo.** *(Ehx-tee-ehn-deh-loh)*
Flex it.	**Dóblalo.** *(Doh-blah-loh)*
Rotate it.	**Rótalo/dale vuelta.** *(Roh-tah-loh/dah-leh boo-ehl-tah)*
Bend your elbow.	**Dobla el codo.** *(Doh-blah ehl koh-doh)*
I am going to palpate your elbow.	**Voy a palpar el codo.** *(Boy ah pahl-pahr ehl koh-doh)*
I am going to palpate your nodes.	**Voy a palpar los nodos.** *(Boy ah pahl-pahr lohs noh-dohs)*
Turn your forearm.	**Voltea el antebrazo.** *(Bohl-tee-ah ehl ahn-teh brah-soh)*
I am going to palpate your shoulder.	**Voy a palpar el hombro.** *(Boy ah pahl-pahr ehl ohm-broh)*
Place your arms behind your back.	**Pon los brazos atrás.** *(Pohn lohs brah-sohs ah-trahs)*
Place your hands behind your head.	**Pon tus manos detrás de tu cabeza.** *(Pohn toos mah-nohs deh-trahs deh too kah-beh-sah)*
Flex your arm.	**Dobla tu brazo.** *(Doh-blah too brah-soh)*

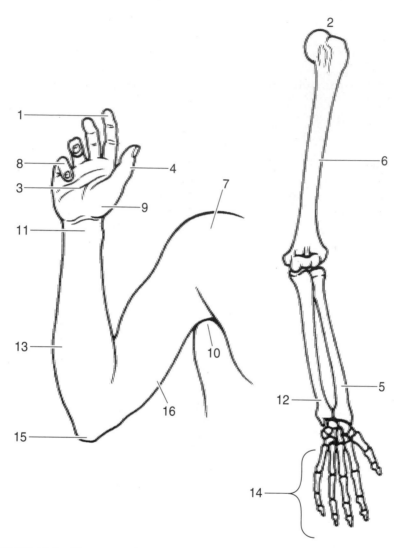

FIGURE 14-3   The arm and hand. (1) El dedo índice (index finger), (2) los huesos (bones), (3) la palma de la mano (palm of the hand), (4) el dedo pulgar (thumb), (5) el radio (radius), (6) el húmero (humerus), (7) el hombro (shoulder), (8) el dedo meñique (little finger), (9) la mano derecha (right hand), (10) la axila/el sobaco (armpit/axilla), (11) la muñeca (wrist), (12) la ulna (ulna), (13) el antebrazo (forearm), (14) las falanges (phalanges), (15) el codo (elbow), (16) el brazo (arm).

Don't let me extend it.

No me dejes extenderlo.
(Noh meh deh-hehs ehx-tehn-dehr-loh)

I am going to check your hand.

Voy a revisar la mano.
(Boy ah reh-bee-sahr lah mah-noh)

I am going to palpate it.

Voy a palparla.
(Boy ah pahl-pahr-lah)

Open your hand.

Abre tu mano.
(Ah-breh too mah-noh)

Close it.

Ciérrala.
(See-eh-rrah-lah)

Open your fingers wide.

Separa bien los dedos.
(Seh-pah-rah bee-ehn lohs deh-dohs)

Don't let me close them.

No me dejes cerrarlos.
(Noh meh deh-hehs seh-rrahr-lohs)

Make a fist.

Haz un puño.
(Ahs oon poo-nyoh)

Hold my finger.

Agarra mi dedo.
(Ah-gah-rrah mee deh-doh)

Tighten!

¡Aprieta!
(Ah-pree-eh-tah)

Lift your hand.

Levanta tu mano.
(Leh-bahn-tah too mah-noh)

Bend your wrist.

Dobla la muñeca.
(Doh-blah lah moo-nyeh-kah)

Extend your wrist.

Extiende la muñeca.
(Ehx-tee-ehn-deh lah moo-nyeh-kah)

I am going to examine your nailbeds.

Voy a examinar la base de tus uñas.
(Boy ah ehx-ah-mee-nahr lah bah-seh deh toos oo-nyahs)

LOWER EXTREMITIES

EXTREMIDADES INFERIORES

I am going to examine the leg.

Voy a examinar tu pierna.
(Boy ah ehx-ah-mee-nahr too pee-ehr-nah)

Lift your leg.

Levanta la pierna.
(Leh-bahn-tah lah pee-ehr-nah)

Bend it.

Dóblala.
(Doh-blah-lah)

Bend your hip.

Dobla tu cadera.
(Doh-blah too kah-deh-rah)

Straighten your knee.

Endereza la rodilla.
(Ehn-deh-reh-sah lah roh-dee-yah)

Move your leg.	**Mueve tu pierna.** *(Moo-eh-beh too pee-ehr-nah)*
Forward.	**Adelante.** *(Ah-deh-lahn-teh)*
Backward.	**Atrás.** *(Ah-trahs)*

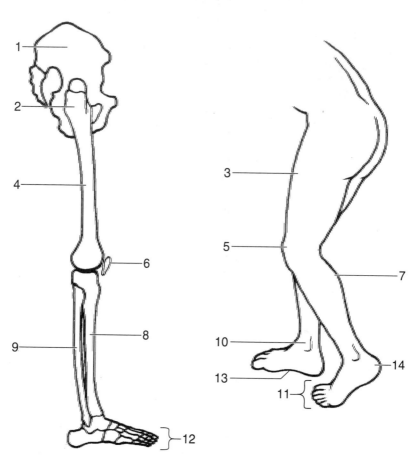

FIGURE 14-4 *The leg and foot. (1) La pelvis (pelvis), (2) la cabeza del fémur (head), (3) el muslo (thigh), (4) el fémur (femur), (5) la rodilla (knee), (6) la rótula (knee cap), (7) la pantorrilla (calf), (8) el peroné (fibula), (9) la tibia (tibia), (10) el tobillo (ankle), (11) los dedos (toes), (12) las falanges (phalanges), (13) la planta (plantar area), (14) el talón (heel).*

I am going to examine your foot.	**Voy a examinar tu pie.** *(Boy ah ehx-ah-mee-nahr too pee-eh)*
Turn it to the left.	**Voltéalo hacia la izquierda.** *(Bohl-teh-ah-loh ah-see-ah lah ees-kee-ehr-dah)*
Turn it to the right.	**Voltéalo hacia la derecha.** *(Bohl-teh-ah-loh ah-see-ah lah deh-reh-chah)*
Push.	**Haz fuerza, empuja.** *(Ahs foo-ehr-sah, ehm-poo-hah)*
Lift your foot.	**Levanta el pie.** *(Leh-bahn-tah ehl pee-eh)*
Bend your toes.	**Dobla los dedos.** *(Doh-blah lohs deh-dohs)*
Lower your foot.	**Baja el pie.** *(Bah-hah ehl pee-eh)*
I am going to palpate your feet and ankles.	**Voy a palpar tus pies y tobillos.** *(Boy ah pahl-pahr toos pee-ehs ee toh-bee-yohs)*
Flex your foot upwardly.	**Dobla el pie hacia arriba.** *(Doh-blah ehl pee-eh ah-see-ah ah-ree-bah)*
Hold it like this.	**Mantenlo así.** *(Mahn-tehn-loh ah-see)*
I am going to press on your big toe.	**Voy a apretar tu dedo gordo.** *(Boy ah ah-preh-tahr too deh-doh gohr-doh)*
I am going to palpate your knees.	**Voy a palpar tus rodillas.** *(Boy ah pahl-pahr toos roh-dee-yahs)*
Pull your knee to your chest.	**Estira la rodilla hacia el pecho.** *(Ehs-tee-rah lah roh-dee-yah ah-see-ah ehl peh-choh)*
Place your foot on the opposite knee.	**Pon el pie sobre la rodilla opuesta.** *(Pohn ehl pee-eh soh-breh lah roh-dee-yah oh-poo-ehs-tah)*
Flex your knee and turn to the middle.	**Dobla la rodilla y voltéala hacia adentro.** *(Doh-blah lah roh-dee-yah ee bohl-teh-ah-lah ah-see-ah ah-dehn-troh)*
Cross your legs.	**Cruza las piernas.** *(Kroo-sah lahs pee-ehr-nahs)*
Straighten your leg.	**Endereza la pierna.** *(Ehn-deh-reh-sah lah pee-ehr-nah)*

Don't let me bend it.	**No me dejes que la doble.**
	(Noh meh deh-hehs keh lah doh-bleh)
Relax your muscle.	**Relaja tu músculo.**
	(Reh-lah-hah too moos-koo-loh)
Stand up!	**¡Levántate!**
	(Leh-bahn-tah-teh)
Please walk.	**Camina, por favor.**
	(Kah-mee-nah pohr fah-bohr)
Stop!	**¡Para! ¡Deténte!**
	(Pah-rah, deh-tehn-teh)
Jump on one foot.	**Brinca con un pie.**
	(Breen-kah kohn oon pee-eh)
Take your shoes off.	**Quítate tus zapatos.**
	(Kee-tah-teh toos sah-pah-tohs)
Take your socks off.	**Quítate los calcetines.**
	(Kee-tah-teh lohs kahl-seh-tee-nehs)
Now I am going to examine your skin.	**Ahora voy a revisar tu piel.**
	(Ah-oh-rah boy ah reh-bee-sahr too pee-ehl)
You have bruises and white spots.	**Tienes moretones y manchas blancas.**
	(Tee-eh-nehs moh-reh-toh-nehs ee mahn-chahs blahn-kahs)
Now I am going to examine your chest.	**Ahora, voy a revisar tu pecho.**
	(Ah-oh-rah boy ah reh-bee-sahr too peh-choh)
I am going to listen to your heart.	**Voy a escuchar el corazón.**
	(Boy ah ehs-koo-chahr ehl koh-rah-sohn)
Don't talk.	**No hables.**
	(Noh ah-blehs)
Breathe!	**¡Respira!**
	(Rehs-pee-rah)
Breathe regularly.	**Respira normalmente.**
	(Rehs-pee-rah nohr-mahl-mehn-teh)
Now take a deep breath.	**Ahora, respira hondo.**
	(Ah-oh-rah, rehs-pee-rah ohn-doh)
Hold it!	**¡Deténlo!**
	(Deh-tehn-loh)
Does it hurt to breathe?	**¿Te duele al respirar?**
	(Teh doo-eh-leh ahl rehs-pee-rahr)
Cough!	**¡Tose!**
	(Toh-seh)

TABLE 14-2 SKIN RELATED TERMS		*TABLA 14-2* ***TERMINOS RELACIONADOS CON LA PIEL***
ENGLISH	*SPANISH*	*PRONUNCIATION*
dry	**seca**	*seh-kah*
bruises/echymosis	**moretones/equimosis**	*moh-reh-tohn-ehs/eh-kee-moh-sees*
hematoma	**hematoma**	*eh-mah-toh-mah*
scratch	**raspón**	*rahs-pohn*
acne	**acné**	*ahk-neh*
burns	**quemaduras**	*keh-mah-doo-rahs*
wound	**herida**	*eh-ree-dah*
infection	**infección**	*een-fehk-see-ohn*
inflammation	**inflamación**	*een-flah-mah-see-ohn*
ulcers	**úlceras**	*ool-seh-rahs*
fungus	**hongos**	*ohn-gohs*
red/white spots	**manchas rojas/ blancas**	*mahn-chahs roh-hahs/blahn-kahs*
birthmark	**lunares**	*loo-nah-rehs*
mole	**verrugas**	*beh-rroo-gahs*
psoriasis	**psoriasis**	*soh-ree-ah-sees*
eczema	**eczema**	*ehk-seh-mah*
freckles	**pecas**	*peh-kahs*

Cough deeply!

¡Tose más fuerte!
(Toh-seh mahs foo-ehr-teh)

I am going to palpate your chest.

Voy a palpar el pecho.
(Boy ah pahl-pahr ehl peh-choh)

Relax.

Descansa.
(Dehs-kahn-sah)

Sit upright!

¡Siéntate derecho!
(See-ehn-tah-teh deh-reh-choh)

Please lie down.

Acuéstate, por favor.
(Ah-koo-ehs-tah-teh pohr fah-bohr)

I am going palpate your breast.

Voy a palpar el seno.
(Boy ah pahl-pahr ehl seh-noh)

I am going to palpate your axillary nodes.

Voy a palpar los nodos de la axila.
(Boy ah pahl-pahr lohs noh-dohs deh lah ahx-ee-lah)

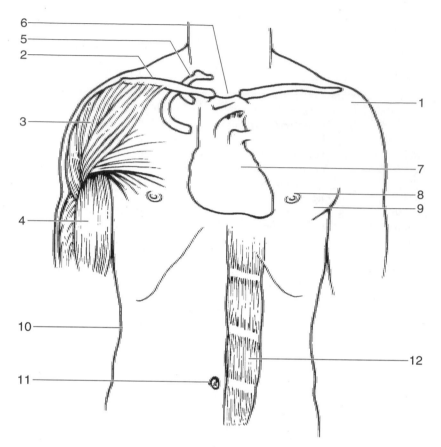

FIGURE 14-5 The chest. (1) El hombro (shoulder), (2) la clavícula (clavicle), (3) los deltoides (deltoid), (4) el bíceps (biceps), (5) la costilla (rib), (6) el esternón (sternum), (7) el corazón (heart), (8) la aréola/el pezón (areola/nipple), (9) el pecho/seno (chest/breast), (10) la cintura (waist), (11) el ombligo (umbilicus), (12) el músculo abdominal (abdominal muscle).

I am going to tap.	**Voy a percutir/golpear.**
	(Boy ah pehr-koo-teer/gohl-peh-ahr)
I am going to listen.	**Voy a auscultar/escuchar.**
	(Boy ah ah-oos-kool-tahr/ehs-koo-chahr)
I am going to listen to your apical pulse.	**Voy a oír tu pulso apical/latidos del corazón.**
	(Boy ah oh-eer too pool-soh ah-pee-kahl/lah-tee-dohs dehl koh-rah-sohn)

I am going to palpate your carotid pulse.	**Voy a palpar tu pulso en la carótida/cuello.** *(Boy ah pahl-pahr too pool-soh ehn lah kah-roh-tee-dah/koo-eh-yoh)*
I am going to take your radial pulse.	**Voy a tomar tu pulso radial.** *(Boy ah toh-mahr too pool-soh rah-dee-ahl)*
I am going to observe your jugular vein.	**Voy a observar tu vena yugular.** *(Boy ah ohb-sehr-bahr too beh-nah yoo-goo-lahr)*

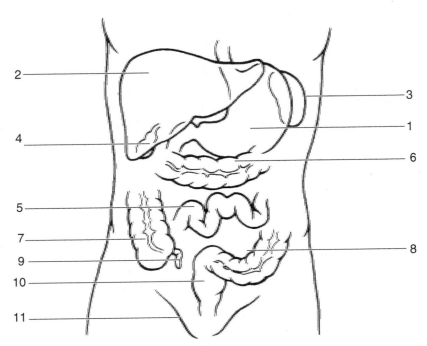

FIGURE 14-6   *The abdomen. (1) El estómago (stomach), (2) el hígado (liver), (3) el bazo (spleen), (4) la vesícula biliar (gallbladder), (5) el intestino delgado (small intestine), (6) el intestino transverso (transverse intestine), (7) el colon ascendente (ascending colon), (8) el área pélvica (lower pelvic area), (9) el apéndice (appendix), (10) el recto (rectum), (11) la ingle (groin).*

Now I am going to examine your abdomen.	Ahora, voy a revisar tu abdomen/vientre.
	(Ah-oh-rah boy ah reh-bee-sahr too ahb-doh-mehn/bee-ehn-treh)
I am going to check your liver.	Voy a revisar tu hígado.
	(Boy ah reh-bee-sahr too eeh-gah-doh)
I am going to palpate lightly.	Voy a palpar/tocar ligeramente.
	(Boy ah pahl-pahr/toh-kahr lee-heh-rah-mehn-teh)
I am going to palpate deeply.	Voy a palpar hondo.
	(Boy ah pahl-pahr ohn-doh)
Tell me if it hurts.	Dime si duele.
	(Dee-meh see doo-eh-leh)
Does it hurt when I press?	¿Duele cuando presiono?
	(Doo-eh-leh koo-ahn-doh preh-see-oh-noh?)
Does it hurt when I let go?	¿Duele cuando retiro la mano?
	(Doo-eh-leh koo-ahn-doh reh-tee-roh lah mah-noh)
I am going to palpate with both hands.	Voy a palpar/tocar con las dos manos.
	(Boy ah pahl-pahr/toh-kahr kohn lahs dohs mah-nohs)
Raise your head.	Levanta la cabeza.
	(Leh-bahn-tah lah kah-beh-sah)
I am going to check how strong your abdominal muscle is.	Voy a ver la fuerza del músculo abdominal.
	(Boy ah behr lah foo-ehr-sah dehl moos-koo-loh ahb-doh-mee-nahl)
Turn onto your side.	Voltéate de lado.
	(Bohl-teh-ah-teh deh lah-doh)
left	izquierdo
	(ees-kee-ehr-doh)
right	derecho
	(deh-reh-choh)
Take a deep breath.	Respira hondo.
	(Rehs-pee-rah ohn-doh)
Let it out.	Exhala.
	(Ehx-ah-lah)
I am going to palpate your groin.	Voy a palpar las ingles.
	(Boy ah pahl-pahr lahs een-glehs)
Push down.	Empuja.
	(Ehm-poo-hah)

I am going to examine your
    rectum.
I am going to collect a stool
    sample.

Voy a examinar el recto.
(Boy ah ehx-ah-mee-nahr ehl rehk-toh)
**Voy a recojer una muestra de
    excremento.**
*(Boy ah reh-koh-hehr oo-nah moo-ehs-
    trah deh ehx-kreh-mehn-toh)*

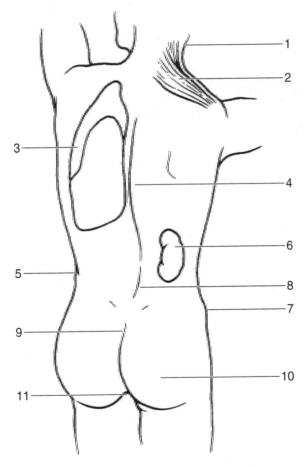

FIGURE 14-7   *The back. (1) La nuca (nape), (2) el trapezoide (trapezius), (3) el pul-
món (lung), (4) la vertebra (spine), (5) la cintura (waist), (6) el riñón (kidney), (7) la
cadera (hip), (8) el lumbar (lumbar), (9) el sacro (sacrum), (10) la nalga (buttock), (11)
el ano/la cola (anus).*

I am going to examine your genitalia.	**Voy a examinar los genitales.** *(Boy ah ehx-ah-mee-nahr lohs heh-nee-tah-lehs)*
I am going to examine your back.	**Voy a examinar tu espalda.** *(Boy ah ehx-ah-mee-nahr too ehs-pahl-dah)*
I am going to listen to your lungs.	**Voy a escuchar los pulmones.** *(Boy ah ehs-koo-chahr lohs pool-moh-nehs)*
Breathe through your mouth.	**Respira con la boca abierta.** *(Rehs-pee-rah kohn lah boh-kah ah-bee-ehr-tah)*
Again.	**Otra vez.** *(Oh-trah behs)*
Repeat one, two, three.	**Repite uno, dos, tres.** *(Reh-pee-teh oo-noh, dohs, trehs)*
Now stand up.	**Ahora, levántate.** *(Ah-oh-rah, leh-bahn-tah-teh)*
Now bend over.	**Ahora, agáchate.** *(Ah-oh-rah, ah-gah-chah-teh)*
Cross your arms.	**Cruza tus brazos.** *(Kroo-sah toos brah-sohs)*
Twist your waist.	**Tuerce la cintura.** *(Too-ehr-seh lah seen-too-rah)*
Repeat the word "99."	**Repite la palabra "noventa y nueve."** *(Reh-pee-teh lah pah-lah-brah noh-behn-tah ee noo-eh-beh)*
Say your name.	**Dí tu nombre.** *(Dee too nohm-breh)*
Bend your shoulder.	**Dobla tu hombro.** *(Doh-blah too ohm-broh)*
I have finished the exam.	**Terminé de revisarte.** *(Tehr-mee-neh deh reh-bee-sahr-teh)*
Do you have any questions?	**¿Alguna pregunta?** *(Ahl-goo-nah preh-goon-tah)*

Greetings and Common Expressions

Saludos y Expresiones Comunes

Greetings and expressions are used to address a person or to get a person's attention. Hispanics are generally very friendly and will greet you even when they do not know you. In this chapter, you will study some commonly used greetings and expressions.

Los saludos y expresiones se usan para dirigirse a una persona o para llamar la atención. Los hispanos generalmente son muy amigables y saludan aún sin conocer a la otra persona. En este capítulo estudiará algunos saludos y expresiones que se usan con más frequencia.

Hi!	**¡Hola!** *(Oh-lah)*
Good morning.	**Buenos días.** *(Boo-eh-nohs dee-ahs)*
Good afternoon.	**Buenas tardes.** *(Boo-eh-nahs tahr-dehs)*
Good evening.	**Buenas noches.** *(Boo-eh-nahs noh-chehs)*
Good night.	**Buenas noches.** *(Boo-eh-nahs no-chehs)*
Do you speak English?	**¿Habla inglés?** *(Ah-blah een-glehs)*
Yes, I speak English.	**Sí, yo hablo inglés.** *(See yoh ah-bloh een-glehs)*
No, I do not speak English.	**No, no hablo inglés.** *(Noh noh ah-bloh een-glehs)*
Do you speak Spanish?	**¿Habla español?** *(Ah-blah ehs-pah-nyohl)*
Yes, I speak Spanish.	**Sí hablo español.** *(See ah-bloh ehs-pah-nyohl)*

FIGURE 15-1   Hispanics are generally very friendly.

No, I do not speak Spanish.	**No no hablo español.**
	(Noh noh ah-bloh ehs-pah-nyohl)
Yes, a little.	**Sí un poco.**
	(See, oon poh-koh)
No, I don't understand.	**No, no comprendo/no entiendo.**
	(Noh noh kohm-prehn-doh/noh ehn-tee-ehn-doh)
Please speak slowly.	**Hable despacio por favor.**
	(Ah-bleh dehs-pah-see-oh pohr fah-bohr)
Thank you very much!	**¡Muchas gracias!**
	(Moo-chahs grah-see-ahs)
It's nothing/you are welcome.	**De nada.**
	(Deh nah-dah)
I am . . .	**Yo soy . . .**
	(Yoh soh-ee)
the doctor.	**el doctor.**
	(ehl dohk-tohr)

FIGURE 15-2 *Friendliness is a trait which is developed at a young age.*

the doctor. (female)	**la doctora.** *(lah dohk-tohr-ah)*
the nurse. (female)	**la enfermera.** *(Lah ehn-fehr-meh-rah)*
the nurse. (male)	**el enfermero.** *(ehl ehn-fehr-meh-roh)*
What is your name? (formal)	**¿Cómo se llama usted?** *(Koh-moh seh yah-mah oos-tehd)*
What is your name? (informal)	**¿Cómo se llama?** *(Koh-moh seh yah-mah)*
My name is . . .	**Me llamo . . .** *(Meh yah-moh)*
Can I join you?	**¿Te puedo acompañar?** *(Teh poo-eh-doh ah-kohm-pah-nyahr)*

Commands

Ordenes o Mandatos

Commands are used in hospitals, private offices, and health centers. This gives responsibility to patients regarding their health and well being. These commands should be given firmly and with confidence. In this manner, the patient is able to understand the outcome of such commands.

Las órdenes o mandatos se usan en los hospitales, consultorios privados o en los centros de salud. Esto crea en los pacientes una responsa-

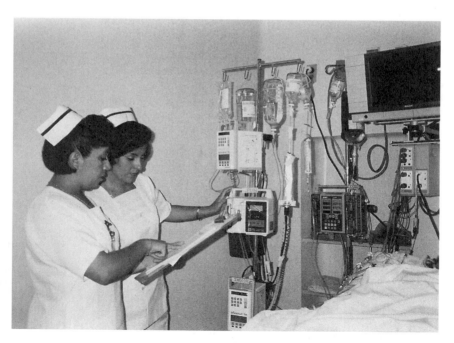

FIGURE 16-1 *Knowledge of commands is useful in the clinical setting.*

bilidad acerca de su salud y bienestar. Estas órdenes deben darse con mucha firmeza y seguridad. De esta manera el paciente capta en su totalidad la finalidad que se persigue al indicárselas.

Wake up!

Get up!

Do not get up!

Sit up!

Walk!

Stop!

Look up/down.

¡Despierte!
(Dehs-pee-ehr-teh)
¡Levántese!
(Leh-bahn-teh-seh)
¡No se levante!
(Noh seh leh-bahn-teh)
¡Siéntese!
(See-ehn-teh-seh)
¡Camine!
(Kah-mee-neh)
¡Párese!
(Pah-reh-seh)
Mire hacia arriba/abajo.
(Mee-reh ah-see-ah ah-ree-bah/ah-bah-
hoh)

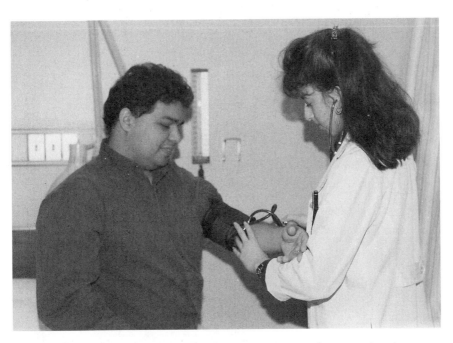

FIGURE 16-2 The patient will follow your instructions when you give the appropriate commands.

Move!	**¡Muévase!**
	(Moo-eh-bah-seh)
Listen!	**¡Oiga/Escuche!**
	(Oh-ee-gah/ehs-koo-cheh)
Don't talk!	**¡No hable!**
	(Noh ah-bleh)
Open your mouth!	**¡Abra la boca!**
	(Ah-brah lah boh-kah)
Show me your tongue!	**¡Muéstreme la lengua!**
	(Moo-ehs-treh-meh lah lehn-goo-ah)
Close your mouth!	**¡Cierre la boca!**
	(See-eh-rreh lah boh-kah)
Bite!	**¡Muerda!**
	(Moo-ehr-dah)
Talk!	**¡Hable!**
	(Ah-bleh)
Breathe deeply!	**¡Respire hondo/profundo!**
	(Rehs-pee-reh ohn-doh/proh-foon-doh)
Don't breathe!	**¡No respire!**
	(Noh rehs-pee-reh)
Turn!	**¡Voltee!**
	(Bohl-teh-eh)
Take a bath!	**¡Báñese!**
	(Bah-nyeh-seh)
Wash your face!	**¡Lávese la cara!**
	(Lah-beh-seh lah kah-rah)
Brush your teeth!	**¡Cepíllese los dientes!**
	(Seh-pee-yeh-seh lohs dee-ehn-tehs)
Bend over!	**¡Agáchese!**
	(Ah-gah-cheh-seh)
Kneel down!	**¡Póngase de rodillas!**
	(Pohn-gah-seh deh roh-dee-yahs)
Open your eyes!	**¡Abra los ojos!**
	(Ah-brah lohs oh-hohs)
Close your eyes!	**¡Cierre los ojos!**
	(See-eh-reh lohs oh-hohs)
Lie down!	**¡Acuéstese!**
	(Ah-koo-ehs-teh-seh)
Eat!	**¡Coma!**
	(Koh-mah)
Swallow!	**¡Trague!**
	(Trah-geh)

Drink!	¡Beba! ¡Tome! *(Beh-bah Toh-meh)*
Relax!	¡Relájese! ¡Descanse! *(Reh-lah-heh-seh Dehs-kahn-seh)*
Run!	¡Corra! *(Koh-rah)*
Wait!	¡Espere! *(Ehs-peh-reh)*
Don't sit down!	¡No se siente! *(Noh seh see-ehn-teh)*
Bend your knees!	¡Doble su rodilla! *(Doh-bleh soo roh-dee-yah)*
Move your eyes!	¡Mueva sus ojos! *(Moo-eh-bah soos oh-hohs)*
Squeeze my hand!	¡Apriete mi mano! *(Ah-pree-eh-teh mee mah-noh)*
Cough!	¡Tosa! *(Toh-sah)*
Don't push!	¡No haga esfuerzo! *(Noh ah-gah ehs-foo-ehr-soh)*
Watch your bleeding!	¡Vigile su sangrado! *(Bee-hee-leh soo sahn-grah-doh)*
Take care of yourself!	¡Cuídese mucho! *(Koo-ee-deh-seh moo-choh)*

Chapter Seventeen

Phrases

Frases

Phrases consist of a series of words that add feeling to a short conversation. (They also mean more than they express.) For example, if you ask a person, "How are you?" and he or she replies, "marvelous," you understand that the person feels well and is happy.

Las frases son una serie de palabras, que le dan sentido a una conversación corta. Significan más de lo que se expresa en ellas. Por ejemplo, al preguntarle a una persona "¿Cómo se siente?" y nos contesta "maravillosamente," entendemos que se siente muy bien y está contenta.

Find out . . .	**Descubrir . . .**
	(Dehs-koo-breer)
From time to time . . .	**De vez en cuando . . .**
	(Deh behs ehn koo-ahn-doh)
For the most part . . .	**Por la mayor parte . . .**
	(Pohr lah mah-yohr pahr-teh)
. . . deal with . . .	**. . . tratar . . .**
	(trah-tahr)
Don't be afraid!	**¡No tenga miedo!**
	(Noh tehn-gah mee-eh-doh)
. . . call for . . .	**. . . llamar . . .**
	(yah-mahr)
As a whole . . .	**En conjunto . . . En todo . . .**
	(Ehn kohn-hoon-toh Ehn toh-doh)
According to . . .	**De acuerdo con . . .**
	(Deh ah-koo-ehr-doh kohn)
. . . go through . . .	**. . . atravesar/cruzar . . .**
	(ah-trah-beh-sahr/kroo-sahr)
. . . go by . . .	**. . . pasar . . .**
	(pah-sahr)

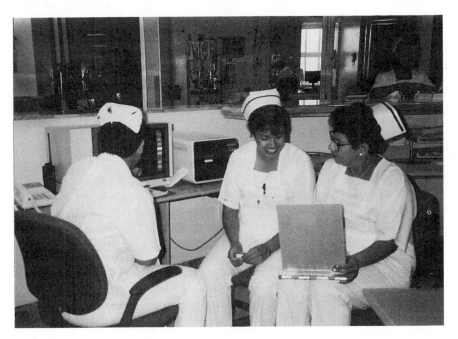

FIGURE 17-1   *Specific phrases make conversation interesting and meaningful.*

. . . gain by . . .	**. . . ganar con . . .** *(gah-nahr kohn)*
. . . helpful . . .	**. . . útil . . .** *(oo-teel)*
. . . in addition . . .	**. . . además . . .** *(ah-deh-mahs)*
. . . in large part . . .	**. . . en gran parte . . .** *(ehn grahn pahr-teh)*
. . . in the middle of . . .	**. . . a mediados de . . .** *(ah meh-dee-ah-dohs deh)*
All of a sudden . . .	**De golpe . . .** *(Deh gohl-peh)*
. . . keep up . . .	**. . . continuar . . .** *(kohn-tee-noo-ahr)*
. . . leave behind . . .	**. . . abandonar . . .** *(ah-bahn-doh-nahr)*
. . . meet with . . .	**. . . encontrarse con . . .** *(ehn-kohn-trahr-seh kohn)*

Never mind.	**No importa.** *(Noh eem-pohr-tah)*
. . . none the less . . .	**. . . sin embargo . . .** *(seen ehm-bahr-goh)*
. . . not at all . . .	**. . . de ningún modo . . .** *(deh neen-goon moh-doh)*
Of course.	**Desde luego.** *(Dehs-deh loo-eh-goh)*
. . . registered/on record . . .	**. . . registrado . . .** *(reh-hees-trah-doh)*
Over a period . . .	**Durante un período . . .** *(Doo-rahn-teh oon peh-ree-oh-doh)*
On the one hand . . .	**Por un lado . . .** *(Pohr oon lah-doh)*
Point out . . .	**Señalar/Apuntar . . .** *(Seh-nyah-lahr/Ah poon-tahr)*
. . . modern/present day . . .	**. . . moderno . . .** *(moh-dehr-noh)*
. . . each hour . . .	**. . . cada una hora . . .** *(kah-dah oo-nah oh-rah)*
. . . every 2 hours . . .	**. . . cada dos horas . . .** *(kah-dah dohs oh-rahs)*
. . . four times . . .	**. . . cuatro veces . . .** *(koo-ah-troh beh-sehs)*
. . . recall . . .	**. . . recordar . . .** *(reh-kohr-dahr)*
. . . rather than . . .	**. . . más bien que . . .** *(mahs bee-ehn keh)*
. . . rely on . . .	**. . . confiar . . .** *(kohn-fee-ahr)*
Say it again.	**Dígalo otra vez/Repita.** *(Dee-gah-loh oh-trah behs/Reh-pee-tah)*
. . . so far/until now . . .	**. . . hasta ahora . . .** *(ahs-tah ah-oh-rah)*
. . . select . . .	**. . . seleccionar . . .** *(seh-lehk-see-ohn-ahr)*
. . . sort out . . .	**. . . escoger . . .** *(ehs-koh-hehr)*
. . . such as . . .	**. . . tal como . . .** *(tahl koh-moh)*
. . . thought to be/ considering . . .	**. . . considerando . . .** *(kohn-see-deh-rahn-doh)*

. . . to some extent . . .   **. . . hasta cierto punto . . .**
                                              (ahs-tah see-ehr-toh poon-toh)
Try again!   **¡Pruebe otra vez!**
                                              (Proo-eh-beh oh-trah behs)
. . . buzzing in ears . . .   **. . . zumbido en los oídos . . .**
                                              (soom-bee-doh ehn lohs oh-ee-dohs)
. . . sore throat . . .   **. . . dolor de garganta . . .**
                                              (doh-lohr deh gahr-gahn-tah)
. . . toothache . . .   **. . . dolor de muelas . . .**
                                              (doh-lohr deh moo-eh-lahs)
. . . difficulty swallowing . . .   **. . . dificultad al tragar . . .**
                                              (dee-fee-kool-tahd ahl trah-gahr)
I am continuously . . .   **Continuamente estoy . . .**
                                              (Kohn-tee-noo-ah-mehn-teh ehs-tohy)
Have you had this happen   **¿Le ha pasado esto antes?**
  before?   *(Leh ha pah-sah-doh ehs-toh ahn-tehs)*
Don't worry.   **No se preocupe.**
                                              (Noh seh preh-oh-koo-peh)
See you later!   **¡Hasta luego!**
                                              (Ahs-tah loo-eh-goh)

UNIT IV

UNIDAD IV

Useful Vocabulary for Home Use

Vocabulario Util Sobre la Vivienda

Vocabulary is a group of words which forms a language. Here we will use the most common words that you will use during an interview or conversation with a patient. This will give you an idea how the patient lives at home or what is available to him.

El vocabulario es un conjunto de palabras de un idioma. En esta ocasión usaremos las palabras más usuales o útiles que usará en una en-

FIGURE 18-1 *The appearance of a patient's home tells a lot about how the patient lives.*

trevista o una conversación con el paciente. Esto nos indicará la forma de vivir del paciente.

house	**casa**	*(kah-sah)*
home	**hogar**	*(oh-gahr)*
address	**dirección**	*(dee-rehk-see-ohn)*
street/avenue	**calle/avenida**	*(kah-yeh/ah-beh-nee-dah)*
number	**número**	*(noo-meh-roh)*
living room	**sala**	*(sah-lah)*
sofa	**sofá**	*(soh-fah)*
chair	**silla**	*(see-yah)*
bedroom	**recámara**	*(reh-kah-mah-rah)*
room	**cuarto**	*(koo-ahr-toh)*
bed	**cama**	*(kah-mah)*
mirror	**espejo**	*(ehs-peh-hoh)*
lamp	**lámpara**	*(lahm-pah-rah)*
window	**ventana**	*(behn-tah-nah)*
door	**puerta**	*(poo-ehr-tah)*

FIGURE 18-2   *The home environment tells much about a patient's disposition.*

bathroom	**baño**	*(bah-nyoh)*
shower	**regadera**	*(reh-gah-deh-rah)*
towel	**toalla**	*(toh-ah-yah)*
basin	**lavabo**	*(lah-bah-boh)*
toilet	**escusado**	*(ehs-koo-sah-doh)*
toothbrush	**cepillo de dientes**	*(seh-pee-yoh deh dee-ehn-tehs)*
toothpaste	**pasta de dientes**	*(pahs-tah deh dee-ehn-tehs)*
comb	**peine**	*(peh-ee-neh)*
hairbrush	**cepillo de pelo**	*(seh-pee-yoh deh peh-loh)*
kitchen	**cocina**	*(koh-see-nah)*
pots/pans	**trastes/vasijas**	*(trahs-tehs/bah-see-hahs)*
glass	**vaso**	*(bah-soh)*
cup	**tasa**	*(tah-sah)*
plate	**platón**	*(plah-tohn)*
dish	**plato**	*(plah-toh)*
table	**mesa**	*(meh-sah)*

Chapter Nineteen

Cognates

Cognados

Cognates are terms that may be identical or that have small variations in spelling between two languages. In this chapter, we will mention some cognate words which will be useful for you in a medical environment.

Los cognados son aquellos términos que se escriben y se pronuncian casi igual en ambos idiomas ya que tienen pequeñas variaciones entre

FIGURE 19-1 *Similarities in written words make communication between languages easier.*

sí. En este capítulo mencionaremos algunos cognados útiles en la práctica de la medicina.

abdomen	**abdomen**	*(ahb-doh-mehn)*
accident	**accidente**	*(ahk-see-dehn-teh)*
acetic	**acético**	*(ah-seh-tee-koh)*
acid	**ácido**	*(ah-see-doh)*
acne	**acne**	*(ahk-neh)*
acoustic	**acústico**	*(ah-koos-tee-koh)*
adenoid	**adenoide**	*(ah-deh-noh-ee-deh)*
adrenalism	**adrenalismo**	*(ah-dreh-nah-lees-moh)*
air	**aire**	*(ah-ee-reh)*
alcohol	**alcohol**	*(ahl-kohl)*
alcoholic	**alcohólico**	*(ahl-koh-lee-koh)*
allergy	**alergia**	*(ah-lehr-hee-ah)*
amebic	**amébico**	*(ah-meh-bee-koh)*
amygdala	**amígdala**	*(ah-meeg-dah-lah)*
analyze	**analizar**	*(ah-nah-lee-sahr)*
anemia	**anemia**	*(ah-neh-mee-ah)*
anesthesia	**anestesia**	*(ah-nehs-teh-see-ah)*
angioma	**angioma**	*(ahn-hee-oh-mah)*
angle	**ángulo**	*(ahn-goo-loh)*
antibiotic	**antibiótico**	*(ahn-tee-bee-oh-tee-koh)*
anticoagulant	**anticoagulante**	*(ahn-tee-koh-ah-goo-lahn-teh)*
asthma	**asma**	*(ahs-mah)*
bacteria	**bacteria**	*(bahk-teh-ree-ah)*
barbaric	**bárbaro**	*(bahr-bah-roh)*
bradycardia	**bradicardia**	*(brah-dee-kahr-dee-ah)*
cafe (coffee)	**café**	*(kah-feh)*
caffeine	**cafeína**	*(kah-feh-ee-nah)*
callus	**callo**	*(kah-yoh)*
calm	**calma**	*(kah-mah)*
cancer	**cáncer**	*(kahn-sehr)*
cardiac	**cardíaco**	*(kahr-dee-ah-koh)*
caries	**caries**	*(kah-ree-ehs)*
carotid	**carótida**	*(kah-roh-tee-dah)*
cause	**causa**	*(kah-oo-sah)*
cavity	**cavidad**	*(kah-bee-dahd)*
chancre	**chancro**	*(chahn-kroh)*
chemotherapy	**quimioterapia**	*(kee-mee-oh-teh-rah-pee-ah)*
chocolate	**chocolate**	*(choh-koh-lah-teh)*
claustrophobia	**claustrofobia**	*(klah-oos-troh-foh-bee-ah)*
coagulation	**coagulación**	*(koh-ah-goo-lah-see-ohn)*

coma	**coma**	*(koh-mah)*
comatose	**comatoso**	*(koh-mah-toh-soh)*
common	**común**	*(koh-moon)*
communication	**comunicación**	*(koh-moon-ee-kah-see-ohn)*
compromise	**compromiso**	*(kohm-proh-mee-soh)*
consultant	**consultante**	*(kohn-sool-tahn-teh)*
continued	**continuado**	*(kohn-tee-noo-ah-doh)*
control	**control**	*(kohn-trohl)*
cortisone	**cortisona**	*(kohr-tee-soh-nah)*
deficiency	**deficiencia**	*(deh-fee-see-ehn-see-ah)*
dehydration	**deshidratación**	*(deh-see-drah-tah-see-ohn)*
delirious	**delirio**	*(deh-lee-ree-oh)*
demented	**demente**	*(deh-mehn-teh)*
dental	**dental**	*(dehn-tahl)*
dentrifice	**dentífrico**	*(dehn-tee-free-koh)*
echymosis	**equimosis**	*(eh-kee-moh-sees)*
eczema	**eczema**	*(ehk-seh-mah)*
embolism	**embolismo**	*(ehm-boh-lees-moh)*
emetic	**emético**	*(ehm-eh-tee-koh)*
employ	**emplear**	*(ehm-pleh-ahr)*
English	**inglés**	*(een-glehs)*
epilepsy	**epilepsia**	*(eh-peel-ehp-see-ah)*
error	**error**	*(eh-rohr)*
exercise	**ejercicio**	*(eh-hehr-see-see-oh)*
explain	**explicar**	*(ehx-plee-kahr)*
extraction	**extracción**	*(ehx-trahk-see-ohn)*
exudate	**exudado**	*(ehx-oo-dah-doh)*
facial	**facial**	*(fah-see-ahl)*
fail	**fallar**	*(fah-yahr)*
false	**falso**	*(fahl-soh)*
family	**familia**	*(fah-mee-lee-ah)*
fatal	**fatal**	*(fah-tahl)*
fever	**fiebre**	*(fee-eh-breh)*
fibroid	**fibroide**	*(fee-broh-ee-deh)*
fistula	**fístula**	*(fees-too-lah)*
form	**forma**	*(fohr-mah)*
fremitus	**frémito**	*(freh-mee-toh)*
fresh	**fresco**	*(frehs-koh)*
frontal	**frontal**	*(frohn-tahl)*
function	**función**	*(foon-see-ohn)*
fundamental	**fundamental**	*(foon-dah-mehn-tahl)*
gastroenteritis	**gastroenteritis**	*(gahs-troh-ehn-teh-ree-tees)*
generic	**genérico**	*(heh-neh-ree-koh)*

genial	genial	*(heh-nee-ahl)*
glaucoma	glaucoma	*(glah-oo-koh-mah)*
globule	glóbulo	*(gloh-boo-loh)*
grave	grave	*(grah-beh)*
gynecologist	ginecólogo	*(hee-neh-koh-loh-goh)*
hematoma	hematoma	*(eh-mah-toh-mah)*
hemolysis	hemólisis	*(eh-moh-lee-sees)*
hepatitis	hepatitis	*(eh-pah-tee-tees)*
history	historia	*(ees-toh-ree-ah)*
hygienist	higienista	*(ee-hee-eh-nees-tah)*
ignore	ignorar	*(eeg-noh-rahr)*
impression	impresión	*(eem-preh-see-ohn)*
independence	independencia	*(een-deh-pehn-dehn-see-ah)*
indigestion	indigestión	*(een-dee-hehs-tee-ohn)*
infancy	infancia	*(een-fahn-see-ah)*
infection	infección	*(een-fehk-see-ohn)*
inflammation	inflamación	*(een-flah-mah-see-ohn)*
injection	inyección	*(een-yehk-see-ohn)*
insect	insecto	*(een-sehk-toh)*
instrument	instrumento	*(een-stroo-mehn-toh)*
insulin	insulina	*(een-soo-lee-nah)*
intimate	íntimo	*(een-tee-moh)*
jugular	yugular	*(yoo-goo-lahr)*
July	Julio	*(hoo-lee-oh)*
just	justo	*(hoos-toh)*
juvenile	juvenil	*(hoo-beh-neel)*
kleptomania	cleptomanía	*(klehp-toh-mah-nee-ah)*
laboratory	laboratorio	*(lah-boh-rah-toh-ree-oh)*
lancet	lanceta	*(lahn-seh-tah)*
laparoscopy	laparoscopia	*(lah-pah-rohs-koh-pee-ah)*
ligament	ligamento	*(lee-gah-mehn-toh)*
linen	lino	*(lee-noh)*
lingual	lingual	*(leen-goo-ahl)*
lithium	litio	*(lee-tee-oh)*
lupus	lupus	*(loo-poos)*
manual	manual	*(mah-noo-ahl)*
material	material	*(mah-teh-ree-ahl)*
maternal	maternal	*(mah-tehr-nahl)*
mathematics	matemáticas	*(mah-teh-mah-tee-kahs)*
medication	medicamento	*(meh-dee-kah-mehn-toh)*
medicine	medicina	*(meh-dee-see-nah)*
medulla	médula	*(meh-doo-lah)*
memory	memoria	*(meh-moh-ree-ah)*

meningitis	meningitis	*(meh-neen-hee-tees)*
minimum	mínimo	*(mee-nee-moh)*
model	modelo	*(moh-deh-loh)*
modern	moderno	*(moh-dehr-noh)*
molar	muela	*(moo-eh-lah)*
moral	moral	*(moh-rahl)*
nasal	nasal	*(nah-sahl)*
nausea	náusea	*(nah-oo-seh-ah)*
neonatal	neonatal	*(neh-oh-nah-tahl)*
nervous	nervioso	*(nehr-bee-oh-soh)*
neurotic	neurótico	*(neh-oo-roh-tee-koh)*
neutral	neutral	*(neh-oo-trahl)*
normal	normal	*(nohr-mahl)*
note	nota	*(noh-tah)*
novocain	novocaína	*(noh-boh-kah-ee-nah)*
nutrition	nutrición	*(noo-tree-see-ohn)*
obsession	obsesión	*(ohb-seh-see-ohn)*
obstruction	obstrucción	*(ohb-strook-see-ohn)*
occipital	occipital	*(ohk-see-pee-tahl)*
occur	ocurrir	*(oh-koo-reer)*
office	oficina	*(oh-fee-see-nah)*
opinion	opinión	*(oh-pee-nee-ohn)*
optic	óptico	*(ohp-tee-koh)*
organ	órgano	*(ohr-gah-noh)*
ovary	ovario	*(oh-bah-ree-oh)*
oxygen	oxígeno	*(ohx-ee-heh-noh)*
palate	paladar	*(pahl-ah-dahr)*
palmar	palmar	*(pahl-mahr)*
palpation	palpación	*(pahl-pah-see-ohn)*
pancreas	páncreas	*(pahn-kreh-ahs)*
panic	pánico	*(pah-nee-koh)*
paralytic	paralítico	*(pah-rah-lee-tee-koh)*
pathogen	patogénico	*(pah-toh-heh-nee-koh)*
pathological	patológico	*(pah-toh-loh-hee-koh)*
pelvis	pelvis	*(pehl-bees)*
pharmacy	farmacia	*(fahr-mah-see-ah)*
philosophy	filosofía	*(fee-loh-soh-fee-ah)*
physique	físico	*(fee-see-koh)*
piece	pieza	*(pee-eh-sah)*
plan	plan	*(plahn)*
porcelain	porcelana	*(pohr-seh-lah-nah)*
practice	práctica	*(prahk-tee-kah)*
prepare	prepara	*(preh-pah-rah)*

preventive	**preventivo**	*(preh-behn-tee-boh)*
probable	**probable**	*(proh-bah-bleh)*
problem	**problema**	*(proh-bleh-mah)*
pruritic	**prurítico**	*(proo-ree-tee-koh)*
pubic	**púbico**	*(poo-bee-koh)*
pulse	**pulso**	*(pool-soh)*
pure	**puro**	*(poo-roh)*
pyorrhea	**piorrea**	*(pee-oh-rreh-ah)*
racial	**racial**	*(rah-see-ahl)*
radical	**radical**	*(rah-dee-kahl)*
radioactive	**radiactivo**	*(rah-dee-ahk-tee-boh)*
rare	**raro**	*(rah-roh)*
rectal	**rectal**	*(rehk-tahl)*
repel	**repeler**	*(reh-peh-lehr)*
residue	**residuo**	*(reh-see-doo-oh)*
resin	**resina**	*(reh-see-nah)*
respect	**respeto**	*(rehs-peh-toh)*
rheumatic	**reumático**	*(reh-oo-mah-tee-koh)*
roseola	**roséola**	*(roh-seh-oh-lah)*
rubeola	**rubéola**	*(roo-beh-oh-lah)*
saliva	**saliva**	*(sah-lee-bah)*
salt	**sal**	*(sahl)*
sanitary	**sanitario**	*(sah-nee-tah-ree-oh)*
science	**ciencia**	*(see-ehn-see-ah)*
scleral	**escleral**	*(ehs-kleh-rahl)*
sebaceous	**sebáceo**	*(seh-bah-seh-oh)*
secrete	**secretar**	*(seh-kreh-tahr)*
selection	**selección**	*(seh-lehk-see-ohn)*
serology	**serología**	*(seh-roh-loh-hee-ah)*
sex	**sexo**	*(sehx-oh)*
sexual	**sexual**	*(sehx-oo-ahl)*
situation	**situación**	*(see-too-ah-see-ohn)*
social	**social**	*(soh-see-ahl)*
solution	**solución**	*(soh-loo-see-ohn)*
solvent	**solvente**	*(sohl-behn-teh)*
somatic	**somático**	*(soh-mah-tee-koh*
Spanish	**español**	*(ehs-pah-nyohl)*
spectrum	**espectro**	*(ehs-pehk-troh)*
spinal	**espinal**	*(ehs-pee-nahl)*
spirit	**espíritu**	*(ehs-pee-ree-too)*
stethoscope	**estetoscopio**	*(ehs-teh-tohs-koh-pee-oh)*
stupor	**estupor**	*(ehs-too-pohr)*
subaxillary	**subaxilar**	*(soob-ahx-ee-lahr)*

subnormal	**subnormal**	*(soob-nohr-mahl)*
substernal	**subesternal**	*(soob-ehs-tehr-nahl)*
suffer	**sufrir**	*(soo-freer)*
syncope	**síncope**	*(seen-koh-peh)*
systole	**sístole**	*(sees-toh-leh)*
tea	**té**	*(teh)*
technical	**técnico**	*(tehk-nee-koh)*
temporal	**temporal**	*(tehm-poh-rahl)*
tension	**tensión**	*(tehn-see-ohn)*
tetanus	**tétanos**	*(teh-tah-nohs)*
thermometer	**termómetro**	*(tehr-moh-meh-troh)*
tolerant	**tolerante**	*(toh-leh-rahn-teh)*
torso	**torso**	*(tohr-soh)*
treatment	**tratamiento**	*(trah-tah-mee-ehn-toh)*
tube	**tubo**	*(too-boh)*
tumor	**tumor**	*(too-mohr)*
ulcer	**úlcera**	*(ool-seh-rah)*
union	**unión**	*(oo-nee-ohn)*
universal	**universal**	*(oo-nee-behr-sahl)*
urea	**urea**	*(oo-reh-ah)*
uremia	**uremia**	*(oo-reh-mee-ah)*
ureteritis	**uretritis**	*(oo-reh-tree-tees)*
urticaria	**urticaria**	*(oor-tee-kah-ree-ah)*
use	**usar**	*(oo-sahr)*
uterus	**útero**	*(oo-teh-roh)*
uvula	**úvula**	*(oo-boo-lah)*
vaginal	**vaginal**	*(bah-hee-nahl)*
vagus	**vago**	*(bah-goh)*
valve	**válvula**	*(bahl-boo-lah)*
vapor	**vapor**	*(bah-pohr)*
varicocele	**varicocele**	*(bah-ree-koh-seh-leh)*
vein	**vena**	*(beh-nah)*
venereal	**venéreo**	*(beh-neh-reh-oh)*
vertebrate	**vertebrado**	*(behr-teh-brah-doh)*
vertigo	**vértigo**	*(behr-tee-goh)*
vestibule	**vestíbulo**	*(behs-tee-boo-loh)*
veterinary	**veterinaria**	*(beh-teh-ree-nah-ree-ah)*
vinegar	**vinagre**	*(bee-nah-greh)*
visible	**visible**	*(bee-see-bleh)*
vision	**visión**	*(bee-see-ohn)*
vital	**vital**	*(bee-tahl)*
volume	**volúmen**	*(boh-loo-mehn)*
vomit	**vómito**	*(boh-mee-toh)*

FIGURE 19-2 *Words that look alike in both languages help in many routine transactions.*

X-rays	**rayos X**	*(rah-yohs eh-kiss)*
xiphoid	**xifoides**	*(see-foh-ee-dehs)*
yogurt	**yogur**	*(yoh-goohr)*
zone	**zona**	*(soh-nah)*
zoology	**zoología**	*(soh-oh-loh-hee-ah)*
zygomatic	**cigomático**	*(see-goh-mah-tee-koh)*

Chapter Twenty

Numbers

Números

Knowing numbers is as important as knowing names and verbs. Everybody needs to know numbers to buy, sell, mention dates, indicate hours of the day, determine temperature, and state measurements and quantities. Numbers are also needed to make phone calls, are used in the sciences and in thousands of other areas. There is a difference between knowing numbers and knowing how to use them. In medicine, especially, errors can be made if one is not careful.

El conocimiento de los números es tan importante como el de los nombres y los verbos. Todas las personas necesitan conocer los números para comprar, vender, mencionar fechas, indicar la hora, la temperatura y expresar medidas y cantidades. También son necesarios para telefonear, para aplicar en todas las ciencias y para miles de cosas más. Hay diferencia entre saber los números y cómo usarlos. Especialmente en la medicina, se pueden cometer muchos errores si no somos cuidadosos con su uso.

1	one	**uno**	*(oo-noh)*
2	two	**dos**	*(dohs)*
3	three	**tres**	*(trehs)*
4	four	**cuatro**	*(koo-ah-troh)*
5	five	**cinco**	*(seen-koh)*
6	six	**seis**	*(seh-ees)*
7	seven	**siete**	*(see-eh-teh)*
8	eight	**ocho**	*(oh-choh)*
9	nine	**nueve**	*(noo-eh-beh)*
10	ten	**diez**	*(dee-ehs)*
11	eleven	**once**	*(ohn-seh)*
12	twelve	**doce**	*(doh-seh)*
13	thirteen	**trece**	*(treh-seh)*
14	fourteen	**catorce**	*(kah-tohr-seh)*

FIGURE 20-1 *Numbers are used in a variety of verbal and written transactions.*

15	fifteen	**quince**	*(keen-seh)*
16	sixteen	**dieciséis**	*(dee-ehs-ee-seh-ees)*
17	seventeen	**diecisiete**	*(dee-ehs-ee-see-eh-teh)*
18	eighteen	**dieciocho**	*(dee-ehs-ee-oh-choh)*
19	nineteen	**diecinueve**	*(dee-ehs-ee-noo-eh-beh)*
20	twenty	**veinte**	*(beh-een-teh)*

After the number 20, use the root of the number (20) and add the first nine numbers in order. See Table 20-1.

Después del número veinte, use la raíz de ese número y agregue los primeros nueve números en orden. Vea la tabla 20-1.

30	thirty	**treinta**	*(treh-een-tah)*
40	forty	**cuarenta**	*(koo-ah-rehn-tah)*
50	fifty	**cincuenta**	*(seen-koo-ehn-tah)*
60	sixty	**sesenta**	*(seh-sehn-tah)*
70	seventy	**setenta**	*(seh-tehn-tah)*
80	eighty	**ochenta**	*(oh-chehn-tah)*
90	ninety	**noventa**	*(noh-behn-tah)*
100	one hundred	**cien**	*(see-ehn)*

TABLE 20-1 ADD THE ROOTS	TABLA 20-1 AGREGUE LA RAÍZ	
ENGLISH	SPANISH	PRONUNCIATION
twenty-one	**veintiuno**	*beh-een-tee-oo-noh*
twenty-two	**veintidós**	*beh-een-tee-dohs*
twenty-three	**veintitrés**	*beh-een-tee-trehs*
twenty-four	**veinticuatro**	*beh-een-tee-koo-ah-troh*
twenty-five	**veinticinco**	*beh-een-tee-seen-koh*
twenty-six	**veintiséis**	*beh-een-tee-seh-ees*
twenty-seven	**veintisiete**	*beh-een-tee-see-eh-teh*
twenty-eight	**veintiocho**	*beh-een-tee-oh-choh*
twenty-nine	**veintinueve**	*beh-een-tee-noo-eh-beh*

FIGURE 20-2 *Numbers are helpful when inquiring about prices, buying merchandise, or working on a budget.*

When forming hundreds in Spanish, add the first nine numbers before the word *cientos*. The exceptions are *one hundred, five hundred, seven hundred,* and *nine hundred.* See Table 20-2.

Cuando en español se forman números en los cientos, se añaden los primeros nueve números antes de la palabra *cientos*. Las excepciones son *cien* (1); *quinientos* (5); *setecientos* (7) y *novecientos* (9). Vea la tabla 20-2.

Larger numbers are easier to deal with. Add the first nine numbers before or after, as shown below.

Los números mayores ofrecen menos problemas. A la raíz se le agregan los primeros números antes o después. Vea los siguientes ejemplos.

1,000	one thousand	**mil**	*(meel)*
1,001	one thousand one	**mil uno**	*(meel oo-noh)*
2,000	two thousand	**dos mil**	*(dohs meel)*
2,001	two thousand one	**dos mil uno**	*(dohs meel oo-noh)*

Fractions are often used in medicine. It is necessary to know exact quantities, since doses vary, especially for children. See below.

Las fracciones, o números fraccionarios, se usan en medicina frecuentemente. Es necesario saber las cantidades exactas ya que las dósis varían mucho, especialmente para niños. Vea abajo.

$1/3$	one-third	**un tercio**	*(oon tehr-see-oh)*
$1/4$	one-fourth	**un cuarto**	*(oon koo-ahr-toh)*
$1/2$	one-half	**un medio**	*(oon meh-dee-oh)*
$3/4$	three-fourths	**tres cuartos**	*(trehs koo-ahr-tohs)*

TABLE 20-2 IN THE HUNDREDS	TABLA 20-2 *EN LOS CIENTOS*	
ENGLISH	SPANISH	PRONUNCIATION
two hundred	**doscientos**	*doh-see-ehn-tohs*
three hundred	**trescientos**	*treh-see-ehn-tohs*
four hundred	**cuatrocientos**	*koo-ah-troh-see-ehn-tohs*
five hundred	**quinientos**	*kee-nee-ehn-tohs*
six hundred	**seiscientos**	*seh-ee-see-ehn-tohs*
seven hundred	**setecientos**	*seh-teh-see-ehn-tohs*
eight hundred	**ochocientos**	*oh-choh-see-ehn-tohs*
nine hundred	**novecientos**	*noh-beh-see-ehn-tohs*

When there is a need to emphasize degree or a category of items or persons, you must use ordinal numbers, as listed below.

Cuando hay necesidad de enfatizar ciertos grados o categorías se deben usar los números ordinales como se listan abajo.

1st	first	**primero(a)**	*(pree-meh-roh[rah])*
2nd	second	**segundo(a)**	*(seh-goon-doh[dah])*
3rd	third	**tercero(a)**	*(tehr-seh-roh[rah])*
4th	fourth	**cuarto(a)**	*(koo-ahr-toh[tah])*
5th	fifth	**quinto(a)**	*(keen-toh[tah])*
6th	sixth	**sexto(a)**	*(sehx-toh[tah])*
7th	seventh	**séptimo(a)**	*(sehp-tee-moh[mah])*
8th	eighth	**octavo(a)**	*(ohk-tah-boh[bah])*
9th	ninth	**noveno(a)**	*(noh-beh-noh[nah])*
10th	tenth	**décimo(a)**	*(deh-see-moh[mah])*

Chapter Twenty-one

Time

Capítulo Veintiuno

Tiempo

Time is so important throughout the world that all of us want to know: What time is it? At what time do we eat? At what time do we go to the movies? Time varies depending on the time zone in which you reside. There are places where time schedules are very different. If you wish to travel to far-away places, you must consult a travel agent or a time chart that shows the standard times in various parts of the

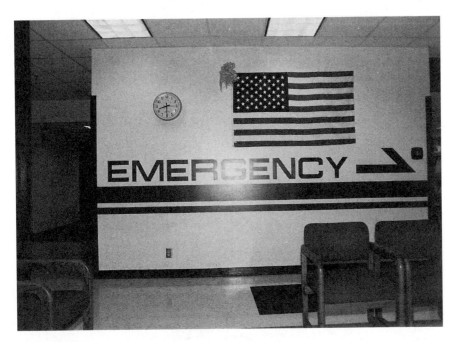

FIGURE 21-1 In a hospital, time is essential.

world. In hospitals, time is of the essence, since a life can be lost or saved in seconds.

El tiempo es tan importante en el mundo entero que todos queremos saber: ¿Qué hora es? ¿A qué hora comemos? ¿A qué hora nos vamos al cine? El tiempo varía de acuerdo con el huso horario donde nos encontremos. Hay lugares en los que el horario es muy diferente. Por lo tanto, debemos consultar con nuestro agente de viajes o un esquema que muestre el tiempo estándar en diferentes partes del mundo con referencia a un lugar específico. En los hospitales, el tiempo es la esencia, ya que una vida se puede salvar o perder en segundos.

In some hospitals, standard time is used; in others, military time is used.

En algunos hospitales se usa el tiempo estándar. En otros se usa el tiempo militar.

TIME	*STANDARD*	*MILITARY*
one o'clock	**la una**	**las trece horas**
	(lah oo-nah)	*(lahs-treh-seh oh-rahs)*
two o'clock	**las dos**	**las catorce horas**
	(lahs dohs)	*(lahs kah-tohr-seh oh-rahs)*

FIGURE 21-2   *Time changes from country to country.*

three o'clock	**las tres** *(lahs trehs)*	**las quince horas** *(lahs keen-seh oh-rahs)*
four o'clock	**las cuatro** *(lahs koo-ah-troh)*	**las dieciséis horas** *(lahs dee-ehs-ee-seh-ees oh-rahs)*
five o'clock	**las cinco** *(lahs seen-koh)*	**las diecisiete horas** *(lahs dee-ehs-ee-see-eh-teh oh-rahs)*
six o'clock	**las seis** *(lahs seh-ees)*	**las dieciocho horas** *(lahs dee-ehs-ee-oh-choh oh-rahs)*
seven o'clock	**las siete** *(lahs see-eh-teh)*	**las diecinueve horas** *(lahs dee-ehs-ee-noo-eh-beh oh-rahs)*
eight o'clock	**las ocho** *(lahs oh-choh)*	**las veinte horas** *(lahs beh-een-teh oh-rahs)*
nine o'clock	**las nueve** *(lahs noo-eh-beh)*	**las veintiuna horas** *(lahs beh-een-tee-oo-nah oh-rahs)*
ten o'clock	**las diez** *(lahs dee-ehs)*	**las veintidós horas** *(lahs beh-een-tee-dohs oh-rahs)*
eleven o'clock	**las once** *(lahs ohn-seh)*	**las veintitrés horas** *(lahs beh-een-tee-trehs oh-rahs)*
twelve o'clock	**las doce** *(lahs doh-seh)*	**las veinticuatro horas** *(lahs beh-een-tee-koo-ah-troh oh-rahs)*

Chapter Twenty-two

The Colors, The Seasons, The Months, The Days, Cardinal Points

Los Colores, Las Estaciones del Año, Los Meses, Los Días, Los Puntos Cardinales

THE COLORS

LOS COLORES

Colors are used frequently in medicine. In daily care, the physician notes the condition of the patient through observation of the color of the skin, hair, eyes, tongue, lips, etc. Colors also assist in making a medical diagnosis. For example, a reddish tint in the urine could be caused by kidney problems.

Los colores se utilizan a menudo en el área médica. En el cuidado diario, el médico observa la condición del paciente y vigila el color de la piel, pelo, ojos, lengua, labios, etc. Los colores también apoyan el diagnóstico médico. Por ejemplo, al notar una orina color rojizo, podría indicar que hay problemas de riñón.

yellow	amarillo	(ah-mah-ree-yoh)
amber	ámbar	(ahm-bahr)
clear	claro	(klah-roh)
white	blanco	(blahn-koh)
albino	albino	(ahl-bee-noh)
brown	café/moreno (skin tone)	(kah-feh/moh-reh-noh)
hazel	castaño	(kahs-tah-nyoh)
gold	dorado	(doh-rah-doh)
emerald	esmeralda	(ehs-meh-rahl-dah)
gray	gris	(grees)
grayish-white	canoso	(kah-noh-soh)
orange	naranja	(nah-rahn-hah)
black	negro	(neh-groh)
blue	azul	(ah-sool)
red	rojo	(roh-hoh)
pink	rosa	(roh-sah)
blonde	rubio	(roo-bee-oh)

green	**verde**	*(behr-deh)*
violet	**violeta**	*(bee-oh-leh-tah)*

THE SEASONS   LAS ESTACIONES DEL AÑO

We also use the seasons of the year to guide us during our practice. The human body reacts differently when exposed to temperature variations. These variations cause the skin to be sweaty, dry, cold, or warm. One can detect potential dangers, such as dehydration or burns, caused by very low temperatures.

También usamos las estaciones del año para guiarnos durante nuestra práctica. El cuerpo humano reacciona de manera diferente cuando se expone a variaciones en la temperatura. Estas variaciones causan que la piel se sienta caliente, húmeda, fría, o seca. Uno puede detectar posibles peligros tales como la deshidratación por el calor durante el verano, o las quemaduras causadas por una temperatura muy baja en el invierno.

season	**estación**	*(ehs-tah-see-ohn)*
spring	**primavera**	*(pree-mah-beh-rah)*
summer	**verano**	*(beh-rah-noh)*
fall	**otoño**	*(oh-toh-nyoh)*
winter	**invierno**	*(een-bee-ehr-noh)*

TABLE 22-1   ***TABLA 22-1***
DESCRIPTIVE WORDS   ***PALABRAS DESCRIPTIVAS***

ENGLISH	SPANISH	PRONUNCIATION
opaque	**opaco**	*(oh-pah-koh)*
transparent	**transparente**	*(trahns-pah-rehn-teh)*
grayish	**grisáceo**	*(gree-sah-seh-oh)*
icteric	**ictérico**	*(eek-teh-ree-koh)*
pinkish	**rosado**	*(roh-sah-doh)*
amber	**ambarino**	*(ahm-bah-ree-noh)*
orangy	**anaranjado**	*(ah-nah-rahn-hah-doh)*
bluish	**azulosa**	*(ah-soo-loh-sah)*
cianotic	**cianótico/violáceo**	*(see-ah-noh-tee-koh/bee-oh-lah-seh-oh)*
pale	**pálido**	*(pah-lee-doh)*

THE MONTHS   LOS MESES

Months become important during a pregnancy, since one can calculate a tentative delivery date. One can give instruction to the mother and prepare her for the birth date. Also, months help us map the growth and development of babies, since they require scheduled vaccinations at specific ages.

Los meses son importantes durante el embarazo, ya que se puede calcular una fecha probable de parto. Se puede entonces instruir a la madre y prepararla para el parto. Los meses también nos ayudan a vigilar el desarrollo de los bebés, ya que ellos requieren de vacunación en ciertas edades.

month	**mes**	*(mehs)*
January	**enero**	*(eh-neh-roh)*
February	**febrero**	*(feh-breh-roh)*
March	**marzo**	*(mahr-soh)*
April	**abril**	*(ah-breel)*
May	**mayo**	*(mah-yoh)*
June	**junio**	*(hoo-nee-oh)*
July	**julio**	*(hoo-lee-oh)*
August	**agosto**	*(ah-gohs-toh)*
September	**septiembre**	*(sehp-tee-ehm-breh)*
October	**octubre**	*(ohk-too-breh)*
November	**noviembre**	*(noh-bee-ehm-breh)*
December	**diciembre**	*(dee-see-ehm-breh)*

THE DAYS OF   LOS DIAS
THE WEEK   DE LA SEMANA

The use of days is indispensable in a hospital. We use them in all medical records, appointments, visits to the laboratory, X-Ray department, rehabilitation, or home visits. The days serve as a control. We use the number of hospital days to determine the cost of a hospitalization.

El uso de los días es indispensable en un hospital. Se usan en todas las notas de evolución de los pacientes, citas en el laboratorio, rayos X, rehabilitación o visitas comunitarias. Los días sirven para controlar la estancia del paciente en el hospital. Se usa el número de días de estancia para determinar el costo de la hospitalización.

Monday	**lunes**	*(loo-nehs)*
Tuesday	**martes**	*(mahr-tehs)*

Wednesday	miércoles	*(mee-ehr-koh-lehs)*
Thursday	jueves	*(hoo-eh-behs)*
Friday	viernes	*(bee-ehr-nehs)*
Saturday	sábado	*(sah-bah-doh)*
Sunday	domingo	*(doh-meen-goh)*

CARDINAL POINTS   **LOS PUNTOS CARDINALES**

Cardinal points serve as orientation, especially when one asks for directions.

Los puntos cardinales sirven de orientación, especialmente cuando uno requiere direcciones.

North	**Norte**	*(Nohr-teh)*
South	**Sur**	*(Soor)*
East	**Este**	*(Ehs-teh)*
West	**Oeste**	*(Oh-ehs-teh)*

Chapter Twenty-three	Capítulo Veintitrés

The Members of the Family

Los Miembros de la Familia

In the past, due to the fact that families were much larger, it was difficult to enumerate all of the members of a family. One could easily confuse the relationships between members. Today, because families are smaller, one knows who makes up the nuclear family and where we find the best relationships.

En épocas pasadas era muy difícil enumerar o contar a todos los miembros que integraban una familia, ya que éstas eran muy numero-

FIGURE 23-1 *Sometimes we find several family generations in a group.*

sas. Fácilmente se podía confundir el parentesco. Ahora que las familias son más pequeñas, se pueden conocer mejor a los integrantes del núcleo familiar y en dónde encontramos mejor convivencia.

English	Spanish	Pronunciation
the family	**la familia**	*(lah fah-mee-lee-ah)*
father	**padre**	*(pah-dreh)*
dad	**papá**	*(pah-pah)*
mother	**madre**	*(mah-dreh)*
mom	**mamá**	*(mah-mah)*
husband	**esposo**	*(ehs-poh-soh)*
wife	**esposa**	*(ehs-poh-sah)*
grandchildren	**nietos**	*(nee-eh-tohs)*
godparents	**padrinos**	*(pah-dree-nohs)*
godfather	**padrino**	*(pah-dree-noh)*
godmother	**madrina**	*(mah-dree-nah)*

It is important to determine the family composition soon after you interview the patient. This will give you an idea how much family

FIGURE 23-2 *Potential health problems may be prevented if you know the family background.*

TABLE 23-1 COMMON CHRONIC ILLNESSES	TABLA 23-1 ENFERMEDADES CRONICAS COMUNES	
ENGLISH	SPANISH	PRONUNCIATION
asthma	asma	ahs-mah
arthritis	artritis	ahr-tree-tees
diabetes	diabetes	dee-ah-beh-tees
epilepsy	epilépsia	eh-pee-lehp-see-ah
gout	gota	goh-tah
hypertension	hipertensión	ee-pehr-tehn-see-ohn
obesity	obesidad	oh-beh-see-dahd
mental retardation	retraso mental	reh-trah-soh mehn-tahl

FIGURE 23-3   *The American family is changing. It is important to determine family composition during your interview with the patient.*

support the patient has. It may also show potential familial problems. Many problems may be prevented if we know which members of the family have chronic illnesses.

Es muy importante determinar la composición de la familia inmediatamente después de la entrevista. Esto le dará una idea de cuanto apoya la familia al paciente. También puede demostrar posibles problemas hereditarios. Muchos problemas se pueden prevenir si sabemos cuáles de los miembros de la familia tienen enfermedades crónico-degenerativas.

We must keep in mind that the family composition is changing. A parent may be missing due to death, divorce, or abandonment. This means that we must be alert to potential problems, especially when the family has few economic resources, is educationally deprived, or is new to an area.

Debemos considerar que la composición de la familia está evolucionando. El padre o la madre pueden faltar debido a muerte, divorcio o abandono. Esto nos debe alertar de posibles problemas, especialmente cuando la familia posee escasos recursos económicos, está privada educacionalmente, o acaba de integrarse en la comunidad.

UNIT V

UNIDAD V

Chapter Twenty-four

The Alphabet

El Abecedario

The alphabet consists of a series of letters in a language in alphabetical order. It is also used by deaf and dumb persons, who use finger signals so they can be understood.

El abecedario es una serie de letras de un idioma en orden alfabético. También es usado por personas sordomudas que lo emplean con signos en los dedos de sus manos para darse a entender.

A	*B*	*C*	*D*	*E*
ah	beh	zeh	deh	eh
(arm)	(bell)	(cassette)	(day)	(bet)

F	*G*	*H**	*I*	*J*	*K*
eh-feh	jeh	ah-cheh	ie	joh-tha	kah
(effeminate)	(hen)	(hour)	(dear)	(holly)	(car)

L	*M*	*N*	*Ñ*	*O*
eh-leh	eh-meh	eh-neh	eh-nyeh	oh
(electric)	(emeritus)	(energy)	(canyon)	(opera)

P	*Q*	*R*	*S*	*T*
peh	kuh	errh	eh-seh	teh
(pay)	(cook)	(air)	(essence)	(tell)

U	*V*	*W*	*X*	*Y*	*Z*
uh	veh	double u	ehkiss	igriega	zehtah
(oo)	(verdict)	(unusual)	(a kiss)	(yo-yo)	(gazette)

*In Spanish pronunciation, the *h* is always silent.

211

RULES FOR PRONUNCIATION	REGLAS PARA LA PRONUNCIACION

Spanish is pronounced as it is written. Pay special attention to the five vowel sounds:

El español se escribe como se pronuncia. Ponga atención particularmente a los cinco sonidos de las vocales:

A (ah)	**asma** *(ahs-mah)*	asthma
E (eh)	**vena** *(beh-nah)*	vein
I (ee)	**herida** *(eh-ree-dah)*	wound
O (aw)	**obeso** *(oh-beh-soh)*	fat
U (oo)	**úlcera** *(ool-seh-rah)*	ulcer

Now pay attention to the consonants:
Ahora ponga atención a las consonantes:

C (seh)	**célula** *(seh-loo-lah)*	cell
C (see)	**ciencia** *(see-ehn-see-ah)*	science
C (cah)	**cama** *(kah-mah)*	bed
C (coh)	**comer** *(koh-mehr)*	to eat
C (koo)	**cuerpo** *(kee-ehr-poh)*	body
C (kree)	**crisis** *(kree-sees)*	crisis
CH (cheh)	**chancro** *(chahn-kroh)*	chancre
D (deh)	**dosis** *(doh-sees)*	dose
F (eh-feh)	**fiebre** *(fee-eh-breh)*	fever
G (heh)	**genital** *(heh-nee-tahl)*	genital
G (he)	**gingivitis** *(heen-hee-bee-tees)*	gingivitis
G (gahn)	**gangrena** *(gahn-greh-nah)*	gangrene
G (goh)	**gota** *(goh-tah)*	gout
G (goos)	**gusto** *(goos-toh)*	taste
G (glah)	**glaucoma** *(glah-oo-koh-mah)*	glaucoma
*H (hache)	***hernia** *(ehr-nee-ah)*	hernia
J (ha)	**jeringa** *(heh-reen-gah)*	syringe
K (kah)	**kilogramo** *(kee-loh-grah-moh)*	kilogram
L (eh-leh)	**laringitis** *(lah-reen-hee-tees)*	laryngitis
LL (eh-yeh)	**llorar** *(yoh-rahr)*	to cry
M (eh-meh)	**meningitis** *(meh-neen-hee-tees)*	meningitis
N (eh-neh)	**náuseas** *(nah-oo-seh-ahs)*	nausea
N (eh-nyeh)	**baño** *(bah-nyoh)*	bath

*Note that the *h* is always silent.

P (peh)	**palpitación** *(pahl-pee-tah-see-ohn)*	palpitation
Q (koo)	**quejar** *(keh-hahr)*	to complain
R (eh-reh)	**curar** *(koo-rahr)*	to cure
RR (doh-bleh-eh-rreh)	**carro** *(kah-rroh)*	car
	hemorragia *(eh-moh-rah-hee-ah)*	hemorrhage
S (eh-seh)	**síntomas** *(seen-toh-mahs)*	symptoms
T (teh)	**tensión** *(tehn-see-ohn)*	tension
V (beh)	**vértigo** *(behr-tee-goh)*	vertigo
W (double v/doh-bleh-beh)	**watusi** *(oo-ah-too-see)*	watusi
X (equis)	**extra** *(ehx-trah)*	extra
Y (y griega)	**y** *(ee)*	and
Y (yoh)	**yodo** *(yoh-doh)*	iodine
Z (zeta)	**zumbido** *(soom-bee-doh)*	buzzing

Accents

Acentos

The acute accent is the only mark of its kind in Spanish. It is a small oblique line (´) drawn from left to right and specifies a syllable that has a stronger sound when pronouncing it. Accents are also used to distinguish words that are written alike and are identical in form to other parts of speech, but have a different meaning. For example: papá (father), papa (vegetable); monte (hill), monté (verb).

El acento es la intensidad con que se marca determinada sílaba al pronunciar una palabra. Es una rayita oblícua (´) que se escribe de derecha a izquierda y se coloca en ciertos casos sobre la vocal de la sílaba en que se enfatiza la pronunciación. En español es muy importante acentuar las palabras para darles el significado correcto que llevan. Por ejemplo: papá (padre), papa (vegetal); monte (terreno elevado), monté (verbo).

I love	yo amo	*(ah-moh)*
he loved	el amó	*(ehl ah-moh)*
the owner	el dueño/amo	*(ehl doo-eh-nyoh/ah-moh)*
road	camino	*(kah-mee-noh)*
he walked	el caminó	*(ehl kah-mee-noh)*
copper	cobre	*(koh-breh)*
I charged	yo cobré	*(yoh koh-breh)*
volume	volúmen	*(boh-loo-mehn)*
never	jamás	*(hah-mahs)*
pencil	lápiz	*(lah-pees)*

Chapter Twenty-six

Capítulo Veintiséis

Gender of Nouns

Género de los Sustantivos

In Spanish, the gender of a noun corresponds to its sex. Therefore, to differentiate between them, masculine (el), feminine (la), and, for certain abstract nouns, neuter (lo) articles are used. A bone is masculine, the head is feminine, and a table is neuter.

En español, el género de los sustantivos corresponde al sexo. Por lo tanto, para diferenciarlos, se utilizan los artículos masculino (el), femenino (la), y, para ciertos sustantivos abstractos, neutro (lo). *Un hueso* **es masculino,** *la cabeza* **es femenina, y** *lo bueno* **es neutro.**

All Spanish nouns must be masculine or feminine.

The definite article *the* has the following singular forms in Spanish:

el (masculine)   **la** (feminine)

The indefinite article *a* or *an* has the following forms in Spanish:

un (masculine)   **una** (feminine)

Masculine nouns require a masculine article, feminine nouns require a feminine article:

the man	**el hombre**	the woman	**la mujer**
the boy	**el muchacho**	the back	**la espalda**
the friend	**el amigo**	a rib	**una costilla**
the eye	**el ojo**	the bladder	**la vejiga**
a skeleton	**un esqueleto**	the clavicle	**la clavícula**

IMPORTANT EXCEPTION: **la mano.** Note the ending *o;* la mano is feminine.

Nouns ending in *al, ante, ador,* or *on* are usually masculine.

the hospital	**el hospital**
the tranquilizer	**el tranquilizante**
the worker	**el trabajador**
the heart	**el corazón**

The days of the week, months of the year, and names of languages are all masculine:

Spanish	**el español**
Wednesday	**el miércoles**
the month of April	**el mes de abril**

Nouns ending in *tad, dad, cion, sion, tion, ez, ie, ud,* or *umbre* are usually feminine:

(the) dehydration	**la deshidratación**	the habit	**la costumbre**
the age	**la edad**	(the) friendship	**la amistad**
the series	**la serie**	the health	**la salud**

Nouns ending in *e* should be memorized with the definite article.

the blood	**la sangre**	. penis	**el pene**

THE PLURAL OF NOUNS

A noun ending in a vowel forms the plural by adding *s;* a noun ending in a consonant forms the plural by adding *es.*

the physician	**el médico**	the physicians	**los médicos**
the doctor	**el doctor**	the doctors	**los doctores**

A noun ending in *z* changes to *c* and then adds *es.*

the nose	**la nariz**	the noses	**las narices**

Nouns ending in a stressed vowel form the plural by adding *es.*

the tumor	**el tumor**	the tumors	**los tumores**

Nouns ending in unstressed *es* or *is* are considered to be both singular and plural. Number is expressed by the article.

Monday	**el lunes**	Monday	**los lunes**
dose	**la dosis**	doses	**las doses**

SPECIAL USES OF ARTICLES

The definite article is used in Spanish, but omitted in English as follows:

1. Before the names of languages, except after *hablar, en,* or *de:*

Spanish is important.	**El español es importante.**
My friend speaks French.	**Mi amigo habla francés.**
The whole book is in German.	**Todo el libro es en alemán.**

2. Before titles, except when addressing the person. (The article is omitted, however, before *Don, Doña, Santo, Santa, San.*):

Mr. Gomez left yesterday.	**El señor Gómez salió ayer.**
How are you, Mrs. Garcia?	**¿Cómo está, Señora García?**

3. With parts of the body or personal possessions (clothing, etc.):

He has black hair.	**El tiene el pelo negro.**
Mary has a broken foot.	**María tiene el pie quebrado.**

4. With the time of day (la hora, las horas = hour, hours):

It is one o'clock.	**Es la una.**
I go to sleep at eleven.	**Me duermo a las once.**

5. With the names of seasons:

I like summer.	**Me gusta el verano.**

6. With the days of the week, except after the verb *ser* (to be):

I go downtown on Tuesday.	**Los martes voy al centro.**
Today is Monday.	**Hoy es lunes.**

7. Before certain geographic areas:

The United States	**Los Estados Unidos**
Canada	**El Canadá**
Argentina	**La Argentina**

NEUTER ARTICLE *LO*

1. The neuter article *lo* precedes an adjective used as a noun to express a quality or an abstract idea:

I like red (that which is red).	**Me gusta lo rojo.**
I think the same as you.	**Pienso lo mismo que usted.**

2. *Lo* + adjective or adverb + *que* = how:

I see how good she is. **Ya veo lo buena que es.**

Since the article *lo* is neuter, it has no plural form. Therefore, *lo* is used whether the adjective is masculine or feminine, singular or plural.

OMISSION OF ARTICLES

1. The article is omitted:

A. Before nouns in opposition:

Austin, the Capital of Texas, is at the center of the state. **Austin, capital de Texas, está en el centro del estado.**

B. Before numerals expressing the numerical order of rules:

Charles V (the fifth) **Carlos V (quinto)**
Mary II (the second) **María II (segunda)**

2. The indefinite article is omitted:

A. Before predicate nouns denoting a class or group, social class, occupation, nationality, religion, etc.:

He is a barber. **Es barbero.**
I am Mexican. **Soy mexicana.**
I want to be a nurse. **Quiero ser enfermera.**

If the predicate noun is modified, the indefinite article is stated:

He is a hard working barber. **Es un barbero muy trabajador.**
I want to be a good nurse. **Quiero ser una buena enfermera.**

B. Before or after certain words that in English ordinarily have the article: *otro* (another), *cierto* (a certain), or *mil* (a thousand):

another bus **otro autobus**
a certain day **cierto dia**
one (a) thousand persons **mil personas**

Chapter Twenty-seven

Adjectives and Pronouns

Adjetivos y Pronombres

Adjectives describe nouns and pronouns. In Spanish, adjectives are placed after the noun. They agree in number and gender with the noun they modify.

ADJECTIVES ENDING IN *O*

Masculine singular:
The patient is happy.
El paciente está contento.
(Ehl pah-see-ehn-teh ehs-tah kohn-tehn-toh)

Feminine singular:
She is happy.
Ella está contenta.
(Eh-yah ehs-tah kohn-tehn-tah)

Masculine plural:
They are happy.
Ellos están contentos.
(Eh-yohs ehs-tahn kohn-tehn-tohs)

Feminine plural:
They are happy.
Ellas están contentas.
(Eh-yahs ehs-tahn kohn-tehn-tahs)

ADJECTIVES ENDING IN *E*

Masculine singular:
He is sad.
El es (está) triste.
(Ehl ehs (ehs-tah) trees-teh)

Feminine singular:
She is sad.
Ella es (está) triste.
(Eh-yah ehs (ehs-tah) trees-teh)

219

Masculine plural:	They are sad.
	Ellos son (están) tristes.
	(Eh-yohs sohn (ehs-tahn) trees-tehs)
Feminine plural:	They are sad.
	Ellas son (están) tristes.
	(Eh-yahs sohn (ehs-tahn) trees-tehs)

ADJECTIVES ENDING IN A CONSONANT

Masculine singular:	The procedure is difficult.
	El procedimiento es difícil.
	(Ehl proh-seh-dee-mee-ehn-toh ehs dee-fee-seel)
Feminine singular:	The test is difficult.
	La prueba es difícil.
	(Lah proo-eh-bah ehs dee-fee-seel)
Masculine plural:	The exams are difficult.
	Los exámenes son difíciles.
	(Lohs ehx-ah-meh-nehs sohn dee-fee-see-lehs)
Feminine plural:	The tests are difficult.
	Las pruebas son difíciles.
	(Lahs proo-eh-bahs sohn dee-fee-see-lehs)

TABLE 27-1
FEMININE AND MASCULINE ADJECTIVES

TABLA 27-1
ADJETIVOS FEMENINOS Y MASCULINOS

ADJECTIVE	FEMININE	MASCULINE
this	**esta**	**este**
	(ehs-tah)	*(ehs-teh)*
those	**estas**	**estos**
	(ehs-tahs)	*(ehs-tohs)*
that	**aquella**	**aquel**
	(ah-keh-yah)	*(ah-kehl)*
that	**esa**	**ese**
	(eh-sah)	*(eh-seh)*
those	**esas**	**esos**
	(eh-sahs)	*(eh-sohs)*
those	**aquellas**	**aquellos**
	(ah-keh-yahs)	*(ah-keh-yohs)*

Demonstrative adjectives precede the nouns they modify and agree with them in number and gender:

| This book . . . | **Este libro . . .** | *(Ehs-teh lee-broh . . .)* |
| This pencils . . . | **Estas plumas . . .** | *(Ehs-tahs ploo-mahs . . .)* |

Este (this) refers to what is near or directly concerns me.
Esos (those) refers to what is near or directly concerns you.
Aquel (that) refers to what is remote to the speaker or the person addressed.

This pencil is red.	**Este lápiz es rojo.**
	(Ehs-teh lah-pees ehs rroh-hoh)
John, give me that bone.	**Juan, déme aquel hueso.**
	(Hoo-ahn deh-meh ah-kehl oo-eh-soh)

SOME COMMON LIMITING ADJECTIVES

more	**mucho, más**	*(moo-choh, mahs)*
little, few	**poco**	*(poh-koh)*
all, everything	**todo**	*(toh-doh)*
nothing	**nada**	*(nah-dah)*
one, a, an	**un**	*(oon)*
first	**primero**	*(pree-meh-roh)*
fourth	**cuarto**	*(koo-ahr-toh)*
good	**bueno**	*(boo-eh-noh)*
bad	**mal**	*(mahl)*
big (age)	**grande**	*(grahn-deh)*
small (age, fit)	**pequeño/chico**	*(peh-keh-nyoh/chee-koh)*
less	**menos**	*(meh-nohs)*
better	**mejor**	*(meh-hohr)*

POSSESSIVE PRONOUNS

	SINGULAR	*PLURAL*
mine	**el mío, la mía**	**los míos, las mías**
	(ehl mee-oh, lah mee-ah)	*(lohs mee-ohs, lahs mee-ahs)*
yours	**el tuyo, la tuya**	**los tuyos, las tuyas**
	(ehl too-yoh, lah too-yah)	*(lohs too-yohs, lahs too-yahs)*
his, hers	**el suyo, la suya**	
	(ehl soo-yoh, lah soo-yah)	
theirs	**los suyos**	
	(lohs soo-yohs)	

TABLE 27-2 PERSONAL PRONOUNS		TABLA 27-2 PRONOMBRES PERSONALES	
SINGULAR		*PLURAL*	
I	**yo** *(yoh)*	we we	**nosotros** (masculine) *(noh-soh-trohs)* **nosotras** (feminine) *(noh-soh-trahs)*
you	**tú** (familiar) *(too)*	you	**vosotros/as** *(boh-soh-trohs/ahs)*
you	**usted** (formal) *(oos-tehd)*	you	**ustedes** *(oos-teh-dehs)*
he	**él** *(ehl)*	they	**ellos** (masculine) *(eh-yohs)*
she	**ella** *(eh-yah)*	they	**ellas** (feminine) *(eh-yahs)*

ours	**el nuestro, la nuestra** *(ehl noo-ehs-troh, lah noo-ehs-trah)*	**los nuestros, las nuestras** *(lohs noo-ehs-trohs, lahs noo-ehs-trahs)*

Possessive pronouns are formed by the definite article + the long form of the possessive adjective:

My nose is prettier than yours.	**Mi nariz es más bonita que la tuya.** *(Mee nah-rees ehs mahs boh-nee-tah keh lah too-yah)*
These books and mine.	**Estos libros y los míos.** *(Ehs-tohs lee-brohs ee lohs mee-ohs)*
His pens and yours.	**Sus plumas y las de usted.** *(Soos ploo-mahs ee lahs deh oos-tehd)*

After the verb *ser*, the article preceding the possessive pronoun is generally omitted:

The bones are mine.	**Los huesos son míos.** *(Lohs oo-eh-sohs soh mee-ohs)*
That gown is yours.	**Aquella bata es suya.** *(Ah-keh-yah bah-tah ehs soo-yah)*

Possession is expressed by *de* + the possessor. This corresponds to 's or *s'* in English.

Martin's pencil.	**El lápiz de Martín.** *(Ehl lah-pees deh Mahr-teen)*
My book and Louisa's.	**Mi libro y el de Luisa.** *(Mee lee-broh ee ehl deh Loo-ee-sah)*
Our patient.	**Nuestro paciente.** *(Noo-ehs-troh pah-see-ehn-teh)*
Her rings.	**Sus anillos.** *(Soos ah-nee-yohs)*
A friend of theirs.	**Un amigo de ellos.** *(Oon ah-mee-goh deh eh-yohs)*

WHOSE?

The interrogative pronoun *whose* is expressed in Spanish by *De quien es?*

Whose pen is it?	**¿De quién es la pluma?** *(Deh kee-ehn ehs lah ploo-mah)*
It belongs to the doctor.	**Es del doctor.** *(Ehs dehl dohk-tohr)*
Whose card is it?	**¿De quién es la tarjeta?** *(Deh kee-ehn ehs lah tahr-heh-tah)*
Mr. Garcia's.	**Del señor García.** *(Dehl seh-nyohr Gahr-see-ah)*
Whose X-rays are these?	**¿De quién son estos rayos X's?** *(Deh kee-ehn sohn ehs-tohs rah-yohs eh-kiss)*
They are Mrs. Luna's.	**Son de la señora Luna.** *(Sohn de lah seh-nyoh-rah Loo-nah)*

SOME COMMON PREPOSITIONS

to, at	**a**	*(ah)*
about	**acerca de**	*(ah-sehr-kah deh)*
around	**alrededor de**	*(ahl-rreh-deh-dohr deh)*
in front of	**enfrente de**	*(ehn-frehn-teh deh)*
in front of	**delante de**	*(deh-lahn-teh deh)*
within	**dentro de**	*(dehn-troh deh)*
beneath, under	**debajo de**	*(deh-bah-hoh deh)*

outside of	**fuera de**	*(foo-eh-rah deh)*
besides	**además de**	*(ah-deh-mahs deh)*
far	**lejos de**	*(leh-hohs deh)*
behind	**detrás de**	*(deh-trahs deh)*
near	**cerca de**	*(sehr-kah deh)*
since	**desde**	*(dehs-deh)*
before	**antes de**	*(an-tehs deh)*
after	**después de**	*(dehs-poo-ehs deh)*
during	**durante**	*(doo-rahn-teh)*
with	**con**	*(kohn)*
in, on	**en**	*(ehn)*
against	**contra**	*(kohn-trah)*
from, of	**de**	*(deh)*
among, between	**entre**	*(ehn-treh)*
for	**para**	*(pah-rah)*
toward	**hacia**	*(ah-see-ah)*
for, by, therefore	**por**	*(pohr)*
until	**hasta**	*(ahs-tah)*
according	**según**	*(seh-goon)*
over, above	**sobre**	*(soh-breh)*

Simple Questions, Exclamations

Preguntas Sencillas, Exclamaciones

Simple questions are used most frequently. They are used in short form to ask a question or give a command. In Spanish, questions have an inverted question mark (¿) before and a regular one after (?). We use questions to let the patient tell us what they know or how they feel.

FIGURE 28-1 *Simple questions are used frequently. Remember to give simple answers.*

The exclamation points indicate emotion or the mood that the patient is in (¡ !).

Las preguntas sencillas son las que usamos con mayor frecuencia. Se usan en forma corta ya sea interrogando o exclamando. En la lengua española las preguntas tienen signos de interrogación (¿ ?) invertidos al inicio y al final como los conocemos. Las interrogativas son preguntas que se hacen para que nos respondan lo que saben o sienten en ese momento. Las exclamaciones reflejan una emoción o estado de ánimo de la persona.

What?	¿Qué/Qué tal?	*(keh/keh tahl)*
When?	¿Cuándo?	*(koo-ahn-doh)*
Where?	¿Dónde?	*(dohn-deh)*
Why?	¿Por qué?	*(pohr keh)*
For whom?	¿Para quién?	*(pah-rah kee-ehn)*
For what?	¿Para qué?	*(pah-rah keh)*
Which?	¿Cuál?	*(koo-ahl)*
Who?	¿Quién?	*(kee-ehn)*
What is it?	¿Qué es?	*(keh ehs)*
What happens?	¿Qué pasa?	*(keh pah-sah)*

FIGURE 28-2 *Questions are often asked to clarify messages.*

What's going on?	¿Qué pasa?	(keh pah-sah)
Why not?	¿Por qué no?	(pohr keh noh)
Always!	¡Siempre!	(see-ehm-preh)
Since when?	¿Desde cuándo?	(dehs-deh koo-ahn-doh)
How many?	¿Cuántos?	(koo-ahn-tohs)
How much?	¿Cuánto?	(koo-ahn-toh)
Do you understand?	¿Comprende?	(kohm-prehn-deh)
Do you understand?	¿Entiende?	(ehn-tee-ehn-deh)
Never!	¡Nunca!	(noon-kah)
None!	¡Ninguno!	(neen-goo-noh)
Do you wish to use the bedpan?	¿Quiere el pato/quiere el bacín?	(kee-eh-reh ehl pah-toh/kee-eh-reh ehl bah-seen)
Do you wish to urinate?	¿Quiere orinar?	(kee-eh-reh oh-ree-nahr)
Do you wish to have a bowel movement?	¿Quiere evacuar/mover el intestino?	(kee-eh-reh eh-bah-koo-ahr/moh-behr ehl een-tehs-tee-noh)
Do you want . . .	¿Quiere . . .	(kee-eh-reh)
a glass of water?	un vaso con agua?	(oon bah-soh kohn ah-goo-ah)
a glass of juice?	un vaso con jugo?	(oon bah-soh kohn hoo-goh)
something to eat?	algo de comer?	(ahl-goh deh koh-mehr)
something to drink?	algo de tomar/beber?	(ahl-goh deh toh-mahr/beh-behr)
something to read?	algo de leer?	(ahl-goh deh leh-ehr)
I want . . .	Yo quiero . . .	(yoh kee-eh-roh)
Are you cold?	¿Tiene frío?	(tee-eh-neh free-oh)
Are you hot?	¿Tiene calor?	(tee-eh-neh kah-lohr)
Are you hungry?	¿Tiene hambre?	(tee-eh-neh ahm-breh)
Are you sleepy?	¿Tiene sueño?	(tee-eh-neh soo-eh-nyoh)
Are you thirsty?	¿Tiene sed?	(tee-eh-neh sehd)
Is that enough?	¿Es suficiente?	(ehs soo-fee-see-ehn-teh)
Is that a lot?	¿Es mucho?	(ehs moo-choh)
Is that too much?	¿Es demasiado?	(ehs deh-mah-see-ah-doh)

Are you comfortable?	¿Está cómodo(a)?	*(ehs-tah koh-moh-doh[a])*
Can you feel this?	¿Siente esto?	*(see-ehn-teh ehs-toh)*
Don't worry!	¡No se preocupe!	*(noh seh preh-oh-koo-peh)*
Be patient!	¡Tenga paciencia!	*(tehn-gah pah-see-ehn-see-ah)*

Chapter Twenty-nine

Negatives, Affirmatives

Negativos, Afirmativos

The principal negative words and their affirmative opposites are:
Las principales palabras negativas y sus opuestas afirmativas son:

You do not know the plan.	**Usted no sabe el plan.** *(Oos-tehd noh sah-beh ehl plahn)*
I see no one here.	**No veo a nadie aquí.** *(Noh beh-oh ah nah-dee-eh ah-kee)*
I have neither paper nor pencil.	**No tengo ni papel ni lápiz.** *(Noh tehn-goh nee pah-pehl nee lah-pees)*
He left without saying anything.	**Salió sin decir nada.** *(Sah-lee-oh seen deh-seer nah-dah)*

BUT

PERO, SINO

Though both *pero* (but, nevertheless) and *sino* (on the contrary) are translated as *but,* their use differs as follows: *Sino* is used only if the first clause of the sentence is negative and the second clause is in direct contrast to the first. *Pero* is used in all other cases where *but* is required.

Aunque *pero* y *sino* se tranducen *but,* su uso se distingue como lo siguiente: *Sino* se usa solo si la primera cláusula de la oración es negativa y la segunda cláusula está en contraste directo con la primera. *Pero* se usa en todos los otros casos cuando se requiere.

He doesn't speak English, but Spanish.	**No habla inglés sino español.** *(Noh ah-blah een-glehs see-noh ehs-pah-nyohl)*
He is not wearing a green shirt, but a blue one.	**No usa camisa verde sino azul.** *(Noh oo-sah kah-mee-sah behr-deh see-noh ah-sool)*

TABLE 29-1   TABLA 29-1
NEGATIVES AND   NEGATIVOS Y AFIRMATIVOS
AFFIRMATIVES

NEGATIVE		AFFIRMATIVE	
no, not	**no**	yes	**sí**
	(noh)		*(see)*
no one, nobody	**nadie**	someone,	**alguien**
	(nah-dee-eh)	somebody	*(ahl-ggee-ehn)*
nothing	**nada**	something	**algo**
	(nah-dah)		*(ahl-goh)*
never, not ever	**nunca, jamás**	always	**siempre**
	(noon-kah, hah-mahs)		*(see-ehm-preh)*
neither	**tampoco**	also	**también**
	(tahm-poh-koh)		*(tahm-bee-ehn)*
neither . . . nor	**ni . . . ni**	either . . . or	**o . . . o**
	(nee . . . nee)		*(oh . . . oh)*
none, not any	**ninguno**	some, any	**alguno**
	(neen-goo-noh)		*(ahl-goo-noh)*
without	**sin**	with	**con**
	(seen)		*(kohn)*

I don't like to study, but to go   **No me gusta estudiar sino ir al teatro.**
  to the theater.   *(Noh meh goos-tah ehs-too-dee-ahr see-*
                                     noh eer ahl teh-ah-troh)

Verbs

Verbos

Verbs are to a sentence what the spinal cord is to the body. Verbs give structure to a sentence because they tell us what is being done and when it is being done; for example: *I talk to the nurse* (present), *I talked to the nurse* (past), *I will talk to the nurse* (future).

Los verbos son para una oración lo que la espina dorsal es para el cuerpo. Los verbos dan estructura a una oración al indicar qué es lo que se está haciendo y cuándo se está haciendo; por ejemplo: *Yo hablo con la enfermera* (presente), *Yo hablé con la enfermera ayer* (pasado), *Yo hablaré con la enfermera mañana* (futuro).

Regular verbs end in *ar, er,* or *ir* in Spanish. They are easy to conjugate because one usually only has to take the stem of the verb and add the endings *-o, -as, -a, -amos, -an.* See Table 30-1.

En español los verbos regulares tienen la terminación *ar, er,* o *ir.* Son fáciles de conjugar ya que usualmente se toma la raíz del verbo y se le agrega la terminación *-o, -as, -a, -amos, -an.* Vea la tabla 30-1.

to name	**nombrar**	*(nohm-brahr)*
to call	**llamar**	*(yah-mahr)*
to hear	**escuchar**	*(ehs-koo-chahr)*
to listen	**oír**	*(oh-eer)*
to see	**ver**	*(behr)*
to operate	**operar**	*(oh-peh-rahr)*
to examine	**examinar**	*(ehx-ah-mee-nahr)*
to revise	**revisar**	*(reh-bee-sahr)*
to auscultate	**auscultar**	*(ah-oos-kool-tahr)*
to palpate	**palpar**	*(pahl-pahr)*
to heal	**sanar**	*(sah-nahr)*
to get better	**mejorar**	*(meh-hoh-rahr)*
to become ill	**enfermar**	*(ehn-fehr-mahr)*

TABLE 30-1 REGULAR VERB		TABLA 30-1 EL VERBO REGULAR	
VERB	STEM	ENDING	PERSONS

to live vivir (bee-beer)	viv	o	yo vivo (yoh bee-boh)
		es	tú vives (too bee-behs)
		e	éll/ella vive (ehl/eh-yah bee-beh)
		imos	nosotros vivimos (noh-soh-trohs bee-bee-mohs)
		en	ellos/ellas viven (eh-yohs/eh-yahs bee-behn)

to hurt	**doler**	*(doh-lehr)*
to vomit	**vomitar**	*(boh-mee-tahr)*
to die	**morir**	*(moh-reer)*
to be born	**nacer**	*(nah-sehr)*
to live	**vivir**	*(bee-beer)*
to leave	**dejar**	*(deh-hahr)*
to eat	**comer**	*(koh-mehr)*
to bring near	**acercar**	*(ah-sehr-kahr)*
to remain	**quedar**	*(keh-dahr)*
to come	**venir**	*(beh-neer)*
to reach	**alcanzar**	*(ahl-kahn-sahr)*
to take out	**sacar**	*(sah-kahr)*
to finish	**acabar**	*(ah-kah-bahr)*
to walk	**caminar**	*(kah-mee-nahr)*
to go out	**salir**	*(sah-leer)*
to let go	**soltar**	*(sohl-tahr)*
to stop	**parar**	*(pah-rahr)*
to need	**necesitar**	*(neh-seh-see-tahr)*
to agree	**acordar**	*(ah-kohr-dahr)*
to bore	**aburrir**	*(a-boo-rrecr)*
to deserve	**merecer**	*(meh-reh-sehr)*

Personal pronouns designate who is performing the action. Many times it is not necessary to include the personal pronouns when conjugating a verb or using it in a sentence.

| TABLE 30-2 | TABLA 30-2 |
| PRESENT AND PAST TENSE | TIEMPO PRESENTE Y PASADO |

Verb: to eat   **comer** *(koh-mehr)*

PRESENT TENSE   **TIEMPO PRESENTE**

I eat	**yo como**	*(yoh koh-moh)*
you eat	**tú comes**	*(too koh-mehs)*
he/she/you eat	**él/ella come**	*(ehl/eh-yah koh-meh)*
we eat	**nosotros comemos**	*(noh-soh-trohs koh-meh-mohs)*
they eat	**ellos/ellas comen**	*(eh-yohs/eh-yahs koh-mehn)*

PAST TENSE   **TIEMPO PASADO**

I ate	**yo comí**	*(yoh koh-mee)*
you ate	**tú comistes**	*(too koh-mees-tehs)*
he/she/you ate	**él/ella comió**	*(ehl/eh-yah koh-mee-oh)*
we ate	**nosotros comimos**	*(noh-soh-trohs koh-mee-mohs)*
they ate	**ellos/ellas comieron**	*(eh-yohs/eh-yahs koh-mee-eh-rohn)*

Los pronombres personales designan a las personas. Muchas veces no es necesario usar la persona al conjugar verbos o al usarlos en una oración.

PERSONAL PRONOUNS   PRONOMBRES PERSONALES

I	**yo**	*(yoh)*
you	**tú (informal)**	*(too)*
he/she/you	**él/ella/usted**	*(ehl/eh-yah/oos-tehd)*
we	**nosotros**	*(noh-soh-trohs)*
they/you (plural)	**ellos/ellas/ustedes**	*(eh-yohs/eh-yahs/oos-teh-dehs)*

TO FEEL	*SENTIR*	*(SEHN-TEER)*
I feel	**siento**	*(see-ehn-toh)*
you feel	**sientes**	*(see-ehn-tehs)*
he/she/you feel	**siente**	*(see-ehn-teh)*
we feel	**sentimos**	*(sehn-tee-mohs)*
they feel	**sienten**	*(see-ehn-tehn)*

TO SIT (MYSELF)	SENTAR	(SEHN-TAHR)
I sit	me siento	(meh see-ehn-toh)
you sit	te sientas	(teh see-ehn-tahs)
he/she/you sit	se sienta	(seh see-ehn-tah)
we sit	nos sentamos	(nohs sehn-tah-mohs)
they sit	se sientan	(seh see-ehn-tahn)

The direct object pronouns change the verb's action.

Los pronombres del objeto directo cambian la acción del verbo.

MOVER (MOVE)—ACTION ON SELF

yo me muevo
  (yoh meh moo-eh-boh)
tú te mueves
  (too teh moo-eh-behs)
él/ella se mueve
  (ehl/eh-yah seh moo-eh-beh)
nosotros nos movemos
  (noh-soh-trohs nohs moh-beh-mohs)
ellos/ellas se mueven
  (eh-yohs/eh-yahs seh moo-eh-behn)

MOVER (MOVE)—ACTION ON OBJECT

yo muevo
  (yoh moo-eh-boh)
tú mueves
  (too moo-eh-behs)
él/ella mueve
  (ehl/eh-yah moo-eh-beh)
nosotros movemos
  (noh-soh-trohs moh-beh-mohs)
ellos/ellas mueven
  (eh-yohs/eh-yahs moo-eh-behn)

to advise	aconsejar	(ah-kohn-seh-hahr)
to deny	negar	(neh-gahr)
to remember	acordar	(ah-kohr-dahr)
to thank for	agradecer	(ah-grah-deh-sehr)
to lose	perder	(pehr-dehr)
to turn off	apagar	(ah-pah-gahr)
to step	pisar	(pee-sahr)
to drink	beber	(beh-behr)
to take	tomar	(toh-mahr)
to change	cambiar	(kahm-bee-ahr)
to go to bed	acostarse	(ah-kohs-tahr-seh)
to sleep	dormir	(dohr-meer)
to lay down	acostar	(ah-kohs-tahr)
to get up, raise	levantar	(leh-bahn-tahr)
to sit	sentar	(sehn-tahr)
to feel	sentir	(sehn-teer)
to jump	saltar	(sahl-tahr)
to wash	lavar	(lah-bahr)

to clean	**limpiar**	*(leem-pee-ahr)*
to bathe	**bañar**	*(bah-nyahr)*
to turn	**voltear**	*(bohl-teh-ahr)*
to go	**ir**	*(eer)*
to do/make	**hacer**	*(ah-sehr)*
to promise	**prometer**	*(proh-meh-tehr)*
to ask	**preguntar**	*(preh-goon-tahr)*
to communicate	**comunicar**	*(koh-moo-nee-kahr)*
to respond	**responder**	*(rehs-pohn-dehr)*
to embrace	**abrazar**	*(ah-brah-sahr)*
to kiss	**besar**	*(beh-sahr)*
to believe	**creer**	*(kreh-ehr)*
to recognize	**reconocer**	*(reh-koh-noh-sehr)*
to confuse	**confundir**	*(kohn-foon-deer)*
to remember	**recordar**	*(reh-kohr-dahr)*
to discover, find	**descubrir**	*(dehs-koo-breer)*
to joke, kid	**bromear**	*(broh-meh-ahr)*
to complain	**quejar**	*(keh-hahr)*
to cry	**llorar**	*(yoh-rahr)*
to want	**querer**	*(keh-rehr)*
to wish	**desear**	*(deh-seh-ahr)*
to give	**dar**	*(dahr)*
to marry	**casar**	*(kah-sahr)*
to hunt	**cazar**	*(kah-sahr)*
to paint	**pintar**	*(peen-tahr)*
to cook	**cocinar**	*(koh-see-nahr)*
to build	**construir**	*(kohns-troo-eer)*
to receive	**recibir**	*(reh-see-beer)*
to start	**comenzar**	*(koh-mehn-sahr)*
to conduct	**conducir**	*(kohn-doo-seer)*
to fix	**componer**	*(kohm-poh-nehr)*
to destroy	**destruir**	*(dehs-troo-eer)*
to disappear	**desaparecer**	*(deh-sah-pah-reh-sehr)*
to find	**hallar**	*(ah-yahr)*
to break	**romper**	*(rohm-pehr)*
to cut	**cortar**	*(kohr-tahr)*
to carry	**llevar**	*(yeh-bahr)*
to return	**regresar**	*(reh-greh-sahr)*
to know	**conocer**	*(koh-noh-sehr)*
to cover	**cubrir**	*(koo-breer)*
to point	**señalar**	*(seh-nyah-lahr)*
to serve	**servir**	*(sehr-beer)*
to eat breakfast	**desayunar**	*(deh-sah-yoo-nahr)*

to suffer	**sufrir**	*(soo-freer)*
to shake	**temblar**	*(tehm-blahr)*
to be afraid	**temer**	*(teh-mehr)*
to scream	**gritar**	*(gree-tahr)*
to speak	**hablar**	*(ah-blahr)*
to employ	**emplear**	*(ehm-pleh-ahr)*
to take	**tomar**	*(toh-mahr)*
to work	**trabajar**	*(trah-bah-hahr)*
to have	**haber**	*(ah-behr)*
to try	**tratar**	*(trah-tahr)*
to sell	**vender**	*(behn-dehr)*

TABLE 30-3	TABLA 30-3
VERB TENSES	*TIEMPO DE LOS VERBOS*

Verb: to speak   **hablar** *(ah-blahr)*

PRESENT TENSE   **TIEMPO PRESENTE**

I speak	**yo hablo**	*(yoh ah-bloh)*
you speak	**tú hablas**	*(too ah-blahs)*
he/she/you speak	**él/ella habla**	*(ehl/eh-yah ah-blah)*
we speak	**nosotros hablamos**	*(noh-soh-trohs ah-blah-mohs)*
they speak	**ellos/ellas hablan**	*(eh-yohs/eh-yahs ah-blahn)*

PAST TENSE   **TIEMPO PASADO**

I spoke	**yo hablé**	*(yoh ah-bleh)*
you spoke	**tú hablaste**	*(too ah-blahs-teh)*
he/she/you spoke	**él/ella habló**	*(ehl/eh-yah ah-bloh)*
we spoke	**nosotros hablamos**	*(noh-soh-trohs ah-blah-mohs)*
they spoke	**ellos/ellas hablaron**	*(eh-yohs/eh-yahs ah-blah-rohn)*

FUTURE TENSE   **TIEMPO FUTURO**

I will speak	**yo hablaré**	*(yoh ah-blah-reh)*
you will speak	**tú hablarás**	*(too ah-blah-rahs)*
he/she/you will speak	**él/ella hablará**	*(ehl/eh-yah ah-blah-rah)*
we will speak	**nosotros hablaremos**	*(noh-soh-trohs ah-blah-reh-mohs)*
they will speak	**ellos/ellas hablarán**	*(eh-yohs/eh-yahs ah-blah-rahn)*

to see	ver	(behr)
to boil	hervir	(ehr-beer)
to fly	volar	(boh-lahr)
to return	volver	(bohl-behr)
to fill	llenar	(yeh-nahr)
to beat, knock	golpear	(gohl-peh-ahr)
to hit	pegar	(peh-gahr)
to bleed	sangrar	(sahn-grahr)
to activate	activar	(ahk-tee-bahr)
to present	presentar	(preh-sehn-tahr)
to administer	administrar	(ahd-mee-nees-trahr)
to provoke	provocar	(proh-boh-kahr)
to authorize	autorizar	(ahu-toh-ree-sahr)
to reduce	reducir	(reh-doo-seer)
to protect	proteger	(proh-teh-hehr)
to evaluate	evaluar	(eh-bah-loo-ahr)
to accept	aceptar	(ah-sehp-tahr)
to write	escribir	(ehs-kree-beer)
to interpret	interpretar	(een-tehr-preh-tahr)
to control	controlar	(kohn-troh-lahr)
to conserve	conservar	(kohn-sehr-bahr)
to inform	informar	(een-fohr-mahr)
to select	seleccionar	(seh-lehk-see-oh-nahr)
to revise	revisar	(reh-bee-sahr)
to separate	separar	(seh-pah-rahr)
to suspend	suspender	(soos-pehn-dehr)

The verbs *ser* and *estar* both translate in English as *to be,* but they are not interchangeable. Both are irregular in the present and the past tense.

Los verbos *ser* y *estar* se traducen al inglés *to be,* pero no se intercambian. Los dos verbos son irregulares en el tiempo presente y en el pasado.

	SER	ESTAR
I am	**yo soy**	**yo estoy**
	(yo soh-ee)	*(yoh ehs-tohy)*
you are	**usted es/tú eres**	**usted está/tú estás**
	(oos-tehd ehs/too eh-rehs)	*(oos-tehd ehs-tah/too ehs-tahs)*
he/she/it is	**él/ella/eso es**	**él/ella/eso está**
	(ehl/eh-yah/eh-soh ehs)	*(ehl/eh-yah/eh-soh ehs-tah)*

we are	nosotros somos	nosotros estamos
	(noh-soh-trohs soh-mohs)	*(noh-soh-trohs ehs-tah-mohs)*
they are	ellos/ellas son	ellos/ellas están
	(eh-yohs/eh-yahs sohn)	*(eh-yohs/eh-yahs ehs-tahn)*

USES OF *SER:*   **USO DEL VERBO** *SER*

Ser expresses a relatively permanent quality.

Age:	You are old.	**Usted *es* viejo.**
Characteristic:	The snow is cold.	**La nieve *es* fría.**
Color:	The urine is yellow.	**La orina *es* amarilla.**
Shape:	The glass is round.	**El vaso *es* redondo.**
Size:	You are tall.	**Usted *es* alto.**
Possession:	The pencil is mine.	**El lápiz *es* mío.**
Wealth:	The man is rich.	**El hombre *es* rico.**

Ser is used with predicate nouns, pronouns, or adjectives.

He is a dentist.	**El *es* dentista.**
Who am I?	**¿Quién *soy* yo?**
We are protestant.	**Nosotros *somos* protestantes.**

Ser indicates material, origin, or ownership.

material:	The needle is metal.	**La aguja *es* de metal.**
origin:	The doctor is from Texas.	**El doctor *es* de Texas.**
ownership:	The dentures are mine.	**Las dentaduras *son* mías.**

Ser tells time.

It is one o'clock.	***Es* la una.**
It is 10 o'clock.	***Son* las diez.**

USES OF *ESTAR*   **USO DEL VERBO** *ESTAR*

Estar expresses location (permanent and temporary).

Dallas is in Texas.	**Dallas *está* en Texas.**
I am in the room.	**Yo *estoy* en el cuarto.**

Estar expresses status of health.

How are you?	**¿Cómo *está* usted?**
I am fine.	***Estoy* bien.**
We are sick.	***Estamos* enfermos.**

Estar expresses a temporary characteristic or quality.

He is nervous.	**El *está* nervioso.**
I am ready.	***Estoy* lista.**
You are far away.	**Usted *está* lejos.**

UNIT VI

UNIDAD VI

Chapter Thirty-one

A Cultural
Perspective

—

Perspectiva
Cultural

—

Hispanics is a term often used to identify people who speak Spanish and who have Cuban, Central and South American, Mexican, or Puerto Rican backgrounds. Currently, Mexican-Americans and Puerto Ricans are the two largest Hispanic groups in the United States. The movement of Hispanics into the United States seems to have occurred in phases. In 1910, many Mexicans entered the United States with permanent visas. In the early 1940s, the *Bracero* program (source of cheap agricultural labor) further increased the Mexican population in the United States. During the 1950s, Puerto Ricans were recruited to work as laborers in the United States. In the 1960s, many Cubans and Latin Americans migrated to the United States in an attempt to better their social and economic status. A second influx of Cubans occurred in the early 1970s, when entire families were ousted or chose to leave the country that was battling communist oppression. Living conditions in Mexico and in South and Central America have fluctuated considerably over the years, forcing many to immigrate or to illegally settle in the United States year after year. Although one can find Hispanics almost everywhere, most of them are concentrated in Arizona, California, Colorado, Florida, New Mexico, New York, and Texas.

As a group, Hispanics have certain similarities. They are young (median age ranges from 17 to 28 years), their median level of education ranges from 9 to 12 years, they are mostly employed in blue-collar jobs (well over 50%), and their median income is about $15,000.00. If one relates the socio-economic conditions of a group to their level of health, then one can agree that Hispanics (with the statistics presented above), in general, are at risk for health problems. This risk doubles when Hispanics are not able to communicate with health providers due to language barriers. The use of interpreters is not uncommon. In major university hospitals, where Hispanic patient populations are large, one often is called in to be an interpreter. Very often, hospitals refuse to

FIGURE 31-1 *Hispanics have many similar characteristics.*

hire translators that would facilitate communication; but instead, housekeepers, orderlies, physical plant, or transportation employees are burdened with this task. The medical staff who are not able to communicate in Spanish are at a disadvantage because they cannot verify if the information that the patient is receiving is being translated adequately.

Hispanics have lived in the United States for decades. Many members of the third and fourth generations may not have retained Spanish as their primary language. However, in large cities where Hispanics concentrate, one commonality is evident: the use of Spanish, especially among teenagers and the elderly, is still practiced. Perhaps the current use of Spanish among the young relates to a new influx of Hispanic immigrants.

Hispanics tend to cluster, as do other cultural groups who share similar ethnicity, socio-economic level, or belief systems. Because Hispanics value camaraderie and rely on familiar support systems, they are often seen in large numbers when one of the members is sick in the hospital. This is often annoying to medical staff who are often understaffed, who have to complete myriads of documents, who have to deal with multiple services, and who have no clue why these people insist on visiting the patient even when the crisis is over. Determining the severity of the condition of the patient, reviewing the hospital's policies and procedures, and identifying the benefits/liabilities of having family members present may help the medical staff to alleviate the discomfort provided by the many visitors.

The concept of health varies in many cultures. For most Hispanics, being healthy means being free from pain. It also means that the person is able to perform all daily activities. Many think that health is a gift from God and that there is very little that one can do to avoid illness. In all cultures, behavior is learned; and as it is shared through the years, it tends to change and new behaviors are added. For some Hispanics, being sick is viewed as a punishment. Penance may include going to confession, making a long pilgrimage to a church, wearing a habit for a prescribed number of days, or keeping a *promesa* or *mandas* (promise) made to a patron saint. Many times people kneel and "walk" on their knees several blocks to church, thus helping the illness disappear.

Music plays an important role in Hispanics' lives. One often hears

FIGURE 31-2 *Consideration must be given to the cultural and religious habits of people.*

popular ballads while traveling through Hispanic communities. It is not unusual for hospitalized patients to ask to see a favorite Spanish program. Again, this is not only observed in the elderly population, but also in the younger population (teenagers).

Catholicism is predominant in many Hispanic groups. However, other religions such as Baptist, Jehovah's Witnesses, and Methodist claim to have large numbers of Hispanic members. It is not unusual to see some patients take candles (*veladoras*) or their favorite religious medals to the hospital. Understanding the importance of religion (for any ethnic group) will facilitate the care and treatment of the patient.

Vibrant colors in clothes, jewelry, and makeup are trademarks of Hispanics. These, along with what appear to be loud intonations, rapid speech and hand movements, often confuse medical staff who may not be aware of Hispanic cultural characteristics. It is extremely important to assess the patient's cultural background before diagnosing any unusual behavior or weird mannerisms.

Hospital food, traditionally, will not win any awards. Besides not

FIGURE 31-3 *Patients like some foods and dislike others. It is necessary to assess cultural tendencies.*

being hot (temperature), it is often too bland (not enough condiments/spices) for Hispanic (and many other) tastes. It is important to communicate the availability of foods to the patient. It is also helpful to assist in the decision-making process when selecting a menu. Often the patient's religion, ethnicity, age, and illness make it difficult to choose a menu.

Acculturation to a different group is often difficult. While parents may resent having to change, young members of an ethnic group may embrace the new group's ideologies and way of living. This often causes stress within the family and outside the family. Careful assessment must be made by medical staff who may not be aware of the degree of acculturation of Hispanic patients. This is a great opportunity to provide anticipatory guidance and teaching related to assimilation to a new group.

REFERENCES

Bonuck, K., & Arno, P. (1992). What is access and what does it mean for nursing? *Scholarly Inquiry for Nursing Practice*, 6(3), 211–216.

Clemon-Stone, S. A., Eigsti, D. G., & McGuire, S. L. (1991). *Comprehensive family and community health nursing* (3rd ed.). New York: Mosby Year Book.

Dancy, B., & Logan, B. (1994). Culture and ethnicity. In V. Bolander (ed.), *Sorensen and Luckmann's basic nursing* (3rd ed.) (pp. 331–342). Philadelphia: W. B. Saunders.

Fong, C. M. (1985). Ethnicity and nursing practice. *Topics in Clinical Nursing*, 7(3), 1–9.

Friedman, M. M. (1992). *Family nursing: Theory and practice* (3rd ed.). East Norwalk, CT: Appleton and Lange.

González, H. (1972). *Becoming aware of cultural differences in nursing*. Missouri: American Nurses Association, 1–2.

Howard, A. (1981). *Ethnicity and medical care*. Cambridge, MA: Harvard University Press.

Leininger, M. (1978). *Transcultural nursing: Concepts, theories and practice*. New York: John Wiley.

Maduro, R. (1983). Curanderismo and latino views of disease and curing. *The Western Journal of Medicine*, 139(6), 868–874.

Marroquin, M. (1983). *Los indocumentados*. Mexico: COPEC/CECOPE.

Orque, M. S., Bloch, B., & Monrroy, L. S. A. (1983). *Ethnic nursing care: A multicultural approach*. St. Louis: Mosby.

Osterling, J. P. (1985). The society and its environment. In J. D. Rudolph (ed.), *Mexico: A country study* (pp. 81–164). Washington, DC: The American University.

Poma, P. A. (1983). Hispanic cultural influences on medical practice. *Journal of the National Medical Association*, 75(10), 941–946.

Reinert, B. R. (1986). The health care beliefs and values of Mexican-Americans. *Home Health Care Nurse*, Sept.–Oct. 86, 32–38.

Robertson, I. (1987). *Sociology: Cultural responses to illness* (3rd ed.). New York: Worth Publishing.

Rooda, L. A. (1993). Knowledge and attitudes of nurses towards culturally different patients: Implications for nursing education. *Journal of Nursing Education*, 32(5). 209–213.

Santiago, J. M. (1993). Taking issue. *Hospital and Community Psychiatry*, 44(7), 613.

Satariano, W. A. (1986). Race, socioeconomic status, and health: A study of age differences in a depressed area.

American Journal of Preventive Medicine, *2*(1), 1–5.

Spector, R. E. (1993–94). Diversifying your approach. *Minority Nursing,* Winter/ Spring, (4)4, 28–31, 49–51.

United States Department of Health and Human Services. (1991). *Health status of minorities and low-income groups* (3rd ed.). Washington, DC: U.S. Government Printing Office.

U.S. Census Bureau. (1990). Census Data, Washington, DC: U.S. Government Printing Office.

Zuckerman, M. (1990). Some dubious premises in research and theory on racial differences: Scientific social and ethical issues. *American Psychologist, 45*(19), 1297–1303.

Home Cures and Popular Beliefs

Remedios Caseros y Creencias Populares

Each society has a different way of life. Data about many cultures have been collected by anthropologists, nursing scientists, sociologists, psychologists, and others with interest in studying behaviors exhibited by different ethnic groups. Since behaviors are transmitted from generation to generation, it is beneficial to understand a Hispanic's cultural background in order to understand his/her behavior.

FIGURE 32-1 People in a society have diverse customs and beliefs.

In times of crisis or physical distress, a patient may revert to treatment modalities used during childhood. It is not uncommon to find, during the initial interview, that Hispanic patients favor a variety of home-treatment modalities even when complying with Western medical regimens. It is imperative that the health care provider be nonjudgmental regarding these differences in beliefs and practices because it is the patient's perception of the illness that governs his/her behavior. Failure to assess the use of treatment modalities may result in frustration both for the patient and for the health care provider. It is also important not to stereotype patients within a specific culture. Ideally, each patient must be viewed as a unique individual with plans of care that incorporate his beliefs and practices.

For years, medicinal plants have been used throughout the world. According to Dr. Hero Gali (1985), there are over 20,000 plants being used for medicinal purposes in Mexico. It is not difficult to find *hierberias* in open markets where vendors are allowed to recommend dried herbs that have been successful in alleviating certain ailments. Along the Texas-Mexico border, in rural areas and in larger cities where a high concentration of Mexican-Americans is found, many (especially the

FIGURE 32-2   *Home remedies have been used for centuries.*

older generations) still shop at *hierberias* and have tailor-made prescriptions for their ailments. Popular among Hispanics is tea. Chamomile (*manzanilla*), mint (*hierba buena*), eucalyptus (*eucalipto*), ginger (*jengibre*), vanilla (*vainilla*), and olive (*olivo*) are often used for common ailments such as colic, colds, cough, and indigestion.

Folk-medicine belief and practice can be traced to the Greeks. Those beliefs were elaborated by the Arabs and brought to Spain by the Moslems. Eventually, those beliefs were transmitted to America at the time of the Spanish conquest of Mexico. The combination of Spanish-Catholic tradition in Mexico with the Indian heritages (Aztecs, Mayans, etc.) yielded the practice of *curanderismo* as it is observed today.

Expensive and time-consuming treatment is avoided by the lower socio-economic groups when they visit a *curandero*. The *curandero* successfully integrates concepts and practices from diverse sources. He combines psychotherapeutic skills and ritualistic herbal remedies. Much of the *curandero*'s tools are religious in nature. In his office he usually has a large number of crosses and pictures of saints. He centers his thinking about illness on Christ and encourages patients to feel that they are doing what Christ did, suffer on earth. The *curandero* is usually sought for minor illnesses and chronic conditions that are feared to be supernatural. He is also seen for febrile conditions in children, convulsions, apathy, and disruptive behavior. Most *curanderos* do not charge for their services but they accept donations. The practitioners of *curanderismo* offer no barriers to care and have no waiting lists. This makes it attractive to many patients who do not have insurance or who find the health care system inaccessible. Other Hispanic groups rely on health care providers similar to the *curandero*. *Sobadoras* (female healers) are very popular in Puerto Rico. They use oils (*aceite de culebra, aceite de olivo*) in their treatment of patients. The *sobadoras* combine their listening skills with massage skills to assist the patient.

Acculturation and assimilation of persons of Hispanic origin has been slowed by various social mechanisms of the larger society that tend to keep massive numbers of people separate (in vast housing projects), and by a tendency on their part to separate themselves from the larger community by living in *barrios*. This isolation is not unusual. People tend to group because they find commonalities, acceptance, and comfort in the group. This socio-cultural isolation results in the preservation of many folk beliefs of Spanish origin.

Prominent among health disease concepts are *mal de ojo* (evil eye), *empacho* (surfeit/indulgence), and *susto* (fright).

Mal de ojo is an illness to which children and adults are susceptible. When a person with "stronger" vision looks at another admiringly, but

FIGURE 32-3 *It is important to assess the patient's degree of acculturation and as-similation. Many customs prevail through the years.*

does not touch him, he/she gives the person *mal de ojo*. Symptoms of fever, headache, restlessness, crying, and vomiting are most commonly reported. When the stronger-visioned person actually touches the other, the symptoms disappear. When the person is not available to touch the other, the treatment of choice is sweeping. To sweep *(barrer)* means both to pass an unbroken raw egg over the body without touching, or actually rub the body with the egg. Prayers are recited during the sweeping. After the sweeping, to extract the fever from the patient's body and transmit it to the egg, the egg is broken and placed in a bowl of water. The bowl is placed under the head of the patient's bed. The egg is said to absorb the fever and by morning it should be cooked. The cooked egg is a sign that the patient had *ojo*.

Empacho is caused by a bolus of poorly digested or uncooked food sticking to the wall of the stomach. This is a disease primarily seen in children and attributed to overeating foods such as bread and bananas. Most common symptoms are lack of appetite, stomachache, diarrhea, and vomiting. Other reported symptoms include fever, crying, and rest-lessness in children. The treatment includes rubbing the stomach and rubbing and pinching the back. In order to dislodge the bolus, grasp a fold of skin on the back, pull it up, and release it. This procedure is done with both hands at least three times before breakfast. The patient is then administered a tea made with *estafiate* (larkspur) or *manzanilla* (chamomile). It is important to determine how long the child has been ill and what procedures have been performed. There could be intestinal blockage that may lead to toxic megacolon if medical attention is not sought.

Susto is the result of a traumatic experience that may be anything from a simple scare at night (lightning, loud noises) to the witnessing of an accident. Children are more susceptible than adults, but groups of individuals may develop symptoms at the same time. The most common symptom of *susto* is sleeping. Also, anorexia, insomnia, hallucinations, or weakness often accompanies this condition. Treatment of *susto* involves sweeping. The sweeping of the body is generally done by the healer (usually a grandmother) with orange or lemon tree branches or with palm leaves while reciting or chanting prayers. An herbal tea is usually administered after the sweeping.

Hispanics tend to use the "hot and cold" theory of disease. This theory is often used to explain the cause of an ailment and to choose a form of treatment. When a person has a "hot" disease, he/she may refuse to eat hot foods, medicines, or teas because he/she may think that the condition will worsen. Cold treatments and cold beverages are assumed to be beneficial in this case. On the other hand, when a person has a "cold" disease, he/she may ingest hot teas to alleviate his/her symptoms. Hot and cold diseases are often labeled differently by different cultural groups (Hispanic, Chinese, etc.). It is pertinent to ask a patient during the history-taking phase of the visit if he/she has determined to what category a certain disease belongs.

There is a widespread fatalistic attitude among many Hispanics, specifically in the low-income, low-education segments. Because of lack of education related to health promotion and health prevention, many Hispanics leave their health status up to God. Many also believe that the hospital is the place where one goes to die. Mr. T., one of our diabetic patients, believed that his son was murdered by doctors who gave him too much medicine and, thus, refused to go to the hospital when he needed help.

Many Hispanics may secure health information and treatment from many sources including relatives, magazines, radio, religion, and tradition. Given a choice, they often consult medical doctors but they may be ingesting their own home remedies. It is appropriate to ask what treatment modalities they have been using prior to the visit. It is important to respect cultural and value differences, and when possible, attempt to incorporate these treatments into the plan of care. Perhaps if this is done, patient compliance with medical treatment will increase.

REFERENCES

Clark, M. J. (1992). *Nursing in the community.* East Norwalk, CT: Appleton and Lange.

Ellis, J. R., & Hartley, C. L. (1992). *Nursing in today's world* (4th ed.). Philadelphia: J. B. Lippincott Company.

Fong, C. M. (1985). Ethnicity and nursing practice. *Topics in Clinical Nursing,* 7(3), 1–10.

Foreman, J. T. (1985). Susto and the health needs of the Cuban refugee population. *Topics in Clinical Nursing,* 7(3), 40–47.

Gali, H. (1985). *Las hierbas del indio.* Mexico City: Gómez Gómez Hnos.

———. (1985). *Hojas que curan.* Mexico City: Gómez Gómez Hnos.

Harwood, A. The hot-cold theory of disease: Implications for treatment of Puerto Rican patients. *Journal of the American Medical Association, 216*(7), 1153–1158.

Selby, H. A. (1987). Battling urban poverty from below. *American Anthropology, 89*(6), 419–423.

Spector, R. E. (1991). *Cultural diversity in health and illness* (3rd ed.). East Norwalk, CT: Appleton and Lange.

Torres, E. (1989). *Green medicine.* Kingsville, Texas: Nieves Press.

———. (1989). *The folk healer.* Kingsville, Texas: Nieves Press.

Vigil, J. D. (1984). *From Indians to Chicanos.* Prospect Heights, Illinois: Waveland Press.

Sentence Index

A bowel movement.
Mover el intestino.
(Moh-behr ehl een-tehs-tee-noh)

A friend of theirs.
Un amigo de ellos.
(Oon ah-mee-goh deh eh-yohs)

A nurse will see you.
Una enfermera lo/la atenderá.
(Oon-nah ehn-fehr-meh-rah loh/lah ah-tehn-deh-rah)

A pharmacist assists with patient education.
Un farmacéutico asiste con la educación del paciente.
(Oon fahr-mah-seh-oo-tee-koh ah-sees-teh kohn lah eh-doo-kah-see-ohn dehl pah-see-ehn-teh)

A standard schedule is used.
Se usa un horario estándar.
(Seh oo-sah oon oh-rah-ree-oh ehs-tahn-dahr)

About your baby.
En cuanto a su bebé.
(Ehn koo-ahn-toh ah soo beh-beh)

According to . . .
De acuerdo con . . .
(Deh ah-koo-ehr-doh kohn)

After meals.
Después de las comidas.
(Dehs-poo-ehs deh lahs koh-mee-dahs)

Again . . .
Otra vez . . .
(Oh-trah behs)

All of a sudden . . .
De golpe . . .
(Deh gohl-peh)

Always!
¡Siempre!
(See-ehm-preh)

The technician always comes at 6A.M.
El técnico siempre viene a las seis de la mañana.
(Ehl tehk-nee-koh see-ehm-preh bee-eh-neh ah lahs seh-ees deh lah mah-nyah-nah)

Among the vegetables that we serve are:
Entre los vegetales/verduras que servimos hay:
(Ehn-treh lohs beh-heh-tah-lehs/behr-doo-rahs keh sehr-bee-mohs ah-ee:)

Are there elevators?
¿Hay elevadores?
(Ah-ee eh-leh-bah-doh-rehs)

Are there ramps?
¿Hay rampas?
(Ah-ee rahm-pahs)

Are you a widow/widower?
¿Es usted viudo(a)?
(Ehs oos-tehd bee-oo-doh[-dah])

Are you allergic to any foods?
¿Es alérgico a ciertas comidas?
(Ehs ah-lehr-hee-koh ah see-ehr-tahs koh-mee-dahs)

Are you allergic to any drugs?
¿Es alérgico a ciertas drogas?
(Ehs ah-lehr-hee-koh ah see-ehr-tahs droh-gahs)

Are you allergic to any plants?
¿Es alérgico a ciertas plantas?
(Ehs ah-lehr-hee-koh ah see-ehr-tahs plahn-tahs)

Are you cold?
¿Tiene frío?
(Tee-eh-neh free-oh)

Are you comfortable?
¿Está cómodo(a)?
(Ehs-tah koh-moh-doh[-dah])

Are you divorced?
¿Es usted divorciado(a)?
(Ehs oos-tehd dee-bohr-see-ah-doh[-dah])

Are you dizzy?
¿Tiene mareos?
(Tee-eh-neh mah-reh-ohs)

Are you employed?
¿Trabaja usted?
(Trah-bah-hah oos-tehd)

Are you hot?
¿Tiene calor?
(Tee-eh-neh kah-lohr)

Are you hungry?
¿Tiene hambre?
(Tee-eh-neh ahm-breh)

Are you hurting?
¿Tiene dolor?
(Tee-eh-neh doh-lohr)

Are you in a hurry?
¿Tiene prisa?
(Tee-eh-neh pree-sah)

Are you married?
¿Es usted casado(a)?
(Ehs oos-tehd kah-sah-doh[-dah])

Are you O.K.?
¿Está bien/Se siente bien?
(Ehs-tah bee-ehn/Seh see-ehn-teh bee-ehn)

Are you on vacation?
¿Está de vacaciones?
(Ehs-tah deh bah-kah-see-oh-nehs)

Are you single?
¿Es usted soltero(a)?
(Ehs oos-tehd sohl-teh-roh[-rah])

Are you sleepy?
¿Tiene sueño?
(Tee-eh-neh soo-eh-nyoh)

Are you taking your medicine?
¿Está tomando sus medicinas?
(Ehs-tah toh-mahn-doh soos meh-dee-see-nahs)

Are you the patient?
¿Es usted el/la paciente?
(Ehs oos-tehd ehl/lah pah-see-ehn-teh)

Are you thirsty?
¿Tiene sed?
(Tee-eh-neh sehd)

Are your teeth sensitive to cold?
¿Sus dientes son sensibles al frío?
(Soos dee-ehn-tehs sohn sehn-see-blehs ahl free-oh)

Arm and hand . . .
Brazo y mano . . .
(Brah-soh ee mah-noh)

As a whole . . .
En conjunto . . ./En todo . . .
(Ehn kohn-hoon-toh/Ehn toh-doh)

As soon as you can go to your doctor.
En cuanto pueda acuda a su médico.
(Ehn koo-ahn-toh poo-eh-dah ah-koo-dah ah soo meh-dee-koh)

Ask for unit six-A.
Pregunte por la unidad Seis A.
(Preh-goon-teh pohr lah oo-nee-dahd seh-ees ah)

Ask the receptionist for a number.
Pídale un número a la recepcionista.
(Pee-dah-leh oon noo-meh-roh ah lah reh-sehp-see-ohn-ees-tah)

At bedtime.
Al acostarse.
(Ahl ah-kohs-tahr-seh)

At least 30 minutes!
¡Por lo menos treinta minutos!
(Pohr loh meh-nohs treh-een-tah mee-noo-tohs)

At the same time, we will take the X-rays.
Al mismo tiempo, tomamos los rayos X.
(Ahl mees-moh tee-ehm-poh, toh-mah-mohs lohs rah-yohs eh-kiss)

At what time do they close?
¿A qué hora cierran?
(Ah keh oh-rah see-eh-rahn)

At what time do you get up?
¿A qué hora se levanta?
(Ah keh oh-rah seh leh-bahn-tah)

At what time do you go to bed?
¿A qué hora se acuesta?
(Ah keh oh-rah seh ah-koo-ehs-tah)

Austin is at the center of the state.
Austin está en el centro del estado.
(Aoos-teen ehs-tah ehn ehl sehn-troh dehl ehs-tah-doh)

Avoid sunlight.
Evite asolearse/los rayos del sol.
(Eh-bee-teh ah-soh-leh-ahr-seh/lohs rah-yohs dehl sohl)

Backward.
Atrás.
(Ah-trahs)

Do you have bad breath?
¿Tiene mal aliento?
(Tee-eh-neh mahl ah-lee-ehn-toh)

Bathe him every day.
Báñelo diariamente.
(Bah-nyeh-loh dee-ah-ree-ah-mehn-teh)

Be patient!
¡Tenga paciencia!
(Tehn-gah pah-see-ehn-see-ah)

Before/after meals.
Antes/después de las comidas.
(Ahn-tehs/dehs-poo-ehs deh lahs koh-mee-dahs)

Bend it.
Dóblala.
(Doh-blah-lah)

Bend over!
¡Agáchese!
(Ah-gah-cheh-seh)

Bend the elbow.
Doble el codo.
(Doh-bleh ehl koh-doh)

Bend the wrist.
Doble la muñeca.
(Doh-bleh lah moo-nyeh-kah)

Bend your hip.
Dobla tu cadera.
(Doh-blah too kah-deh-rah)

Bend your shoulder.
Dobla tu hombro.
(Doh-blah too ohm-broh)

Bend your toes.
Dobla tus dedos.
(Doh-blah toos deh-dohs)

Bite!
¡Muerda!
(Moo-ehr-dah)

Boil all water that he drinks.
Hierva el agua que tome.
(Ee-ehr-bah ehl ah-goo-ah keh toh-meh)

Breast-feed or give a bottle every three hours.
Dele pecho o biberón cada tres horas.
(Deh-leh peh-choh oh bee-beh-rohn kah-dah trehs oh-rahs)

Breathe!
¡Respire!
(Rehs-pee-reh)

Breathe, deep!
¡Respire, hondo/profundo!
(Rehs-pee-reh ohn-doh/proh-foon-doh)

Breathe deep; let it out slowly.
Respira hondo; exhala despacio.
(Rehs-pee-rah ohn-doh; ehx-ah-lah dehs-pah-see-oh)

Breathe out!
¡Exhale/respire!
(Ehx-ah-leh/rehs-pee-reh)

Breathe regularly.
Respire regularmente/normalmente.
(Rehs-pee-reh reh-goo-lahr-mehn-teh/nohr-mahl-mehn-teh)

Breathe through your mouth.
Respire por la boca.
(Rehs-pee-reh pohr lah boh-kah)

Brush your teeth!
¡Cepíllese los dientes!
(Seh-pee-yeh-seh lohs dee-ehn-tehs)

But, I don't have a pencil.
Pero no tengo un lápiz.
(Peh-roh noh tehn-goh oon lah-pees)

But, we will give you something to drink.
Pero le daremos algo que tomar.
(Peh-roh leh dah-reh-mohs ahl-goh keh toh-mahr)

Buzzing in your ears . . .
Zumbido en los oídos . . .
(Soom-bee-doh ehn lohs oh-ee-dohs)

Call for . . .
Llamar . . .
(Yah-mahr)

Call your friends.
Llame a sus amigos.
(Yah-meh ah soos ah-mee-gohs)

Call your physician.
Llame a su médico.
(Yah-meh ah soo meh-dee-koh)

Can I join you?
¿Te puedo acompañar?
(Teh poo-eh-doh ah-kohm-pah-nyahr)

Can you do housework?
¿Puede hacer quehaceres domésticos?
*(Poo-eh-deh ah-sehr keh-ah-seh-rehs
doh-mehs-tee-kohs)*

Can you feel this?
¿Siente esto?
(See-ehn-teh ehs-toh)

Can you get out of bed?
¿Puede salir de la cama?
(Poo-eh-deh sah-leer deh lah kah-mah)

Can you give me directions?
¿Me puede dar direcciones?
*(Meh poo-eh-deh dahr dee-rehk-see-ohn-
ehs)*

Can you go with me?
¿Puede ir conmigo?
(Poo-eh-deh eer kohn-mee-goh)

Can you read?
¿Puede leer?
(Poo-eh-deh leh-ehr)

Can you see the blackboard well?
¿Puede(s) ver bien la pizarra/pizarrón?
*(Poo-eh-deh[s] behr bee-ehn lah pee-sah-
rrah/pee-sah-rrohn)*

Can you see the fire extinguisher?
¿Ve el extintor de fuego?
(Beh ehl ehx-teen-tohr deh foo-eh-goh)

Can you take off work?
¿Puede faltar al trabajo?
(Poo-eh-deh fahl-tahr ahl trah-bah-hoh)

Can you take a vacation?
¿Puede tomar vacaciones?
*(Poo-eh-deh toh-mahr bah-kah-see-ohn-
ehs)*

Can you tell me what kind of diet you
have?
¿Puede decirme qué dieta tiene?
*(Poo-eh-deh deh-seer-meh keh dee-eh-tah
tee-eh-neh)*

Can you write?
¿Puede escribir usted?
(Poo-eh-deh ehs-kree-beer oos-tehd)

Can you write the name?
¿Puede escribir el nombre?
*(Poo-eh-deh ehs-kree-beer ehl nohm-
breh)*

Have you ever been in a car accident?
¿Accidente automovilístico?
*(Ahk-see-dehn-teh ah-oo-toh-moh-bee-
lees-tee-koh)*

Clean your breast thoroughly.
Lave muy bien sus senos/pechos.
*(Lah-beh moo-ee bee-ehn soohs seh-
nohs/peh-chohs)*

Clean your nipples before you breast-
feed.
Lave sus pezones antes de darle el pecho.
*(Lah-beh soos peh-sohn-ehs ahn-tehs deh
dahr-leh ehl peh-choh)*

Close it.
Ciérrala(lo).
(See-eh-rrah-lah[-loh])

Please close your books.
Por favor, cierren sus libros.
*(Pohr fah-bohr, see-eh-rrehn soos lee-
brohs)*

Close your eyes!
¡Cierre los ojos!
(See-eh-reh lohs oh-hohs)

Close your mouth!
¡Cierre la boca!
(See-eh-reh lah boh-kah)

Come in.
Pase/entre usted.
(Pah-seh/ehn-treh oos-tehd)

Cough!
¡Tose!
(Toh-seh)

Cough deeply.
Tosa más fuerte.
(Toh-sah mahs foo-ehr-teh)

Cross your arms.
Cruza tus brazos.
(Kroo-sah toos brah-sohs)

Cross your legs.
Cruza tus piernas.
(Kroo-sah toos pee-ehr-nahs)

Daily.
Diariamente/Una por día/Cada día.
*(Dee-ah-ree-ah-mehn-teh/Oo-nah pohr
dee-ah/Kah-dah dee-ah)*

Date.
Fecha.
(Feh-chah)

Deal with . . .
Tratar . . .
(Trah-tahr)

Dial '9', wait for the tone, then dial the
number you want to call.
**Marque el nueve, espere el tono, luego
marque el número que quiera llamar.**
*(Mahr-keh ehl noo-eh-beh, ehs-peh-reh
ehl toh-noh, loo-eh-goh mahr-keh ehl
noo-meh-roh keh kee-eh-rah yah-
mahr)*

Did you arrive in a wheelchair?
¿Llegó en silla de ruedas?
(Yeh-goh ehn see-yah deh roo-eh-dahs)

Did you bring a hearing aid?
¿Trajo un aparato para oír?
*(Trah-hoh oon ah-pah-rah-toh pah-rah
oh-eer)*

Did you bring an artificial eye?
¿Trajo un ojo artificial?
*(Trah-hoh oon oh-hoh ahr-tee-fee-see-
ahl)*

Did you bring an artificial limb?
¿Trajo una prótesis?
(Trah-hoh oo-nah proh-teh-sees)

Did you bring contact lenses?
¿Trajo lentes de contacto?
(Trah-hoh lehn-tehs deh kohn-tahk-toh)

Did you bring dentures?
¿Trajo una dentadura postiza?
*(Trah-hoh oon-ah dehn-tah-doo-rah
pohs-tee-sah)*

Did you bring glasses?
¿Trajo anteojos?/lentes?
(Trah-hoh ahn-teh-oh-hohs/lehn-tehs)

Did you bring jewelry?/cash?
¿Trajo joyería?/dinero?
(Trah-hoh hoh-yeh-ree-ah/dee-neh-roh)

Did you bring any valuables?
¿Trajo algo de valor?
(Trah-hoh ahl-goh deh bah-lohr)

Did you come in a car?
¿Vino en un carro?
(Bee-noh ehn oon kah-rroh)

Did you faint?
¿Se desmayó?
(Seh dehs-mah-yoh)

Did you fall?
¿Se cayó?
(Seh kah-yoh)

Did you have a bowel movement?
¿Movió el intestino?
(Moh-bee-oh ehl een-tehs-tee-noh)

Did you lose consciousness?
¿Perdió el conocimiento?
*(Pehr-dee-oh ehl koh-noh-see-mee-ehn-
toh)*

Did you walk?
¿Caminó?
(Kah-mee-noh)

Difficulty in swallowing . . .
Dificultad al tragar . . .
(Dee-fee-kool-tahd ahl trah-gahr)

Do all of you go to school?
¿Todos van a la escuela?
(Toh-dohs bahn ah lah ehs-koo-eh-lah)

Do any of your children have asthma?
¿Algunos de sus niños tienen asma?
*(Ahl-goo-nohs deh soos nee-nyohs tee-
eh-nehn ahs-mah)*

Do any of your children have bad
coordination?
**¿Algunos de sus niños tienen mala
coordinación?**
*(Ahl-goo-nohs deh soos nee-nyohs tee-
eh-nehn mah-lah kohr-dee-nah-see-
ohn)*

Do any of your children have
chickenpox?
¿Algunos de sus niños tienen viruelas?
*(Ahl-goo-nohs deh soos nee-nyohs tee-
eh-nehn bee-roo-eh-lahs)*

Do any of your children have a cold?
¿Algunos de sus niños tienen resfriado?
*(Ahl-goo-nohs deh soos nee-nyohs tee-
eh-nehn rehs-free-ah-doh)*

Do any of your children have
convulsions?
**¿Algunos de sus niños tienen
convulsiones?**
*(Ahl-goo-nohs deh soos nee-nyohs tee-
eh-nehn kohn-bool-see-ohn-ehs)*

Do any of your children have delayed speech?
¿Algunos de sus niños tienen retraso del habla?
(Ahl-goo-nohs deh soos nee-nyohs tee-eh-nehn reh-trah-soh dehl ah-blah)

Do any of your children have diphtheria?
¿Algunos de sus niños tienen difteria?
(Ahl-goo-nohs deh soos nee-nyohs tee-eh-nehn deef-teh-ree-ah)

Do any of your children have hearing defects?
¿Algunos de sus niños tienen defectos del oído?
(Ahl-goo-nohs deh soos nee-nyohs tee-eh-nehn deh-fehk-tohs dehl oh-ee-doh)

Do any of your children have measles?
¿Algunos de sus niños tienen sarampión?
(Ahl-goo-nohs deh soos nee-nyohs tee-eh-nehn sah-rahm-pee-ohn)

Do any of your children have mumps?
¿Algunos de sus niños tienen paperas?
(Ahl-goo-nohs deh soos nee-nyohs tee-eh-nehn pah-peh-rahs)

Do any of your children have nausea and vomiting?
¿Algunos de sus niños tienen náusea y vómitos?
(Ahl-goo-nohs deh soos nee-nyohs tee-eh-nehn nah-oo-seh-ah ee boh-mee-tohs)

Do any of your children have pneumonia?
¿Algunos de sus niños tienen pulmonía?
(Ahl-goo-nohs deh soos nee-nyohs tee-eh-nehn pool-moh-nee-ah)

Do any of your children have visual defects?
¿Algunos de sus niños tienen defectos de la vista?
(Ahl-goo-nohs deh soos nee-nyohs tee-eh-nehn deh-fehk-tohs deh lah bees-tah)

Do exercise number . . .
Hagan el ejercicio número . . .
(Ah-gahn ehl eh-hehr-see-see-oh noo-meh-roh)

Do I have time?
¿Tengo tiempo?
(Tehn-goh tee-ehm-poh)

Do not bend your leg!
¡No doble la pierna!
(Noh doh-bleh lah pee-ehr-nah)

Do not drink alcohol with this medication.
No tome alcohol con esta medicina.
(Noh toh-meh ahl-kol kohn ehs-tah meh-dee-see-nah)

Do not drive!
¡No maneje/conduzca!
(Noh mah-neh-heh/kohn-doos-kah)

Do not eat or drink anything for thirty minutes.
No coma o beba nada por treinta minutos.
(Noh koh-mah oh beh-bah nah-dah pohr treh-een-tah mee-noo-tohs)

Do not get up!
¡No se levante!
(Noh seh leh-bahn-teh)

Do not hold onto the wall.
No se agarre de la pared.
(Noh seh ah-gah-rreh deh lah pah-rehd)

Do not move!
¡No se mueva!
(Noh seh moo-eh-bah)

Do not operate machinery!
¡No maneje/opere una máquina/maquinaria!
(Noh mah-neh-heh/oh-peh-reh oo-nah mah-kee-nah/mah-kee-nah-ree-ah)

Do not put on plastic panties.
No le ponga calzón de plástico.
(Noh leh pohn-gah kahl-sohn deh plahs-tee-koh)

Do they live close to you?
¿Viven cerca de usted?
(Bee-behn sehr-kah deh oos-tehd)

Do you drink alcohol?
¿Toma bebidas alcohólicas?
(Toh-mah beh-bee-dahs ahl-koh-lee-kahs)

Do you drink coffee?
¿Toma café?
(Toh-mah kah-feh)

Do you eat breakfast?
¿Toma desayuno/almuerzo?
(Toh-mah deh-sah-yoo-noh/ahl-moo-ehr-soh)

Do you feed the baby every three hours?
¿Le da de comer cada tres horas?
(Leh dah deh koh-mehr kah-dah trehs
oh-rahs)

Do you feel all right?
¿Se siente bien?
(Seh see-ehn-teh bee-ehn)

Do you feel dizzy?
¿Se siente mareado?
(Seh see-ehn-teh mah-reh-ah-doh)

Do you feel nauseated?
¿Tiene náusea?
(Tee-eh-neh naoo-seh-ah)

Do you feel weak?
¿Se siente débil?
(Seh see-ehn-teh deh-beel)

Do you get distracted easily?
¿Se distrae fácilmente?
(Seh dees-trah-eh fah-seel-mehn-teh)

Do you get tired easily?
¿Se cansa con facilidad?
(Seh kahn-sah kohn fah-see-lee-dahd)

Do you have . . .
Tiene . . .
(Tee-eh-neh)

Do you have a driver's license?
¿Tiene licencia de manejar?
(Tee-eh-neh lee-sehn-see-ah deh mah-
neh-hahr)

Do you have a husband?
¿Tiene esposo?
(Tee-eh-neh ehs-poh-soh)

Do you have a family doctor?
¿Tiene usted doctor particular?
(Tee-eh-neh oos-tehd dohk-tohr pahr-
tee-koo-lahr)

Do you have a hospital card?
¿Tiene usted tarjeta de hospital?
(Tee-eh-neh oos-tehd tahr-heh-tah deh
ohs-pee-tahl)

Do you have a phone?
¿Tiene teléfono?
(Tee-eh-neh teh-leh-foh-noh)

Do you have any allergies?
¿Tiene alergias?
(Tee-eh-neh ah-lehr-hee-ahs)

Do you have another car?
¿Tiene otro carro?
(Tee-eh-neh oh-troh kah-rroh)

Do you have any children?
¿Tiene niños?
(Tee-eh-neh nee-nyohs)

Do you have any questions?
¿Tiene preguntas?
(Tee-eh-neh preh-goon-tahs)

Do you have any brothers/sisters?
¿Tiene hermanos/hermanas?
(Tee-eh-neh ehr-mah-nohs/ehr-mah-
nahs)

Do you have cancer?
¿Tiene cáncer?
(Tee-eh-neh kahn-sehr)

Do you have car insurance?
¿Tiene seguro de carro?
(Tee-eh-neh seh-goo-roh deh kah-rroh)

Do you have chest pain?
¿Tiene dolor en el pecho?
(Tee-eh-neh doh-lohr ehn ehl peh-choh)

Do you have diabetes?
¿Tiene diabetes?
(Tee-eh-neh dee-ah-beh-tehs)

Do you have health insurance?
¿Tiene seguro de salud?
(Tee-eh-neh seh-goo-roh deh sah-lood)

Do you have help at home?
¿Tiene ayuda en casa?
(Tee-eh-neh ah-yoo-dah ehn kah-sah)

Do you have high blood pressure?
¿Tiene alta presión?
(Tee-eh-neh ahl-tah preh-see-ohn)

Do you have hospital insurance?
¿Tiene seguro de hospital?
(Tee-eh-neh seh-goo-roh deh ohs-pee-
tahl)

Do you have Medicare?
¿Tiene Medicare?
(Tee-eh-neh meh-dee-kehr)

Do you have problems with your teeth?
¿Tiene(s) problemas en los dientes?
(Tee-eh-neh[s] proh-bleh-mahs ehn lohs
dee-ehn-tehs)

Do you have any problems you want the
nurse to know about?
¿Tiene problemas que quiera decirle a la
enfermera?
(Tee-eh-neh proh-bleh-mahs keh kee-eh-
rah deh-seer-leh ah lah ehn-fehr-meh-
rah)

Do you have any questions?
¿Tiene(s) preguntas?
(Tee-eh-neh[s] preh-goon-tahs)

Do you have any relatives?
¿Tiene parientes?
(Tee-eh-neh pah-ree-ehn-tehs)

Do you have any special problems?
¿Tiene problemas especiales?
(Tee-eh-neh proh-bleh-mahs ehs-peh-see-ah-lehs)

Do you have time?
¿Tiene(s) tiempo?
(Tee-eh-neh[s] tee-ehm-poh)

Do you have tuberculosis?
¿Tiene tuberculosis?
(Tee-eh-neh too-behr-koo-loh-sees)

Do you have vision problems?
¿Tiene(s) problemas con la visión?
(Tee-eh-neh[s] proh-bleh-mahs kohn lah bee-see-ohn)

Do you have your Medicare card?
¿Tiene usted su tarjeta de Medicare?
(Tee-eh-neh oos-tehd soo tahr-heh-tah deh meh-dee-kehr)

Do you know?
¿Sabe?
(Sah-beh)

Do you know his phone number?
¿Sabe su teléfono?
(Sah-beh soo teh-leh-foh-noh)

Do you know how to return?
¿Sabe cómo regresar?
(Sah-beh koh-moh reh-greh-sahr)

Do you know what day today is?
¿Qué día es hoy?
(Keh dee-ah ehs oh-ee)

Do you know the name of the hospital?
¿Sabe el nombre del hospital?
(Sah-beh ehl nohm-breh dehl ohs-pee-tahl)

Do you know the name of the street?
¿Sabe el nombre de la calle?
(Sah-beh ehl nohm-breh deh lah kah-yeh)

Do you like going to school?
¿Te/le gusta ir a la escuela?
(Teh-leh goos-tah eer ah lah ehs-koo-eh-lah)

Do you like them hot/cold?
¿Le gustan calientes/fríos?
(Leh goos-tahn kah-lee-ehn-tehs/free-ohs)

Do you live by yourself?
¿Vive solo?
(Bee-beh soh-loh)

Do you miss a lot of school?
¿Falta(s) mucho a la escuela?
(Fahl-tah[s] moo-choh ah lah ehs-koo-eh-lah)

Do you need help?
¿Necesita ayuda?
(Neh-seh-see-tah ah-yoo-dah)

Do you need help with school work?
¿Necesita(s) ayuda con la tarea/trabajo?
(Neh-seh-see-tah[s] ah-yoo-dah kohn lah tah-reh-ah/trah-bah-hoh)

Do you need ice?
¿Necesita hielo?
(Neh-seh-see-tah ee-eh-loh)

Do you need more pillows?
¿Necesita más almohadas?
(Neh-seh-see-tah mahs ahl-moh-ah-dahs)

Do you need the headboard up?
¿Necesita levantar la cabecera más alto?
(Neh-seh-see-tah leh-bahn-tahr lah kah-beh-seh-rah mahs ahl-toh)

Do you need to call a taxi?
¿Necesita llamar un taxi?
(Neh-seh-see-tah yah-mahr oon tahx-ee)

Do you need to see a dietitian?
¿Necesita ver a la dietista?
(Neh-seh-see-tah behr ah lah dee-eh-tees-tah)

Do you play sports?
¿Practica(s) deportes?
(Prak-tee-kah[s] deh-pohr-tehs)

Do you remember me?
¿Se acuerda de mí?
(Seh ah-koo-ehr-dah deh mee)

Do you remember the name of the street?
¿Recuerda la calle?
(Reh-koo-ehr-dah lah kah-yeh)

Do you sleep during the day?
¿Duerme durante el día?
(Doo-ehr-meh doo-rahn-teh ehl dee-ah)

Do you smoke?
¿Fuma?
(Foo-mah)

Do you speak English?
¿Habla usted inglés?
(Ah-blah oos-tehd een-glehs)

Do you speak Spanish?
¿Habla español?
(Ah-blah ehs-pah-nyohl)

Do you have a special diet?
¿Hace dieta especial?
(Ah-seh dee-eh-tah ehs-peh-see-ahl)

Do you understand?
¿Comprende/entiende?
(Kohm-prehn-deh/ehn-tee-ehn-deh)

Do you take drugs?
¿Toma drogas?
(Toh-mah droh-gahs)

Do you wake up at night?
¿Se despierta en la noche?
(Seh dehs-pee-ehr-tah ehn lah noh-cheh)

Do you walk to school?
¿Camina(s) a la escuela?
(Kah-mee-nah[s] ah lah ehs-koo-eh-lah)

Do you want a cup of coffee?
¿Quiere una taza de café?
(Kee-eh-reh oo-nah tah-sah deh kah-feh)

Do you want to go home?
¿Quiere ir a su casa?
(Kee-eh-reh eer ah soo kah-sah)

Do you want to see a priest?
¿Necesita ver al sacerdote?
(Neh-seh-see-tah behr ahl sah-sehr-doh-teh)

Do you want to see our doctor?
¿Quiere ver a nuestro doctor?
(Kee-eh-reh behr ah noo-ehs-troh dohk-tohr)

Do you want to take the stairs?
¿Quiere tomar las escaleras?
(Kee-eh-reh toh-mahr lahs ehs-kah-leh-rahs)

Do you want water?
¿Quiere agua?
(Kee-eh-reh ah-goo-ah)

Do you wear glasses?
¿Usa(s) anteojos?/lentes?
(Oo-sah[s] ahn-teh-oh-hohs/lehn-tehs)

Do you wish . . .
Quiere . . .
(Kee-eh-reh)

Do you want a glass of juice?
¿Quiere un vaso con jugo?
(Kee-eh-reh oon bah-soh kohn hoo-goh)

Do you want a glass of water?
¿Quiere un vaso con agua?
(Kee-eh-reh oon bah-soh kohn ah-goo-ah)

Do you want to use the bedpan?
¿Quiere el bacín?
(Kee-eh-reh ehl bah-seen)

Do you have to have a bowel movement?
¿Quiere evacuar?
(Kee-eh-reh eh-bah-koo-ahr)

Do you have to urinate?
¿Quiere orinar?
(Kee-eh-reh oh-ree-nahr)

Do you want something to eat?
¿Quiere algo de comer?
(Kee-eh-reh ahl-goh deh koh-mehr)

Do you want a drink?
¿Quiere tomar/beber?
(Kee-eh-reh toh-mahr/beh-behr)

Do you wish/want to read?
¿Quiere leer?
(Kee-eh-reh leh-ehr)

Do you work?
¿Trabaja usted?
(Trah-bah-hah oos-tehd)

Do you work everyday?
¿Trabaja todos los días?
(Trah-bah-hah toh-dohs lohs dee-ahs)

Do your gums bleed?
¿Le sangran las encías?
(Leh sahn-grahn lahs ehn-see-ahs)

Doctor's name?
¿Nombre del doctor?
(Nohm-breh dehl dohk-tohr)

Does he cough only at night?
¿Tose sólo de noche?
(Toh-seh soh-loh deh noh-cheh)

Does he cry a lot?
¿Llora mucho?
(Yoh-rah moo-choh)

Does he go to school?
¿Va a la escuela?
(Bah ah lah ehs-koo-eh-lah)

Does he have any friends?
¿Tiene amigos?
(Tee-eh-neh ah-mee-gohs)

Does he have fever/diarrhea/colic?
¿Tiene fiebre/diarrea/cólico?
*(Tee-eh-neh fee-eh-breh/dee-ah-rreh-ah/
koh-lee-koh)*

Does he play outdoors?
¿Juega afuera de la casa?
*(Hoo-eh-gah ah-foo-eh-rah deh lah kah-
sah)*

Does he/she speak English?
¿Él/ella habla inglés?
(Ehl/eh-yah ah-blah een-glehs)

Does he sleep well?
¿Duerme bien?
(Doo-ehr-meh bee-ehn)

Does he wet the bed?
¿Moja la cama?
(Moh-hah lah kah-mah)

Does it hurt to cough?
¿Te duele al toser?
(Teh doo-eh-leh ahl toh-sehr)

Does it hurt to breathe?
¿Te duele al respirar?
(Teh doo-eh-leh ahl rehs-pee-rahr)

Does it hurt when you chew very hard?
¿Le duele al masticar con fuerza?
*(Leh doo-eh-leh ahl mahs-tee-kahr kohn
foo-ehr-sah)*

Does it still hurt?
¿Todavía le duele?
(Toh-dah-bee-ah leh doo-eh-leh)

Does the baby sleep all night?
¿Duerme el bebé toda la noche?
*(Doo-ehr-meh ehl beh-beh toh-dah lah
noh-cheh)*

Does the air hurt your teeth?
¿Le molesta el aire en los dientes?
*(Leh moh-lehs-tah ehl ahee-reh ehn lohs
dee-ehn-tehs)*

Don't be afraid!
¡No tenga miedo!
(Noh tehn-gah mee-eh-doh)

Don't breathe!
¡No respire!
(Noh rehs-pee-reh)

Don't change clothes.
No se cambie de ropa.
(Noh seh kahm-bee-eh deh roh-pah)

Don't eat foods that can cause
constipation.
Trate de no estreñirse.
(Trah-teh deh noh ehs-treh-nyeer-seh)

Don't hold the rail.
No se agarre del barandal.
*(Noh seh ah-gah-rreh dehl bah-rahn-
dahl)*

Don't let him put dirt in his mouth.
No deje que se meta tierra en la boca.
*(Noh deh-heh keh seh meh-tah tee-eh-
rrah ehn lah boh-kah)*

Don't let me bend it.
No dejes que la doble.
(Noh deh-hehs keh lah doh-bleh)

Don't let me close them.
No me dejes cerrarlos.
(Noh meh deh-hehs seh-rrahr-lohs)

Don't let me extend it.
No me dejes extenderlo.
(Noh meh deh-hehs ehx-tehn-dehr-loh)

Don't let the baby sleep more than three
hours during the day.
**No deje que el bebé duerma más de tres
horas durante el día.**
*(Noh deh-heh keh ehl beh-beh doo-ehr-
mah mahs deh trehs oh-rahs doo-
rahn-teh ehl dee-ah)*

Don't move!
¡No se mueva!
(Noh seh moo-eh-bah)

Don't sit!
¡No se siente!
(Noh seh see-ehn-teh)

Don't talk!
¡No hable!
(Noh ah-bleh)

Don't turn.
No voltee.
(Noh bohl-teh-eh)

Don't walk barefoot.
No camine descalzo.
(Noh kah-mee-neh dehs-kahl-soh)

Don't worry.
No se preocupe.
(Noh seh preh-oh-koo-peh)

Dosage?
¿Dósis?
(Doh-sees)

Dress him with loose clothes.
Póngale ropa cómoda.
(Pohn-gah-leh roh-pah koh-moh-dah)

Dress the baby with few clothes.
Vista al bebé con poca ropa.
(Bees-tah ahl beh-beh kohn poh-kah roh-pah)

Drink!
¡Beba/tome!
(Beh-bah/toh-meh)

Drink a lot of water and juices.
Tome mucha agua y jugos.
(Toh-meh moo-chah ah-goo-ah ee hoo-gohs)

Drug carts are checked for quantity, number, and expiration dates on all items.
Los carros de drogas se revisan para verificar cantidad, número y fecha de caducidad de todos los artículos.
(Lohs kah-rohs deh droh-gahs seh reh-bee-sahn pah-rah beh-ree-fee-kahr kahn-tee-dahd, noo-meh-roh ee feh-chah deh kah-doo-see-dahd deh toh-dohs lohs ahr-tee-koo-lohs)

Drugs are dispensed only upon the order of a physician.
Los medicamentos son distribuidos solamente por ordenes de un doctor.
(Lohs meh-dee-kah-mehn-tohs sohn dees-tree-boo-ee-dohs sohl-ah-mehn-teh pohr ohr-dehn-ehs deh oon dohk-tohr)

Each hour . . .
Cada hora . . .
(Kah-dah oh-rah)

Eat!
¡Coma!
(Koh-mah)

Every time you go to the bathroom to urinate, you must place the urine in this container.
Cada vez que vaya al baño a orinar, debe poner la orina en el recipiente.
(Kah-dah behs keh bah-yah ahl bah-nyoh ah oh-ree-nahr, deh-beh poh-nehr lah oh-ree-nah ehn ehl reh-see-pee-ehn-teh)

Every two (2) hours . . .
Cada dos horas . . .
(Kah-dah dohs oh-rahs)

Everything will be all right.
Todo saldrá con éxito.
(Toh-doh sahl-drah kohn ehx-ee-toh)

Excuse me!
¡Excúseme!
(Ehx-koo-seh-meh)

Exit to the right.
Salga a la derecha.
(Sahl-gah ah lah deh-reh-chah)

Expiration date.
Caducidad.
(Kah-doo-see-dahd)

Extend it.
Extiéndelo.
(Ehx-tee-ehn-deh-loh)

Extend your arm.
Extiende tu brazo.
(Ehx-tee-ehn-deh too brah-soh)

Extend your leg and foot.
Extiende tu pierna y tu pie.
(Ehx-tee-ehn-deh too pee-ehr-nah ee too pee-eh)

Extend your wrist.
Extiende tu muñeca.
(Ehx-tee-ehn-deh too moo-nyeh-kah)

Find out.
Descubrir.
(Dehs-koo-breer)

Flex it
¡Dóblalo!
(Doh-blah-loh)

Flex the foot upwardly.
Dobla el pie hacia arriba.
(Doh-blah ehl pee-eh ah-see-ah ah-ree-bah)

Flex your arm.
Dobla tu brazo.
(Doh-blah too brah-soh)

Flex your arm; don't let me extend it.
Dobla tu brazo; no me dejes extenderlo.
(Doh-blah too brah-soh; noh meh deh-hehs ehx-tehn-dehr-loh)

Flex your knee and turn to the middle.
Dobla tu rodilla y volteala para adentro.
*(Doh-blah too roh-dee-yah ee bohl-teh-
ah-lah pah-rah ah-dehn-troh)*

Follow my finger.
Sigue mi dedo.
(See-geh mee deh-doh)

Follow the green line.
Siga la línea verde.
(See-gah lah lee-neh-ah behr-deh)

Follow the instructions carefully.
Siga las instrucciones con cuidado.
*(See-gah lahs eens-trook-see-ohn-ehs
kohn koo-ee-dah-doh)*

Follow the red arrows.
Siga las flechas rojas.
(See-gah lahs fleh-chahs roh-hahs)

Foods you may not eat:
Comidas que no debe comer:
*(Koh-mee-dahs keh noh deh-beh koh-
mehr:)*

For breakfast:
Para el desayuno:
(Pah-rah ehl deh-sah-yoo-noh:)

For now, change into this gown.
Por ahora, póngase esta bata.
*(Pohr ah-oh-rah, pohn-gah-seh ehs-tah
bah-tah)*

For the birth control plan that you wish
to have.
Para el control de fertilidad que desee.
*(Pah-rah ehl kohn-trohl deh fehr-tee-lee-
dahd keh deh-seh-eh)*

For the most part . . .
Por la mayor parte . . .
(Pohr lah mah-yohr pahr-teh)

For what purpose?
¿Para qué?
(Pah-rah keh)

For whom?
¿Para quién?
(Pah-rah kee-ehn)

Forward.
Adelante.
(Ah-deh-lahn-teh)

Four times . . .
Cuatro veces . . .
(Koo-ah-troh beh-sehs)

Four times a day.
Cuatro veces al día.
(Koo-ah-troh beh-sehs ahl dee-ah)

Frequent blisters?
Ulceraciones frecuentes?
*(Ool-seh-rah-see-oh-nehs freh-koo-ehn-
tehs)*

From here, turn to the left, then turn to
the right.
**De aquí, de vuelta a la izquierda, luego
voltee a la derecha.**
*(Deh ah-kee, deh boo-ehl-tah ah lah ees-
kee-ehr-dah, loo-eh-goh bohl-teh-eh
ah lah deh-reh-chah)*

From time to time . . .
De vez en cuando . . .
(Deh behs ehn koo-ahn-doh)

Gain by . . .
Ganar con . . .
(Gah-nahr kohn)

Gas-producing foods.
Comidas que producen gases.
*(Koh-mee-dahs keh proh-doo-sehn gah-
sehs)*

Get up!
¡Levántese!
(Lah-bahn-teh-seh)

Give it to the clerk.
Déselo a la secretaria.
(Deh-seh-loh ah lah seh-kreh-tah-ree-ah)

Give the medicine to him every four
hours.
Déle la medicina cada cuatro horas.
*(Deh-leh lah meh-dee-see-nah kah-dah
koo-ah-troh oh-rahs)*

Give the medicine to him with a
dropper.
Déle la medicina con gotero.
*(Deh-leh lah meh-dee-see-nah kohn goh-
teh-roh)*

Go by . . .
Pasar . . .
(Pah-sahr)

Go immediately to the hospital!
**Vaya inmediatamente/en seguida al
hospital!**
*(Bah-yah een-meh-dee-ah-tah-mehn-teh/
ehn seh-ggee-dah ahl ohs-pee-tahl)*

Go on, please.
Continúe/Siga, por favor.
(Kohn-tee-noo-eh/See-gah, pohr fah-bohr)

Go through . . .
Atravesar/Cruzar . . .
(Ah-trah-beh-sahr/Kroo-sahr)

Go to page . . .
Vayan a la página . . .
(Bah-yahn ah lah pah-hee-nah)

Go to the blackboard, please.
Vaya a la pizarra, por favor.
(Bah-yah ah lah pee-sah-rrah, pohr fah-bohr)

Go to the glass doors.
Vaya hasta las puertas de vidrio.
(Bah-ya ahs-tah lahs poo-ehr-tahs deh bee-dree-oh)

Go to the hospital right away.
Acuda inmediatamente al hospital.
(Ah-koo-dah een-meh-dee-ah-tah-mehn-teh ahl ohs-pee-tahl)

Good!
¡Bueno!
(Boo-eh-noh)

Good afternoon.
Buenas tardes.
(Boo-eh-nahs tahr-dehs)

Good afternoon, Ms. Gonzalez.
Buenas tardes, señorita González.
(Boo-eh-nahs tahr-dehs seh-nyoh-ree-tah Gohn-sah-lehs)

Good evening.
Buenas noches.
(Boo-eh-nahs noh-chehs)

Good luck!
¡Buena suerte!
(Boo-eh-nah soo-ehr-teh)

Good morning!
¡Buenos días!
(Boo-eh-nohs dee-ahs)

Good morning miss.
Buenos días señorita.
(Boo-eh-nohs dee-ahs seh-nyoh-ree-tah)

Good morning, Mr. Martinez.
Buenos días, señor Martínez.
(Boo-eh-nohs dee-ahs seh-nyohr Mahr-tee-nehs)

Good night.
Buenas noches.
(Boo-eh-nahs noh-chehs)

Has the child been ill?
¿Ha estado enfermo el niño?
(Ah ehs-tah-doh ehn-fehr-moh ehl nee-nyoh)

Have a good day!
¡Pase un buen día!
(Pah-seh oon boo-ehn dee-ah)

Have you been a patient here before?
¿Ha sido un paciente de este lugar antes?
(Ah see-doh oon pah-see-ehn-teh deh ehs-teh loo-gahr ahn-tehs)

Have you been here before?
¿Ha estado aquí antes?
(Ah ehs-tah-doh ah-kee ahn-tehs)

Have you been sick?
¿Ha estado enfermo?
(Ah ehs-tah-doh ehn-fehr-moh)

Have you ever been in this hospital?
¿Ha estado en este hospital?
(Ah ehs-tah-doh ehn ehs-teh ohs-pee-tahl)

Have you ever been to the emergency room?
¿Ha estado en el cuarto de emergencias/urgencias.
(Ah ehs-tah-doh ehn ehl koo-ahr-toh deh eh-mehr-hehn-see-ah/oor-hehn-se-ahs)

Have you had . . . ?
¿Ha tenido . . .?
(Ah teh-nee-doh)

Have you had any accidents?
¿Ha tenido algún accidente?
(Ah teh-nee-doh ahl-goon ahk-see-dehn-teh)

Have you ever broken anything?
¿Se ha quebrado/fracturado alguna vez?
(Seh ah keh-brah-doh/frahk-too-rah-doh ahl-goo-nah behs)

Have you ever had blood drawn before?
¿Le han sacado/tomado muestras de sangre antes?
(Leh ahn sah-kah-doh/toh-mah-doh moo-ehs-trahs deh sahn-greh ahn-tehs)

Have you ever had a blood transfusion?
¿Ha tenido transfusiones de sangre?
(Ah teh-nee-doh trahns-foo-see-ohn-ehs deh sahn-greh)

Have you ever broken any bones?
**¿Ha tenido huesos quebrados/
fracturados?**
*(Ah teh-nee-doh oo-eh-sohs keh-brah-
dohs/frahk-too-rah-dohs)*

Have you ever had a reaction to a
transfusion?
**¿Ha tenido alguna reacción a las
transfusiones?**
*(Ah teh-nee-doh ahl-goo-nah reh-ahk-
see-ohn ah lahs trahns-foo-see-ohn-
ehs)*

Have you ever had surgery?
¿Ha tenido operaciones?
(Ah teh-nee-doh oh-peh-rah-see-ohn-ehs)

Have you had swelling?
¿Ha tenido hinchazón?
(Ah teh-nee-doh een-chah-sohn)

Have you had swelling in the ankles?
¿Ha tenido hinchazón en los tobillos?
*(Ah teh-nee-doh een-chah-sohn ehn lohs
toh-bee-yohs)*

Have you had swelling in the eyelids?
¿Ha tenido hinchazón en los parpados?
*(Ah teh-nee-doh een-chah-sohn ehn lohs
pahr-pah-dohs)*

Have you had swelling on your feet?
¿Ha tenido hinchazón en los pies?
*(Ah teh-nee-doh een-chah-sohn ehn lohs
pee-ehs)*

Have you had this happen before?
¿Le ha pasado esto antes?
(Leh ah pah-sah-doh ehs-toh ahn-tehs)

The doctor also tells the patient that she
must follow directions carefully so
that everything turns out all right.
**El doctor también le dice al paciente que
debe seguir cuidadosamente las recomendaciones que se le den para que
todo salga bien.**
*(Ehl dohk-tohr tahm-bee-ehn leh dee-seh
ahl pah-see-ehn-teh keh deh-beh seh-
ggeer koo-ee-dah-doh-sah-mehn-teh
lahs reh-koh-mehn-dah-see-ohn-ehs
keh seh leh dehn pah-rah keh toh-
doh sahl-gah bee-ehn)*

The doctor assigns a dosage schedule to
the order in the computer.
**El asigna un horario de dósis para cargar
en la computadora.**

*(Ehl dohk-tohr ah-seeg-nah oon oh-rah-
ree-oh deh doh-sees pah-rah kahr-
gahr ehn lah kohm-poo-tah-doh-rah)*

He bought me the book.
Me compró el libro.
(Meh kohm-proh ehl lee-broh)

He collected the money from me.
Me cobró el dinero.
(Meh koh-broh ehl dee-neh-roh)

He doesn't speak English, but Spanish.
No habla inglés, sino español.
*(Noh ah-blah een-glehs, see-noh ehs-pah-
nyohl)*

He gave me the money.
Me dió el dinero.
(Meh dee-oh ehl dee-neh-roh)

He has black hair.
El tiene el pelo negro.
(Ehl tee-ehn-eh ehl peh-loh neh-groh)

He is a barber.
Es barbero.
(Ehs bahr-beh-roh)

He is a hard-working barber.
Es un barbero muy trabajador.
*(Ehs oon bahr-beh-roh moo-ee trah-bah-
hah-dohr)*

He is content.
El está contento.
(Ehl ehs-tah kohn-tehn-toh)

He is happy.
El es (está) alegre.
(Ehl ehs [ehs-tah] ah-leh-greh)

He is not wearing a green shirt, but a
blue one.
No usa camisa verde, sino azul.
*(Noh oo-sah kah-mee-sah behr-deh, see-
noh ah-sool)*

He is not wearing a white shirt, but a
blue one.
No usa camisa blanca, sino azul.
*(Noh oo-sah kah-mee-sah blahn-kah,
see-noh ah-sool)*

He is sad.
El es (está) triste.
(Ehl ehs [ehs-tah] trees-teh)

He left without saying anything.
Salió sin decir nada.
(Sah-lee-oh seen deh-seer nah-dah)

He loved . . .
El amó . . .
(Ehl ah-moh)

He tells her that she will be discharged
tomorrow.
**Le comunica que mañana será dada de
alta.**
*(Leh koh-moo-nee-kah keh mah-nyah-
nah seh-rah dah-dah deh ahl-tah)*

He will talk to you.
El hablará con usted.
(Ehl ah-blah-rah kohn oos-tehd)

He will take you.
El lo llevará.
(Ehl loh yeh-bah-rah)

Head and neck . . .
Cabeza y cuello . . .
(Kah-beh-sah ee koo-eh-yoh)

Hello, Mr. Martinez.
Hola, señor Martínez.
(Oh-lah seh-nyohr Mahr-tee-nehs)

Hello, Mr. Gonzalez, I am the nurse in
charge.
**Hola, señor González, yo soy la enfer-
mera encargada.**
*(Oh-lah seh-nyohr Gohn-sah-lehs yoh
soh-ee lah ehn-fehr-meh-rah ehn-
kahr-gah-dah)*

Hello, Mrs. Garza, I am here to draw
your blood.
**Hola, señora Garza, estoy aquí para sa-
carle una muestra de sangre.**
*(Oh-lah seh-nyoh-rah Gahr-sah ehs-tohy
ah-kee pah-rah sah-kahr-leh oo-nah
moo-ehs-trah deh sahn-greh)*

Hello, Mrs. Mora.
Hola, señora Mora.
(Oh-lah seh-nyoh-rah Moh-rah)

Burp him.
Hágalo eructar/repetir.
(Ah-gah-loh eh-rook-tahr/reh-peh-teer)

Helpful . . .
Util . . .
(Oo-teel)

Her rings.
Sus anillos.
(Soos ah-nee-yohs).

Hi!
¡Hola!
(Oh-lah)

His pens and yours.
Sus plumas y las de usted.
(Soos ploo-mahs ee lahs deh oos-tehd)

Hold it!
¡Deténlo!
(Deh-tehn-loh)

Hold my finger.
Detén mi dedo.
(Deh-tehn mee deh-doh)

Hold your breath.
No respire.
(Noh rehs-pee-reh)

Hospital policy.
Reglas del hospital.
(Reh-glahs dehl ohs-pee-tahl)

How?
¿Cómo?
(Koh-moh)

How are you?
¿Cómo está?
(Koh-moh ehs-tah)

How are you, Mrs. Garcia?
¿Cómo está, Señora García?
*(Koh-moh ehs-tah sehn-nyoh-rah Gahr-
see-ah)*

How did you do it?
¿Cómo lo hizo?
(Koh-moh-loh ee-soh)

How did you get here?
¿Cómo llegó aquí?
(Koh-moh yeh-goh ah-kee)

How do you feel?
¿Cómo se siente?
(Koh-moh seh see-ehn-teh)

How do you like your eggs cooked?
¿Cómo le gustan los huevos?
(Koh-moh leh goos-tahn lohs oo-eh-bohs)

How do you like hot dogs?
**¿Cómo le gustan los emparedados de
salchicha/perros calientes?**
*(Koh-moh leh goos-tahn lohs ehm-pah-
reh-dah-dohs deh sahl-chee-chah/
peh-rohs kah-lee-ehn-tehs)*

How do you like your coffee?
¿Cómo le gusta el café?
(Koh-moh leh goos-tah ehl kah-feh)

How do you spend the day?
¿Cómo pasa el día?
(Koh-moh pah-sah ehl dee-ah)

How far?
¿Qué tan lejos?
(Keh tahn leh-hohs)

How long?
¿Cuánto tiempo?
(Koo-ahn-toh tee-ehm-poh)

How long ago?
¿Cuánto tiempo hace?
(Koo-ahn-toh tee-ehm-poh ah-seh)

How long have you been sick?
¿Cuánto tiempo hace que está enfermo?
(Koo-ahn-toh tee-ehm-poh ah-seh keh ehs-tah ehn-fehr-moh)

How many?
¿Cuántos?
(Koo-ahn-tohs)

How many boys/girls?
¿Cuántos niños/niñas?
(Koo-ahn-tohs nee-nyohs/nee-nyahs)

How many cigarettes per day?
¿Cuántos cigarrillos por día?
(Koo-ahn-tohs see-gah-rree-yohs pohr dee-ah)

How many cups per day?
¿Cuántas tazas diarias?
(Koo-ahn-tahs tah-sahs dee-ah-ree-ahs)

How many diapers have you changed since yesterday?
¿Cuántos pañales ha cambiado desde ayer?
(Koo-ahn-tohs pah-nyah-lehs ah kahm-bee-ah-doh dehs-deh ah-yehr)

How many friends do you have?
¿Cuántos amigos tiene?
(Koo-ahn-tohs ah-mee-gohs tee-eh-neh)

How many hours do you sleep?
¿Cuántas horas duerme?
(Koo-ahn-tahs oh-rahs doo-ehr-meh)

How many hours do you work?
¿Cuántas horas trabaja?
(Koo-ahn-tahs oh-rahs trah-bah-hah)

How many ounces does he take?
¿Cuántas onzas toma?
(Koo-ahn-tahs ohn-sahs toh-mah)

How many persons are there in your family?
¿Cuántas personas constituyen su familia?
(Koo-ahn-tahs pehr-soh-nahs kohns-tee-too-yehn soo fah-mee-lee-ah)

How many times a day?
¿Cuántas veces al día?
(Koo-ahn-tahs beh-sehs ahl dee-ah)

How many times do you eat per day?
¿Cuántas veces come por día?
(Koo-ahn-tahs beh-sehs koh-meh pohr dee-ah)

How many times does he wake up?
¿Cuántas veces se despierta durante la noche?
(Koo-ahn-tahs beh-sehs seh dehs-pee-ehr-tah doo-rahn-teh lah noh-che)

How many times has he vomited?
¿Cuántas veces ha vomitado?
(Koo-ahn-tahs beh-sehs ah boh-mee-tah-doh)

For how many years did you go to school?
¿Cuántos años fué a la escuela?
(Koo-ahn-tohs ah-nyohs foo-eh ah lah ehs-koo-eh-lah)

How much?
¿Cuánto?
(Koo-ahn-toh)

How much do you drink per day?
¿Cuánto alcohol toma por día?
(Koo-ahn-toh ahl-kohl toh-mah pohr dee-ah)

How much water do you drink?
¿Cuánta agua toma?
(Koo-ahn-tah ah-goo-ah toh-mah)

How often do you feed the baby?
¿Qué tan a menudo alimenta al bebé?
(Keh tahn ah meh-noo-doh ah-lee-mehn-tah ahl beh-beh)

How often do you urinate?
¿Cuántas veces orina?
(Koo-ahn-tahs beh-sehs oh-ree-nah)

How old are you/they?
¿Cuántos años tiene/tienen?
(Koo-ahn-tohs ah-nyohs tee-eh-neh/tee-ehn-ehn)

Husband/Wife/Children?
¿Esposo/Esposa/Hijos?
(Ehs-poh-soh/ehs-poh-sah/ee-hohs)

I am . . .
Yo soy . . .
(Yoh soh-ee)

I am afraid of getting lost.
Tengo miedo de perderme.
(Tehn-goh mee-eh-doh deh pehr-dehr-meh)

I am back.
Ya regresé.
(Yah reh-greh-seh)

I am continuously . . .
Continuamente estoy . . .
(Kohn-tee-noo-ah-mehn-teh ehs-tohy)

I am Dr. Blanco.
Yo soy el doctor Blanco.
(Yoh soh-ee ehl dohk-tohr Blahn-koh)

I am going to ask you several questions!
¡Voy a hacerle muchas preguntas!
(Boy ah ah-sehr-leh moo-chahs preh-goon-tahs)

I am going to cover you.
Lo voy a cubrir.
(Loh boy ah koo-breer)

I am going to cover you with a sheet.
Voy a cubrirlo con una sábana.
(Boy ah koo-breer-loh kohn oo-nah sah-bah-nah)

I am going to examine you.
Voy a examinarte.
(Boy ah ehx-ah-mee-nahr-teh)

I am going to explain the collection of urine.
Le voy a explicar la colección de orina.
(Leh boy ah ehx-plee-kahr lah koh-lehk-see-ohn deh oh-ree-nah)

I am going to help you.
Voy a ayudarlo a acostarse.
(Boy ah ah-yoo-dahr-loh ah ah-kohs-tahr-seh)

I am going to give you a list.
Voy a darle una lista.
(Boy ah dahr-leh oo-nah lees-tah)

I am going to give you a tour of the floor.
Voy a darle un recorrido por el piso.
(Boy ah dahr-leh oon reh-koh-rree-doh pohr ehl pee-soh)

I am going to help you lie on the stretcher.
Voy a ayudarlo a acostarse en la camilla.

(Boy ah ah-yoo-dahr-loh ah ah-kohs-tahr-seh ehn lah kah-mee-yah)

I am going to hit you gently.
Voy a darle golpecitos.
(Boy ah dahr-leh gohl-peh-see-tohs)

I am going to let you rest.
Voy a dejarlo descansar.
(Boy ah deh-hahr-loh dehs-kahn-sahr)

I am going to lift your sleeve.
Voy a levantar la manga.
(Boy ah leh-bahn-tahr lah mahn-gah)

I am going to put on a Band-Aid.
Voy a ponerle una cinta adhesiva/un curita/bandaid.
(Boy ah poh-nehr-leh oo-nah seen-tah ah-deh-see-bah/oon koo-ree-tah/bahn-dah-eed)

I am going to put a splint on the leg.
Voy a ponerle una tablilla en la pierna.
(Boy ah poh-nehr-leh oo-nah tah-blee-yah ehn lah pee-ehr-nah)

I am going to take X-rays of the abdomen, first.
Primero voy a tomar rayos X del abdomen.
(Pree-meh-roh boy ah toh-mahr rah-yohs eh-kiss dehl ahb-doh-mehn)

I am hurting a lot.
Tengo mucho dolor.
(Tehn-goh moo-choh doh-lohr)

I am Mexican.
Soy mexicana.
(Soh-ee meh-hee-kah-nah)

I am putting a casette under your waist.
Estoy poniendo una casetera abajo de la cintura.
(Ehs-toh-ee poh-nee-ehn-doh oo-nah kah-seh-teh-rah ah-bah-hoh deh lah seen-too-rah)

I am putting in a temporary filling.
Le aplicaré empaste temporal.
(Leh ah-plee-kah-reh ehm-pahs-teh tehm-poh-rahl)

I am sorry, we have no toothpicks.
Lo siento, no hay palillos.
(Loh see-ehn-toh noh ah-ee pah-lee-yohs)

I am the dentist.
Yo soy el/la dentista.
(Yo soh-ee ehl/lah dehn-tees-tah)

I am the doctor(m).
Yo soy el doctor/médico.
(Yoh soh-ee ehl dohk-tohr/meh-dee-koh)

I am the doctor(f).
Yo soy la doctora/médica.
(Yo soh-ee lah dohk-tohr-ah/meh-dee-kah)

I am the nurse.
Yo soy el/la enfermero(a).
(Yoh soh-ee ehl/lah ehn-fehr-meh-roh[-rah])

I am the medical student.
Yo soy el/la estudiante de medicina.
(Yo soh-ee ehl/lah ehs-too-dee-ahn-teh deh meh-dee-see-nah)

I am the social worker.
Yo soy el/la trabajador(a) social.
(Yo soh-ee ehl/lah trah-bah-hah-dohr [-doh-rah] soh-see-ahl)

I am the technician.
Yo soy el/la técnico(a).
(Yo soh-ee ehl/lah tehk-nee-koh[-kah])

I am the therapist.
Yo soy el/la terapista.
(Yoh soh-ee ehl/lah teh-rah-pees-tah)

I am through.
Ya terminé.
(Yah tehr-mee-neh)

I can stop.
Puedo pararme.
(Poo-eh-doh pah-rahr-meh)

I cannot read English, can you help me?
No puedo leer inglés, ¿puede ayudarme?
(Noh poo-eh-doh leh-ehr een-glehs poo-eh-deh ah-yoo-dahr-meh)

I charged.
Yo cobré.
(Yoh koh-breh)

I checked your X-rays.
Revisé sus ratos X.
(Reh-bee-seh soos rah-yos eh-kiss)

I don't have a pen, either.
Tampoco tengo una pluma.
(Tahm-poh-koh tehn-goh oo-nah ploo-mah)

I don't like to study, but to go to the movies.
No me gusta estudiar, sino ir al cine.

(Noh meh goos-tah ehs-too-dee-ahr see-noh eer ahl see-neh)

I don't like to study, but to go to the theater.
No me gusta estudiar, sino ir al teatro.
(Noh meh goos-tah ehs-too-dee-ahr see-noh eer ahl teh-ah-troh)

I don't think so.
No lo creo.
(Noh loh kreh-oh)

I go downtown on Tuesdays.
Los martes voy al centro.
(Lohs mahr-tehs boy ahl sehn-troh)

I go to sleep at eleven.
Me duermo a las once.
(Meh doo-ehr-moh ah lahs ohn-seh)

I have a piece of paper.
Tengo un pedazo de papel.
(Tehn-goh oon peh-dah-soh deh pah-pehl)

I have finished the exam.
Terminé de revisarte/revisarlo[la].
(Tehr-mee-neh deh reh-bee-sahr-teh/rreh-bee-sahr-loh[lah])

I have first-hand information.
Tengo información directa.
(Tehn-goh een-fohr-mah-see-ohn dee-rek-tah)

I have neither paper nor pencil.
No tengo ni papel ni lápiz.
(Noh tehn-goh nee pah-pehl nee lah-pees)

I have some paper.
Tengo papel.
(Tehn-goh pah-pehl)

I have to enter the information into the computer.
Tengo que poner la información en la computadora.
(Tehn-goh keh poh-nehr lah een-fohr-mah-see-ohn ehn lah kohm-poo-tah-doh-rah)

I have to pull your tooth.
Tengo que extraer/sacar la muela.
(Tehn-goh keh ehx-trah-ehr/sah-kahr lah moo-eh-lah)

I hope you do well.
Que siga bien.
(Keh see-gah bee-ehn)

I like green (that which is green).
Me gusta lo verde.
(Meh goos-tah loh behr-deh)

I like summer.
Me gusta el verano.
(Meh goos-tah ehl beh-rah-noh)

I need better directions.
Necesito mejores direcciones.
*(Neh-seh-see-toh meh-hoh-rehs dee-rehk-
see-ohn-ehs)*

I need to ask you some questions.
Necesito hacerle unas preguntas.
*(Neh-seh-see-toh ah-sehr-leh oo-nahs
preh-goon-tahs)*

I need to cut your pants.
Necesito cortar el pantalón.
*(Neh-seh-see-toh kohr-tahr ehl pahn-tah-
lohn)*

I need to go to the surgery clinic.
Necesito ir a la clínica de cirugía.
*(Neh-seh-see-toh eer ah lah klee-nee-kah
deh see-roo-hee-ah)*

I need to see Doctor White.
Necesito ver al doctor White.
*(Neh-seh-see-toh behr ahl dohk-tohr
White)*

I need to see if you are hurt.
Necesito ver si está lastimado.
*(Neh-seh-see-toh behr see ehs-tah lahs-
tee-mah-doh)*

I need to use a tourniquet.
**Necesito usar un torniquete/una
ligadura.**
*(Neh-seh-see-toh oo-sahr oon tohr-nee-
keh-teh/oon-ah lee-gah-doo-rah)*

I need two tubes of blood.
Necesito dos tubos de sangre.
*(Neh-seh-see-toh dohs too-bohs deh
sahn-greh)*

I pulled your tooth.
Le saqué la muela.
(Leh sah-keh lah moo-eh-lah)

I see how good she is.
Ya veo lo buena que es.
(Yah beh-oh loh boo-eh-nah keh ehs)

I see no one.
No veo a nadie.
(Noh beh-oh ah nah-dee-eh)

I see no one here.
No veo a nadie aquí.
(Noh beh-oh ah nah-dee-eh ah-kee)

I think the same as you.
Pienso lo mismo que usted.
(Pee-ehn-soh loh mees-moh keh oos-tehd)

I want . . .
Yo quiero . . .
(Yoh kee-eh-roh . . .)

I want something to drink!
¡Yo quiero algo de tomar/beber!
*(Yoh kee-eh-roh ahl-goh deh toh-mahr/
beh-behr)*

I want something to eat!
¡Yo quiero algo de comer!
(Yoh kee-eh-roh ahl-goh deh koh-mehr)

I want something to read!
¡Yo quiero algo para leer!
(Yoh kee-eh-roh ahl-goh pah-rah leh-ehr)

I want to see if the X-rays are good.
Quiero ver si los rayos X salieron bien.
*(Kee-eh-roh behr see lohs rah-yohs eh-
kiss sah-lee-eh-rohn bee-ehn)*

I want to talk to you.
Quiero hablar con usted.
(Kee-eh-roh ah-blahr kohn oos-tehd)

I want to talk to you about plaque.
**Quiero platicarle acerca de la placa
bacteriana.**
*(Kee-eh-roh plah-tee-kahr-leh ah-sehr-
kah deh lah plah-kah bahk-teh-ree-
ah-nah)*

I want to test your sugar level.
Quiero ver el nivel de azúcar.
*(Kee-eh-roh behr ehl nee-behl deh ah-
soo-kahr)*

I want to be a nurse.
Quiero ser enfermera.
(Kee-eh-roh sehr ehn-fehr-meh-rah)

I want to be a good nurse.
Quiero ser una buena enfermera.
*(Kee-eh-roh sehr oo-nah boo-eh-nah ehn-
fehr-meh-rah)*

I want to examine the older child.
Quiero examinar al niño mayor.
*(Kee-eh-roh ehx-ah-mee-nahr ahl nee-
nyoh mah-yohr)*

I want to take a blood sample from your finger.
Quiero tomar una muestra de sangre del dedo.
(Kee-eh-roh toh-mahr oo-nah moo-ehs-trah deh sahn-greh dehl deh-doh)

I want you to write your name and to-day's date.
Quiero que escriba su nombre y la fecha de hoy.
(Kee-eh-roh keh ehs-kree-bah soo nohm-breh ee lah feh-chah deh oh-ee)

I was told to come here.
Me dijeron que viniera.
(Meh dee-heh-rohn keh bee-nee-eh-rah)

I will ask you to urinate.
Le diré que orine.
(Leh dee-reh keh oh-ree-neh)

I am going to auscultate.
Voy a auscultar/escuchar.
(Boy ah ah-oos-kool-tahr/ehs-koo-chahr)

I am going to call the radiologist.
Voy a hablarle al radiólogo.
(Boy ah ah-blahr-leh ahl rah-dee-oh-loh-goh)

I will call transportation.
Llamaré al transporte.
(Yah-mah-reh ahl trahns-pohr-teh)

I am going to check your arm.
Voy a revisar el brazo.
(Boy ah reh-bee-sahr ehl brah-soh)

I am going to check your ears.
Voy a revisar las orejas.
(Boy ah reh-bee-sahr lahs oh-reh-hahs)

I am going to check your eyes.
Voy a revisar los ojos.
(Boy ah reh-bee-sahr lohs oh-hohs)

I am going to check your hand.
Voy a revisar la mano.
(Boy ah reh-bee-sahr lah mah-noh)

I am going to check your mouth.
Voy a revisar la boca.
(Boy ah reh-bee-sahr lah boh-kah)

I am going to check your nose.
Voy a revisar la nariz.
(Boy ah reh-bee-sahr lah nah-rees)

I am going to check your throat.
Voy a revisar la garganta.
(Boy ah reh-bee-sahr lah gahr-gahn-tah)

I am going to check your abdomen.
Voy a revisar el abdomen.
(Boy ah reh-bee-sahr ehl ahb-doh-mehn)

I am going to check your gums.
Voy a revisar tus encías.
(Boy ah reh-bee-sahr toos ehn-see-ahs)

I am going to check your head.
Voy a revisar tu cabeza.
(Boy ah reh-bee-sahr too kah-beh-sah)

I am going to check your liver.
Voy a revisar tu hígado.
(Boy ah reh-bee-sahr too ee-gah-doh)

I am going to check your teeth.
Voy a revisar tus dientes.
(Boh ah reh-bee-sahr toos dee-ehn-tehs)

I am going to collect a stool sample.
Voy a recoger una muestra de excremento.
(Boh ah reh-koh-hehr oo-nah moo-ehs-trah deh ehx-kreh-mehn-toh)

I am going by examine your anus, strain down.
Voy a examinar el ano. Empuja, haz fuerza.
(Boy ah ehx-ah-mee-nahr ehl ah-noh. Ehm-poo-hah, ahs foo-ehr-sah)

I am going to examine your back.
Voy a examinar la espalda.
(Boh ah ehx-ah-mee-nahr lah ehs-pahl-dah)

I am going to examine your foot.
Voy a examinar el pie.
(Boy an ehx-ah-mee-nahr ehl pee-eh)

I am going to examine your genitalia.
Voy a examinar los genitales.
(Boy ah ehx-ah-mee-nahr lohs heh-nee-tah-lehs)

I am going to examine your leg.
Voy a examinar la pierna.
(Boy ah ehx-ah-mee-nahr lah pee-ehr-nah)

I am going to examine your rectum.
Voy a examinar el recto.
(Boy ah ehx-ah-mee-nahr ehl rehk-toh)

I am going to examine your fingernails.
Voy a examinar la base de tus uñas.
(Boy ah ehx-ah-mee-nahr lah bah-seh deh toos oo-nyahs)

I will give you recommendations for you and your baby.
Le daré recomendaciones para usted y para su bebé.
(Leh dah-reh reh-koh-mehn-dah-see-ohn-ehs pah-rah oos-tehd ee pah-rah soo beh-beh)

I will help you sit.
Le ayudaré a sentarse.
(Leh ah-yoo-dah-reh ah sehn-tahr-seh)

I am going to inspect your chest.
Voy a revisar tu pecho.
(Boy ah reh-bee-sahr too peh-choh)

I am going to inspect your skin.
Voy a inspeccionar tu piel.
(Boy ah eens-pehk-see-oh-nahr too pee-ehl)

First, I am going to listen.
Primero voy a escuchar.
(Pree-meh-roh boy ah ehs-koo-chahr)

I am going to listen to your heart.
Voy a escuchar el corazón.
(Boy ah ehs-koo-chahr ehl koh-rah-sohn)

I am going to listen to your lungs.
Voy a escuchar los pulmones.
(Boy ah ehs-koo-chahr lohs pool-mohn-ehs)

I am going to listen to your apical pulse.
Voy a escuchar el latido del corazón.
(Boy ah ehs-koo-chahr ehl lah-tee-doh dehl koh-rah-sohn)

I will not find the street.
No encontraré la calle.
(Noh ehn-kohn-trah-reh lah kah-yeh)

I am going to observe the jugular vein.
Voy a observar tu vena yugular.
(Boy ah ohb-sehr-bahr too beh-nah yoo-goo-lahr)

I am going to palpate.
Voy a palpar/tocar.
(Boy ah pahl-pahr/toh-kahr)

I am going to palpate deeply.
Voy a palpar hondo.
(Boy ah pahl-pahr ohn-doh)

I am going to palpate it.
Voy a palparla.
(Boy ah pahl-pahr-lah)

I am going to palpate lightly.
Voy a palpar ligero.
(Boy ah pahl-pahr lee-heh-roh)

I am going to palpate your abdomen.
Voy a palpar el abdomen.
(Boy ah pahl-pahr ehl ahb-doh-mehn).

I am going to palpate your axillary nodes.
Voy a palpar los nodos de la axila.
(Boy ah pahl-pahr lohs noh-dohs deh lah ahx-ee-lah)

I am going to palpate your breast.
Voy a palpar el seno.
(Boy ah pahl-pahr ehl seh-noh)

I am going to palpate your elbow.
Voy a palpar el codo.
(Boy ah pahl-pahr ehl koh-doh)

I am going to palpate your groin. Strain down.
Voy a palpar las ingles. Empuja/empuje.
(Boy ah pahl-pahr lahs een-glehs. Ehm-poo-hah/ehm-poo-heh)

I am going to palpate the hand.
Voy a palpar la mano.
(Boy ah pahl-pahr lah mah-noh)

I am going to palpate nodes.
Voy a palpar los nodos.
(Boy ah pahl-pahr lohs noh-dohs)

I am going to palpate the rectum.
Voy a palpar el recto.
(Boy ah pahl-pahr ehl rehk-toh)

I am going to palpate the shoulder.
Voy a palpar el hombro.
(Boy ah pahl-pahr ehl ohm-broh)

I am going to palpate with both hands.
Voy a palpar con las dos manos.
(Boy ah pahl-pahr kohn lahs dohs mah-nohs)

I am going to palpate your carotid pulse.
Voy a palpar el pulso de la carótida.
(Boy ah pahl-pahr ehl pool-soh deh lah kah-roh-tee-dah)

I am going to palpate your chest.
Voy a palpar el pecho.
(Boy ah pahl-pahr ehl peh-choh)

I am going to palpate your feet and ankles.
Voy a palpar tus pies y tus tobillos.
(Boy ah pahl-pahr toos pee-ehs ee toos toh-bee-yohs)

I am going to palpate your knees.
Voy a palpar tus rodillas.
(Boy ah pahl-pahr toos roh-dee-yahs)

I am going to tap.
Voy a percutir.
(Boy ah pehr-koo-teer)

I am going to tap your side.
Voy a percutir tu costado.
(Boy ah pehr-koo-teer too kohs-tah-doh)

I am going to press on your big toe.
Voy a apretar tu dedo gordo.
(Boy ah ah-preh-tahr too deh-doh gohr-doh)

I am going to put you on the stretcher.
Voy a ponerlo en la camilla.
(Boy ah poh-nehr-loh ehn lah kah-mee-yah)

I will remind you during the day.
Le recordaré durante el día.
(Leh reh-kohr-dah-reh doo-rahn-teh ehl dee-ah)

I will return!
¡Regresaré!
(Reh-greh-sah-reh)

I will return shortly.
Regreso en seguida.
(Reh-greh-soh ehn seh-ggee-dah)

I will return to ask you more questions.
Regresaré para hacerle más preguntas.
(Reh-greh-sah-reh pah-rah ah-sehr-leh mahs preh-goon-tahs)

I am going to see the strength of the abdominal muscle.
Voy a ver la fuerza del músculo abdominal.
(Boy ah behr lah foo-ehr-sah dehl moos-koo-loh ahb-doh-mee-nahl)

I will see you, Mrs. Garcia.
Hasta luego, señora García.
(Ahs-tah loo-eh-goh seh-nyoh-rah Gahr-see-ah)

I will see you tomorrow.
La veré mañana.
(Lah beh-reh mah-nyah-nah)

I will see you tomorrow at 9 A.M.
Lo veré mañana a las nueve.
(Loh beh-reh mah-nyah-nah ah lahs noo-eh-beh)

I will show you your room.
Le mostraré su cuarto.
(Leh mohs-trah-reh soo koo-ahr-toh)

I am going to start by taking your vital signs.
Voy a empezar por tomar los signos vitales.
(Boy ah ehm-peh-sahr pohr toh-mahr lohs seeg-nohs bee-tah-lehs)

I am going to take the radial pulse.
Voy a tomar su pulso radial.
(Boy ah toh-mahr soo pool-soh rah-dee-ahl)

I am going to take your blood pressure.
Voy a tomar tu presión de sangre.
(Boy ah toh-mahr too preh-see-ohn deh sahn-greh)

I will talk to your mother again.
Hablaré con tu mamá otra vez.
(Ah-blah-reh kohn too mah-mah oh-trah behs)

I will use a local anesthetic.
Le pondré/aplicaré anestesia local.
(Leh pohn-dreh/ah-plee-kah-reh ah-nehs-teh-see-ah loh-kahl)

I will use resins.
Usaré resinas.
(Oo-sah-reh reh-see-nahs)

I am going to wake you up in the morning.
La voy a despertar en la mañana.
(Lah boy ah dehs-pehr-tahr ehn lah mah-nyah-nah)

I would like to talk to you.
Me gustaría hablar contigo (con usted).
(Meh goos-tah-ree-ah ah-blahr kohn-tee-goh [kohn oos-tehd])

I'll call for a wheelchair.
Pediré una silla de ruedas.
(Peh-dee-reh oo-nah see-yah deh roo-eh-dahs)

I'm going to clean your teeth.
Voy a limpiarle los dientes.
(Boy ah leem-pee-ahr-leh lohs dee-ehn-tehs)

I'm going to polish your teeth.
Voy a pulir sus dientes.
(Boy ah poo-leer soos dee-ehn-tehs)

I will take X-rays.
Le tomaré radiografías.
(Leh toh-mah-reh rah-dee-oh-grah-fee-ahs)

If it hurts, tell me.
Si le duele, avíseme.
(See leh doo-eh-leh, ah-bee-seh-meh)

If it is abundant, or there is fever.
Si es abundante, o aparece fiebre.
(See ehs ah-boon-dahn-teh, oh ah-pah-reh-seh fee-eh-breh)

If it is far, could I drive?
¿Si está lejos, podría manejar?
(See ehs-tah leh-hohs, poh-dree-ah mah-neh-hahr)

If nurses find expired items on the unit, they return them to the pharmacy for replacement.
Si las enfermeras encuentran artículos con fecha vencida, los regresan a la farmacia donde son reemplazados.
(See lahs ehn-fehr-meh-rahs ehn-koo-ehn-trahn ahr-tee-koo-lohs kohn feh-chah behn-see-dah, lohs reh-greh-sahn ah lah fahr-mah-see-ah dohn-deh sohn reh-ehm-plah-sah-dohs)

If you do not have ice in the bucket, please call me.
Si no tiene hielo en la tina, llámeme.
(See noh tee-eh-neh ee-eh-loh ehn lah tee-nah, yah-meh-meh)

If you do not understand, please let me know.
Si no entiende, dígame, por favor.
(See noh ehn-tee-ehn-deh, dee-gah-meh pohr fah-bohr)

If you follow these recommendations.
Si usted sigue estos consejos.
(See oos-tehd see-geh ehs-tohs kohn-seh-hohs)

If you have been here, I need your card.
Si ha estado aquí, necesito su tarjeta.
(See ah ehs-tah-doh ah-kee, neh-seh-see-toh soo tahr-heh-tah)

If you haven't, please fill out these papers.
Si no, por favor llene estos papeles.
(See noh, pohr fah-bohr yeh-neh ehs-tohs pah-peh-lehs)

If you need more sheets, call the assistant.
Si necesita más sábanas, llame a la asistente.
(See neh-seh-see-tah mahs sah-bah-nahs, yah-meh ah lah ah-sees-tehn-teh)

If you see anything wrong, take him to the doctor.
Si nota algo malo, llévelo a su médico.
(See noh-tah ahl-goh mah-loh, yeh-beh-loh ah soo meh-dee-koh)

If you want to watch T.V., you have to pay a fee.
Si quiere ver el televisor, tiene que pagar una cuota.
(See kee-eh-reh behr ehl teh-leh-bee-sohr, tee-eh-neh keh pah-gahr oo-nah koo-oh-tah)

In addition . . .
Además . . .
(Ah-deh-mahs)

In case of fire, take the stairs.
En caso de fuego, use las escaleras.
(Ehn kah-soh deh foo-eh-goh, oo-seh lahs ehs-kah-leh-rahs)

In case of a medication error, the doctor is notified.
En caso de un error con el medicamento, se le notifica al doctor.
(Ehn kah-soh deh oon eh-rohr kohn ehl meh-dee-kah-mehn-toh, seh leh noh-tee-fee-kah ahl dohk-tohr)

In large . . .
En gran parte . . .
(Ehn grahn pahr-teh)

In that case, tell me your full name.
En ese caso, dígame su nombre completo.
(Ehn eh-seh kah-soh, dee-gah-meh soo nohm-breh kohm-pleh-toh)

In the middle of . . .
A mediados de . . .
(Ah meh-dee-ah-dohs deh)

In your case, eat nothing after 8 P.M.
En su caso, no coma nada después de las ocho de la noche.
(Ehn soo kah-soh, noh koh-mah nah-dah dehs-poo-ehs deh lahs oh-choh deh lah noh-cheh)

Is he at work?
¿Está trabajando?
(Ehs-tah trah-bah-hahn-doh)

Is he breast-feeding?
¿Está tomando el pecho?
(Ehs-tah toh-mahn-doh ehl peh-choh)

Is he coughing?
¿Está tosiendo?
(Ehs-tah toh-see-ehn-doh)

Is he eating well?
¿Está comiendo bien?
(Ehs-tah koh-mee-ehn-doh bee-ehn)

Is he with you?
¿El viene con usted?
(Ehl bee-ehn-eh kohn oos-tehd)

Is he sleeping well?
¿Está durmiendo bien?
(Ehs-tah door-mee-ehn-doh bee-ehn)

Is he taking formula?
¿Está tomando fórmula?
(Ehs-tah toh-mahn-doh fohr-moo-lah)

Is he urinating well?
¿Orina bien?
(Oh-ree-nah bee-ehn)

Is it a dry cough?
¿Es tos seca?
(Ehs tohs seh-kah)

Is it a house?
¿Es una casa?
(Ehs oo-nah kah-sah)

Is it a lot?
¿Es mucho?
(Ehs moo-choh)

Is it far?
¿Está lejos?
(Ehs-tah leh-hohs)

Is it here in town?
¿Está en esta ciudad?
(Ehs-tah ehn ehs-tah see-oo-dahd)

Is it the same color?
¿Es del mismo color?
(Ehs dehl mees-moh koh-lohr)

Is parking available?
¿Hay estacionamiento?
(Ah-ee ehs-tah-see-oh-nah-mee-ehn-toh)

Is someone with you?
¿Hay alguien con usted?
(Ah-ee ahl-ggee-ehn kohn oos-tehd)

Is that a lot?
¿Es mucho?
(Ehs moo-choh)

Is that an apartment?
¿Es apartamento?
(Ehs ah-pahr-tah-mehn-toh)

Is that enough?
¿Es suficiente?
(Ehs soo-fee-see-ehn-teh)

Is that too much?
¿Es mucho/demasiado?
(Ehs moo-choh/deh-mah-see-ah-doh)

Is there a policeman?
¿Hay algún policía?
(Ah-ee ahl-goon poh-lee-see-ah)

Is there anything that worries you?
¿Hay algo que te/le preocupa?
(Ah-ee ahl-goh keh teh/leh preh-oh-koo-pah)

Is this _____ Hospital?
¿Es éste el Hospital _____?
(Ehs ehs-teh ehl ohs-pee-tahl _____)

Is this your first time in the hospital?
¿Es su primera vez en el hospital?
(Ehs soo pree-meh-rah behs ehn ehl ohs-pee-tahl)

Is your appetite bad?
¿Tiene mal apetito?
(Tee-eh-neh mahl ah-peh-tee-toh)

Is your family in town?
¿Está su familia en la ciudad?
(Ehs-tah soo fah-mee-lee-ah ehn lah see-oo-dahd)

It also causes pyorrhea and tooth loss.
Causa pérdida de dientes y piorrea.
(Kah-oo-sah pehr-dee-dah deh dee-ehn-tehs ee pee-oh-rreh-ah)

It belongs to the doctor.
Es del doctor.
(Ehs dehl dohk-tohr)

It belongs to the teacher.
Es de la maestra.
(Ehs deh lah mah-ehs-trah)

It can cause drowsiness.
Le puede causar somnolencia.
(Leh poo-eh-deh kah-oo-sahr sohm-noh-lehn-see-ah)

It causes dental caries.
Causa caries dental.
(Kah-oo-sah kah-ree-ehs dehn-tahl)

It feels like a board.
Se siente como una tabla.
(Seh see-ehn-teh koh-moh oo-nah tah-blah)

It has the film inside.
Tiene la película adentro.
(Tee-eh-neh lah peh-lee-koo-lah ah-dehn-troh)

Does it hurt when I let go?
¿Duele cuando suelto?
(Doo-eh-leh koo-ahn-doh soo-ehl-toh)

It hurts when I press?
¿Duele cuando aprieto?
(Doo-eh-leh koo-ahn-doh ah-pree-eh-toh)

It is a six-story building.
Es un edificio de seis pisos.
(Ehs oon eh-dee-fee-see-oh deh seh-ees pee-sohs)

It is one o'clock.
Es la una.
(Ehs lah oo-nah)

It is open from 7 A.M. to 1 A.M.
Está abierta de siete de la mañana a una de la mañana.
(Ehs-tah ah-bee-ehr-tah deh see-eh-teh deh lah mah-nyah-nah ah oo-nah deh lah mah-nyah-nah)

It is open from 7 A.M. to midnight.
Está abierta de siete de la mañana a doce de la noche/medianoche.
(Ehs-tah ah-bee-ehr-tah deh see-eh-teh deh lah mah-nyah-nah ah doh-seh deh lah noh-cheh/meh-dee-ah-noh-cheh)

It is open Saturday, Sunday, and Holidays.
Está abierta los sábados, domingos y días festivos.
(Ehs-tah ah-bee-ehr-tah lohs sah-bah-dohs, doh-meen-gohs ee dee-ahs fehs-tee-bohs)

It is the next day.
Es el día siguiente.
(Ehs ehl dee-ah see-ggee-ehn-teh)

It keeps the food warm.
Guarda la comida tibia.
(Goo-ahr-dah lah koh-mee-dah tee-bee-ah).

It will take a minute.
Va a tomar un minuto.
(Bah ah toh-mahr oon mee-noo-toh)

It will take ten minutes.
Tomará diez minutos.
(Toh-mah-rah dee-ehs mee-noo-tohs)

It is in the middle of the wall.
Está en la mitad de la pared.
(Ehs-tah ah lah mee-tahd deh lah pah-rehd)

It is not very far.
No está muy lejos.
(Noh ehs-tah moo-ee leh-hohs)

You are welcome.
De nada.
(Deh nah-dah)

John, give me that bone.
Juan, déme aquel hueso.
(Hoo-ahn, deh-meh ah-kehl oo-eh-soh)

John, give me that book.
Juan, déme aquel libro.
(Hoo-ahn, deh-meh ah-kehl lee-broh)

Jump with one foot.
Brinca con un pie.
(Breen-kah kohn oon pee-eh)

Keep the baby awake.
Mantenga al bebé despierto.
(Mahn-tehn-gah ahl beh-beh dehs-pee-ehr-toh)

Keep your leg straight.
Mantenga la pierna derecha.
(Mahn-tehn-gah lah pee-ehr-nah deh-reh-chah)

Keep the siderails up at night.
Mantenga los barandales levantados durante la noche.
(Mahn-tehn-gah lohs bah-rahn-dah-lehs leh-bahn-tah-dohs doo-rahn-teh lah noh-cheh)

Keep up . . .
Continuar . . .
(Kohn-tee-noo-ahr)

Keep your feet together!
¡Ponga los pies juntos!
(Pohn-gah lohs pee-ehs hoon-tohs)

Keep your leg elevated.
Mantenga la pierna elevada.
(Mahn-tehn-gah lah pee-ehr-nah eh-leh-
bah-dah)

Kitchen personnel bring the food trays.
Los empleados de la cocina traen las ban-
dejas con comida.
(Lohs ehm-pleh-ah-dohs deh lah koh-see-
nah trah-ehn lahs bahn-deh-hahs
kohn koh-mee-dah)

Kneel down!
¡Póngase de rodillas!
(Pohn-gah-seh deh roh-dee-yahs)

Leave behind.
Abandonar.
(Ah-bahn-doh-nahr)

Leave the area uncovered.
Deje el área descubierta.
(Deh-heh ehl ah-reh-ah dehs-koo-bee-
ehr-tah)

Left . . .
Izquierdo . . .
(Ees-kee-ehr-doh . . .)

Let it go.
Exhala.
(Ehx-ah-lah)

Let it out slowly.
Exhala despacio.
(Ehx-ah-lah dehs-pah-see-oh)

Let me know how you feel.
Dígame cómo se siente.
(Dee-gah-meh koh-moh seh see-ehn-teh)

Lie down!
¡Acuéstese!
(Ah-koo-ehs-teh-seh)

Lie down, please.
Acuéstate, por favor.
(Ah-koo-ehs-tah-teh, pohr fah-bohr)

Lift your foot.
Levante el pie.
(Leh-bahn-teh ehl pee-eh)

Lift your arm.
Levanta tu brazo.
(Leh-bahn-tah too brah-soh)

Lift your hand.
Levanta tu mano.
(Leh-bahn-tah too mah-noh)

Lift your head.
Levante la cabeza.
(Leh-bahn-teh lah kah-beh-sah)

Lift your leg.
Levante la pierna.
(Leh-bahn-teh lah pee-ehr-nah)

Lift your right foot.
Levante el pie derecho.
(Leh-bahn-teh ehl pee-eh deh-reh-choh)

The lips should not be dry.
Los labios no deben estar secos.
(Lohs lah-bee-ohs noh deh-behn ehs-tahr
seh-kohs)

Listen!
¡Escuche/Oiga!
(Ehs-koo-cheh/Oh-ee-gah)

Listen, please.
Escuchen, por favor.
(Ehs-koo-chehn, pohr fah-bohr)

Look down.
Vea abajo.
(Beh-ah ah-bah-hoh)

Look straight ahead.
Vea directo.
(Beh-ah dee-rehk-toh)

Look straight at the light.
Mire directo a la luz.
(Mee-reh dee-rehk-toh ah lah loos)

Look up.
Mire hacia arriba.
(Mee-reh ah-see-ah ah-ree-bah)

Look down!
¡Mire hacia abajo!
(Mee-reh ah-see-ah ah-bah-hoh)

Lot number.
Número de lote.
(Noo-meh-roh deh loh-teh)

Lower your foot.
Baja el pie.
(Bah-hah ehl pee-eh)

Lower your head.
Baja la cabeza.
(Bah-hah lah kah-beh-sah)

Hold it like this.
Manténlo así.
(Mahn-tehn-loh ah-see)

Make a fist!
¡Cierre la mano/haga un puño!
(See-eh-reh lah mah-noh/ah-gah oon poo-nyoh)

Burp the baby.
Haga que el bebé eructe/repita.
(Ah-gah keh ehl beh-beh eh-rook-teh/ reh-pee-tah)

Martin's pencil.
El lápiz de Martín.
(Ehl lah-pees deh Mahr-teen)

Mary has a broken foot.
María tiene el pie quebrado.
(Mah-ree-ah tee-eh-neh ehl pee-eh keh-brah-doh)

Mary II (the second) is queen.
María II (segunda) es reina.
(Mah-ree-ah seh-goon-dah ehs reh-ee-nah)

May I help you?
¿En qué puedo servirle?
(Ehn keh poo-eh-doh sehr-beer-leh)

Meet with . . .
Encontrarse con . . .
(Ehn-kohn-trahr-seh kohn)

Modern/Present day . . .
Moderno . . .
(Moh-dehr-noh)

Moist cough?
¿Tos húmeda?
(Tohs oo-meh-dah)

Monthly, the pharmacy staff inspects the medication area.
Cada mes, los empleados de la farmacia inspeccionan el área de medicamentos.
(Kah-dah mehs lohs ehm-pleh-ah-dohs deh lah fahr-mah-see-ah eens-pehk-see-ohn-ahn ehl ah-reh-ah deh meh-dee-kah-mehn-tohs)

Move it from side to side.
Muévela de lado a lado.
(Moo-eh-beh-lah deh lah-doh ah lah-doh)

Move!
¡Muévase!
(Moo-eh-bah-seh)

Move your leg.
Mueve tu pierna.
(Moo-eh-beh too pee-ehr-nah)

Move your leg backward.
Mueve tu pierna hacia atrás.
(Moo-eh-beh too pee-ehr-nah ah-see-ah ah-trahs)

Move your leg forward.
Mueve tu pierna hacia adelante.
(Moo-eh-beh too pee-ehr-nah ah-see-ah ah-deh-lahn-teh)

Mr. and Mrs. Garcia.
El señor y la señora García.
(Ehl seh-nyohr ee lah seh-nyoh-rah Gahr-see-ah)

Mr. Gomez left yesterday.
El señor Gómez salió ayer.
(Ehl seh-nyohr Goh-mehs sah-lee-oh ah-yehr)

Mr. Martinez arrives at the department.
El señor Martínez llega al departamento.
(Ehl seh-nyohr Mahr-tee-nehs yeh-gah ahl deh-pahr-tah-mehn-toh)

Mr. Rios, how are you?
Señor Ríos, ¿cómo está?
(Seh-nyohr Ree-ohs, koh-moh ehs-tah)

Mrs. Garcia, tomorrow you will be discharged from the hospital.
Señora García, mañana sale usted del hospital.
(Seh-nyoh-rah Gahr-see-ah, mah-nyah-nah sah-leh oos-tehd dehl ohs-pee-tahl)

Mrs. Garza, I want you to get up and go to the bathroom to urinate.
Señora Garza, quiero que se levante y vaya al baño a orinar.
(Seh-nyoh-rah Gahr-sah, kee-eh-roh keh seh leh-bahn-teh ee bah-yah ahl bah-nyoh ah oh-ree-nahr)

Mrs. Garza, the doctor ordered blood samples.
Señora Garza, el doctor ordenó muestras de sangre.
(Seh-nyoh-rah Gahr-sah, ehl dohk-tohr ohr-deh-noh moo-ehs-trahs deh sahn-greh)

My book and Louisa's.
Mi libro y el de Luisa.
(Mee lee-broh ee ehl deh Loo-ee-sah).

My car is prettier than yours.
Mi carro es más bonito que el tuyo.
(Mee kah-rroh ehs mahs boh-nee-toh keh ehl too-yoh)

My friend speaks French.
Mi amigo habla francés.
(Mee ah-mee-goh ah-blah Frahn-sehs)

My name is . . .
Mi nombre es . . .
(Mee nohm-breh ehs)

My name is John.
Me llamo Juan.
(Meh yah-moh Joo-ahn)

My nose is prettier than yours.
Mi nariz es más bonita que la tuya.
(Mee nah-rees ehs mahs boh-nee-tah keh lah too-yah)

Name of the drug.
Nombre de la droga/del medicamento.
(Nohm-breh deh lah droh-gah/dehl meh-dee-kah-mehn-toh)

Name of the patient.
Nombre del paciente.
(Nohm-breh dehl pah-see-ehn-teh)

Never?
¿Nunca?
(Noon-kah)

Never mind.
No importa.
(Noh eem-pohr-tah)

No, I do not speak English.
No, no hablo inglés.
(Noh, noh ah-bloh een-glehs)

No, I do not speak Spanish.
No, no hablo español.
(Noh, noh ah-bloh ehs-pah-nyohl).

No, I don't understand.
No, no comprendo/entiendo.
(Noh, noh kohm-prehn-doh/ehn-tee-ehn-doh)

No problem!
¡No hay problema!
(Noh ah-ee proh-bleh-mah)

No smoking.
No se permite fumar.
(Noh seh pehr-mee-teh foo-mahr)

None the less . . .
Sin embargo . . .
(Seen ehm-bahr-goh)

None!
¡Ninguno!
(Neen-goo-noh)

Not at all.
De ningún modo.
(Deh neen-goon moh-doh)

Now, bend over.
Ahora, agáchate.
(Ah-oh-rah, ah-gah-chah-teh)

Now, I need to X-ray the chest.
Ahora, necesito radiografiar el pecho.
(Ah-oh-rah, neh-seh-see-toh rah-dee-oh-grah-fee-ahr ehl peh-choh)

Now, I will examine your abdomen.
Ahora, voy a revisar tu abdomen/vientre.
(Ah-oh-rah, boy ah reh-bee-sahr too ahb-doh-mehn/bee-ehn-treh)

Now, I will examine your skin and chest.
Ahora, voy a examinar tu piel y tu pecho.
(Ah-oh-rah, boy ah ehx-ah-mee-nahr too pee-ehl ee too peh-choh)

Now, raise the left arm.
Ahora, levante el brazo izquierdo.
(Ah-oh-rah, leh-bahn-teh ehl brah-soh ees-kee-ehr-doh)

Now, stand up!
Ahora, ¡levántate!
(Ah-oh-rah, leh-bahn-tah-teh)

Now, stand up and walk.
Ahora, levántese y camine.
(Ah-oh-rah, leh-bahn-teh-seh ee kah-mee-neh)

Now, take a deep breath.
Ahora, respira hondo/profundo.
(Ah-oh-rah, rehs-pee-rah ohn-doh/proh-foon-doh)

Now, turn to the screen.
Ahora, voltee hacia la placa.
(Ah-oh-rah, bohl-teh-eh ah-see-ah lah plah-kah)

Now you can change clothes.
Ahora se puede cambiar de ropa.
(Ah-oh-rah seh poo-eh-deh kahm-bee-ahr deh roh-pah)

Nursing staff take STAT orders to the pharmacy.
Los empleados de enfermería llevan órdenes STAT/de emergencia a la farmacia.

(Lohs ehm-pleh-ah-dohs deh ehn-fehr-
meh-ree-ah yeh-bahn ohr-deh-nehs
EHS-TAHT/deh eh-mehr-hehn-see-ah
ah lah fahr-mah-see-ah)

Of course.
Desde luego.
(Dehs-deh loo-eh-goh)

On the one hand . . .
Por un lado . . .
(Pohr oon lah-doh)

One more time.
Una vez más.
(Oo-nah behs mahs)

One, two, three.
Uno, dos, tres.
(Oo-noh, dohs, trehs)

Open again.
Abre otra vez.
(Ah-breh oh-trah behs)

Open the fingers wide.
Abre bien los dedos.
(Ah-breh bee-ehn lohs deh-dohs)

Open your books, please.
Abran sus libros, por favor.
(Ah-brahn soos lee-brohs, pohr fah-bohr)

Open your eyes.
Abra los ojos.
(Ah-brah lohs oh-hohs)

Open your hand!
¡Abra la mano!
(Ah-brah lah mah-noh)

Open your mouth.
Abra la boca.
(Ah-brah lah boh-kah)

Open your mouth, please.
Abra la boca, por favor.
(Ah-brah lah boh-kah pohr fah-bohr)

Our country.
Nuestro país.
(Noo-ehs-troh pah-ees)

Our patient.
Nuestro paciente.
(Noo-ehs-troh pah-see-ehn-teh)

Outpatient prescriptions are filled by the
pharmacy.
Las recetas para pacientes de consulta ex-
terna son distribuidas por la farmacia.

(Lahs reh-seh-tahs pah-rah pah-see-ehn-
tehs deh kohn-sool-tah ehx-tehr-nah
sohn dees-tree-boo-ee-dahs pohr lah
fahr-mah-see-ah)

Over a period . . .
Durante un período . . .
(Doo-rahn-teh oon peh-ree-oh-doh)

Over the stool.
Sobre el taburete.
(Soh-breh ehl tah-boo-reh-teh)

Pain?
¿Dolor?
(Doh-lohr)

Pardon me!
¡Perdóneme!
(Pehr-doh-neh-meh)

Pat his back gently.
Déle palmaditas en la espalda.
(Deh-leh pahl-mah-dee-tahs ehn lah ehs-
pahl-dah)

Peanut-butter sandwich;
Emparedado de crema de cacahuate;
(Ehm-pah-reh-dah-doh deh kreh-mah
deh kah-kah-oo-ah-teh)

Phone for local calls.
Teléfono para llamadas locales.
(Teh-leh-foh-noh pah-rah yah-mah-dahs
loh-kahl-ehs)

Place the urine in the brown plastic
bottle.
Ponga la orina en la botella de plástico
café.
(Pohn-gah lah oh-ree-nah ehn lah boh-
teh-yah deh plahs-tee-koh kah-feh)

Place your arms behind the back.
Pon los brazos atrás.
(Pohn lohs brah-sohs ah-trahs)

Place your hands behind your head.
Pon tus manos detrás de tu cabeza.
(Pohn toos mah-nohs deh-trahs deh too
kah-beh-sah)

Place your feet here.
Ponga los pies aquí.
(Pohn-gah lohs pee-ehs ah-kee)

Place your foot on the opposite knee.
Pon tu pie en la rodilla opuesta.
(Pohn too pee-eh ehn lah roh-dee-yah
oh-poo-ehs-tah)

Plaque can be prevented by brushing and flossing.
La placa se evita usando hilo dental y cepillo.
(Lah plah-kah seh eh-bee-tah oo-sahn-doh ee-loh dehn-tahl ee seh-pee-yoh)

Plaque is a sticky, colorless layer of bacteria.
La placa es una capa pegajosa sin color y con bacterias.
(Lah plah-kah ehs oo-nah kah-pah peh-gah-hoh-sah seen koh-lohr ee kohn bahk-teh-ree-ahs)

Please!
¡Por favor!
(Pohr fah-bohr)

Please bend your arm for about five minutes.
Por favor, doble el brazo por cinco minutos.
(Pohr fah-bohr, doh-bleh ehl brah-soh pohr seen-koh mee-noo-tohs)

Please change your clothes.
Por favor, cámbiese de ropa.
(Pohr fah-bohr, kahm-bee-eh-seh deh roh-pah)

Please come back in a few minutes.
Por favor, regrese en unos minutos.
(Pohr fah-bohr, reh-greh-seh ehn oo-nohs mee-noo-tohs)

Please cross your legs.
Por favor, cruce las piernas.
(Pohr fah-bohr, kroo-seh lahs pee-ehr-nahs)

Please do not eat anything after midnight.
Por favor, no coma nada después de medianoche.
(Pohr fah-bohr, noh koh-mah nah-dah dehs-poo-ehs deh meh-dee-ah-noh-cheh)

Please don't move.
Por favor, no se mueva.
(Pohr fah-bohr, noh seh moo-eh-bah)

Please lie down.
Por favor, acuéstate.
(Pohr fah-bohr, ah-koo-ehs-tah-teh)

Please open your mouth some more.
Por favor, abra más la boca.
(Pohr fah-bohr, ah-brah mahs lah boh-kah)

Please raise this arm.
Por favor, levante este brazo.
(Pohr fah-bohr, leh-bahn-teh ehs-teh brah-soh)

Please raise your arm.
Por favor, levanta tu brazo.
(Pohr fah-bohr, leh-bahn-tah too brah-soh)

Please repeat slowly!
¡Por favor, repita despacio!
(Pohr fah-bohr, reh-pee-tah dehs-pah-see-oh)

Please return as needed.
En caso necesario, puede regresar.
(Ehn kah-soh neh-seh-sah-ree-oh, poo-eh-deh reh-greh-sahr)

Please return in six months.
Por favor, regrese en seis meses.
(Pohr fah-bohr, reh-greh-seh ehn seh-ees meh-sehs)

Please sign.
Por favor, firme.
(Pohr fah-bohr, feer-meh)

Please sign here.
Por favor, firme aquí.
(Pohr fah-bohr, feer-meh ah-kee)

Please sit down.
Por favor, siéntese.
(Pohr fah-bohr, see-ehn-teh-seh)

Please sit down in the waiting room.
Por favor, siéntese en la sala de espera.
(Pohr fah-bohr, see-ehn-teh-seh ehn lah sah-lah deh ehs-peh-rah)

Please sit up on the bed.
Por favor, siéntate en la cama.
(Pohr fah-bohr, see-ehn-tah-teh ehn lah kah-mah)

Please stay/remain in bed.
Por favor, quédese en la cama.
(Pohr fah-bohr, keh-deh-seh ehn lah kah-mah)

Please tell the nurse to call me.
Por favor, dígale a la enfermera que me llame.
(Pohr fah-bohr, dee-gah-leh ah lah ehn-fehr-meh-rah keh meh yah-meh)

Please wait a few minutes.
Por favor, espere unos minutos.
(Pohr fah-bohr, ehs-peh-reh oo-nohs mee-noo-tohs)

Please wait about 30 minutes.
Por favor, espere treinta minutos.
(Pohr fah-bohr, ehs-peh-reh treh-een-tah mee-noo-tohs)

Point out.
Señalarlo/Apuntarlo.
(Seh-nyah-lahr-loo/Ah-poon-tahr-loh)

Point when it hurts.
Señale donde le duela.
(Seh-nyah-leh dohn-deh leh doo-eh-lah)

Pronounce, please.
Pronuncien, por favor.
(Proh-noon-see-ehn, pohr fah-bohr)

Pull the emergency cord in the bathroom.
Jale el cordón de emergencia en el baño.
(Hah-leh ehl kohr-dohn deh eh-mehr-hehn-see-ah ehn ehl bah-nyoh)

Pull the knee to the chest.
Levanta la rodilla hasta pecho.
(Leh-bahn-tah lah roh-dee-yah ahs-tah peh-choh)

Push.
Haz fuerza/empuja/puja.
(Ahs foo-ehr-sah/ehm-poo-hah/poo-hah)

Raise your head.
Levanta tu cabeza.
(Leh-bahn-tah too kah-beh-sah)

Rather than . . .
Más bien que . . .
(Mahs bee-ehn keh)

Read this, please.
Lea, por favor.
(Leh-ah, pohr fah-bohr)

Recall?
¿Recuerda?
(Reh-koo-ehr-dah)

Registered/on record . . .
Registrado . . .
(Reh-hees-trah-doh)

Relax!
¡Relájese/Descanse!
(Reh-lah-heh-seh/Dehs-kahn-seh)

Relax, calm down.
Relájese, cálmese.
(Reh-lah-heh-seh, kahl-meh-seh)

Relax, it will not hurt!
¡Relájese, no le va a doler!

(Reh-lah-heh-seh, noh leh bah ah doh-lehr)

Relax your muscle.
Relaja tu músculo.
(Reh-lah-hah too moos-koo-loh)

Rely on . . .
Confiar . . .
(Kohn-fee-ahr)

Remember that you are to urinate and put it into the container.
Recuerde que debe orinar y poner la orina en el recipiente.
(Reh-koo-ehr-deh keh deh-beh oh-ree-nahr ee poh-nehr lah oh-ree-nah ehn ehl reh-see-pee-ehn-teh)

Remember that you will do this for 24 hours.
Recuerde que hará esto por veinticuatro horas.
(Reh-koo-ehr-deh keh ah-rah ehs-toh pohr beh-een-tee-koo-ah-troh oh-rahs)

Remember to bring them back.
Acuérdese de traerlos.
(Ah-koo-ehr-deh-seh deh trah-ehr-lohs)

Repeat one, two, three.
Repite uno, dos, tres.
(Reh-pee-teh oo-noh, dohs, trehs)

Repeat, please.
Repitan, por favor.
(Reh-pee-tahn, pohr fah-bohr)

Repeat the word "99."
Repite la palabra "noventa y nueve."
(Reh-pee-teh lah pah-lah-brah noh-behn-tah ee noo-eh-beh)

Return in 10 days.
Regrese en diez días.
(Reh-greh-seh ehn dee-ehs dee-ahs)

Right . . .
Derecho . . .
(Deh-reh-choh)

Rinse your mouth.
Enjuague su boca.
(Ehn-hoo-ah-ggeh soo boh-kah)

Rotate it.
Rótalo/dale vuelta.
(Roh-tah-loh/dah-leh boo-ehl-tah)

Rotate your arm.
Rota tu brazo.
(Roh-tah too brah-soh)

Route?
¿Vía/ruta?
(Bee-ah/roo-tah)

Run!
¡Corra!
(Koh-rah)

Say "aah."
Di "aah."
(Dee aah)

Say it again.
Dígalo otra vez/Repita.
(Dee-gah-loh oh-trah behs/Reh-pee-tah)

Say your name.
Di tu nombre.
(Dee too nohm-breh)

See you later!
¡Hasta luego!
(Ahs-tah loo-eh-goh)

See your doctor before you refill the prescription.
Vea al doctor antes de surtir la receta.
(Beh-ah ahl dohk-tohr ahn-tehs deh soohr-teer lah reh-seh-tah)

Select . . .
Seleccionar . . .
(Seh-lek-see-oh-nahr)

Select your foods after breakfast.
Seleccione las comidas después del desayuno.
(Seh-lehk-see-oh-neh lahs koh-mee-dahs dehs-poo-ehs del deh-sah-yoo-noh)

Select your foods from the menu after breakfast.
Seleccione las comidas del menú después del desayuno.
(Seh-lehk-see-oh-neh lahs koh-mee-dahs dehl meh-noo dehs-poo-ehs dehl deh-sah-yoo-noh)

She assigns a dosage schedule to the order in the computer.
Ella asigna un horario de dósis para cargar en la computadora.
(Eh-yah ah-seeg-nah oon oh-rah-ree-oh deh doh-sees pah-rah kahr-gahr ehn lah kohm-poo-tah-doh-rah)

She is content.
Ella está contenta.
(Eh-yah ehs-tah kohn-tehn-tah)

She is happy.
Ella es (está) alegre.
(Eh-yah ehs (ehs-tah) ah-leh-greh)

She is sad.
Ella es (está) triste.
(Eh-yah ehs (ehs-tah) trees-teh).

Shock?
¿Crisis?
(Kree-sees)

Should I drive?
¿Debo manejar?
(Deh-boh mah-neh-hahr)

Show me your tongue!
¡Muéstreme la lengua!
(Moo-ehs-treh-meh lah lehn-goo-ah)

Since when?
¿Desde cuándo?
(Dehs-deh koo-ahn-doh)

Sit down please.
Siéntese por favor.
(See-ehn-teh-seh pohr fah-bohr)

Sit here and wait.
Siéntese aquí y espere.
(See-ehn-teh-seh ah-kee ee ehs-peh-reh)

Sit in the chair.
Siéntese en la silla.
(See-ehn-teh-seh ehn lah see-yah)

Sit up!
¡Siéntese!
(See-ehn-teh-seh)

Sit upright!
¡Siéntate derecho!
(See-ehn-tah-teh deh-reh-choh)

Six to eleven (6 to 11) servings of starches.
De seis a once porciones de almidones.
(Deh seh-ees ah ohn-seh pohr-see-ohn-ehs deh ahl-mee-doh-nehs)

Sleep at least 6 hours daily.
Duerma por lo menos seis horas diarias.
(Doo-ehr-mah pohr loh meh-nohs seh-ees oh-rahs dee-ah-ree-ahs)

Sleep at least 8 hours.
Duerma al menos ocho horas.
(Doo-ehr-mah ahl meh-nohs oh-choh oh-rahs)

Slowly, please.
Despacio, por favor.
(Dehs-pah-see-oh, pohr fah-bohr)

Smile.
Sonríe.
(Sohn-ree-eh)

So far . . .
Hasta ahora...
(Ahs-tah ah-oh-rah)

Some people cannot tolerate gas-producing foods and should avoid eating
them.
**Algunas personas no toleran comidas que
producen gases y deben evitar
comerlas.**
*(Ahl-goo-nahs pehr-soh-nahs noh toh-
leh-rahn koh-mee-dahs keh proh-doo-
sehn gahs-ehs ee deh-behn eh-bee-
tahr koh-mehr-lahs)*

Someone will take you to your hospital
room.
Alguien lo llevará a su cuarto.
*(Ahl-ggee-ehn loh yeh-bah-rah ah soo
koo-ahr-toh)*

Sore throat . . .
Dolor de garganta...
(Doh-lohr deh gahr-gahn-tah.)

Sorry, we have no toothpicks.
Lo siento, no hay palillos.
*(Loh see-ehn-toh, noh ah-ee pah-lee-
yohs)*

Spanish is important.
El español es importante.
*(Ehl ehs-pah-nyohl ehs eehm-pohr-tahn-
teh)*

Speak slowly, please.
Hable despacio, por favor.
(Ah-bleh dehs-pah-see-oh, pohr fah-bohr)

Stand up straight.
Párese derecho(a).
(Pah-reh-seh deh-reh-choh[-chah].)

Stand up!
¡Levántate!
(Leh-bahn-tah-teh)

Start at the beginning.
Empiece desde el principio.
*(Ehm-pee-eh-seh dehs-deh ehl preen-see-
pee-oh)*

Stay as you are.
Quédese como está.
(Keh-deh-seh koh-moh ehs-tah)

Stay like this for a while.
Quédese así por un rato.
(Keh-deh-seh ah-see pohr oon rah-toh)

Stay seated.
Quédese sentado.
(Keh-deh-seh sehn-tah-doh)

Sterilize the bottles.
Esterilice las botellas.
(Ehs-teh-ree-lee-seh lahs boh-teh-yahs)

Stick out your tongue.
Saca la lengua.
(Sah-kah lah lehn-goo-ah)

Stop!
¡Párese/Deténte/Deténgase!
*(Pah-reh-seh/Deh-tehn-teh/Deh-tehn-
gah-seh)*

Stop breathing.
No respire.
(Noh rehs-pee-reh)

Straighten your knee.
Estira la rodilla.
(Ehs-tee-rah lah roh-dee-yah)

Straighten your leg.
Endereza tu pierna.
(Ehn-deh-reh-sah too pee-ehr-nah)

Strain down.
Empuja.
(Ehm-poo-hah)

Study the lesson.
Estudien la lección.
(Ehs-too-dee-ehn lah lehk-see-ohn)

Such as . . .
Tal cómo . . .
(Tahl koh-moh)

Swallow!
¡Trague!
(Trah-ggeh)

Swallow, please.
Traga, por favor.
(Trah-gah, pohr fah-bohr)

Take a bath!
¡Báñese!
(Bah-nyeh-seh)

Take a bath every day.
Báñese todos los días.
(Bah-nyeh-seh toh-dohs lohs dee-ahs)

Take a deep breath.
Respire hondo/profundo.
(Rehs-pee-reh ohn-doh/proh-foon-doh)

Take a deep breath; hold it.
Respire hondo; deténlo.
(Rehs-pee-reh ohn-doh; deh-tehn-loh)

Take a deep breath; let it go.
Respire hondo; exhala.
(Rehs-pee-rah ohn-doh; ehx-ah-lah)

Take all the medicine in this prescription.
Tome toda la medicina de esta receta.
*(Toh-meh toh-dah lah meh-dee-see-nah
deh ehs-tah reh-seh-tah)*

Take him for vaccinations at two
months.
Llévelo a vacunar a los dos meses.
*(Yeh-beh-loh ah bah-koo-nahr ah lohs
dohs meh-sehs)*

Take it with a full glass of water.
Tómela con un vaso lleno de agua.
*(Toh-meh-lah kohn oon bah-soh yeh-noh
deh ah-goo-ah)*

Take it on an empty stomach.
Tómela con el estómago vacío.
*(Toh-meh-lah kohn ehl ehs-toh-mah-goh
bah-see-oh)*

Take it one hour before eating.
Tómela una hora antes de comer.
*(Toh-meh-lah oo-nah oh-rah ahn-tehs
deh koh-mehr)*

Take the elevator to the sixth floor.
Tome el elevador al sexto piso.
*(Toh-meh ehl eh-leh-bah-dohr ahl sehx-
toh pee-soh)*

Take the medicine with food.
Tome la medicina con comida.
*(Toh-meh lah meh-dee-see-nah kohn
koh-mee-dah)*

Take the medicine with juice.
Tome la medicina con jugo.
*(Toh-meh lah meh-dee-see-nah kohn
hoo-goh)*

Take the temperature rectally.
Tome la temperatura por el recto.
*(Toh-meh lah tehm-peh-rah-too-rah pohr
ehl rehk-toh)*

Take these pills after your meal.
**Tómese estas pastillas después de la
cena.**
*(Toh-meh-seh ehs-tahs pahs-tee-yahs
dehs-poo-ehs deh lah seh-nah)*

Take two aspirin.
Tome dos aspirinas.
(Toh-meh dohs ahs-pee-ree-nahs)

Take your hospital card.
Lleve su tarjeta del hospital.
*(Yeh-beh soo tahr-heh-tah dehl ohs-pee-
tahl)*

Take your medical file.
Lleve su archivo.
(Yeh-beh soo ahr-chee-boh)

Take your shoe off.
Quítate tu zapato.
(Kee-tah-teh too sah-pah-toh)

Take your socks off.
Quítate los calcetines.
(Kee-tah-teh lohs kahl-seh-tee-nehs)

Talk!
¡Hable!
(Ah-bleh)

Tell me if it hurts.
Dime si duele.
(Dee-meh see doo-eh-leh)

Tell me what foods.
Dígame qué alimentos.
(Dee-gah-meh keh ah-lee-mehn-tohs)

Tell me when it feels numb.
Avíseme cuando sienta dormido.
*(Ah-bee-seh-meh koo-ahn-doh see-ehn-
tah dohr-mee-doh)*

Tell me why you are here?
¿Dígame por qué está aquí?
(Dee-gah-meh pohr keh ehs-tah ah-kee)

Thank you!
¡Gracias!
(Grah-see-ahs)

Thank you for talking to me!
¡Gracias por hablar conmigo!
*(Grah-see-ahs pohr ah-blahr kohn-mee-
goh)*

Thank you for the information.
Gracias por la información.
*(Grah-see-ahs pohr lah een-fohr-mah-
see-ohn)*

Thank you very much!
¡Muchas gracias!
(Moo-chahs grah-see-ahs)

That bracelet is hers.
Aquella pulsera es suya.
(Ah-keh-yah pool-seh-rah ehs soo-yah)

That gown is yours.
Aquella bata es suya.
(Ah-keh-yah bah-tah ehs soo-yah)

That is all!
¡Es todo!
(Ehs toh-doh)

The bed has one blanket.
La cama tiene una frazada/colcha.
(Lah kah-mah tee-eh-neh oo-nah frah-sah-dah/kohl-chah)

The bell will sound.
La campana sonará.
(Lah kahm-pah-nah soh-nah-rah)

The bones are mine.
Los huesos son míos.
(Lohs oo-eh-sohs sohn mee-ohs)

The bottle will be kept in a bucket with ice.
La botella se mantendrá en una tina con hielo.
(Lah boh-teh-yah seh mahn-tehn-drah ehn oo-nah tee-nah kohn ee-eh-loh)

The building has beige bricks.
El edificio tiene ladrillo crema.
(Ehl eh-dee-fee-see-oh tee-eh-neh lah-dree-yoh kreh-mah)

The clerical staff is very important.
Las secretarias son muy importantes.
(Lahs seh-kreh-tah-ree-ahs sohn moo-ee eem-pohr-tahn-tehs)

The clinic is in another building.
La clínica está en otro edificio.
(Lah klee-nee-kah ehs-tah ehn oh-troh eh-dee-fee-see-oh)

Your appointment is listed on the computer.
Su cita está registrada en la computadora.
(Soo see-tah ehs-tah reh-gees-trah-dah ehn lah kohm-poo-tah-doh-rah)

The cover is hot.
La cubierta está caliente.
(Lah koo-bee-ehr-tah ehs-tah kah-lee-ehn-teh)

The doctor will give you something for your pain.
El doctor le dará algo para el dolor.

(Ehl dohk-tohr leh dah-rah ahl-goh pah-rah ehl doh-lohr)

The doctor will see you in the emergency room.
Lo verá el doctor en el cuarto de emergencias.
(Loh beh-rah ehl dohk-tohr ehn ehl koo-ahr-toh deh eh-mehr-hehn-see-ahs)

The doctor will see you there.
El doctor lo verá ahí.
(Ehl dohk-tohr loh beh-rah ah-ee)

The doctor has to prescribe it.
La doctora debe recetarla.
(Lah dohk-tohr-ah deh-beh reh-seh-tahr-lah)

The elevators are slow.
Los elevadores son lentos.
(Lohs eh-leh-bah-doh-rehs sohn lehn-tohs)

The elevators work twenty-four hours a day.
Los elevadores trabajan veinticuatro horas.
(Lohs eh-leh-bah-doh-rehs trah-bah-hahn beh-een-tee-koo-ah-troh oh-rahs)

The exam is difficult.
El examen es difícil.
(Ehl ehx-ah-mehn ehs dee-fee-seel)

The exams are difficult.
Los exámenes son difíciles.
(Lohs ehx-ah-mee-nehs sohn dee-fee-see-lehs)

The following information is included in the label:
La siguiente información se incluye en la etiqueta:
(Lah see-ggee-ehn-teh een-fohr-mah-see-ohn seh een-kloo-yeh ehn lah eh-tee-keh-tah)

The following should be included in your diet every day:
Lo siguiente se debe incluir en su dieta todos los días:
(Loh see-ggee-ehn-teh seh deh-beh een-kloo-eer ehn soo dee-eh-tah toh-dohs lohs dee-ahs)

The fork, spoon, and knife are wrapped in the napkin.
El tenedor, la cuchara y el cuchillo están envueltos en la servilleta.

(Ehl teh-neh-dohr, lah koo-chah-rah ee ehl koo-chee-yoh ehs-tahn ehn-boo-ehl-tohs ehn lah sehr-bee-yeh-tah)

The hospital is not responsible.
El hospital no se hace responsable.
(Ehl ohs-pee-tahl noh seh ah-seh rehs-pohn-sah-bleh)

The hours of operation of the inpatient pharmacy are: Monday through Friday, 7:00 A.M. to 1:00 A.M.
El horario de la farmacia para pacientes internados es de lunes a viernes de 7 de la mañana a una de la mañana.
(Ehl oh-rah-ree-oh deh lah fahr-mah-see-ah pah-rah pah-see-ehn-tehs een-tehr-nah-dohs ehs deh loo-nehs ah bee-ehr-nehs deh see-eh-teh deh lah mah-nyah-nah ah oo-nah deh lah mah-nyah-nah)

The inpatient pharmacy is open.
La farmacia para pacientes internados está abierta.
(Lah fahr-mah-see-ah pah-rah pah-see-ehn-tehs een-tehr-nah-dohs ehs-tah ah-bee-ehr-tah)

The line is on the wall.
La línea está en la pared.
(Lah lee-neh-ah ehs-tah ehn lah pah-rehd)

The meals are served at 11:30 A.M.
Los alimentos se sirven a las once y media.
(Lohs ah-lee-mehn-tohs seh seer-behn ah lahs ohn-seh ee meh-dee-ah)

The meals are served at 5 P.M.
Los alimentos se sirven a las cinco de la tarde.
(Lohs ah-lee-mehn-tohs seh seer-behn ah lahs seen-koh deh lah tahr-deh)

The meals are served at 7 A.M.
Los alimentos se sirven a las siete de la mañana.
(Lohs ah-lee-mehn-tohs seh seer-behn ah lahs see-eh-teh deh lah mah-nyah-nah)

The measurements are difficult.
Las medidas son difíciles.
(Lahs meh-dee-dahs sohn dee-fee-see-lehs).

The test is difficult.
La prueba es difícil.
(Lah proo-eh-bah ehs dee-fee-seel).

The next day, the bottle will be sent to the laboratory.
Al día siguiente, la botella se mandará al laboratorio.
(Ahl dee-ah see-ggee-ehn-teh, lah boh-teh-yah seh mahn-dah-rah ahl lah-boh-rah-toh-ree-oh)

The nurse orders the medication from the pharmacy.
La enfermera ordena la medicina a la farmacia.
(Lah ehn-fehr-meh-rah ohr-deh-nah lah meh-dee-see-nah ah lah fahr-mah-see-ah)

The nurse explains the procedure and hospital routine.
La enfermera le explica el procedimiento y la rutina del hospital.
(Lah ehn-fehr-meh-rah leh ehx-plee-kah ehl proh-seh-dee-mee-ehn-toh ee lah roo-tee-nah dehl ohs-pee-tahl)

The nurse wants to talk to you.
La enfermera quiere hablarle.
(Lah ehn-fehr-meh-rah kee-eh-reh ah-blahr-leh)

The nurse will ask you how you feel.
La enfermera le preguntará cómo se siente.
(Lah ehn-fehr-meh-rah leh preh-goon-tah-rah koh-moh seh see-ehn-teh)

The one who is 6 years old.
El que tiene seis años.
(Ehl keh tee-eh-neh seh-ees ah-nyohs)

The outpatient pharmacy opens daily from 9 A.M. to 6 P.M.
La farmacia de consulta externa abre diariamente de nueve de la mañana a seis de la tarde.
(Lah fahr-mah-see-ah deh kohn-sool-tah ehx-tehr-nah ah-breh dee-ah-ree-ah-mehn-teh deh noo-eh-beh deh lah mah-nyah-nah ah seh-ees deh lah tahr-deh)

The owner . . .
Dueño/Amo . . .
(Doo-eh-nyoh/Ah-moh)

The patient is happy.
El paciente está contento.

(Ehl pah-see-ehn-teh ehs-tah kohn-tehn-toh)

The pharmacist interprets the physician's order.
El farmacéutico interpreta la orden del doctor.
(Ehl fahr-mah-seh-oo-tee-koh een-tehr-preh-tah lah ohr-dehn dehl dohk-tohr)

The pharmacy is open Monday through Friday.
La farmacia está abierta de lunes a viernes.
(Lah fahr-mah-see-ah ehs-tah ah-bee-ehr-tah deh loo-nehs ah bee-ehr-nehs)

The pharmacy provides services which are an integral part of total patient care.
La farmacia provee servicios como parte integral del cuidado total del paciente.
(Lah fahr-mah-see-ah proh-beh-eh sehr-bee-see-ohs koh-moh pahr-teh een-teh-grahl dehl koo-ee-dah-doh toh-tahl dehl pah-see-ehn-teh)

The pharmacy staff deliver and pick up orders every hour from the floors.
Los empleados de la farmacia recogen y surten órdenes en los pisos cada hora.
(Lohs ehm-pleh-ah-dohs deh lah fahr-mah-see-ah reh-koh-hehn ee soor-tehn ohr-deh-nehs ehn lohs pee-sohs kah-dah oh-rah)

The plates are made of plastic.
Los platos son de plástico.
(Lohs plah-tohs sohn deh plahs-tee-koh)

The prescription will be ready at _____.
La receta estará lista a las _____.
(Lah reh-seh-tah ehs-tah-rah lees-tah ah lahs _____)

The procedure is difficult.
El procedimiento es difícil.
(Ehl proh-seh-dee-mee-ehn-toh ehs dee-fee-seel).

The rails lower.
El barandal se baja.
(Ehl bah-rahn-dahl seh bah-hah)

The rings are mine.
Los anillos son míos.
(Lohs ah-nee-yohs sohn mee-ohs)

The salt and pepper are in these packets.
La sal y la pimienta están en estos paquetes.
(Lah sahl ee lah pee-mee-ehn-tah ehs-tahn ehn ehs-tohs pah-keh-tehs)

The secretary will help you.
La secretaria lo ayudará.
(Lah seh-kreh-tah-ree-ah loh ah-yoo-dah-rah)

The stairs are at the end of the hallway.
Las escaleras están al final del pasillo.
(Lahs ehs-kah-leh-rahs ehs-tahn ahl feen-ahl dehl pah-see-yoh)

The stairs will take you to a walkway.
Las escaleras lo llevarán a un pasillo.
(Lahs ehs-kah-leh-rahs loh yeh-bah-rahn ah oon pah-see-yoh)

The surgery floor is in the hospital towers.
El piso de cirugía está en las torres del hospital.
(Ehl pee-soh deh see-roo-hee-ah ehs-tah ehn lahs toh-rrehs dehl ohs-pee-tahl)

The television has 4 channels.
El televisor tiene cuatro canales.
(Ehl teh-leh-bee-sohr tee-eh-neh koo-ah-troh kah-nah-lehs)

The United States, Canada, and Argentina are important.
Los Estados Unidos, el Canadá, y la Argentina son importantes.
(Lohs ehs-tah-dohs oo-nee-dohs, ehl kah-nah-dah, ee lah ahr-hehn-tee-nah sohn eehm-pohr-tahn-tehs)

The water is in the glass/pitcher.
El agua está en el vaso/la jarra.
(Ehl ah-goo-ah ehs-tah ehn ehl bah-soh/ lah hah-rrah)

The whole book is in German.
Todo el libro es en alemán.
(Toh-doh ehl lee-broh ehs ehn ah-leh-mahn)

Their ability to be pleasant, to be courteous, and to give the appropriate information will speed up the process of admitting.
La habilidad de ser amables, atentas y de dar información apropiada asegura el proceso de admitir.

(Lah ah-bee-lee-dahd deh sehr ah-mah-blehs, ah-tehn-tahs ee deh dahr een-fohr-mah-see-ohn ah-proh-pee-ah-dah ah-seh-goo-rah ehl proh-seh-soh deh ahd-mee-teer)

Then, turn to the left.
Luego, voltee a la izquierda.
(Loo-eh-goh, bohl-teh-eh ah lah ees-kee-ehr-dah)

There are a lot of patients.
Hay muchos pacientes.
(Ah-ee moo-chohs pah-see-ehn-tehs)

There are bathrooms for guests in the corner.
Hay baños para las visitas en la esquina.
(Ah-ee bah-nyohs pah-rah lahs bee-see-tahs ehn lah ehs-kee-nah)

There are many diets available to patients.
Hay muchas dietas para los pacientes.
(Ah-ee moo-chahs dee-eh-tahs pah-rah lohs pah-see-ehn-tehs)

There is a front desk.
Hay un escritorio al frente.
(Ah-ee oon ehs-kree-toh-ree-oh ahl frehn-teh)

There is a shower.
Hay una ducha.
(Ah-ee oo-nah doo-chah)

There is a straw.
Hay un popote.
(Ah-ee oon poh-poh-teh)

There is also a bathtub/tub.
También hay una bañera/tina.
(Tahm-bee-ehn ah-ee oo-nah bah-nyeh-rah/tee-nah)

There is an educational channel.
Hay un canal educativo.
(Ah-ee oon kah-nahl eh-doo-kah-tee-boh)

There is an emergency light.
Hay una luz para emergencias.
(Ah-ee oo-nah loos pah-rah eh-mehr-hehn-see-ahs)

There, turn to the left.
Ahí, de vuelta a la izquierda.
(Ah-ee, deh boo-ehl-tah ah lah ees-kee-ehr-dah)

These books are mine.
Estos libros son los míos.
(Ehs-tohs lee-brohs sohn lohs mee-ohs)

These buttons move the bed up/down.
Estos botones mueven la cama hacia arriba/abajo.
(Ehs-tohs boh-toh-nehs moo-eh-behn lah kah-mah ah-see-ah ah-rree-bah/ah-bah-hoh)

These meats can be substituted.
Estas carnes se pueden sustituir.
(Ehs-tahs kahr-nehs seh poo-eh-dehn soos-tee-too-eer)

These pens . . .
Estas plumas . . .
(Ehs-tahs ploo-mahs)

They are around the corner.
Están alrededor de la esquina.
(Ehs-tahn ahl-rreh-deh-dohr deh lah ehs-kee-nah)

They are contented.
Ellas están contentas.
(Eh-yahs ehs-tahn kohn-tehn-tahs)

They are Mario's.
Son de Mario.
(Sohn deh Mah-ree-oh)

They are men.
Ellos son hombres.
(Eh-yohs sohn ohm-brehs)

They are Mrs. Luna's.
Son de la señora Luna.
(Sohn de lah seh-nyoh-rah Loo-nah)

They are sad.
Ellas están tristes.
(Eh-yahs ehs-tahn trees-tehs).

They are the ones that first greet the patient.
Ellas son las primeras personas que saludan al paciente.
(Eh-yahs sohn lahs pree-meh-rahs pehr-soh-nahs keh sahl-oo-dahn ahl pah-see-ehn-teh)

They can help clean.
Pueden ayudar a limpiar.
(Poo-eh-dehn ah-yoo-dahr ah leem-pee-ahr)

They can't break.
No se pueden quebrar.
(Noh seh poo-eh-dehn keh-brahr)

They will let you talk to your family.
Le permitirán hablar con su familia.
(Leh pehr-mee-tee-rahn ah-blahr kohn soo fah-mee-lee-ah)

This book . . .
Este libro . . .
(Ehs-teh lee-broh)

This button lowers (raises) the
    headboard.
Este botón baja la cabecera de la cama.
*(Ehs-teh boh-tohn bah-hah lah kah-beh-
    seh-rah deh lah kah-mah)*

This chair turns into a bed.
Esta silla se hace cama.
(Ehs-tah see-yah seh ah-seh kah-mah)

This is a brochure that describes the hos-
    pital's guidelines.
**Este es un folleto que trata de las reglas
    del hospital.**
*(Ehs-teh ehs oon foh-yeh-toh keh trah-
    tah deh lahs reh-glahs dehl ohs-pee-
    tahl)*

This is a large place.
Este es un lugar grande.
(Ehs-teh ehs oon loo-gahr grahn-deh)

This is a new formula.
Esta es una fórmula nueva.
*(Ehs-tah ehs oo-nah fohr-moo-lah noo-
    eh-bah)*

This is a sedative.
Este es un sedante.
(Ehs-teh ehs oon seh-dahn-teh)

This is an antacid.
Este es un antiácido.
(Ehs-teh ehs oon ahn-tee-ah-see-doh)

This is an employee.
Este es un empleado.
(Ehs-teh ehs oon ehm-pleh-ah-doh)

This is done quickly.
Esto se hace rápido.
(Ehs-toh seh ah-seh rah-pee-doh)

This is my first time here.
Esta es la primera vez que estoy aquí.
*(Ehs-tah ehs lah pree-meh-rah behs keh
    ehs-tohy ah-kee)*

This is the call bell.
Esta es la campana.
(Ehs-tah ehs lah kahm-pah-nah)

This is the call buzzer.
Este es el timbre.
(Ehs-teh ehs ehl teem-breh)

This is the clinic.
Esta es la clínica.
(Ehs-tah ehs lah klee-nee-kah)

This is the lobby.
Esta es la sala de espera.
*(Ehs-tah ehs lah-sah-lah deh ehs-peh-
    rah)*

This is the radio.
Este es el radio.
(Ehs-teh ehs ehl rah-dee-oh)

This is the service area.
Esta es el área de servicio.
*(Ehs-tah ehs ehl ah-reh-ah deh sehr-bee-
    see-oh)*

This is the tray.
Esta es la bandeja/charola.
*(Ehs-tah ehs lah bahn-deh-hah/chah-roh-
    lah)*

This is your room.
Este es el cuarto.
(Ehs-teh ehs ehl koo-ahr-toh)

This medicine is a pain killer.
Esta medicina quita/alivia el dolor.
*(Ehs-tah meh-dee-see-nah kee-tah/ah-lee-
    bee-ah ehl doh-lohr)*

This pencil is red.
Este lápiz es rojo.
(Ehs-teh lah-pees ehs roh-hoh)

This prescription may not be refilled.
Esta receta no se puede surtir de nuevo.
*(Ehs-tah reh-seh-tah noh seh poo-eh-deh
    soohr-teer deh noo-eh-boh)*

This will feel cold.
Esto se sentirá frío.
(Ehs-toh seh sehn-tee-rah free-oh)

This will take you to the end of the hall.
Esta la llevará al fin del pasillo.
*(Ehs-tah lah yeh-bah-rah ahl feen dehl
    pah-see-yoh)*

Thought to be/considering . . .
Considerando . . .
(Kohn-see-deh-rahn-doh)

Three times a day.
Tres veces al día.
(Trehs beh-sehs ahl dee-ah)

Three to five servings of vegetables.
De tres a cinco porciones de vegetales.
*(Deh trehs ah seen-koh pohr-see-oh-nehs
    deh beh-heh-tah-lehs)*

Tighten!
¡Aprieta!
(Ah-pree-eh-tah)

To some extent . . .
Hasta cierto punto . . .
(Ahs-tah see-ehr-toh poon-toh)

Today I am here to examine the baby.
Estoy aquí para examinar al bebé.
(Ehs-tohy ah-kee pah-rah ehx-ah-mee-nahr ahl beh-beh)

Today is Monday.
Hoy es lunes.
(Oh-ee ehs loo-nehs)

Tomorrow, bring a stool specimen in this container.
Mañana traiga una muestra de su excremento en este frasco.
(Mah-nyah-nah trah-ee-gah oo-nah moo-ehs-trah deh soo ehx-kreh-mehn-toh ehn ehs-teh frahs-koh)

Tomorrow they will give you a special test.
Mañana le harán un análisis especial.
(Mah-nyah-nah leh ah-rahn oon ah-nah-lee-sees ehs-peh-see-ahl)

Tonight, eat lightly.
Esta noche coma poco.
(Ehs-tah noh-cheh koh-mah poh-koh)

Toothache . . .
Dolor de muelas . . .
(Doh-lohr deh moo-eh-lahs)

Total number of pills?
¿Número total de pastillas?
(Noo-meh-roh toh-tahl deh pahs-tee-yahs)

Transportation is here.
El transporte está aquí.
(Ehl trahns-pohr-teh ehs-tah ah-kee)

Transportation will take you back to your room.
Transportación lo regresará a su cuarto.
(Trahns-pohr-tah-see-ohn loh reh-greh-sah-rah ah soo koo-ahr-toh)

Try again!
¡Pruebe otra vez!
(Proo-eh-beh oh-trah behs)

Try to calm down.
Trate de calmarse.
(Trah-teh deh kahl-mahr-seh)

Try to have a bowel movement daily.
Procure hacer del baño diariamente.
(Proh-koo-reh ah-sehr dehl bah-nyoh dee-ah-ree-ah-mehn-teh)

Turn!
¡Voltee!
(Bohl-teh-eh)

Turn it to the right.
Voltéalo a la derecha.
(Bohl-teh-ah-loh ah lah deh-reh-chah)

Turn it to the left.
Voltéalo a la izquierda.
(Bohl-teh-ah-loh ah lah ees-kee-ehr-dah)

Turn left.
Voltéate a la izquierda.
(Bohl-teh-ah-teh ah lah ees-kee-ehr-dah)

Turn on your side.
Voltéese de lado.
(Bohl-teh-eh-seh deh lah-doh)

Turn right.
Voltéate a la derecha.
(Bohl-teh-ah-teh ah lah deh-reh-chah)

Turn the forearm.
Voltea el antebrazo.
(Bohl-teh-ah ehl ahn-teh-brah-soh)

Turn to the right.
Voltee a la derecha.
(Bohl-teh-eh ah lah deh-reh-chah)

Turn to your side.
Voltéate de lado.
(Bohl-teh-ah-teh deh lah-doh)

Turn your head to the left.
Voltea la cabeza a la izquierda.
(Bohl-teh-ah lah kah-beh-sah ah lah ees-kee-ehr-dah)

Turn your head to the right.
Voltea la cabeza a la derecha.
(Bohl-teh-ah lah kah-beh-sah ah lah deh-reh-chah)

Twice a day.
Dos veces al día.
(Dohs beh-sehs ahl dee-ah)

Twist your upper extremities.
Tuerce las extremidades superiores.
(Too-ehr-seh lahs ehx-treh-mee-dah-dehs soo-peh-ree-oh-rehs)

Twist your waist.
Tuerce la cintura.
(Too-ehr-seh lah seen-too-rah)

Two to four servings of milk should be
included.
**Se debe incluir de dos a cuatro porciones
de leche.**
*(Seh deh-beh een-kloo-eer deh dohs ah
koo-ah-troh pohr-see-ohn-ehs deh
leh-cheh.)*

Two to three servings daily of meat, fish,
or poultry.
**Dos a tres porciones diarias de carne, pes-
cado o aves de corral.**
*(Dohs ah trehs pohr-see-oh-nehs dee-ah-
ree-ahs deh kahr-neh, pehs-kah-doh
oh ah-behs deh koh-rrahl)*

Two to four servings of fruit.
Dos a cuatro porciones de fruta.
*(Dohs ah koo-ah-troh pohr-see-ohn-ehs
deh froo-tah)*

Frequent ulcerations?
¿Ulceraciones frecuentes?
*(Ool-seh-rah-see-oh-nehs freh-koo-ehn-
tehs)*

Until now . . .
Hasta ahora . . .
(Ahs-tah ah-oh-rah)

Use dental floss.
Use hilo dental.
(Oo-seh ee-loh dehn-tahl)

Wear slippers; the floor is cold.
**Use las pantunflas/chanclas; el piso está
frío.**
*(Oo-seh lahs pahn-toon-flahs/chahn-
klahs, ehl pee-soh ehs-tah free-oh)*

Use commands and phrases when performing physical examinations.
**Use comandos/órdenes y frases útiles
cuando realice/prepare el examen
físico.**
*(Oo-seh koh-mahn-dohs/ohr-dehn-ehs ee
frah-sehs oo-tee-lehs koo-ahn-doh/
reh-ah-lee-seh/preh-pah-reh ehl ehx-
ah-mehn fee-see-koh)*

Very good!
¡Muy bien!
(Moo-ee bee-ehn)

Vials, pills, capsules, liquids, and fluids
are available in the pharmacy.
**Botellas, pastillas, cápsulas, líquidos y
sueros se encuentran en la farmacia.**
*(Boh-teh-yahs, pahs-tee-yahs, kahp-soo-
lahs, lee-kee-dohs ee soo-eh-rohs seh
ehn-koo-ehn-trahn ehn lah fahr-mah-
see-ah)*

Visiting hours are from 2 to 8 P.M.
**Las horas de visita son de dos a ocho de
la noche.**
*(Lahs oh-rahs deh bee-see-tah sohn deh
dohs ah oh-choh deh lah noh-cheh)*

Visiting hours are from nine in the morning to nine at night.
**Las horas de visita son de nueve de la ma-
ñana a nueve de la noche.**
*(Lahs oh-rahs deh bee-see-tah sohn deh
noo-eh-beh deh lah mah-nyah-nah ah
noo-eh-beh deh lah noh-cheh)*

Urinate a little, then put the urine in
this cup.
**Orine un poco, luego ponga la orina en
esta taza.**
*(Oh-ree-neh oon poh-koh, loo-eh-goh
pohn-gah lah oh-ree-nah ehn ehs-tah
tah-sah)*

Volume?
¿Volúmen?
(Boh-loo-mehn)

Volume, if liquid.
Volúmen, si es líquido.
(Boh-loo-mehn, see ehs lee-kee-doh)

Wait!
¡Espere!
(Ehs-peh-reh)

Wait in the lobby.
Espere en el vestíbulo.
(Ehs-peh-reh ehn ehl behs-tee-boo-loh)

Wait several minutes!
¡Espera varios minutos!
(Ehs-peh-rah bah-ree-ohs mee-noo-tohs)

Wait your turn.
Espere su turno.
(Ehs-peh-reh soo toor-noh)

Wake up!
¡Despierte!
(Dehs-pee-ehr-teh)

Walk!
¡Camine!
(Kah-mee-neh)

Walk, please.
Camina, por favor.
(Kah-mee-nah, pohr fah-bohr)

Walk six paces.
Camine seis pasos.
(Kah-mee-neh seh-ees pah-sohs)

Walk two blocks.
Camine dos cuadras.
(Kah-mee-neh dohs koo-ah-drahs)

Was he premature?
¿Fue prematuro?
(Foo-eh preh-mah-too-roh)

Was the delivery normal?
¿Fue normal el parto?
(Foo-eh nohr-mahl ehl pahr-toh)

Wash his hands before feeding.
**Lávele las manos antes de darle de
comer.**
*(Lah-beh-leh lahs mah-nohs ahn-tehs
deh dahr-leh deh koh-mehr)*

Wash your face!
¡Lávese la cara!
(Lah-beh-seh lah kah-rah)

Watch for the arrow.
Fíjese en la flecha.
(Fee-heh-seh ehn lah fleh-chah)

Watch his growth and development.
Vigile su crecimiento y desarrollo.
*(Bee-hee-leh soo kreh-see-mee-ehn-toh ee
deh-sah-rroh-yoh)*

Watch his navel.
Vigile su ombligo.
(Bee-hee-leh soo ohm-blee-goh)

Watch his urine and his bowel
movements.
Vigile su orina y sus evacuaciones.
*(Bee-hee-leh soo oh-ree-nah ee soos eh-
bah-koo-ah-see-oh-nehs)*

Watch that his nose is clear.
Vigile que su nariz esté libre.
*(Bee-hee-leh keh soo nah-reehs ehs-teh
lee-breh)*

Watch that your wound doesn't get
infected.
Vigile que su herida no se infecte.
*(Bee-hee-leh keh soo eh-ree-dah noh seh
een-fehk-teh)*

Watch your bleeding.
Vigile su sangrado.
(Bee-hee-leh soo sahn-grah-doh)

We also have desserts.
También tenemos postres.
(Tahm-bee-ehn teh-neh-mohs pohs-trehs)

We are going in the ambulance.
Vamos en la ambulancia.
(Bah-mohs ehn lah ahm-boo-lahn-see-ah)

We are going to pull the sheet at the
count of three.
Vamos a jalar la sábana al contar tres.
*(Bah-mohs ah hah-lahr lah sah-bah-nah
ahl kohn-tahr trehs)*

We are going to the hospital.
Vamos al hospital.
(Bah-mohs ahl ohs-pee-tahl)

We are going to take X-Rays.
Vamos a tomar rayos X.
*(Bah-mohs ah toh-mahr rah-yohs eh-
kiss)*

We are here!
¡Ya llegamos/Estamos aquí!
*(Yah yeh-gah-mohs/Ehs-tah-mohs ah-
kee)*

We don't serve carbonated soda or any
canned drinks.
**No servimos refrescos como coca-colas o
bebidas envasadas.**
*(Noh sehr-bee-mohs reh-frehs-kohs koh-
moh koh-kah-koh-lahs oh beh-bee-
dahs ehn-bah-sah-dahs)*

We have cereals.
Tenemos cereales.
(Teh-neh-mohs seh-reh-ah-lehs)

We have meats.
Tenemos carnes.
(Teh-neh-mohs kahr-nehs)

We have to go far.
Tenemos que ir lejos.
(Teh-neh-mohs keh eer leh-hohs)

We need to bring you back.
Necesitamos que regrese.
(Neh-seh-see-tah-mohs keh reh-greh-seh)

We send the menu to the kitchen.
Mandamos el menú a la cocina.
*(Mahn-dah-mohs ehl meh-noo ah lah
koh-see-nah)*

We serve lunch at twelve noon.
Servimos la comida al mediodía.
(Sehr-bee-mohs lah koh-mee-dah ahl
meh-dee-oh-dee-ah)

We are going to X-ray the abdomen
again.
Vamos a radiografiar el abdomen otra
vez.
(Bah-mohs ah rah-dee-oh-grah-fee-ahr
ehl ahb-doh-mehn oh-trah behs)

Wear this bracelet at all times.
Use esta pulsera todo el tiempo.
(Oo-seh ehs-tah pool-seh-rah toh-doh ehl
tee-ehm-poh)

Were you hit by a car?
¿Lo atropelló un carro?
(Lo ah-troh-peh-yoh oon kah-rroh)

Were you hospitalized?
¿Lo hospitalizaron?
(Loh ohs-pee-tah-lee-sah-rohn)

What?
¿Qué tal?
(Keh tahl)

What a beautiful day!
¡Que día tan hermoso!
(Keh dee-ah tahn ehr-moh-soh)

What are the months of the year?
¿Cuáles son los meses del año?
(Koo-ah-lehs sohn lohs meh-sehs dehl
ah-nyoh)

What brought you to the hospital?
¿Qué lo trajo al hospital?
(Keh loh trah-hoh ahl ohs-pee-tahl)

What can I help you with?
¿En qué puedo ayudarlo?
(Ehn keh poo-eh-doh ah-yoo-dahr-loh)

What color?
¿De qué color?
(Deh keh koh-lohr)

What day, what month?
¿Qué día, qué mes?
(Keh dee-ah, keh mehs)

What did you eat for breakfast?
¿Que comió en el desayuno?
(Keh koh-mee-oh ehn ehl deh-sah-yoo-
noh)

What do you do?
¿Qué hace usted?
(Keh ah-seh oo-sted)

What drugs do you take?
¿Qué drogas toma?
(Keh droh-gahs toh-mah)

What foods do you dislike?
¿Qué alimentos le disgustan?
(Keh ah-lee-mehn-tohs leh dees-goos-
tahn)

What foods do you like?
¿Qué comidas/alimentos le gustan?
(Keh koh-mee-dahs/ah-lee-mehn-tohs leh
goos-tahn)

What formula does he take?
¿Qué fórmula toma?
(Keh fohr-moo-lah toh-mah)

What grade are you in?
¿En qué año estás?
(Ehn keh ah-nyoh ehs-tahs)

What happened to you?
¿Qué le pasó?
(Keh leh pah-soh)

What is the matter?
¿Qué pasa?
(Keh pah-sah)

What house chores do you do?
¿Qué quehaceres haces?
(Keh keh-ah-seh-rehs ah-sehs)

What is . . . ?
¿Qué es . . . ?
(Keh ehs)

What is hurting you?
¿Qué le duele?
(Keh leh doo-eh-leh)

What is it?
¿Qué es?
(Keh ehs)

What is the zip code?
¿Cuál es su código postal?
(Koo-ahl ehs soo koh-dee-goh pohs-tahl)

What is the address?
¿Cuál es la dirección?
(Koo-ahl ehs lah dee-rehk-see-ohn)

What is the main reason you are here
today?
¿Cuál es la razón principal por la que
está aquí?
(Koo-ahl ehs lah rah-sohn preen-see-pahl
pohr lah keh ehs-tah ah-kee)

What is the matter?
¿Qué le pasa/sucede?
(Keh leh pah-sah/soo-seh-deh)

What is the name?
¿Cuál es el nombre?
(Koo-ahl ehs ehl nohm-breh)

What is the name of the company?
¿Cómo se llama la compañía?
(Koh-moh seh yah-mah lah kohm-pah-nyee-ah)

What is the name of the street?
¿Cuál es el nombre de la calle?
(Koo-ahl ehs ehl nohm-breh deh lah kah-yeh)

What is the name of the insurance?
¿Cuál es el nombre del seguro?
(Koo-ahl ehs ehl nohm-breh dehl seh-goo-roh)

What is the name of the school?
¿Cómo se llama la escuela?
(Koh-moh seh yah-mah lah ehs-koo-eh-lah)

What is the number of your house?
¿Qué número tiene su casa?
(Keh noo-meh-roh tee-eh-neh soo kah-sah)

What is the street name?
¿Cuál es el número de la calle?
(Koo-ahl ehs ehl noo-meh-roh deh lah kah-yeh)

What is the worst problem?
¿Cuál es su peor problema?
(Koo-ahl ehs soo peh-ohr proh-bleh-mah)

In what year were you born?
¿En qué año nació?
(Ehn keh ah-nyoh nah-see-oh)

What is this?
¿Qué es esto?
(Keh ehs ehs-toh)

What is your address?
¿Cuál es su dirección?
(Koo-ahl ehs soo dee-rehk-see-ohn)

What is your birthdate/year/month/day?
¿Cuál es la fecha de nacimiento/año/mes/día?
(Koo-ahl ehs lah feh-chah deh nah-see-mee-ehn-toh/ah-nyoh/mehs/dee-ah)

What is your brother's name?
¿Cómo se llama su hermano?
(Koh-moh seh yah-mah soo ehr-mah-noh)

What is your husband's name?
¿Cómo se llama su esposo?
(Koh-moh seh yah-mah soo ehs-poh-soh)

What is your last name?
¿Cómo se apellida?
(Koh-moh seh ah-peh-yee-dah)

What is your name?
¿Cómo se llama usted?
(Koh-moh seh yah-mah oos-tehd)

What is your occupation?
¿Qué clase de trabajo tiene?
(Keh klah-seh deh trah-bah-hoh tee-eh-neh)

What is your work phone number?
¿Cuál es el teléfono de su trabajo?
(Koo-ahl ehs ehl teh-leh-foh-noh deh soo trah-bah-hoh)

What is your religion?
¿Cuál es su religión?
(Koo-ahl ehs soo reh-lee-hee-ohn)

What is your Social Security number?
¿Cuál es su número de Seguro Social?
(Koo-ahl ehs soo noo-meh-roh deh seh-goo-roh soh-see-ahl)

What is your wife's name?
¿Cómo se llama su esposa?
(Koh-moh seh yah-mah soo ehs-poh-sah)

What kind?
¿Qué clase?
(Keh klah-seh)

What kind of coffee?
¿Qué clase de café?
(Keh klah-seh deh kah-feh)

What kind of drinks?
¿Qué clase de bebidas?
(Keh klah-seh deh beh-bee-dahs)

What kind of grades do you get?
¿Qué calcificaciones sacas?
(Keh kah-lee-fee-kah-see-ohn-ehs sah-kahs)

What kind of juices?
¿Qué clase de jugos?
(Keh klah-seh deh hoo-gohs)

What kind of surgery?
¿Qué clase de operaciones?
(Keh klah-seh deh oh-peh-rah-see-oh-nehs)

What medical problem do you have?
¿Qué problema médico tiene?
(Keh proh-bleh-mah meh-dee-koh tee-eh-neh)

What medicines do you take?
¿Qué medicinas toma?
(Keh meh-dee-see-nahs toh-mah)

What subject do you like best?
¿Qué materia le gusta más?
(Keh mah-teh-ree-ah leh goos-tah mahs)

What time is it?
¿Qué hora es?
(Keh oh-rah ehs)

What was the color of the urine?
¿Cuál era el color de la orina?
(Koo-ahl eh-rah ehl koh-lohr deh lah oh-ree-nah)

What work do you do?
¿Qué trabajo hace usted?
(Keh trah-bah-hoh ah-seh oos-ted)

What's going on/happening?
¿Qué pasa?
(Keh pah-sah)

Wheat bread and cereals.
Pan de trigo y cereales.
(Pahn deh tree-goh ee seh-reh-ah-lehs)

When?
¿Cuándo?
(Koo-ahn-doh)

When did this happen?
¿Cuándo le pasó esto?
(Koo-ahn-doh leh pah-soh ehs-toh)

When did you notice the skin rash?
¿Cuándo se dió cuenta de la piel rosada?
(Koo-ahn-doh seh dee-oh koo-ehn-tah deh lah pee-ehl roh-sah-dah)

When did you last see the dentist?
¿Cuándo vió al dentista la última vez?
(Koo-ahn-doh bee-oh ahl dehn-tees-tah lah ool-tee-mah behs)

When I tell you, hold your breath.
Cuando le avise, no respire.
(Koo-ahn-doh leh ah-bee-seh, noh rehs-pee-reh)

When was he born?
¿Cuándo nació?
(Koo-ahn-doh nah-see-oh)

When was the last time he had a bowel movement?

When was the last time that he had a bowel movement?
¿Cuándo fue la última vez que hizo del baño?
(Koo-ahn-doh foo-eh lah ool-tee-mah behs keh ee-soh dehl bah-nyoh)

When was the last time that you took medicine?
¿Cuándo fue la última vez que tomó medicina?
(Koo-ahn-doh foo-eh lah ool-tee-mah behs keh toh-moh meh-dee-see-nah)

When was the last time you went to the bathroom?
¿Cuándo fue la última vez que usó el baño?
(Koo-ahn-doh foo-eh lah ool-tee-mah behs keh oo-soh ehl bah-nyoh)

When was the last time you were here?
¿Cuándo fue la última vez que estuvo aquí?
(Koo-ahn-doh foo-eh lah ool-tee-mah behs keh ehs-too-boh ah-kee)

When you get there, turn right.
Cuando llegue ahí, voltee a la derecha.
(Koo-ahn-doh yeh-ggeh ah-ee, bohl-teh-eh ah lah deh-reh-chah)

Where?
¿Dónde?
(Dohn-deh)

Where are they?
¿Dónde están?
(Dohn-deh ehs-tahn)

Where are you from?
¿De dónde es?
(Deh dohn-deh ehs)

Where do I need to go?
¿A dónde necesito ir?
(Ah dohn-deh neh-seh-see-toh eer)

Where do you live?
¿Dónde vive usted?
(Dohn-deh bee-beh oos-tehd)

Where do you work?
¿Dónde trabaja usted?
(Dohn-deh trah-bah-hah oos-tehd)

Where does it hurt?
¿Dónde le duele?
(Dohn-deh leh doo-eh-leh)

Where is it?
¿Dónde está?
(Dohn-deh ehs-tah)

Where were you born?
¿Dónde nació usted?
(Dohn-deh nah-see-oh oos-tehd)

Where were you going?
¿A dónde iba?
(Ah dohn-deh ee-bah)

Which?
¿Cuál?
(Koo-ahl)

Which book do you want?
¿Qué libro quieres?
(Keh lee-broh kee-eh-rehs)

Which kind?
?Qué clase?
(Keh klah-seh)

Which of the books do you want?
¿Cuál de los libros quieres?
(Koo-ahl deh lohs lee-brohs kee-eh-rehs)

Who?
¿Quién?
(Kee-ehn)

Who can take care of the children?
¿Quién puede cuidar a los niños?
(Kee-ehn poo-eh-deh koo-ee-dahr ah lohs nee-nyohs)

Who can we call in case of an emergency?
¿A quién llamamos en caso de emergencia?
(Ah kee-ehn yah-mah-mohs ehn kah-soh deh eh-mehr-hehn-see-ah)

Who do you talk to?
¿Con quién hablas?
(Kohn kee-ehn ah-blahs)

Who helps you?
¿Quién le ayuda?
(Kee-ehn leh ah-yoo-dah)

Who helps you at home?
¿Quién le ayuda en casa?
(Kee-ehn leh ah-yoo-dah ehn kah-sah)

Who is going to pay the hospital?
¿Quién va a pagar el hospital?
(Kee-ehn bah ah pah-gahr ehl ohs-pee-tahl)

Who takes care of you at home?
¿Quién lo cuida en casa?
(Kee-ehn loh koo-ee-dah ehn kah-sah)

Who takes you to school?
¿Quién te lleva a la escuela?
(Kee-ehn teh yeh-bah ah lah ehs-koo-eh-lah)

Whose books are these?
¿De quién son estos libros?
(Deh kee-ehn sohn ehs-tohs lee-brohs)

Whose car is that?
¿De quién es el carro?
(Deh kee-ehn ehs ehl kah-roh)

Whose card is it?
¿De quién es la tarjeta?
(Deh kee-ehn ehs lah tahr-heh-tah)

Whose pen is it?
¿De quién es la pluma?
(Deh kee-ehn ehs lah ploo-mah)

Whose X-rays are these?
¿De quién son estos rayos X?
(Deh kee-ehn sohn ehs-tohs rah-yohs eh-kiss)

Why?
¿Por qué?
(Pohr keh)

Why not?
¿Por qué no?
(Pohr keh noh)

Will it pay for the hospital?
¿Paga por la hospitalización?
(Pah-gah pohr lah ohs-pee-tah-lee-sah-see-ohn)

Will you need to see a social worker?
¿Necesitará ver a la trabajadora social?
(Neh-seh-see-tah-rah behr ah lah trah-bah-hah-doh-rah soh-see-ahl)

Wrinkle your nose.
Arruga la nariz.
(Ah-rroo-gah lah nah-rees)

Write, please.
Escriban, por favor.
(Ehs-kree-bahn, pohr fah-bohr)

Yes, a little.
Sí, un poco.
(See, oon poh-koh)

Yes, go to the end of the hall.
Sí, vaya al final del pasillo.
(See, bah-yah ahl feen-ahl dehl pah-see-yoh)

Yes, I speak English.
Sí, yo hablo inglés.
(See, yoh ah-bloh een-glehs)

Yes, I speak Spanish.
Sí, yo hablo español.
(See, yoh ah-bloh ehs-pah-nyohl)

Yes, please wait.
Sí, espere por favor.
(See, ehs-peh-reh pohr fah-bohr)

You are giving us permission to treat you.
Nos da usted permiso de tratarla.
(Nohs dah oos-ted pehr-mee-soh de trah-tahr-lah)

You can also buy snacks.
También puede comprar aperitivos.
(Tahm-bee-ehn poo-eh-deh kohm-prahr ah-peh-ree-tee-bohs)

You can breathe now.
Ya puede respirar.
(Yah poo-eh-deh rehs-pee-rahr)

You can breathe.
Puede respirar.
(Poo-eh-deh rehs-pee-rahr)

You can bring your family here.
Puede traer a su familia aquí.
(Poo-eh-deh trah-ehr ah soo fah-mee-lee-ah ah-kee)

You can buy canned drinks in the cafeteria.
Puede comprar bebidas envasadas en la cafetería.
(Poo-eh-deh kohm-prahr beh-bee-dahs ehn-bah-sah-dahs ehn lah kah-feh-teh-ree-ah)

You can call collect.
Puede llamar por cobrar.
(Poo-eh-deh yah-mahr pohr koh-brahr)

You can cross at the walkway.
Puede cruzar por el pasillo.
(Poo-eh-deh kroo-sahr pohr ehl pah-see-yoh.)

You can drink water.
Puede tomar agua.
(Poo-eh-deh toh-mahr ah-goo-ah)

You can eat in your room or in the visitors' room.
Puede comer en su cuarto o en el cuarto para visitas.
(Poo-eh-deh koh-mehr ehn soo koo-ahr-toh oh ehn ehl koo-ahr-toh pah-rah bee-see-tahs)

You can feed him solid foods.
Puede darle alimentos sólidos.
(Poo-eh-deh dahr-leh ah-lee-mehn-tohs soh-lee-dohs)

You can have flowers.
Puede tener flores.
(Poo-eh-deh teh-nehr floh-rehs)

You can make local phone calls.
Puede hacer llamadas locales.
(Poo-eh-deh ah-sehr yah-mah-dahs loh-kah-lehs)

You can order coffee here.
Puede ordenar café aquí.
(Poo-eh-deh ohr-deh-nahr kah-feh ah-kee)

You can order one or two portions.
Puede ordenar una o dos porciones.
(Poo-eh-deh ohr-deh-nahr oo-nah oh dohs pohr-see-oh-nehs)

You can pay on terms.
Puede pagar a plazos.
(Poo-eh-deh pah-gahr ah plah-sohs)

You can put cards on the shelf.
Puede poner tarjetas en el estante.
(Poo-eh-deh poh-nehr tahr-heh-tahs ehn ehl ehs-tahn-teh)

You can raise your feet.
Puede levantar los pies.
(Poo-eh-deh leh-bahn-tahr lohs pee-ehs)

You can raise your head.
Puede levantar la cabeza.
(Poo-eh-deh leh-bahn-tahr lah kah-beh-sah)

You can refill _____ times.
Puede surtir _____ veces.
(Poo-eh-deh soor-teer _____ beh-sehs)

You can smoke on the patio.
Puede fumar en el patio.
(Poo-eh-deh foo-mahr ehn ehl pah-tee-oh)

You can tape pictures to the wall.
Puede pegar retratos en la pared.
(Poo-eh-deh peh-gahr reh-trah-tohs ehn lah pah-rehd)

Can you walk on crutches?
¿Puede caminar con muletas?
(Poo-eh-deh kah-mee-nahr kohn moo-leh-tahs)

Can you write an *X*?
¿Puede escribir una X?
(Poo-eh-deh ehs-kree-beer oo-nah eh-kiss)

You can't miss them!
¡No se puede perder!
(Noh seh poo-eh-deh pehr-dehr)

You cannot hang anything from the ceiling.
No puede colgar nada del techo.
(Noh poo-eh-deh kohl-gahr nah-dah dehl teh-choh)

You cannot hang anything from the door.
No puede colgar nada en la puerta.
(Noh poo-eh-deh kohl-gahr nah-dah ehn lah poo-ehr-tah)

You cannot open the windows.
No puede abrir las ventanas.
(Noh poo-eh-deh ah-breer lahs behn-tah-nahs)

You cannot smoke here.
No puede fumar aquí.
(Noh poo-eh-deh foo-mahr ah-kee)

You cannot smoke in your room.
No puede fumar en el cuarto.
(Noh poo-eh-deh foo-mahr ehn ehl koo-ahr-toh)

You do not know the lesson.
Usted no sabe la lección.
(Oos-tehd noh sah-beh lah lehk-see-ohn)

You do not know the plan?
¿Usted no sabe el plan?
(Oos-tehd noh sah-beh ehl plahn)

You don't have to pay cash.
No tiene que pagar al contado.
(Noh tee-eh-neh keh pah-gahr ahl kohn-tah-doh)

You have a private bathroom.
Tiene un baño privado.
(Tee-eh-neh oon bah-nyoh pree-bah-doh)

You have bruises and white patches.
Tiene moretones y manchas blancas.
(Tee-eh-neh moh-reh-toh-nehs ee mahn-chahs blahn-kahs)

You have to choose three meals a day.
Tiene que escoger tres comidas diarias.
(Tee-eh-neh keh ehs-koh-hehr trehs koh-mee-dahs dee-ah-ree-ahs)

You have to cross the street.
Tiene que cruzar la calle.
(Tee-eh-neh keh kroo-sahr lah kah-yeh

You have to give permission for treatment.
Tiene que dar permiso para que le den tratamiento.
(Tee-eh-neh keh dahr pehr-mee-soh pah-rah keh leh dehn trah-tah-mee-ehn-toh)

You have to go directly to the floor.
Debe de ir al piso directamente.
(Deh-beh deh eer ahl pee-soh dee-rehk-tah-mehn-teh)

You have to wait your turn.
Tendrá que esperar su turno.
(Tehn-drah keh ehs-peh-rahr soo toor-noh)

You may be here for four hours.
Estará aquí aproximadamente cuatro horas.
(Ehs-tah-rah ah-kee ah-proh-xee-mah-dah-mehn-teh koo-ah-troh oh-rahs)

You must pay a deposit.
Debe pagar un depósito.
(Deh-beh pah-gahr oon deh-poh-see-toh)

You need to be admitted.
Necesita internarse al hospital.
(Neh-seh-see-tah een-tehr-nahr-seh ahl ohs-pee-tahl)

You need to brush your teeth better.
Necesita cepillar mejor sus dientes.
(Neh-seh-see-tah seh-pee-yahr meh-hohr soos dee-ehn-tehs)

You need to return.
Necesita regresar.
(Neh-seh-see-tah reh-greh-sahr)

You need to sign this form.
Debe firmar este formulario.
(Deh-beh feer-mahr ehs-teh fohr-moo-lah-ree-oh)

You will be all right!
¡Va a estar bien!
(Bah ah ehs-tahr bee-ehn)

You will feel pain, like a pinprick.
Sentirá dolor como una picadura.

*(Sehn-tee-rah doh-lohr koh-moh oo-nah
pee-kah-doo-rah)*

You will get help.
Se le ayudará.
(Seh leh ah-yoo-dah-rah)

You will have to rest at least seven days.
**Tendrá que guardar reposo al menos siete
días.**
*(Tehn-drah keh goo-ahr-dahr reh-poh-
soh ahl meh-nohs see-eh-teh dee-ahs)*

You will have to wait.
Tendrá que esperar.
(Tehn-drah keh ehs-peh-rahr)

You will need a cast.
Necesitará un yeso.
(Neh-seh-see-tah-rah oon yeh-soh)

You will need help.
Va a necesitar ayuda.
(Bah ah neh-seh-see-tahr ah-yoo-dah)

You will pass the cafeteria.
Va a pasar la cafetería.
(Bah ah pah-sahr lah kah-feh-teh-ree-ah)

You will see the sign on the wall.
Verá el letrero en la pared.
*(Beh-rah ehl leh-treh-roh ehn lah pah-
rehd)*

Is your appetite good?
¿Tiene buen apetito?
(Tee-eh-neh boo-ehn ah-peh-tee-toh)

Your clothes go in the closet.
Su ropa va en el closet/ropero/armario.
*(Soo roh-pah bah ehn ehl kloh-seht/roh-
peh-roh/ahr-mah-ree-oh)*

Your diet should be low in fats and
spices.
**Su dieta debe ser baja en grasas y
picantes.**
*(Soo dee-eh-tah deh-beh sehr bah-hah
ehn grah-sahs ee pee-kahn-tehs)*

Your family can bring you your clothes
tomorrow.
**Su familia le puede traer su ropa
mañana.**
*(Soo fah-mee-lee-ah leh poo-eh-deh trah-
ehr soo roh-pah mah-nyah-nah)*

Your leg is broken.
Tiene la pierna quebrada.
*(Tee-eh-neh lah pee-ehr-nah keh-brah-
dah)*

Your towels are in the bathroom.
Sus toallas están en el baño.
*(Soos too-ah-yahs ehs-tahn ehn ehl bah-
nyoh)*

Word Index

A	a	*(ah)*
a	un	*(oon)*
abdomen	abdomen	*(ahb-doh-mehn)*
about	acerca de/por/acerca	*(ah-sehr-kah deh/pohr/ah-sehr-kah)*
above	arriba/sobre	*(ah-rree-bah/soh-breh)*
accent	acento	*(ah-sehn-toh)*
acceptable	aceptable	*(ah-sehp-tah-bleh)*
accident	accidente	*(ahk-see-dehn-teh)*
according	según	*(seh-goon)*
acetic	acético	*(ah-seh-tee-koh)*
acne	acné	*(ahk-neh)*
acoustic	acústico	*(ah-koos-tee-koh)*
additive	aditivo	*(ah-dee-tee-boh)*
address	dirección	*(dee-rehk-see-ohn)*
adenoid	adenoide	*(ah-deh-noh-ee-deh)*
adhesive	adhesivo	*(ah-deh-see-boh)*
administration	administración	*(ahd-mee-nees-trah-see-ohn)*
admitting	admitiendo	*(ahd-mee-tee-ehn-doh)*
adrenalism	adrenalismo	*(ah-dreh-nah-lees-moh)*
adults	adultos	*(ah-dool-tohs)*
after	después de	*(dehs-poo-ehs deh)*
against	contra	*(kohn-trah)*
age	edad	*(eh-dahd)*
aggressive	agresivo	*(ah-greh-see-boh)*
agree	acordar	*(ah-kohr-dahr)*
air	aire	*(ah-ee-reh)*
albino	albino	*(ahl-bee-noh)*
alcohol	alcohol	*(ahl-kohl)*
alcoholic	alcohólico	*(ahl-koh-lee-koh)*
alert	avísele	*(ah-bee-seh-leh)*
all	todo	*(toh-doh)*
all right	bien	*(bee-ehn)*
allergies	alergias	*(ah-lehr-hee-ahs)*
allergy	alérgico	*(ah-lehr-hee-koh)*
alone	solo	*(soh-loh)*
alphabet	abecedario	*(ah-beh-seh-dah-ree-oh)*
also	también	*(tahm-bee-ehn)*
always	siempre	*(see-ehm-preh)*
amber	ámbar/ambarino	*(ahm-bahr/ahm-bah-ree-noh)*

ambulance	ambulancia	*(ahm-boo-lahn-see-ah)*
amebic	amébico	*(ah-meh-bee-koh)*
ammonia	amonia/amoníaco	*(ah-moh-nee-ah/ah-moh-nee-ah-koh)*
among	entre	*(ehn-treh)*
amygdala	amígdala	*(ah-meeg-dah-lah)*
an	un/una	*(oon/oo-nah)*
analgesic	analgésicos	*(ah-nahl-heh-see-kohs)*
analyze	analizar	*(ah-nah-lee-sahr)*
and	y	*(ee)*
anemia	anemia	*(ah-neh-mee-ah)*
anesthesia	anestesia	*(ah-nehs-teh-see-ah)*
angina	angina	*(ahn-hee-nah)*
angioma	angioma	*(ahn-hee-oh-mah)*
angle	ángulo	*(ahn-goo-loh)*
ant	hormiga	*(ohr-mee-gah)*
antacid	antiácidos	*(ahn-tee-ah-see-dohs)*
antianxiety	contra la ansiedad	*(kohn-trah lah ahn-see-eh-dahd)*
antiarrhythmic	antiarritmias	*(ahn-tee-ah-reeht-mee-ahs)*
antibiotic(s)	antibiótico(s)	*(ahn-tee-bee-oh-tee-koh[s])*
anticonvulsant	anticonvulsivo	*(ahn-tee-kohn-bool-see-boh)*
antidiarrheal	antidiarrea	*(ahn-tee-dee-ah-rreh-ah)*
antiemetic	antiemético	*(ahn-tee-eh-meh-tee-koh)*
antiepileptic	antiepiléptico	*(ahn-tee-eh-pee-lehp-tee-koh)*
antihistamine	antihistamínico	*(ahn-tee-ees-tah-mee-nee-koh)*
antiviral	antivirus	*(ahn-tee-bee-roos)*
anxious	ansioso	*(ahn-see-oh-soh)*
any	alguno	*(ahl-goo-noh)*
apothecary	farmacéuticos	*(fahr-mah-seh-oo-tee-kohs)*
appetizers	aperitivos	*(ah-peh-ree-tee-bohs)*
appetizing	apetitosas	*(ah-peh-tee-toh-sahs)*
apple	manzana	*(mahn-sah-nah)*
approaches	se dirige	*(seh dee-ree-heh)*
April	abril	*(ah-breel)*
are dispensed	son distribuidas	*(sohn dees-tree-boo-ee-dahs)*
are giving	están dando	*(ehs-tahn dahn-doh)*
are not	no son	*(noh sohn)*
around	alrededor de	*(ahl-reh-deh-dohr deh)*
arrow	flecha	*(fleh-chah)*
arteriogram	arteriograma	*(ahr-teh-ree-oh-grah-mah)*
arthritis	artritis	*(ahr-tree-tees)*
articles	artículos	*(ahr-tee-koo-lohs)*
as	por/como	*(pohr/koh-moh)*
asparagus	espárragos	*(ehs-pah-rah-gohs)*
aspirin	aspirina	*(ahs-pee-ree-nah)*
assist them	ayúdeles	*(ah-yoo-deh-lehs)*
asthma	asma	*(ahs-mah)*
at	a	*(ah)*
at the	al	*(ahl)*
attention	atención	*(ah-tehn-see-ohn)*
August	agosto	*(ah-gohs-toh)*
aunt	tía	*(tee-ah)*

author	un autor	*(oon ah-oo-tohr)*
author	autor	*(ah-oo-tohr)*
avenue	avenida	*(ah-beh-nee-dah)*
avocados	aguacates	*(ah-goo-ah-kah-tehs)*
B	b	*(beh)*
baby	bebé	*(beh-beh)*
bacon	tocino	*(toh-see-noh)*
bacteria	bacteria	*(bahk-teh-ree-ah)*
bad	mal	*(mahl)*
baked	asadas	*(ah-sah-dahs)*
baked chicken	pollo asado	*(poh-yoh ah-sah-doh)*
baked potatoes	papas asadas	*(pah-pahs ah-sah-dahs)*
balanced	balanceada	*(bah-lahn-seh-ah-dah)*
banana	plátano	*(plah-tah-noh)*
barbaric	bárbaro	*(bahr-bah-roh)*
barbiturates	barbitúricos	*(bahr-bee-too-ree-kohs)*
basin	lavabo	*(lah-bah-doh)*
bathroom	baño	*(bah-nyoh)*
beans	frijoles	*(free-hoh-lehs)*
because	porqué	*(pohr-keh)*
bed	cama	*(kah-mah)*
bed rails	barandal	*(bah-rahn-dahl)*
bedpan	bacín	*(bah-seen)*
bedroom	recámara	*(reh-kah-mah-rah)*
bedspread	colcha	*(kohl-chah)*
beef	carne de res	*(kahr-neh deh rehs)*
beets	remolacha	*(reh-moh-lah-chah)*
before	antes de	*(ahn-tehs deh)*
beginning	principio	*(preen-see-pee-oh)*
behind	detrás de	*(deh-trahs deh)*
being able	poder	*(poh-dehr)*
bell(s)	campana(s)	*(kahm-pah-nah[s])*
below	abajo	*(ah-bah-hoh)*
bend	doblar	*(doh-blahr)*
beneath	debajo de	*(deh-bah-hoh deh)*
besides	además de	*(ah-deh-mahs deh)*
better	mejor	*(meh-hoh-rahr)*
between	entre	*(ehn-treh)*
big	grande	*(grahn-deh)*
birth control	control de fertilidad	*(kohn-trohl deh fehr-tee-lee-dahd)*
birthmark	lunares	*(loo-nah-rehs)*
biscuits	bisquetes/bizcocho	*(bees-keh-tehs/bees-koh-choh)*
bit	poco	*(poh-koh)*
black	negro	*(neh-groh)*
blanket	frazada/cobertor	*(frah-sah-dah/koh-behr-tohr)*
bleeding	sangrado	*(sahn-grah-doh)*
blocks	cuadras	*(koo-ah-drahs)*
blonde	rubio	*(roo-bee-oh)*
blood	sangre	*(sahn-greh)*
blood bank	banco de sangre	*(bahn-koh deh sahn-greh)*

blood count	biometría hemática	(bee-oh-meh-tree-ah eh-mah-tee-kah)
blouse	blusa	(bloo-sah)
blue	azul	(ah-sool)
bluish	azulosa	(ah-soo-loh-sah)
body	cuerpo	(koo-ehr-poh)
boiled	cocidas	(koh-see-dahs)
book	libro	(lee-broh)
boric acid	ácido bórico	(ah-see-doh boh-ree-koh)
bottle	botella	(boh-teh-yah)
bowel	intestino	(een-tehs-tee-noh)
boy	muchacho	(moo-chah-choh)
boy(s)	niño(s)	(nee-nyoh[s])
bradycardia	bradicardia	(brah-dee-kahr-dee-ah)
brand names	marcas de productos	(mahr-kahs deh proh-dook-tohs)
bread(s)	pan(es)	(pahn[-ehs])
breaded	empanizado	(ehm-pah-nee-sah-doh)
breakfast	desayuno	(deh-sah-yoo-noh)
breast	pechuga	(peh-choo-gah)
broiled	hervidos	(hehr-bee-dohs)
broiled fish	pescado al horno	(pehs-kah-doh ahl ohr-noh)
bronchitis	bronquitis	(brohn-kee-tees)
brother	hermano	(ehr-mah-noh)
brother-in-law	cuñado	(koo-nyah-doh)
brown	café	(kah-feh)
brown(skin tone)	moreno	(moh-reh-noh)
bruises	moretones	(moh-reh-toh-nehs)
build	construir	(kohn-stroo-eer)
building	edificio	(eh-dee-fee-see-oh)
burns	quemaduras	(keh-mah-doo-rahs)
burp	repetir/eructar	(reh-peh-teer/eh-rook-tahr)
burritos	burritos	(boo-ree-tohs)
butter	mantequilla	(mahn-teh-kee-yah)
buttons	botón/botones	(boh-tohn/boh-toh-nehs)
buzzing	zumbido	(soom-bee-doh)
by	por	(pohr)
C	c	(seh)
cabbage	col/repollo	(kohl/reh-poh-yoh)
cafe	café	(kah-feh)
cafeteria	cafetería	(kah-feh-teh-ree-ah)
caffeine	cafeína	(kah-feh-ee-nah)
cake	pastel	(pahs-tehl)
call(for/name)	llamar	(yah-mahr)
call-bell	campana/timbre	(kahm-pah-nah/teem-breh)
callus	callo	(kah-yoh)
calm	calma	(kahl-mah)
can	poder	(poh-dehr)
cancer	cáncer	(kahn-sehr)
candy	dulces	(dool-sehs)
canteloupe	melón	(meh-lohn)
capsule	cápsula	(kahp-soo-lah)

carbonated drinks	bebidas gaseosas	*(beh-bee-dahs gah-seh-oh-sahs)*
card	tarjeta	*(tahr-heh-tah)*
cardiac	cardíaco	*(kahr-dee-ah-koh)*
caries	caries	*(kah-ree-ehs)*
carothid	carótida	*(kah-roh-tee-dah)*
carrots	zanahorias	*(sah-nah-oh-ree-ahs)*
cataract	catarata	*(kah-tah-rah-tah)*
categories	categorías	*(kah-teh-goh-ree-ahs)*
cause	causa	*(kah-oo-sah)*
cavity	cavidad	*(kah-bee-dahd)*
ceiling	techo	*(teh-choh)*
celery	apio	*(ah-pee-oh)*
cell	célula	*(seh-loo-lah)*
centimeter	centímetro	*(sehn-tee-meh-troh)*
cereal(cooked)	cereal/cocido	*(seh-reh-ahl/koh-see-doh)*
cereal(dry)	cereal/seco	*(seh-reh-ahl/seh-koh)*
cereal(s)	cereal(es)	*(seh-reh-ahl[-ehs])*
chair	silla	*(see-yah)*
chancre	chancro	*(chahn-kroh)*
change	cambiar	*(kahm-bee-ahr)*
channel	canal	*(kah-nahl)*
chaplain	capellán	*(kah-peh-yahn)*
chapter	capítulo	*(kah-pee-too-loh)*
chat	charlar	*(chahr-lahr)*
cheek	mejilla	*(meh-hee-yah)*
chemotherapy	quimioterapia	*(kee-mee-oh-teh-rah-pee-ah)*
cherries	cerezas	*(seh-reh-sahs)*
chest	pecho	*(peh-choh)*
chicken	pollo	*(poh-yoh)*
child	niño(a)	*(nee-nyoh[-nyah])*
children	niños/hijos	*(nee-nyohs/ee-hohs)*
chocolate	chocolate	*(choh-koh-lah-teh)*
cholesterol	colesterol	*(koh-lehs-teh-rohl)*
chops	chuletas	*(choo-leh-tahs)*
cianotic	cianótico/violáceo	*(see-ah-noh-tee-koh/bee-oh-lah-seh-oh)*
cirrhosis	cirrosis	*(see-rroh-sees)*
claustrophobia	claustrofobia	*(klah-oos-troh-foh-bee-ah)*
clean	limpiar	*(leem-pee-ahr)*
clear	claro/ámbar	*(klah-roh/ahm-bahr)*
clinic	clínica	*(klee-nee-kah)*
close	cerrar	*(seh-rrahr)*
clothes	ropa	*(roh-pah)*
coagulated	coagulado(a)	*(koh-ah-goo-lah-doh[-dah])*
coagulation	coagulación	*(koh-ah-goo-lah-see-ohn)*
coat	abrigo	*(ah-bree-goh)*
cocaine	cocaína	*(koh-kah-ee-nah)*
coffee	café	*(kah-feh)*
cold	frío	*(free-oh)*
colic	cólico	*(koh-lee-koh)*
collection	coleccionar	*(koh-lehk-see-ohn-ahr)*

colonel	coronel	*(koh-rohn-ehl)*
coma	coma	*(koh-mah)*
comatose	comatoso	*(koh-mah-toh-soh)*
comb	peine	*(peh-ee-neh)*
come	venir	*(beh-neer)*
commands	mandatos	*(mahn-dah-tohs)*
common law	concubina	*(kohn-koo-bee-nah)*
common(s)	común/comunes	*(koh-moon/koh-moon-ehs)*
communicate	comunicar	*(koh-moo-nee-kahr)*
communication	comunicación	*(koh-moon-ee-kah-see-ohn)*
community	comunidad	*(koh-moo-nee-dahd)*
complain	quejar/quejarse	*(keh-hahr/keh-hahr-seh)*
compromise	compromiso	*(kohm-proh-mee-soh)*
condiments	condimentos	*(kohn-dee-mehn-tohs)*
conduct	conducir	*(kohn-doo-seer)*
confuse	confundir	*(kohn-foon-deer)*
consciousness	conocimiento	*(koh-noh-see-mee-ehn-toh)*
constipation	estreñimiento/	*(ehs-treh-nyee-mee-ehn-toh/kohns-*
	constipación	*tee-pah-see-ohn)*
consultant	consultante	*(kohn-sool-tahn-teh)*
content	contenido	*(kohn-teh-nee-doh)*
continued	continuado	*(kohn-tee-noo-ah-doh)*
contraceptives	contraceptivos	*(kohn-trah-sehp-tee-bohs)*
contraction	contracciones	*(kohn-trahk-see-ohn-ehs)*
contrast	contraste	*(kohn-trahs-teh)*
control	control	*(kohn-trohl)*
convenient	conveniente	*(kohn-beh-nee-ehn-teh)*
cook	cocinar	*(koh-see-nahr)*
cookies	galletas	*(gah-yeh-tahs)*
copper	cobre	*(koh-breh)*
corn	maíz/elote	*(mah-ees/eh-loh-teh)*
corn bread	pan de maíz	*(pahn deh mah-ees)*
Corn Flakes	hojitas de maíz	*(oh-hee-tahs deh mah-ees)*
corner	esquina	*(ehs-kee-nah)*
cortisone	cortisona	*(kohr-tee-sohn-ah)*
cosmetics	cosméticos	*(kohs-meh-tee-kohs)*
cottage cheese	requesón	*(reh-keh-sohn)*
cough	tos	*(tohs)*
cousin	primo(a)	*(pree-moh[-mah])*
cousins	primos(as)	*(pree-mohs[-mahs])*
cover	cubrir	*(koo-breer)*
crab	cangrejos	*(kahn-greh-hohs)*
crackers	galletas saladas	*(gah-yeh-tahs sah-lah-dahs)*
cream	crema	*(kreh-mah)*
Cream of Wheat	crema de trigo	*(kreh-mah deh tree-goh)*
crisis	crisis	*(kree-sees)*
cross	cruzar	*(kroo-sahr)*
cry	llorar	*(yoh-rahr)*
cubic	cúbico	*(koo-bee-koh)*
cucumbers	pepinos	*(peh-pee-nohs)*
cup	taza	*(tah-sah)*

cure	curar	*(koo-rahr)*
custard	flan	*(flahn)*
customary	acostumbra	*(ah-kohs-toom-brah)*
cut	cortar	*(kohr-tahr)*
cut down	reduzca	*(reh-doos-kah)*
D	d	*(deh)*
dad	papá	*(pah-pah)*
dark	negro	*(neh-groh)*
daughter	hija	*(ee-hah)*
days	días	*(dee-ahs)*
deal with	tratar	*(trah-tahr)*
decaffeinated	descafeinado	*(dehs-kah-feh-ee-nah-doh)*
December	diciembre	*(dee-see-ehm-breh)*
decent	decente	*(deh-sehn-teh)*
decide that	decide que	*(deh-see-deh keh)*
decongestants	descongestionantes	*(dehs-kohn-hehs-tee-oh-nahn-tehs)*
deficiency	deficiencia	*(deh-fee-see-ehn-see-ah)*
dehydrated	deshidratado	*(deh-see-drah-tah-doh)*
dehydration	deshidratación	*(dehs-see-drah-tah-see-ohn)*
delirious	delirio	*(deh-lee-ree-oh)*
demented	demente	*(deh-mehn-teh)*
dental	dental	*(dehn-tahl)*
dentrific	dentífrico	*(dehn-tee-free-koh)*
deny	negar	*(neh-gahr)*
department	departamento	*(deh-pahr-tah-mehn-toh)*
depressed	deprimido	*(deh-pree-mee-doh)*
deserve	merecer	*(meh-reh-sehr)*
desserts	postres	*(pohs-trehs)*
destroy	destruir	*(dehs-troo-eer)*
determine	determinar	*(deh-tehr-meh-nahr)*
development	desarrollo	*(deh-sah-roh-yoh)*
diabetes	diabetes	*(dee-ah-beh-tees)*
diabetic	diabético(a)	*(dee-ah-beh-tee-koh[-kah])*
diamonds	diamantes	*(deh-ah-mahn-tehs)*
diaper	pañal	*(pah-nyahl)*
diarrhea	diarrea	*(dee-ah-rreh-ah)*
die	morir	*(moh-reer)*
diet(s)	dieta(s)	*(dee-eh-tah[s])*
different	diferente	*(dee-feh-rehn-teh)*
digitalis	digitales	*(dee-hee-tah-lehs)*
diluent	diluente	*(dee-loo-ehn-teh)*
dinner	cena	*(seh-nah)*
direct	directas	*(dee-rehk-tahs)*
directions	direcciones	*(dee-rehk-see-oh-nehs)*
disappear	desaparecer	*(deh-sah-pah-reh-sehr)*
discover	descubrir	*(dehs-koo-breer)*
dish	plato	*(plah-toh)*
division	división	*(dee-bee-see-ohn)*
do	haces	*(ah-sehs)*
doctor(m)	doctor/médico	*(dohk-tohr/meh-dee-koh)*

doctor(f)	doctora/médica	*(dohk-tohr-ah/meh-dee-kah)*
door	puerta	*(poo-ehr-tah)*
dose	dosis	*(doh-sees)*
draw	tirar/dibujar	*(tee-rahr/dee-boo-hahr)*
drawn	sacar	*(sah-kahr)*
dress	vestir	*(behs-teer)*
drink	beber/tomar	*(beh-behr/toh-mahr)*
drop	gota	*(goh-tah)*
drugs	drogas	*(droh-gahs)*
dry	seca	*(seh-kah)*
duck	pato	*(pah-toh)*
during	durante	*(doo-rahn-teh)*
E	e	*(eh)*
each	cada	*(kah-dah)*
east	Este	*(ehs-teh)*
eat	comer	*(koh-mehr)*
eat breakfast	desayunar	*(deh-sah-yoo-nahr)*
echymosis	equimosis	*(eh-kee-moh-sees)*
eczema	eccema	*(ehk-seh-mah)*
egg yolks	clara de huevo	*(klah-rah deh oo-eh-bohs)*
eggplant	berenjena	*(beh-rehn-heh-nah)*
eggs	huevos	*(oo-eh-bohs)*
eight	ocho	*(oh-choh)*
eight hundred	ochocientos	*(oho-choh-see-ehn-tohs)*
8:00 A.M.	las ocho	*(lahs oh-choh)*
8:00 P.M.	las veinte horas	*(lahs beh-een-teh oh-rahs)*
eighteen	dieciocho	*(dee-ehs-ee-oh-choh)*
eighth	octavo(a)	*(ohk-tah-boh[-bah])*
eighty	ochenta	*(oh-chehn-tah)*
either . . . or	o . . . o	*(oh . . . oh)*
elevator	elevador	*(eh-leh-bah-dohr)*
eleven	once	*(ohn-seh)*
11:00 A.M.	las once	*(lahs ohn-seh)*
11:00 P.M.	las veintitrés horas	*(lahs beh-een-tee-trehs oh-rahs)*
embolism	embolismo	*(ehm-bohl-ees-moh)*
embrace	abrazar	*(ah-brah-sahr)*
emerald	esmeralda	*(ehs-meh-rahl-dah)*
emergency	emergencia	*(eh-mehr-hehn-see-ah)*
emergency room	cuarto de emergencias	*(koo-ahr-toh deh eh-mehr-hehn-see-ahs)*
emetic	emético	*(eh-meh-tee-koh)*
employ	emplear	*(ehm-pleh-ahr)*
enchiladas	enchiladas	*(ehn-chee-lah-dahs)*
end	al final	*(ahl fee-nahl)*
enema	enema/sonda	*(eh-neh-mah/sohn-dah)*
English	inglés	*(een-glehs)*
enteritis	enteritis	*(ehn-teh-ree-tees)*
environment	ambiente familiar	*(ahm-bee-ehn-teh fah-mee-lee-ahr)*
epilepsy	epilepsia	*(eh-pee-lehp-see-ah)*
error	error	*(ehr-ohr)*

especially	especialmente	*(ehs-peh-see-ahl-mehn-teh)*
essence	esencia	*(eh-sehn-see-ah)*
essential	esencial	*(eh-sehn-see-ahl)*
euphoric	eufórico	*(eh-oo-foh-ree-koh)*
every	vez	*(behs)*
everything	todo	*(toh-doh)*
examine	examinar	*(ehx-ah-mee-nahr)*
excrement	excremento	*(ehx-kreh-mehn-toh)*
Excuse me!	¡Perdón!	*(pehr-dohn)*
exercise	ejercicio	*(eh-hehr-see-see-oh)*
exit	salida	*(sah-lee-dah)*
explain	explique	*(ehx-plee-keh)*
explains	explica	*(ehx-plee-kah)*
expression	expresión/expresiones	*(ehx-preh-see-ohn/ehx-preh-see-oh-nehs)*
extraction	extracción	*(ehx-trahk-see-ohn)*
exudate	exudado	*(ehx-oo-dah-doh)*
F	f	*(eh-feh)*
facial	facial	*(fah-see-ahl)*
fail	fallar	*(fah-yahr)*
fajitas	fajitas	*(fah-hee-tahs)*
Fall	otoño	*(oh-toh-nyoh)*
false	falso	*(fahl-soh)*
familiar	familiar	*(fah-mee-lee-ahr)*
family	familia	*(fah-mee-lee-ah)*
far	lejos de	*(leh-hohs deh)*
fasting	en ayunas	*(ehn ah-yoo-nahs)*
fat	grasa/obeso	*(grah-sah/oh-beh-soh)*
fatal	fatal	*(fah-tahl)*
father	padre	*(pah-dreh)*
father-in-law	suegro	*(soo-eh-groh)*
fats	grasas	*(grah-sahs)*
February	febrero	*(feh-breh-roh)*
feel	sentir	*(sehn-teer)*
fever	fiebre	*(fee-eh-breh)*
few	poco	*(poh-koh)*
fibroid	fibroide	*(fee-broh-ee-deh)*
fifteen	quince	*(keen-seh)*
fifth	quinto(a)	*(keen-toh[-tah])*
fifty	cincuenta	*(seen-koo-ehn-tah)*
fill	llenar	*(yeh-nahr)*
find	hallar/descubrir	*(ah-yahr/dehs-koo-breer)*
fire	lumbre	*(loom-breh)*
fire escape	escape de fuego	*(ehs-kah-peh deh foo-eh-goh)*
first	primero(a)	*(pree-meh-roh[-rah])*
fish	pescado	*(pehs-kah-doh)*
fistula	fístula	*(fees-too-lah)*
five	cinco	*(seen-koh)*
five hundred	quinientos	*(kee-nee-ehn-tohs)*
5:00 A.M.	las cinco	*(lahs seen-koh)*

5:00 P.M.	las diecisiete horas	*(lahs dee-eh-see-see-eh-teh oh-rahs)*
fix	componer	*(kohm-poh-nehr)*
flat	indiferente	*(een-dee-feh-rehn-teh)*
floor	piso	*(pee-soh)*
flower vase	florero	*(floh-reh-roh)*
fluid	fluido	*(floo-ee-doh)*
following	siguiente	*(see-ggee-ehn-teh)*
foods	comidas	*(koh-mee-dahs)*
for	de/por/para	*(deh/pohr/pah-rah)*
fork	tenedor	*(teh-neh-dohr)*
form	forma(s)	*(fohr-mah[s])*
formula	fórmula	*(fohr-moo-lah)*
forty	cuarenta	*(koo-ah-rehn-tah)*
four	cuatro	*(koo-ah-troh)*
four hundred	cuatrocientos	*(koo-ah-troh-see-ehn-tohs)*
four thousand	cuatro mil	*(koo-ah-troh meel)*
4:00 A.M.	las cuatro	*(lahs koo-ah-troh)*
4:00 P.M.	las dieciseis horas	*(lahs dee-eh-see-seh-ees oh-rahs)*
fourteen	catorce	*(kah-tohr-seh)*
fourth	cuarto(a)	*(koo-ahr-toh[-tah])*
freckles	pecas	*(peh-kahs)*
fremitus	frémito	*(freh-mee-toh)*
french fries	papas fritas	*(pah-pahs free-tahs)*
fresh	fresco	*(frehs-koh)*
Friday	viernes	*(bee-ehr-nehs)*
fried	fritos(as)	*(free-tohs[-tahs])*
fried chicken	pollo frito	*(poh-yoh free-toh)*
friend	amigo(a)	*(ah-mee-goh[-gah])*
friendship	amistad	*(ah-mees-tahd)*
from	de	*(deh)*
frontal	frontal	*(frohn-tahl)*
frozen	helado/congelado	*(eh-lah-doh/kohn-heh-lah-doh)*
fruit	fruta	*(froo-tah)*
function	función	*(foon-see-ohn)*
fundamental	fundamental	*(foon-dah-mehn-tahl)*
fungus	hongos	*(ohn-gohs)*
G	g	*(jeh)*
gallbladder	vesícula biliar	*(beh-see-koo-lah bee-lee-ahr)*
gallon	galón	*(gah-lohn)*
gangrene	gangrena	*(gahn-greh-nah)*
gastroenteritis	gastroenteritis	*(gahs-troh-ehn-teh-ree-tees)*
gel/gelatin	gelatina	*(geh-lah-tee-nah)*
general	general	*(heh-neh-rahl)*
generic	genérico	*(heh-neh-ree-koh)*
genial	genial	*(heh-nee-ahl)*
get	consiga	*(kohn-see-gah)*
girl	niña(s)	*(nee-nyah[s])*
glass	vidrio/vaso/cristal	*(bee-dree-oh/bah-soh/krees-tahl)*
glaucoma	glaucoma	*(glah-oo-koh-mah)*
globule	glóbulo	*(gloh-boo-loh)*

gloves	guantes	*(goo-ahn-tehs)*
go	acuda	*(ah-koo-dah)*
godfather	padrino	*(pah-dree-noh)*
godmother	madrina	*(mah-dree-nah)*
godparents	padrinos	*(pah-dree-nohs)*
gold	dorado	*(doh-rah-doh)*
good	bueno(a)	*(boo-eh-noh[-nah])*
gout	gota	*(goh-tah)*
gown	bata/vestido	*(bah-tah/behs-tee-doh)*
grains	granos	*(grah-nohs)*
grams	gramos	*(grah-mohs)*
grandchildren	nietos	*(nee-eh-tohs)*
grandfather	abuelo	*(ah-boo-eh-loh)*
grandmother	abuela	*(ah-boo-eh-lah)*
grandparents	abuelos	*(ah-boo-eh-lohs)*
grape(s)	uva(s)	*(oo-bah[s])*
grapefruit	toronja	*(toh-rohn-hah)*
grave	grave	*(grah-beh)*
gray	gris	*(grees)*
grayish	grisáceo	*(gree-sah-seh-oh)*
grayish-white	canoso	*(kah-noh-soh)*
great-grandparents	bisabuelos	*(bee-sah-boo-eh-lohs)*
green	verde	*(behr-deh)*
green beans	ejotes/habichuelas	*(eh-hoh-tehs/ah-bee-choo-eh-lahs)*
greetings	saludos	*(sah-loo-dohs)*
growth	crecimiento	*(kreh-see-mee-ehn-toh)*
guide	guía	*(ggee-ah)*
gynecologist	ginecólogo	*(hee-neh-koh-loh-goh)*
H	h	*(ah-cheh)*
hairbrush	cepillo de pelo	*(seh-pee-yoh deh peh-loh)*
hallway	pasillo	*(pah-see-yoh)*
ham	jamón	*(hah-mohn)*
hamburger	hamburguesa	*(ahm-boor-geh-sah)*
hand	mano(s)	*(mah-noh[s])*
handshake	apretón de manos	*(ah-preh-tohn deh mah-nohs)*
handy	convenientes	*(kohn-beh-nee-ehn-tehs)*
hard-boiled	duros	*(doo-rohs)*
has	tiene	*(tee-eh-neh)*
hazel	castaño	*(kahs-tah-nyoh)*
he/she/you	él/ella/usted	*(ehl/eh-yah/oos-tehd)*
head	cabeza	*(kah-beh-sah)*
health	salud	*(sah-lood)*
heart	corazón	*(koh-rah-sohn)*
hearts	corazones	*(koh-rah-sohn-ehs)*
hello	hola	*(oh-lah)*
help	ayuda	*(ah-yoo-dah)*
helpful	útil/útiles/ conveniente	*(oo-teel/oo-tee-lehs/kohn-beh-nee-ehn-teh)*
hematology	hematología	*(eh-mah-toh-loh-hee-ah)*
hematoma	hematoma	*(eh-mah-toh-mah)*

hemolysis	hemólisis	*(eh-moh-lee-sees)*
hemorrhage	hemorragia	*(eh-moh-rah-hee-ah)*
hepatitis	hepatitis	*(eh-pah-tee-tees)*
her	ella	*(eh-yah)*
here	aquí	*(ah-kee)*
hernia	hernia	*(ehr-nee-ah)*
high	alto	*(ahl-toh)*
him	él	*(ehl)*
himself	su	*(soo)*
his	su	*(soo)*
Hispanic(s)	hispano(s)	*(ees-pah-noh[s])*
history	historia	*(ees-toh-ree-ah)*
home	casa/hogar	*(kah-sah/oh-gahr)*
hose	medias	*(meh-dee-ahs)*
hospitals	hospital(es)	*(ohs-pee-tahl[-ehs])*
hot	calor	*(kah-lohr)*
hot dog	emparedado de salchicha/perro caliente	*(ehm-pah-reh-dah-doh deh sahl-chee-chah/peh-roh kah-lee-ehn-teh)*
hot sauce	salsa picante	*(sahl-sah pee-kahn-teh)*
hour	hora	*(oh-rah)*
house	casa	*(kah-sah)*
household	caseras	*(kah-seh-rahs)*
how	como	*(koh-moh)*
however	pero	*(peh-roh)*
hunt	cazar	*(kah-sahr)*
hurt	doler	*(doh-lehr)*
husband	esposo	*(ehs-poh-soh)*
hygienist	higienista	*(ee-hee-eh-nees-tah)*
hypertension	hipertensión	*(ee-pehr-tehn-see-ohn)*
I	i	*(ee)*
I	yo	*(yoh)*
ice	hielo	*(ee-eh-loh)*
ice cream	nieve/helado/ mantecado	*(nee-eh-beh/eh-lah-doh/mahn-teh-kah-doh)*
icteric	ictérico	*(eek-teh-ree-koh)*
idea	idea	*(ee-deh-ah)*
if	si	*(see)*
ignore	ignorar	*(eeg-noh-rahr)*
important	importantes	*(eem-pohr-tahn-tehs)*
impression	impresión	*(eem-preh-see-ohn)*
in	en	*(ehn)*
in front of	enfrente de/delante de	*(ehn-frehn-teh deh/deh-lahn-teh deh)*
independence	independencia	*(een-deh-pehn-dehn-see-ah)*
index	tarjeta	*(tahr-heh-tah)*
indigestion	indigestión	*(een-dee-gehs-tee-ohn)*
induce	inducir	*(een-doo-seer)*
infancy	infancia	*(een-fahn-see-ah)*
infection	infección	*(een-fehk-see-ohn)*
inflammation	inflamación	*(een-flah-mah-see-ohn)*

inhalant	inhalante	*(een-ah-lahn-teh)*
injection	inyección	*(een-yehk-see-ohn)*
insect	insecto	*(een-sehk-toh)*
instant	instantáneo	*(eens-tahn-tah-neh-oh)*
instructions	instrucciones	*(eens-trook-see-ohn-ehs)*
instrument	instrumento	*(eens-troo-mehn-toh)*
insulin	insulina	*(een-soo-lee-nah)*
insurance	seguro	*(seh-goo-roh)*
integral	integral	*(een-teh-grahl)*
interest	interés	*(een-teh-rehs)*
interrogation	interrogativo	*(een-teh-rroh-gah-tee-boh)*
interrogative	interrogativas	*(een-teh-rroh-gah-tee-bahs)*
intimate	íntimo	*(een-tee-moh)*
intramuscular	intramuscular	*(een-trah-moos-koo-lahr)*
intravenous	intravenoso	*(een-trah-beh-noh-soh)*
iodine	yodo	*(yoh-doh)*
irradiate	irradiar	*(ee-rah-dee-ahr)*
irritable	irritable	*(ee-ree-tah-bleh)*
is/it is	es/está	*(ehs/ehs-tah)*
it	lo	*(loh)*
J	j	*(hoh-tah)*
jacket	chaqueta	*(cha-keh-tah)*
jam	mermelada	*(mehr-meh-lah-dah)*
January	enero	*(eh-neh-roh)*
jelly	jalea	*(hah-leh-ah)*
jugular	yugular	*(yoo-goo-lahr)*
juice(s)	jugo(s)	*(hoo-goh[s])*
juicy	jugosas	*(hoo-goh-sahs)*
July	julio	*(joo-lee-oh)*
jump	saltar	*(sahl-tahr)*
June	junio	*(joo-nee-oh)*
just	justo/solo	*(hoos-toh/soh-loh)*
juvenile	juvenil	*(hoo-beh-neel)*
K	k	*(kah)*
keep	guardar/mantener	*(goo-ahr-dahr/mahn-teh-nehr)*
key(s)	clave(s)	*(klah-beh[s])*
kilogram(s)	kilogramo(s)/kilo(s)	*(kee-loh-grah-moh[s]/kee-loh[s])*
kiss	besar	*(beh-sahr)*
kitchen	cocina	*(koh-see-nah)*
kleptomania	cleptomanía	*(klehp-toh-mah-nee-ah)*
knife	cuchillo	*(koo-chee-yoh)*
know	conocer/saber	*(koh-noh-sehr/sah-behr)*
L	l	*(eh-leh)*
laboratory	laboratorio	*(lah-boh-rah-toh-ree-oh)*
lamb	cordero	*(kohr-deh-roh)*
lamp	lámpara	*(lahm-pah-rah)*
lancet	lanceta	*(lahn-seh-tah)*
language	lenguaje	*(lehn-goo-ah-heh)*

laparoscopy	laparascopia	*(lah-pah-rahs-koh-pee-ah)*
laryngitis	laringitis	*(lah-reen-hee-tees)*
lasagna	lasaña	*(lah-sah-nyah)*
last	última	*(ool-tee-mah)*
last name	apellido	*(ah-peh-gee-doh)*
laurel	laurel	*(lah-oo-rehl)*
lavage	lavado	*(lah-bah-doh)*
laxative(s)	laxante(s)/purgante(s)	*(lahx-ahn-teh[s]/poor-gahn-teh[s])*
lay down	acostar	*(ah-kohs-tahr)*
lead	plomo	*(ploh-moh)*
leave	dejar	*(deh-hahr)*
left	izquierdo(a)	*(ees-kee-ehr-doh[dah])*
leg	pierna	*(pee-ehr-nah)*
lemon	limón	*(lee-mohn)*
less	menos	*(meh-nohs)*
let go	soltar	*(sohl-tahr)*
lettuce	lechuga	*(leh-choo-gah)*
level	nivel	*(nee-vehl)*
lift	levantar/elevar	*(leh-bahn-tahr/eh-leh-bahr)*
ligament	ligamento	*(lee-gah-mehn-toh)*
light	luz	*(loos)*
light touch	caricia	*(kah-ree-see-ah)*
like	comparación	*(kohm-pah-rah-see-ohn)*
lima beans	habas	*(ah-bahs)*
lime	lima/limón	*(lee-mah/lee-mohn)*
limitations	limitaciones	*(lee-mee-tah-see-ohn-ehs)*
linen	lino	*(lee-noh)*
lingual	lingual	*(leen-goo-ahl)*
lipstick	lápiz de labios	*(lah-pees deh lah-bee-ohs)*
liquid	líquido(a)	*(lee-kee-doh[-dah])*
list	lista	*(lees-tah)*
liter	litro	*(lee-troh)*
lithium	litio	*(lee-tee-oh)*
little	poco	*(poh-koh)*
liver	hígado	*(ee-gah-doh)*
living room	sala	*(sah-lah)*
lobby	sala de espera/vestíbulo	*(sah-lah deh ehs-peh-rah/behs-tee-boo-loh)*
loose	perder	*(pehr-dehr)*
lotion	loción	*(loh-see-ohn)*
love	amor	*(ah-mohr)*
low	baja	*(bah-hah)*
low cholesterol	poco colesterol/colesterol bajo	*(poh-koh koh-lehs-teh-rohl/koh-lehs-teh-rohl bah-hoh)*
low fat	poca grasa	*(poh-kah grah-sah)*
low sodium	poca sal/baja en sal	*(poh-kah sahl/bah-ha-ahn sahl)*
lower	rebajar/bajar	*(reh-bah-hahr/bah-hahr)*
lubricant	lubricante	*(loo-bree-kahn-teh)*
lunch	comida	*(koh-mee-dah)*
lupus	lupus	*(loo-pohs)*

more	mucho/más	*(moo-choh/mahs)*
morphine	morfina	*(mohr-fee-nah)*
mother	madre	*(mah-dreh)*
mother-in-law	suegra	*(soo-eh-grah)*
mouth	boca/oral	*(boh-kah/oh-rahl)*
move	mover/mueva	*(moh-behr/moo-eh-bah)*
Mr.	señor	*(seh-nyohr)*
Mrs.	señora	*(seh-nyoh-rah)*
mustard	mostaza	*(mohs-tah-sah)*
N	n	*(eh-neh)*
name(s)	nombre(s)	*(nohm-breh[s])*
napkin	servilleta	*(sehr-bee-yeh-tah)*
narcotics	narcóticos	*(nahr-koh-tee-kohs)*
nasal	nasal	*(nah-sahl)*
nausea	náusea	*(nah-oo-seh-ah)*
navel	ombligo	*(ohm-blee-goh)*
near	cerca de	*(sehr-kah deh)*
need	necesita	*(neh-seh-see-tah)*
needle	aguja	*(ah-goo-hah)*
needs	necesidades	*(neh-seh-see-dah-dehs)*
neither	tampoco	*(tahm-poh-koh)*
neither . . . nor	ni . . . ni	*(nee . . . nee)*
neonatal	neonatal	*(neh-oh-nah-tahl)*
nephew	sobrino	*(soh-bree-noh)*
nervous	nervioso	*(nehr-bee-oh-soh)*
neurotic	neurótico	*(neh-oo-roh-tee-koh)*
neutral	neutral	*(neh-oo-trahl)*
never	jamás/nunca	*(hah-mahs/noon-kah)*
next	siguiente	*(see-ggee-ehn-teh)*
nicotine	nicotina	*(nee-koh-tee-nah)*
niece	sobrina	*(soh-bree-nah)*
nightgown	camisa de dormir/ bata	*(kah-mee-sah deh dohr-meer/bah-tah)*
nine	nueve	*(noo-eh-beh)*
nine hundred	novecientos	*(noh-beh-see-ehn-tohs)*
9:00 A.M.	las nueve	*(lahs noo-eh-beh)*
9:00 P.M.	las veintiuna horas	*(lahs beh-een-tee-oo-nah oh-rahs)*
nineteen	diecinueve	*(dee-ehs-ee-noo-eh-beh)*
ninety	noventa	*(noh-behn-tah)*
ninth	noveno(a)	*(noh-beh-noh[-nah])*
nitroglycerin	nitroglicerina	*(nee-troh-glee-seh-ree-nah)*
no	no	*(noh)*
no one	nadie	*(nah-dee-eh)*
no salt	sin sal	*(seen sahl)*
nobody	nadie	*(nah-dee-eh)*
none	ninguno	*(neen-goo-noh)*
normal	normal	*(nohr-mahl)*
north	norte	*(nohr-teh)*
nose	nariz	*(nah-rees)*
noses	narices	*(nah-ree-sehs)*

not	no	*(noh)*
not any	ninguno	*(neen-goo-noh)*
not ever	jamás/nunca	*(hah-mahs/noon-kah)*
not translated	no se traducen	*(noh seh trah-doo-sehn)*
note	note	*(noh-teh)*
nothing	nada	*(nah-dah)*
nouns	nombres	*(nohm-brehs)*
November	noviembre	*(noh-bee-ehm-breh)*
Novocain	novocaína	*(noh-boh-kah-ee-nah)*
now	ahora	*(ah-oh-rah)*
nuclear medicine	medicina nuclear	*(meh-dee-see-nah noo-kleh-ahr)*
number(s)	número(s)	*(noo-meh-roh[s])*
nurse	enfermero(a)	*(ehn-fehr-meh-roh[-rah])*
nurses' station	estación de enfermeras	*(ehs-tah-see-ohn deh ehn-fehr-meh-rahs)*
nutrition	nutrición	*(noo-tree-see-ohn)*
O	o	*(oh)*
oatmeal	avena	*(ah-beh-nah)*
obesity	obesidad	*(oh-beh-see-dahd)*
observe	observe	*(ohb-sehr-beh)*
obsession	obsesión	*(ohb-seh-see-ohn)*
obstruction	obstrucción	*(ohbs-trook-see-ohn)*
occasion	ocasión	*(oh-kah-see-ohn)*
occipital	occipital	*(ohk-see-pee-tahl)*
occur	ocurrir	*(oh-koo-rreer)*
October	octubre	*(ohk-too-breh)*
of	de	*(deh)*
of each other	uno de otro	*(oo-noh deh oh-troh)*
office	oficina	*(oh-fee-see-nah)*
oil	aceite	*(ah-seh-ee-teh)*
ointment	ungüento	*(oon-goo-ehn-toh)*
older	mayores	*(mah-yoh-rehs)*
olive	aceituna	*(ah-seh-ee-too-nah)*
on	en/sobre	*(ehn/soh-breh)*
one	un/uno	*(oon/oo-noh)*
one-fourth	un cuarto	*(oon koo-ahr-toh)*
one-half	un medio	*(oon meh-dee-oh)*
one hundred	cien	*(see-ehn)*
one-third	un tercio	*(oon tehr-see-oh)*
one thousand	mil	*(meel)*
one thousand one	mil uno	*(meel oo-noh)*
1:00 A.M.	la una	*(lah oo-nah)*
1:00 P.M.	las trece horas	*(lahs treh-seh oh-rahs)*
onions	cebolla	*(seh-boh-yah)*
only	solamente	*(sohl-lah-mehn-teh)*
opaque	opaco	*(oh-pah-koh)*
open	abra	*(ah-brah)*
operating room	quirófano/cuarto de cirugía	*(kee-roh-fah-noh/koo-ahr-toh deh see-roo-hee-ah)*
ophthalmic	oftálmico	*(ohf-tahl-mee-koh)*

pepper	pimienta	*(pee-mee-ehn-tah)*
perfume	perfume	*(pehr-foo-meh)*
permission	permiso	*(pehr-mee-soh)*
person	persona(s)	*(pehr-soh-nah[s])*
personal	personales	*(pehr-soh-nah-lehs)*
pharmacy	farmacia	*(fahr-mah-see-ah)*
philosophy	filosofía	*(fee-loh-soh-fee-ah)*
phone	teléfono	*(teh-leh-foh-noh)*
phrases	frases	*(frah-sehs)*
physician (m)	médico/doctor	*(meh-dee-koh/dohk-tohr)*
physician (f)	médica/doctora	*(meh-dee-kah/dohk-toh-rah)*
physicians (m)	médicos/doctores	*(meh-dee-kohs/dohk-toh-rehs)*
physicians (f)	médicas/doctoras	*(meh-dee-kahs/dohk-toh-rahs)*
physique	físico	*(fee-see-koh)*
pickles	pepino	*(peh-pee-noh)*
pie(s)	pastel(es)	*(pahs-tehl[-ehs])*
piece	pieza	*(pee-ehs-ah)*
pill	píldora	*(peel-doh-rah)*
pillow	almohada	*(ahl-moh-ah-dah)*
pillowcase	funda	*(foon-dah)*
pineapple	piña	*(pee-nyah)*
pink	rosa	*(roh-sah)*
pinkish	rosado	*(roh-sah-doh)*
pinprick	picadura	*(pee-kah-doo-rah)*
pinto beans	frijol pinto	*(free-hohl peen-toh)*
pity	lástima	*(lahs-tee-mah)*
pizza	pizza	*(pee-sah)*
place	lugar/poner/colocar	*(loo-gahr/poh-nehr/koh-loh-kahr)*
placing it	colocándolo	*(koh-loh-kahn-doh-loh)*
plan	plan	*(plahn)*
plate	plato	*(plah-toh)*
play	jugar	*(hoo-gahr)*
please	por favor	*(pohr fah-bohr)*
plum(s)	ciruelos(as)	*(see-roo-eh-lohs[-lahs])*
plural	plural	*(ploo-rahl)*
pneumonia	pulmonía/neumonía	*(pool-moh-nee-ah/neh-oo-moh-nee-ah)*
point	señalar/apunte	*(seh-nah-lahr/ah-poon-teh)*
poisons	venenos	*(beh-neh-nohs)*
porcelain	porcelana	*(pohr-seh-lah-nah)*
pork	puerco	*(poo-ehr-koh)*
potatoes	papas	*(pah-pahs)*
potential	posibles	*(poh-see-blehs)*
pots	trastes	*(trahs-tehs)*
pound	libra	*(lee-brah)*
practice	práctica	*(prahk-tee-kah)*
pregnant	embarazada	*(ehm-bah-rah-sah-dah)*
preparation	preparación	*(preh-pah-rah-see-ohn)*
prepare	prepara	*(preh-pah-rah)*
prescribed	ordena	*(ohr-deh-nah)*
present day	moderno	*(moh-dehr-noh)*
preventive	preventivo	*(preh-behn-tee-boh)*

priest	sacerdote	(sah-sehr-doh-teh)
prison	cárcel	(kahr-sehl)
probable	probable	(proh-bah-bleh)
problem	problema	(proh-bleh-mah)
procedure	procedimiento	(proh-seh-dee-mee-ehn-toh)
promise	prometer	(proh-meh-tehr)
pronounce	pronuncia	(pro-noon-see-ah)
pronouns	pronombres	(proh-nohm-brehs)
pronunciation	pronunciación	(proh-noon-see-ah-see-ohn)
provides	provee	(proh-beh-eh)
prune(s)	ciruela(s)	(see-roo-eh-lah[s])
pruritic	prurítico	(proo-ree-tee-koh)
psoriasis	soriasis	(soh-ree-ah-sees)
pubic	púbico	(poo-bee-koh)
pull	jale	(hah-leh)
pulse	pulso	(pool-soh)
puncture	pinchazo/picadura	(peen-chah-soh/pee-kah-doo-rah)
pure	puro	(poo-roh)
pureed	pure	(poo-reh)
pyorrhea	piorrea	(pee-oh-rreh-ah)
Q	q	(koo)
quart	cuarto	(koo-ahr-toh)
question(s)	pregunta(s)	(preh-goon-tah[s])
quite attached	acostumbrados	(ah-kohs-toom-brah-dohs)
R	r	(eh-rreh)
racial	racial	(rah-see-ahl)
radio	radio	(rah-dee-oh)
radioactive	radioactivo	(rah-dee-oh-ahk-tee-boh)
railroad	tren	(trehn)
raisins	pasas	(pah-sahs)
rare	raro	(rah-roh)
raw	crudos	(kroo-dohs)
razor	máquina de afeitar/ navaja	(mah-kee-nah deh ah-feh-ee-tahr/nah- bah-hah)
reach	alcanzar	(ahl-kahn-sahr)
read	leer	(leh-ehr)
reason	razón	(rah-sohn)
reassurance	asegurar	(ah-seh-goo-rahr)
receive	recibir	(reh-see-beer)
receptionist	recepcionista	(reh-sehp-see-ohn-ees-tah)
recognize	reconocer	(reh-koh-noh-sehr)
recommendations	recomendaciones	(reh-koh-men-dah-see-ohn-es)
recovery room	cuarto de recuperación	(koo-ahr-toh deh reh-koo-peh-rah-see- ohn)
rectal	rectal	(rehk-tahl)
rectum	recto	(rehk-toh)
recuperating	recuperando	(reh-koo-peh-rahn-doh)
red	rojo	(roh-hoh)
red meat	carne roja	(kahr-neh roh-hah)

red spots	manchas rojas	*(mahn-chahs roh-hahs)*
refried	refritos	*(reh-free-tohs)*
regular	regular	*(reh-goo-lahr)*
remain	quédese	*(keh-deh-seh)*
remember	recordar/acordarse	*(reh-kohr-dahr/ah-kohr-dahr-seh)*
repel	repeler	*(reh-peh-lehr)*
reports	reportes	*(reh-pohr-tehs)*
residue	residuo	*(reh-see-doo-oh)*
resin	resina	*(reh-see-nah)*
respect	respeto	*(rehs-peh-toh)*
respond	responder	*(rehs-pohn-dehr)*
rest	reposo	*(reh-poh-soh)*
restless	inquieto	*(een-kee-eh-toh)*
restroom	cuarto de baño	*(koo-ahr-toh deh bah-nyoh)*
return	volver/regresar	*(bohl-behr/reh-greh-sahr)*
rheumatic	reumático	*(reh-oo-mah-tee-koh)*
ribs	costillas	*(kohs-tee-yahs)*
rice	arroz	*(ah-rohs)*
right	derecha	*(deh-reh-chah)*
road	camino	*(kah-mee-noh)*
roast	rostizado	*(rohs-tee-sah-doh)*
roast beef	rosbif	*(rohs-beef)*
rolls	panecillos	*(pah-neh-see-yohs)*
room	cuarto	*(koo-ahr-toh)*
roseola	roséola	*(roh-seh-oh-lah)*
route(s)	ruta(s)	*(roo-tah[s])*
routine	rutina	*(roo-tee-nah)*
rub	frotar/restregar	*(froh-tahr/rehs-treh-gahr)*
rubella	rubéola	*(roo-beh-oh-lah)*
S	s	*(eh-seh)*
saccharin	sacarina	*(sah-kah-ree-nah)*
salad	ensalada	*(ehn-sah-lah-dah)*
saliva	saliva	*(sah-lee-bah)*
salt	sal	*(sahl)*
sample	muestra	*(moo-ehs-trah)*
sanitary	sanitario	*(sah-nee-tah-ree-oh)*
Saturday	sábado	*(sah-bah-doh)*
saucer	platillo	*(plah-tee-yoh)*
sausage	chorizo/salchicha	*(choh-ree-soh/sahl-chee-chah)*
science	ciencia	*(see-ehn-see-ah)*
scleral	escleral	*(ehs-kleh-rahl)*
scorpion	alacrán	*(ah-lah-krahn)*
scrambled	revueltos	*(reh-boo-ehl-tohs)*
scratch	raspón	*(rahs-pohn)*
scream	gritar	*(gree-tahr)*
season	estación	*(ehs-tah-see-ohn)*
sebaceous	sebáceo	*(seh-bah-seh-oh)*
second	segundo(a)	*(seh-goon-doh[-dah])*
secrete	secretar	*(seh-kreh-tahr)*
sedatives	sedativo/sedantes	*(seh-dah-tee-boh/seh-dahn-tehs)*

selected	selectas	(seh-lehk-tahs)
selection	selección	(seh-lehk-see-ohn)
sell	vender	(behn-dher)
semisolid	semisólido(a)	(seh-mee-soh-lee-doh[-dah])
sensitive	sensitivo	(sehn-see-tee-boh)
sentence	oración	(oh-rah-see-ohn)
September	septiembre	(sehp-tee-ehm-breh)
series	series	(seh-ree-ehs)
serology	serología	(seh-roh-loh-hee-ah)
serve	servimos	(sehr-bee-mohs)
served	se sirven	(seh seer-behn)
services	servicios	(sehr-bee-see-ohs)
setting	área	(ah-reh-ah)
seven	siete	(see-eh-teh)
seven hundred	setecientos	(seh-teh-see-ehn-tohs)
7:00 A.M.	las siete	(lahs see-eh-teh)
7:00 P.M.	las diecinueve horas	(lahs dee-eh-see-noo-eh-beh oh-rahs)
seventeen	diecisiete	(dee-eh-see-see-eh-teh)
seventh	séptimo(a)	(sehp-tee-moh[-mah])
seventy	setenta	(seh-tehn-tah)
several	varios	(bah-ree-ohs)
sex	sexo	(sehx-oh)
sexual	sexual	(sehx-oo-ahl)
she	ella	(ey-yah)
sheet	sábana	(sah-bah-nah)
shirt	camisa	(kah-mee-sah)
shoes	zapatos	(sah-pah-tohs)
shortening	manteca	(mahn-teh-kah)
should	debe	(deh-beh)
shower	ducha	(doo-chah)
shrimp	camarones	(kah-mah-roh-nehs)
sign	firme/letrero	(feer-meh/leh-treh-roh)
similar	similares	(see-mee-lah-rehs)
simple	sencillas	(sehn-see-yahs)
since	desde/como	(dehs-deh/koh-moh)
single	solo/one	(soh-loh/oo-noh)
singular	singular	(seen-goo-lahr)
sister	hermana	(ehr-mah-nah)
sister-in-law	cuñada	(koo-nyah-dah)
sit!	¡Siéntese!	(see-ehn-teh-seh)
situation	situación	(see-too-ah-see-ohn)
six	seis	(seh-ees)
six hundred	seiscientos	(seh-ees-ee-ehn-tohs)
6:00 A.M.	las seis	(lahs seh-ees)
6:00 P.M.	las dieciocho horas	(lahs dee-eh-see-oh-choh oh-rahs)
sixteen	dieciseís	(dee-eh-see-seh-ees)
sixth	sexto(a)	(sex-toh[-tah])
sixty	sesenta	(seh-sehn-tah)
skirt	falda	(fahl-dah)
sleep	sueño	(soo-eh-nyoh)
small	pequeño/chico	(peh-keh-nyoh/chee-koh)

smile	sonrisa	(sohn-ree-sah)
smoke	fumar	(fooh-mahr)
so	así que	(ah-see keh)
social	social	(soh-see-ahl)
social worker	trabajadora social	(trah-bah-hah-doh-rah soh-see-ahl)
socks	calcetines/calcetas	(kahl-seh-tee-nehs/kahl-seh-tahs)
sofa	sofá	(soh-fah)
soft	suave	(soo-ah-beh)
soldier	soldado	(sohl-dah-doh)
solid	sólido	(soh-lee-doh)
solution	solución	(soh-loo-see-ohn)
solvent	solvente	(sohl-behn-teh)
somatic	somático	(soh-mah-tee-koh)
some	algunos/unos	(ahl-goo-nohs/oo-nohs)
some hearts	unos corazones	(oo-nohs koh-rah-soh-nehs)
some tables	unas mesas	(oo-nahs meh-sahs)
somebody	alguien	(ahl-ggee-ehn)
someone	alguien	(ahl-ggee-ehn)
something	algo	(ahl-goh)
sometimes	a veces/algunas veces	(ah beh-sehs/ahl-goo-nahs beh-sehs)
son	hijo	(ee-hoh)
soup(s)	caldo(s)/sopa(s)	(kahl-doh[s]/soh-pah[s])
south	sur	(soor)
spaghetti	espagüeti	(ehs-pah-geh-tee)
Spanish	español	(ehs-pah-nyohl)
speak	hable	(ah-bleh)
special	especiales	(ehs-peh-see-ah-lehs)
specimen	muestra/espectro	(moo-ehs-trah/ehs-pehk-troh)
spices	especias	(ehs-peh-see-ahs)
spicy	condimentadas	(kohn-dee-mehn-tah-dahs)
spinach	espinaca	(ehs-pee-nah-kah)
spinal	espinal	(ehs-pee-nahl)
spirit	espíritu	(ehs-pee-ree-too)
spread	untar/extender	(oon-tahr/ehx-tehn-dehr)
spring	primavera	(pree-mah-beh-rah)
stairs	escaleras	(ehs-kah-leh-rahs)
start	comenzar	(koh-mehn-sahr)
STAT	STAT	(ehs-taht)
steak	bistec	(bees-tehk)
step	pisar	(pee-sahr)
stepdaughter	hijastra	(ee-hahs-trah)
stepfather	padrastro	(pah-drahs-troh)
stepmother	madrastra	(mah-drahs-trah)
stepson	hijastro	(ee-hahs-troh)
sterile	estéril	(ehs-teh-reel)
stethoscope	estetoscópio	(ehs-teh-tohs-koh-pee-oh)
stockings	medias	(meh-dee-ahs)
straight	derecho	(deh-reh-choh)
straw	popote	(poh-poh-teh)
strawberry	fresa	(freh-sah)
street	calle	(kah-yeh)

stroke	ataque de apoplejía	*(ah-tah-keh deh ah-poh-pleh-hee-ah)*
stupor	estupor	*(ehs-too-pohr)*
subaxillary	subaxilar	*(soob-ahx-ee-lahr)*
subcutaneous	subcutáneo	*(soob-koo-tah-neh-oh)*
sublingual	sublingual	*(soob-leen-goo-ahl)*
subnormal	subnormal	*(soob-nohr-mahl)*
substernal	subesternal	*(soob-ehs-tehr-nahl)*
substitutes	sustitutos	*(soohs-tee-too-tohs)*
successful	con éxito	*(kohn ehx-ee-toh)*
suffer	sufrir	*(soo-freer)*
sugar	azúcar	*(ah-soo-kahr)*
suit	traje	*(trah-heh)*
summer	verano	*(beh-rah-noh)*
Sunday	domingo	*(doh-meen-goh)*
supper	cena	*(seh-nah)*
suppository	supositorio	*(soo-poh-see-toh-ree-oh)*
surgery	cirugía	*(see-roo-hee-ah)*
surroundings	alrededor	*(ahl-reh-deh-dohr)*
sweater	chamarra/suéter	*(cha-mah-rah/soo-eh-tehr)*
symbol	símbolo	*(seem-boh-loh)*
symptoms	síntomas	*(seen-toh-mahs)*
syncope	síncope	*(seen-koh-peh)*
syringe	jeringa	*(heh-reen-gah)*
syrup	jarabe/zumo	*(hah-rah-beh/soo-moh)*
systemic	sistémico	*(sees-teh-mee-koh)*
systemic	sistemico	*(sees-teh-mee-koh)*
systole	sístole	*(sees-toh-leh)*
T	t	*(teh)*
table(s)	mesa(s)	*(meh-sah[s])*
tablespoon	cuchara	*(koo-chah-rah)*
tablet	tableta	*(tah-bleh-tah)*
tacos	tacos	*(tah-kohs)*
tamales	tamales	*(tah-mah-lehs)*
taste	gusto	*(goos-toh)*
tea	té	*(teh)*
teaspoon	cucharita	*(koo-chah-ree-tah)*
technician	técnico	*(tehk-nee-koh)*
television	televisor	*(teh-leh-bee-sohr)*
temperature	temperatura	*(tehm-peh-rah-too-rah)*
temporal	temporal	*(tehm-poh-rahl)*
ten	diez	*(dee-ehs)*
10:00 A.M.	las diez	*(lahs dee-ehs)*
10:00 P.M.	las veintidós horas	*(lahs beh-een-tee-dohs oh-rahs)*
tense	tenso	*(tehn-soh)*
tension	tensión	*(tehn-see-ohn)*
tenth	décimo(a)	*(deh-see-moh[-mah])*
terms	términos	*(tehr-mee-nohs)*
tetanus	tétanos	*(teh-tah-nohs)*
than	que	*(keh)*
thank you	gracias	*(grah-see-ahs)*

that	eso/esa/aquello/ aquella/ese/esa/ aquel/que	*(eh-soh/eh-sah/ah-keh-yoh/ah-keh-yah/eh-seh/eh-sah/ah-kehl/keh)*
that have	que tienen	*(keh tee-eh-nehn)*
the	el/la	*(ehl/lah)*
their	su/sus	*(soo/soos)*
them	ellos	*(eh-yohs)*
therapy	terapia	*(teh-rah-pee-ah)*
there are	hay	*(ah-ee)*
therefore	por lo tanto	*(pohr loh tan-toh)*
thermometer	termómetro	*(tehr-moh-meh-troh)*
these	estos(as)	*(ehs-tohs[-tahs])*
they	ellos(as)	*(eh-yohs[-yahs])*
third	tercero(a)	*(tehr-seh-roh[-rah])*
thirteen	trece	*(treh-seh)*
thirty	treinta	*(treh-een-tah)*
this	esto(a)/este	*(ehs-toh[-tah]/ehs-teh)*
those	esos/esas/estos/estas/ aquellos/aquellas	*(eh-sohs/eh-sahs/ehs-tohs/ehs-tahs/ ah-keh-yohs/ah-keh-yahs)*
three	tres	*(trehs)*
three-fourths	tres cuartos	*(trehs koo-ahr-tohs)*
three hundred	trecientos	*(treh-see-ehn-tohs)*
three thousand	tres mil	*(trehs meel)*
3:00 A.M.	las tres	*(lahs trehs)*
3:00 P.M.	las quince horas	*(lahs keen-seh oh-rahs)*
Thursday	jueves	*(hoo-eh-behs)*
thyroid	tiroide/tiroidea	*(tee-roh-ee-deh/tee-roh-ee-deh-ah)*
tie	corbata	*(kohr-bah-tah)*
time	cada	*(kah-dah)*
tiny	menudo	*(meh-noo-doh)*
tissues	tisú(es)	*(tee-sooh[-ehs])*
to	a/para	*(ah/pah-rah)*
to accept	aceptar	*(ah-sehp-tahr)*
to activate	activar	*(ahk-tee-bahr)*
to administer	administrar	*(ahd-mee-nees-trahr)*
to advise	aconsejar	*(ah-kohn-seh-hahr)*
to agree	acordar	*(ah-kohr-dahr)*
to appreciate	apreciar	*(ah-preh-see-ahr)*
to arrive	llegar	*(yeh-gahr)*
to ask	preguntar	*(preh-goon-tahr)*
to assess	asesorar/evaluar	*(ah-seh-soh-rahr/eh-bah-loo-ahr)*
to auscultate	auscultar	*(ah-oos-kool-tahr)*
to authorize	autorizar	*(ahoo-toh-ree-sahr)*
to avoid	evitar	*(eh-bee-tahr)*
to bathe	bañar	*(bah-nyahr)*
to be	estar/ser	*(ehs-tahr/sehr)*
to be able	poder	*(poh-dehr)*
to be afraid	temer	*(teh-mehr)*
to be available	estar disponible	*(ehs-tahr dees-poh-nee-bleh)*
to be born	nacer	*(nah-sehr)*
to be supportive	apoyar	*(ah-poh-yahr)*

to beat	golpear	*(gohl-peh-ahr)*
to become ill	enfermar	*(ehn-fehr-mahr)*
to believe	creer	*(kreh-ehr)*
to bleed	sangrar	*(sahn-grahr)*
to boil	hervir	*(ehr-beer)*
to bore	aburrir	*(ah-boo-rreer)*
to break	romper	*(rohm-pehr)*
to breathe	respirar	*(rehs-pee-rahr)*
to bring	traer	*(trah-ehr)*
to bring near	acercar	*(ah-sehr-kahr)*
to build	construir	*(kohns-troo-eer)*
to call	llamar	*(yah-mahr)*
to carry	llevar	*(yeh-bahr)*
to change	cambiar	*(kahm-bee-ahr)*
to clean	limpiar	*(leem-pee-ahr)*
to close	cerrar	*(seh-rrahr)*
to come	venir	*(beh-neer)*
to communicate	comunicar	*(koh-moo-nee-kahr)*
to complain	quejar	*(keh-hahr)*
to conduct	conducir	*(kohn-doo-seer)*
to confuse	confundir	*(kohn-foon-deer)*
to conserve	conservar	*(kohn-sehr-bahr)*
to control	controlar	*(kohn-troh-lahr)*
to cook	cocinar	*(koh-see-nahr)*
to cover	cubrir	*(koo-breer)*
to cry	llorar	*(yoh-rahr)*
to cut	cortar	*(kohr-tahr)*
to deny	negar	*(neh-gahr)*
to deserve	merecer	*(meh-reh-sehr)*
to destroy	destruir	*(dehs-troo-eer)*
to die	morir	*(moh-reer)*
to disappear	desaparecer	*(deh-sah-pah-reh-sehr)*
to discover	descubrir	*(dehs-koo-breer)*
to do	hacer	*(ah-sehr)*
to drink	beber	*(beh-behr)*
to eat	comer	*(koh-mehr)*
to eat breakfast	desayunar	*(deh-sah-yoo-nahr)*
to embrace	abrazar	*(ah-brah-sahr)*
to employ	emplear	*(ehm-pleh-ahr)*
to evaluate	evaluar	*(eh-bah-loo-ahr)*
to examine	examinar	*(ehx-ah-mee-nahr)*
to feel	sentir	*(sehn-teer)*
to fill	llenar	*(yeh-nahr)*
to find	descubrir/hallar	*(dehs-koo-breer/ah-yahr)*
to find out	descubrir	*(dehs-koo-breer)*
to finish	acabar	*(ah-kah-bahr)*
to fix	componer	*(kohm-poh-nehr)*
to fly	volar	*(boh-lahr)*
to follow	seguir	*(seh-geer)*
to gain by	ganar	*(gah-nahr)*
to get acquainted	darse a conocer	*(dahr-seh ah koh-noh-sehr)*

to get better	mejorar	*(meh-hoh-rahr)*
to get up	levantar	*(leh-bahn-tahr)*
to give	dar	*(dahr)*
to go	ir	*(eer)*
to go by	pasar	*(pah-sahr)*
to go out	salir	*(sah-leer)*
to go to bed	acostarse	*(ah-kohs-tahr-seh)*
to greet	saludar	*(sah-loo-dahr)*
to hang	colgar	*(kohl-gahr)*
to have	haber/tener	*(ah-behr/teh-nehr)*
to heal	sanar	*(sah-nahr)*
to hear	escuchar	*(ehs-koo-chahr)*
to hear me	oírme	*(oh-eer-meh)*
to hesitate	vacilar	*(bah-see-lahr)*
to hit	pegar	*(peh-gahr)*
to hunt	cazar	*(kah-sahr)*
to hurt	doler	*(doh-lehr)*
to inform	informar	*(een-fohr-mahr)*
to interpret	interpretar	*(een-tehr-preh-tahr)*
to joke	bromear	*(broh-meh-ahr)*
to jump	saltar	*(sahl-tahr)*
to kid	bromear	*(broh-meh-ahr)*
to kiss	besar	*(beh-sahr)*
to knock	golpear	*(gohl-peh-ahr)*
to know	conocer	*(koh-noh-sehr)*
to lay down	acostar	*(ah-kohs-tahr)*
to leave	dejar	*(deh-hahr)*
to let go	soltar	*(sohl-tahr)*
to listen	oír	*(oh-eer)*
to live	vivir	*(bee-beer)*
to lose	perder	*(pehr-dehr)*
to make	hacer	*(ah-sehr)*
to marry	casar	*(kah-sahr)*
to name	nombrar	*(nohm-brahr)*
to need	necesitar	*(neh-seh-see-tahr)*
to operate	operar	*(oh-peh-rahr)*
to paint	pintar	*(peen-tahr)*
to palpate	palpar	*(pahl-pahr)*
to pay	pagar	*(pah-gahr)*
to point	señalar	*(seh-nyah-lahr)*
to present	presentar	*(preh-sehn-tahr)*
to promise	prometer	*(proh-meh-tehr)*
to protect	proteger	*(proh-teh-hehr)*
to provoke	provocar	*(proh-boh-kahr)*
to raise	levantar	*(leh-bahn-tahr)*
to reach	alcanzar	*(ahl-kahn-sahr)*
to receive	recibir	*(reh-see-beer)*
to recognize	reconocer	*(reh-koh-noh-sehr)*
to reduce	reducir	*(reh-doo-seer)*
to remain	quedar	*(keh-dahr)*
to remember	acordar/recordar	*(ah-kohr-dahr/reh-kohr-dahr)*

to respond	responder	*(rehs-pohn-dehr)*
to return	regresar/volver	*(reh-greh-sahr/bohl-behr)*
to revise	revisar	*(reh-bee-sahr)*
to scream	gritar	*(gree-tahr)*
to see	ver	*(behr)*
to select	seleccionar	*(seh-lehk-see-oh-nahr)*
to sell	vender	*(behn-dehr)*
to separate	separar	*(seh-pah-rahr)*
to serve	servir	*(sehr-beer)*
to shake	temblar	*(tehm-blahr)*
to sit	sentar	*(sehn-tahr)*
to sleep	dormir	*(dohr-meer)*
to speak	hablar	*(ah-blahr)*
to start	comenzar	*(koh-mehn-sahr)*
to step	pisar	*(pee-sahr)*
to stop	parar	*(pah-rahr)*
to suffer	sufrir	*(soo-freer)*
to suspend	suspender	*(soos-pehn-dehr)*
to take	tomar/llevar	*(toh-mahr/yeh-bahr)*
to take out	sacar	*(sah-kahr)*
to talk	hablar	*(ah-blahr)*
to talk to	hablar con	*(ah-blahr kohn)*
to tell	decir	*(deh-seer)*
to thank for	agradecer	*(ah-grah-deh-sehr)*
to try	tratar	*(trah-tahr)*
to turn	voltear	*(bohl-teh-ahr)*
to turn off	apagar	*(ah-pah-gahr)*
to visit	visitar	*(bee-see-tahr)*
to vomit	vomitar	*(boh-mee-tahr)*
to wait	esperar	*(ehs-peh-rahr)*
to wake	despertar	*(dehs-pehr-tahr)*
to walk	caminar	*(kah-mee-nahr)*
to want	querer	*(keh-rehr)*
to wash	lavar	*(lah-bahr)*
to wish	desear	*(deh-seh-ahr)*
to work	trabajar	*(trah-bah-hahr)*
to write	escribir	*(ehs-kree-beer)*
toast	pan tostado	*(pahn tohs-tah-doh)*
toilet	inodoro	*(ee-noh-doh-roh)*
tolerant	tolerante	*(toh-leh-rahn-teh)*
tomato	tomate	*(toh-mah-teh)*
tomorrow	mañana	*(mah-nyah-nah)*
tonsillitis	tonsilitis/amigdalitis	*(tohn-see-lee-tees/ah-meeg-dah-lee-tees)*
too much	mucho	*(moo-choh)*
toothache	dolor de muelas	*(doh-lohr deh moo-eh-lahs)*
toothbrush	cepillo de dientes	*(seh-pee-yoh deh dee-ehn-tehs)*
toothpaste	pasta de dientes	*(pahs-tah deh dee-ehn-tehs)*
toothpick	palillo	*(pah-lee-yoh)*
topical	tópico	*(toh-pee-koh)*
torso	torso	*(tohr-soh)*

total	total	*(toh-tahl)*
toward	hacia	*(ah-see-ah)*
towel	toalla	*(too-ah-yah)*
tower	torre	*(toh-rreh)*
translate	traducir/interpretar	*(trah-doo-seer/een-tehr-preh-tahr)*
transparent	transparente	*(trahns-pah-rehn-teh)*
treatment	tratamiento	*(trah-tah-mee-ehn-toh)*
tree	árbol	*(ahr-bohl)*
try	intentar/tratar	*(een-tehn-tahr/trah-tahr)*
tube(s)	tubo(s)	*(too-boh[s])*
Tuesday	martes	*(mahr-tehs)*
tumor	tumor	*(too-mohr)*
tuna	atún	*(ah-toon)*
turkey	pavo/guajolote	*(pah-boh/goo-ah-hoh-loh-teh)*
turn	voltear/girar	*(bohl-teh-ahr/hee-rahr)*
turn	voltee	*(bohl-teh-eh)*
turn off	apagar	*(ah-pah-gahr)*
twelve	doce	*(doh-seh)*
12:00 midnight	las veinticuatro horas	*(lahs beh-een-tee-koo-ah-troh oh-rahs)*
12:00 noon	las doce	*(lahs doh-seh)*
twenty	veinte	*(beh-een-teh)*
twenty-four	veinticuatro	*(beh-een-tee-koo-ah-troh)*
two	dos	*(dohs)*
two hundred	doscientos	*(doh-see-ehn-tohs)*
two thousand	dos mil	*(dohs meel)*
two thousand two	dos mil dos	*(dohs meel dohs)*
2:00 A.M.	las dos	*(lahs dohs)*
2:00 P.M.	las catorce horas	*(lahs kah-tohr-seh oh-rahs)*
type(s)	tipo(s)	*(tee-poh[s])*
U	u	*(oo)*
ulcer(s)	úlcera(s)	*(ool-seh-rah[s])*
ulnar	ulnar	*(ool-nahr)*
ultrasound	ultrasonido	*(ool-trah-soh-nee-doh)*
uncle	tío	*(tee-oh)*
under	debajo de	*(deh-bah-hoh deh)*
underwear	ropa interior	*(roh-pah een-teh-ree-ohr)*
union	unión	*(oo-nee-ohn)*
universal	universal	*(oo-nee-behr-sahl)*
until	hasta	*(ahs-tah)*
urea	urea	*(oo-reh-ah)*
uremia	uremia	*(oo-reh-mee-ah)*
ureteritis	uretritis	*(oo-reh-tree-tees)*
urinal	bacín	*(bah-seen)*
urine	orina	*(oh-ree-nah)*
urticaria	urticaria	*(oor-tee-kah-ree-ah)*
use	usar	*(oo-sahr)*
used	usado	*(oo-sah-doh)*
useful	útiles	*(oo-tee-lehs)*
uterus	útero	*(oo-teh-roh)*
uvula	úvula	*(oo-boo-lah)*

V	v	(beh)
vaccinations	vacunas	(bah-koo-nahs)
vaginal	vaginal	(bah-hee-nahl)
vaginitis	vaginitis	(bah-hee-nee-tees)
vagus	vago	(bah-goh)
valve	válvula	(bal-boo-lah)
vanilla	vainilla	(bah-ee-nee-yah)
vapor	vapor	(bah-pohr)
varicocele	varicocéle	(bah-ree-koh-seh-leh)
variety	variedad	(bah-ree-eh-dahd)
vegetables	vegetales	(beh-heh-tah-lehs)
vein	vena	(beh-nah)
venereal	venéreo	(beh-neh-reh-oh)
ventilation	ventilación	(behn-tee-lah-see-ohn)
verbs	verbos	(behr-bohs)
vermouth	vermut	(behr-moot)
vertebrate	vertebrado	(behr-teh-brah-doh)
vertigo	vértigo	(behr-tee-goh)
vestibule	vestíbulo	(behs-tee-boo-loh)
veterinary	veterinaria	(beh-teh-ree-nah-ree-ah)
vinegar	vinagre	(bee-nah-greh)
violet	violeta	(bee-oh-leh-tah)
virgin	virgen	(beer-hehn)
visible	visible	(bee-see-bleh)
vision	visión	(bee-see-ohn)
visiting hours	horas de visita	(oh-rahs deh bee-see-tah)
vital	vital	(bee-tahl)
vitamins	vitaminas	(bee-tah-mee-nahs)
voice	voz	(bohs)
volume	volúmen	(boh-loo-mehn)
vomit	vómito	(boh-mee-toh)
vomiting	vomitando	(boh-mee-tahn-doh)
W	w	(doh-bleh beh)
wake up	despiértese	(dehs-pee-ehr-teh-seh)
wall(s)	pared(es)	(pah-rehd[pah-reh-dehs])
watch	reloj	(rreh-lohj)
watchman	velador	(beh-lah-dohr)
water	agua	(ah-goo-ah)
water jug	jarra	(hah-rrah)
watermelon	sandía	(sahn-dee-ah)
we	nosotros(as)	(noh-soh-trohs[-ahs])
Wednesday	miércoles	(mee-ehr-koh-lehs)
week	semana	(seh-mah-nah)
went out	salió	(sah-lee-oh)
west	oeste	(oh-ehs-teh)
what	qué	(keh)
wheat	trigo	(tree-goh)
when	cuando	(koo-ahn-doh)
where	donde	(dohn-deh)
which	cual/que	(koo-ahl/keh)

which(ones)	cuáles	*(koo-ahl-ehs)*
white	blanco/ceniza	*(blahn-koh/seh-nee-sah)*
white spots	manchas blancas	*(mahn-chahs blahn-kahs)*
who	quién	*(kee-ehn)*
who(all)	quienes	*(kee-eh-nehs)*
whole milk	leche entera	*(leh-cheh ehn-teh-rah)*
whom	quién es	*(kee-ehn ehs)*
why	por qué	*(pohr keh)*
wife	esposa	*(ehs-poh-sah)*
will have	tendrá	*(tehn-drah)*
will help you	le ayudará	*(leh ah-yoo-dah-rah)*
will remember	recordará	*(reh-kohr-dah-rah)*
will talk	hablará	*(ah-blah-rah)*
window	ventana	*(behn-tah-nah)*
window(pane)	ventana de vidrio	*(behn-tah-nah deh bee-dree-oh)*
wings	alas	*(al-lahs)*
winter	invierno	*(een-bee-ehr-noh)*
with	con	*(kohn)*
within	dentro de	*(dehn-troh deh)*
without	sin	*(seen)*
woman	mujer	*(moo-hehr)*
words	palabras	*(pah-lah-brahs)*
worker	trabajador	*(trah-bah-hah-dohr)*
wound	herida	*(eh-ree-dah)*
writing	escribiendo	*(ehs-kree-bee-ehn-doh)*
X	ex	*(eh-kiss)*
X-rays	rayos X	*(rah-yohs eh-kiss)*
X-ray room	cuarto de rayos X	*(koo-ahr-toh deh rah-yohs eh-kiss)*
xiphoid	xifoides	*(see-foh-ee-dehs)*
Y	y	*(ee-gree-eh-gah)*
year	años	*(ah-nyohs)*
yellow	amarillo	*(ah-mah-ree-yoh)*
yes	sí	*(see)*
yogurt	yogur	*(yoh-goor)*
you	tú/usted/ellos/ellas/ ustedes/vosotros	*(too/oos-tehd/eh-yohs/eh-yahs/oos-teh-dehs/boh-soh-trohs)*
you can	puede	*(poo-eh-deh)*
young	jóvenes	*(hoh-beh-nehs)*
young man	joven	*(hoh-behn)*
your	su/sus	*(soo/soos)*
yourself	tú mismo	*(too mees-moh)*
yourselves	ustedes mismos	*(oos-teh-dehs mees-mohs)*
Z	z	*(seh-tah)*
zone	zona	*(soh-nah)*
zoology	zoología	*(soh-oh-loh-hee-ah)*
zygomatic	cigomático	*(see-goh-mah-tee-koh)*